FIVE MILLION WORDS LATER

FIVE MILLION WORDS LATER

An Autobiography

By BRUCE BLIVEN

THE JOHN DAY COMPANY

New York

*This book is dedicated to the men and women of my own genera-
tion, who tried so hard, who failed (in many cases) so lamenta-
bly, and most of whom have now died quietly in their own beds.*

The John Day Company, 257 Park Avenue South, New York, N.Y. 10010
an Intext publisher

Published on the same day in Canada by Longmans Canada Limited.

Library of Congress Catalogue Card Number: 78–115955
Printed in the United States of America

All the people in this book are real, and any resemblance
to fictional characters is purely coincidental.

Part of Chapter 1 was published in *The Palimpsest,* © 1968
by the State Historical Society of Iowa, and is reprinted by permission.

CONTENTS

FOREWORD

Any working newspaperman who undertakes to write his memoirs ought to have his head examined. (I have had this done, with inconclusive results.) We who are in the trade see so many ghostwritten autobiographies, so much prettying up of the truth for publication, so much general hypocrisy and suppression of the facts, that we could not be blamed for being wary in approaching such a task. Why try it at all?

In my case, the answer is a multiple one. I have been engaged in some great public controversies, and I should like to set the record straight in regard to my share in them. I have known several wonderful people who have never had adequate appreciation, and it would be pleasant to restore the balance at least in some degree. But most of all, I should like to recall to some part of the generation much younger than myself the distant roots of today's problems, which in certain cases help to offer solutions. I was born during the presidency of Benjamin Harrison, and came to maturity during that of William Howard Taft. As a boy I watched some of the last of the covered wagons moving west across the prairie; I have lived to see men walk on the moon, the creation in the test tubes of the elements of life itself, the world balance of nuclear terror. I hope my memory of earlier times may help a little to illumine the character of today's often desperate anxieties.

This book has been written mostly out of my head. Where other people have a bump of acquisitiveness, I seem to have a hollow. I envy men who have treasured every scrap of documentation about themselves back to infancy, but I can never be one of them. I also don't see how they do it in these days when dwelling places no longer have attics to serve as warehouses of memorabilia. For thirty years nearly all my letters were written at *The New Republic*, and both sides of the exchanges went into the office files, which in standard business style were kept seven or eight years, and then destroyed. Nowadays when universities send out what are practically form letters, asking to be the repository for one's "papers," I have to answer that I don't have any.

This may not be an unmixed calamity. My old friend Norman Hapgood, long editor of *Collier's Weekly*, once set out to write the life of Lincoln. He assembled documents for many months, and shipped a trunkful of them to his country home at Windsor, Vermont, intending to spend the summer doing his book. The trunk disappeared in transit, so he sat down and wrote the work from memory. Critics generally agreed it was his best.

I am sure some readers will note that this volume contains mention of the early years of a rather large number of people who afterward became famous. In defense I can plead that I have known a lot of anonymous nobodies, too, whose lives don't seem to lend themselves to reporting.

If here and there the pace of this work seems a little leisurely, I wish to plead guilty with an explanation, Your Honor. For one thing, the digressions usually seem more interesting than the facts of my own life. And for another, like many a veteran journalist, I have spent my life writing under great exigencies of time and word limits. When I was a young man there was a successful, elderly journalist named Ray Stannard Baker, who had two successful careers, one under his own name in the field of affairs in general, and one as "David Grayson," writing of the joys of country living. When a volume of his letters was published, I was struck by the fact that over and over, he begged his editors to be allowed time enough, and room enough, for an adequate performance. The cumulative effect of his appeals was heartrending; here was perhaps the best-known magazine writer in America, down on his knees asking to be allowed to do a good job. To take a little more elbowroom is one of the few compensations of working strictly on your own time, for an audience that may or may not exist.

Since I write mostly from memory, about things that cannot be checked, there may be errors of fact in this book, but I hope not too many. After forty years of editing my own work and that of others, I believe I can spell correctly the full names of about a thousand public figures of the present and past; but as every editor knows, the one you need at any given moment is likely to be the most elusive.

When I speak of "five million words" in this book I refer to the number I have published, in newspapers, magazines, and books, in my lifetime. Necessarily, it is only a rough estimate; but I have tried to counteract this fact, and perhaps neutralize the charge of boasting—of quantity if not quality—by setting the figure a couple of million below what I think is the actual total. Five is a nice round figure.

Throughout these pages I have used "liberal" and "progressive" more or less interchangeably, to conform with current usage, though strictly speaking, "liberal" ought to apply more to theory, and "progressive" to practice. Nowhere have I attempted to define them; if you don't know what these words mean, you are reading the wrong book.

Bruce Bliven

Stanford, California, 1970

Chapter 1

A PRAIRIE BOYHOOD

Every personal memoir must begin, no matter how many circumlocutions are employed, with substantially the same three words: "I was born." I was born in 1889, in Emmetsburg, a pleasant little town of 2,300 people, in northwestern Iowa—thirty-two years after the terrible Spirit Lake Massacre, and about the same number of miles from the scene.

Most people have never heard of this massacre, which finally came to mean a great deal to me. MacKinlay Kantor wrote a novel in 1961 about "Spirit Lake," but did not succeed in bringing it into the general public consciousness. There is such a lake, one of a group of three lying close together, but the massacre actually occurred on the shore of another of the group, West Okoboji, where the town of Arnold's Park now stands. The Indians had called the whole region Spirit Lake, and the whites took over the nomenclature. In the red man's eyes, the entire area was haunted by innumerable ghosts from ancient times.

In the massacre, in 1857, forty people were killed by a small band of the Wakpekutis (the word has various spellings), a subtribe of the Sioux, led by a savagely cruel chief named Inkpadutah. The marauders dragged away three young women and a fourteen-year-old girl into South Dakota Territory. Two of the women were murdered in the course of the march; the other woman and the girl survived.

When I was a boy of twelve, I visited a monument to the victims erected on the spot where the massacre had taken place. A few yards away there was a small log cabin; the kidnapped girl, now in her mid-fifties, lived there and sold—of all things—Indian souvenirs! I bought a tiny birchbark canoe and a twenty-five-cent paperback account by her of the massacre.

If I had not happened to visit the monument, I might have gone on for years without ever hearing of the episode, for nobody in my hometown ever talked of it. By the time I was old enough to look around and take cognizance of my surroundings, Emmetsburg seemed to have been there forever. All traces of pioneer days and the hardships suffered so few years ago had been wiped out. Ours was much like any other pleasant little American community, with wide streets of hard-packed dirt (except in the spring rains), broad lawns, big porches with swings suspended from chains, and a great air of solidity and continuity. Most of the houses were monstrosities of Victorian bad taste, but nobody knew it. We almost never saw an Indian, except an occasional beggar at the back door, dressed and acting like the white tramps, of whom there were a good many. The housewives were afraid of both groups, and reluctantly gave them food to get rid of them.

The changes in a few years had been so amazing that I hope I may be forgiven if I pause a moment to dwell on what life was like for the pioneers.

Less than forty years before my birth, there was not a single settler in that part of Iowa; the only white men ever to visit the region were occasional traders and the fur trappers who camped during the bitter winters by the lakes and streams, and in the spring sold, sometimes for large amounts, the skins they had accumulated. The first settlers on the shore of Medium Lake (today renamed Five-Island Lake), where Emmetsburg was to be located more than a decade later, were seven families of Irish farmers, who kept close together for mutual protection.

Through the 1850's settlers came to this area rather slowly, the reason being well-justified fear of the fierce Sioux warriors who wandered across the prairie. At any hint that the Indians were on the rampage, most of the whites fled with as many of their material possessions as they could gather up, to the safety of the nearest settlement that had a blockhouse, or to a United States Army fort, usually Fort Dodge, about eighty miles to the south. When winter began, the pioneers showed a tendency to go to a fort whether the Indians were on the warpath or not, since the deep snows made the few faint traces of roads across the prairie almost impassable for their heavy vehicles.

Timid as they were, these settlers never stopped drifting westward. They came in covered wagons, mostly ox-drawn, bumping over the rough prairie, herding along a few cattle, and riding or leading a horse or two. They did not travel in long trains like those which struck out from St. Jo for the Pacific Coast, but by ones and twos and threes.

At the age of ten or eleven I saw what must have been one of the very last covered wagons heading west. It was drawn by a pair of huge oxen, their heads down as they strained on through the mud. The canvas top was smaller than those we see nowadays in the movies; it was stretched tightly over a series of semi-circular hoops. The flaps in the rear were fastened open and a woman and a half-grown girl were looking out from the dark interior. A man was leading the oxen, and two or three other men, and a boy of my own age, were on horseback, driving a few cows. They all looked poor and dejected, but I was thrilled by the sight of them.

Forty years earlier, the settlers had halted mostly on the shores of lakes or rivers where there was timber for log cabins (no sawed lumber was available until long afterward). Often they dug a root cellar, which began with a crude flight of steps going down inside the house but extended beyond the walls, so that if the subterranean room caved in, little of the interior of the cabin itself would be damaged. In the long and bitter winters, heat from the stone fireplace at one end of the cabin would reach down into the cellar and keep the food stored there from freezing.

Sometimes the walls were made by setting two rows of poles close together and tamping down hay between them into an almost solid mass. The roofs might be made of sod, held down by heavy weights.[1] Beds were built against the wall, sometimes in tiers; doors were of wood, replaced in summer by a quilt or a skin. In the earliest days, before any glass was available, windows were covered with oiled paper or cloth. Where logs were scarce, the sides as well as the roof might be made of the tough prairie sod, and—in a dry area—the interior might be excavated to lower the floor several feet.

In some cases, one end of the cabin had a false wall. Behind it was a very narrow space in which the members of the family would hide from marauding Indians, trying to keep perfectly silent. True, they would lose all their valuables, but at least they would live—unless the intruders set fire to the structure.

Some early arrivals had no such luxury as a looking glass. One bride of 1838 in southern Iowa recalled her wedding day:

> *We had no mirrors to see ourselves when we were arrayed in our wedding gowns [the wedding was to be a double one]. Just as soon as we were dressed we walked around the corner of the house and looked in the rain barrel. There we saw ourselves as sweet and pretty as we had ever hoped to be.*[2]

[1] I am paraphrasing here passages from *Iowa through the Years*, by Cyrenus Cole, and *Ioway to Iowa*, by Irving Richman, both published by the State Historical Society of Iowa, Iowa City, plus a conversation with Dwight McCarty of Emmetsburg, an authority on the early history of the area.
[2] Quoted in *Ioway to Iowa*.

When the Indians were few, they were beggars or thieves; when they outnumbered the whites whom they encountered, they murdered and scalped, burned the newly erected log cabins, stole everything portable, drove off the stock, and usually headed for the inaccessible Bad Lands of the Dakota Territory.

The picture was not, of course, merely one of peaceful white settlers and savage Indians. The frontier attracted many white desperadoes, who took the Indians' property, by guile or force, and killed them without compunction. The mistreatment of the Indians by the whites, going back to 1607, is a familiar story that need not be repeated here.

While the winters were long and bitter, and the summers very hot, the first white settlers found northwestern Iowa a springtime paradise. It was a well-watered area, with many lakes and rivers, the prairie covered with thick grass, sometimes almost as tall as a man, as far as the eye could reach. The matted vegetation held so much water that there were many sloughs, often difficult to cross. The edges of the waterways were lined with trees, and in spring the open prairie was a mass of flowers. Wildlife was abundant; there were herds of deer, antelope, and elk, and the streams had muskrats, beaver, and mink. The wild fowl included prairie chickens, ducks, geese, and quail; the latter were so abundant that a few years later when the white men began hunting for sport and not just for food, they ate only the breasts.

Abbie Gardner Sharp, the girl kidnapped in the Spirit Lake massacre, wrote a book a quarter of a century later, recalling the scenes in the summer of 1856 as her family bumped along westward over the trackless prairie toward the doom that would befall them the following spring.

> *On the route taken, no traces of civilization were discernible west of Algona in Kossuth County. The Des Moines River was unbridged, and the sloughs, being filled with water, were frequently impassable. On the way we frequently encountered the redskins by day, and were entertained at night by the howling of wolves. Still we went forward unhesitatingly in our lonely journey, driving the slow-footed oxen and wagons, loaded with household goods, agricultural implements, and provisions, making our own road over many miles of desolate prairie.*[3]

But the prairie did not always seem desolate to her.

> *The far-stretching prairie, clothed in its mantle of green, luxuriant grass, studded here and there with the golden stars of the resin weed, and a thousand flowering plants of a humbler growth but no less brilliant hues, presented to the eye a scene of enchanting beauty, beside which the*

[3]Quoted in *The Palimpsest*, published by the State Historical Society of Iowa, Iowa City, April, 1956.

8

things of man's devising fade like stars before the morning sun. Nor were prairies the only attraction. Here and there a babbling brook and sparkling river came together, eager to join hands and be away to the sea; and along their banks were shady groves of maple, oak, and elm, festooned with wild grapes, woodbine, bittersweet, and ivy, in most fantastic forms and prodigality. Herds of elk and deer, in all the grace of their native freedom, fed on the nutritious grasses, and sought shelter in groves. Every variety of wild fowl—in flocks which no man could number—filled the air and nested on the ground.[4]

The Gardner family arrived at what is now Arnold's Park on July 16, 1856. Other settlers drifted in; by November there were six families and several single men.

The massacre took place on the morning of March 8 of the following year. The leader, Inkpadutah, was so wild and savage in his actions that few of the Sioux, none of them exactly models of deportment, would have anything to do with him. There were several cabins scattered among the trees on the shore of the lake; a few Indians entered each of them simultaneously and peacefully, early in the morning, begging for food, a familiar action. What happened in the Gardner cabin was typical of the scenes in the others. Abbie tells the story.

As father turned to get them what remained of our scanty store, they shot him through the heart; he fell upon his right side and died without a struggle. When first the Indian raised his gun to fire, mother or Mrs. Luce [another member of the community] seized the gun and drew it down; but the other Indians instantly turned upon them, seized them by their arms, and beat them over the head with the butts of their guns; then dragged them out of doors and killed them in the most cruel and shocking manner.

They then began an indiscriminate destruction of everything in the house; breaking open trunks and taking out clothing, cutting open feather beds, and scattering the feathers everywhere. When the Indians entered the house, and during these awful scenes, I was seated in a chair, holding my sister's baby in my arms; her little boy on one side, and my little brother on the other, clinging to me in terror. They next seized the children, tearing them from me one by one, while they reached their little arms to me crying piteously for protection that I was powerless to give. Heedless of their cries, they dragged them out of doors and beat them to death with sticks of stove wood.[5]

[4] *Ibid.*
[5] *Ibid.*

FIVE MILLION WORDS LATER

Abbie could not understand at the time why she was made captive, instead of being killed with the others. She was told long afterward that the Indians were struck by her utter fearlessness—she now wished only for death—and this may be true. Probably they also intended to hold her for ransom.

The forty people were killed within an area of a few miles; everything portable was stolen and all the cabins were burned. Abbie and three young married women, Mrs. William Marble, Mrs. Lydia Noble, and Mrs. Elizabeth Thatcher, were laden with loot like pack horses, and the tribe set off toward the west. In that winter of unparalleled cold, the ice was still firm on West Okoboji, and they crossed the lake on it. They passed within a few hundred yards of the spot where, forty years later, I used to sit on the front porch of a family summer cottage and look out at a busy scene of sailboats and motor launches.

Having crossed the lake, the Indians and their prisoners traveled rapidly for many days away from the pioneer towns of the white men. They passed through the southwest corner of Minnesota, and then went west into what is now South Dakota. The four captives were forced to carry almost intolerable loads and were treated with dreadful cruelty, too painful to repeat here. Two of the women, as I have said, were murdered.

The massacre was discovered a few days later by three white men who had intended to join the little colony, and found the cabins burned and surrounded by dead bodies. They hurried back to the nearest colony of white men, the "Irish settlement," on the site of what later became Emmetsburg, and spread the alarm. All over the area, isolated families abandoned all their possessions except their livestock and goods that could easily be carried. Those in the vicinity of the Irish settlement gathered at that point and hastily erected a blockhouse into which they crowded; most of the others struck out for Fort Dodge.

Two rescue expeditions were immediately started from Fort Dodge and from Fort Ridgley, in southwestern Minnesota, but both were forced by the terrible weather to turn back, one of them with the loss of two lives. At last, the Army wisely abandoned the attempt to use its strength, and task forces of friendly Indians were employed to ransom the two surviving captives, separately. The young girl, Abbie, was the last to be saved. Her ransom came high, by the standards of the day: two horses, twelve blankets, two kegs of powder, twenty pounds of tobacco, thirty-two yards of blue "squaw cloth," thirty-seven and a half yards of calico and ribbon, and some other small articles.

The girl and her rescuers got back safely to civilization, the first big town they reached being St. Paul, where Abbie was treated as a heroine

—which indeed she was. A short time later she discovered that a sister, who was living elsewhere at the time of the massacre, was now a married woman, living at Hampton, Iowa. There was a happy reunion, and a few months later Abbie herself married a young man named Cassville Sharp. On the frontier, where men heavily outnumbered girls, not much time was wasted.

Twenty-four years later, now a widow, she moved back to the scene of the massacre and built the souvenir shop where I met and talked with her.

In 1858, Palo Alto County was surveyed, a tremendous forward step, since people could now settle on land and know its boundaries. The railroad at this time ended at Iowa City, far to the southeast, near the Mississippi River (it was extended to Fort Dodge a few years later and in 1870 to Algona, twenty-four miles east of Emmetsburg).

An attempt was made in 1858 to establish Emmetsburg on the shore of Medium Lake, where the Irish families, and a few others, were farming, but it came to nothing. The town was named for Robert Emmet, the great Irish hero who, since he bungled horribly everything he tried to do, but made a glorious speech from the scaffold just before he was hanged, appealed strongly to the feelings of his fellow countrymen. They probably would have named the county for him as well, but other Irishmen had forestalled them by doing this for the next one to the north.

In 1851, when ours needed a patronym, it was called Palo Alto, in honor of the battle of that name five years earlier in the Mexican War.

Another forward step came in 1858 with the opening of mail service from Algona to Spirit Lake, where, in spite of the massacre only a year earlier, there was now the beginning of a town. The mail served all the settlers; every few miles one well-located farmer was chosen as postmaster. When the mail arrived—once a week in good weather—all the letters were dumped into a dishpan in the farmer's living room, and the settlers for miles around came and picked out their own.

In 1862 settlement of the West got a great boost with the Homestead Act, permitting people to take up a quarter section of land (160 acres) which became theirs after they had proved they had lived on it for a specified length of time, and were "improving" it—which in Iowa of course meant starting to farm. By 1864, an informal count of noses indicated that there were 143 people in Palo Alto County. That autumn a terrible prairie fire swept through the area, doing great damage, but the pioneers grimly surveyed their smoking ruins and went back to work.

In 1866, a peripatetic sawmill was set up for a while in the county, providing badly needed sawed lumber. In 1869 another one came; by now there was a handful of houses on the east bank of the West Branch of the Des Moines River, several miles from the lake, and the name Emmetsburg was firmly established. The new sawmill was placed on the bank of the river, and a crude dam, consisting chiefly of compacted brush, was constructed to give the necessary water power. The signboard which years earlier had identified the Emmetsburg that had died a-borning on the edge of the lake was pulled up and planted again on the river bank.

When the Chicago, Milwaukee & St. Paul Railroad reached Algona, in 1870, there was great rejoicing among the little group clustered on the bank of the Des Moines. But this turned to dismay when, after a delay of several years, they discovered that the road had no intention of passing through their settlement but would be several miles away. A furious debate started at once; should they stay where they were, or move the town to the railroad? Some of the settlers were determined to move, no matter what the others did, and they finally won with the plea, "Let's have one good town instead of two poor ones." The railroad owned much land along its right-of-way, under the scandalously generous provisions laid down by Congress some years earlier, and it offered two free lots to everybody in "Old Town." But it cannily included an agreement for a $500 penalty if the recipient failed to move, and this penalty probably turned the tide.

The new community consisted of nothing but stakes, and was naturally called "Stake Town." Many years later a pioneer told Dwight McCarty about it. The land was not yet being farmed, and "the grass was tall, in many places up to our hips, and in some places as high as our heads. Not a tree nor a shrub in sight—just prairie. We got a team and mower and set flags and would mow swaths through so we could see to set and line up the stakes."[6]

With the Yankee flair for promotion, the contingent who wanted to move had put on a hot selling campaign. They set up roadside signs reading "On to Stake Town," "Stake Town—Only Station on This Line," and "Stake Town Will Pay More for Farm Products and Sell Goods Cheaper." They sent persuasive salesmen to talk to the nearby farmers and argue the advantages of having a town on the railroad, a point that needed little emphasizing. The promoters also hired men to drive through Old Town with signs on their wagons reading "Stake Town or Bust."

Most of the buildings were dragged across the prairie to the new site, after locations and ownership had been determined; one hustling storekeeper achieved brief fame by continuing to sell goods out of his

[6] *History of Palo Alto County*, by Dwight M. McCarty, Torch Press, Cedar Rapids, Iowa, 1910.

back door during the whole time that his store was being moved. Intoxicated by the drama of the great removal, a local musician, Miss Mary McGroarty, wrote a stirring composition entitled "The March of Emmetsburg."

The new town had two chief streets at right angles, called, with a flash of inspiration, Main Street and Broadway, and others were quickly added. A whole square in the middle of the town was reserved for the court house, and the citizens volunteered to plant trees around it. Each able-bodied citizen was co-opted to find a suitable tree, transplant it, and take care of it. The practice extended to other streets and by the time I was born, fourteen years later, Emmetsburg proudly called itself "the Shade Tree City of Northwestern Iowa."

During these years, the community had plenty to worry about beyond the question of moving. The panic of 1873, with its terrible "Black Friday," hit Iowa hard. Money disappeared and trade came to a halt. Many families kept themselves alive only by their own vegetable gardens, and by killing wild game, mostly quail and prairie chickens. Palo Alto County memorialized the state legislature in Des Moines, begging for help, but the legislature, doubtless overwhelmed with such pleas from every part of the state, did nothing. The county gradually worked its way out of the problem.

A great curse of these days was prairie fires, usually set by lightning. As a small boy, I remember seeing one of these at night, far on the southwestern horizon, a miles-long, thin red line of flame. By the 1890's much of the land was under cultivation and therefore resisted burning; but in the early days, the menace was frightening indeed. With a wind behind it, the blaze would roar forward, sometimes as fast as a horse could gallop, through the thick, tall grass. If they had enough warning, the pioneers had only one recourse: to go a little way upwind and set a small backfire of their own, to burn off the grass nearest the cabin, though these backfires themselves often got out of control. If the settlers succeeded in creating a patch of smoking bare ground, they put wet cloths over their faces and waited for the fire to go by on either side.

In the 1870's, there were grasshopper plagues in four out of five years, beginning in 1873. These were also years of abnormally heavy rainfall, so that the roads were frequently impassable for days or weeks at a time.

It is hard for anyone today to realize what a disaster the locusts were. Dwight McCarty, who talked with some of the pioneers, tells in his book what happened:

> *These insects . . . breed abundantly every year by boring holes in the ground and filling these holes with eggs during August, and these eggs hatch out the following spring. Hundreds of these eggs are laid by a single insect, and the rate of propagation is enormous. When hatched out, the*

*young feed on the tender vegetation near by, and when they have eaten
everything in sight they migrate in great swarms, devouring grain,
garden vegetables, growing crops, young grass, and everything of a like
nature. These pests traveled in dense swarms, often several miles wide,
obscuring the sun and making a roaring noise like the sound of a water-
fall. They traveled mostly in the warm portion of the day, and in the early
morning and cool evening would gather in loose grass or protected places
for shelter and warmth. This fact was made use of by the farmers to
destroy the pests, which were often shoveled up in great quantities from
sheltered places, and loose straw and hay were scattered around and then
burned when covered with the hoppers. These grasshoppers often covered
twenty miles a day in their flight, leaving in their path a region devastated as though swept by a prairie fire.*

By 1876, after three plagues of grasshoppers in four years, the Palo
Alto farmers had learned more efficient methods. The county bought
large sheets of tin which were bent up into rough boxes, set on wheels,
and partly filled with tar. When they were resting, the grasshoppers were
knocked off the grain into the tar, and then dumped out and burned. Yet
despite the vast quantities thus destroyed, the devastation of crops was
still almost complete. After a visitation, the farmers had almost nothing
to sell. If they were buying their farms from an earlier settler on a
mortgage, as was often the case, they lost their land, and had to hire out
for day labor, at whatever jobs they could find. The lending institutions
usually had little difficulty in reselling the farms to somebody else. Wild
land at this time was worth $2 to $10 an acre, and improved land from
$8 to $20, depending of course on the quality of the soil, nearness to town,
and other factors.

Some historians feel that the grasshoppers were a blessing in dis-
guise. The settlers had gone in heavily for wheat, which exhausts the soil,
and was especially attractive to the insects. The switch was now made
to corn and hogs, because of which Iowa was for many years the most
productive agricultural state in the country.

The quarter century beginning in 1870 saw hard times and severe
political unrest in the Middle West—a fact that was to be of great importance to me throughout my childhood. Men found that their debts, often
incurred when prices were high, had to be repaid when prices were low.
The grain elevators in the little towns, and the railroads which shipped
the grain, had the farmers at their mercy, since there was usually a
monopoly in both cases. Crops were sometimes burned because prices
were so low that it wasn't worth while to send them to market. The
railroads and the moneylenders were growing rich while the farmers
were sinking deeper into poverty.

In 1875, the Greenback Party was formed, demanding, as one might expect, the issuance of more paper money, to cheapen the dollar and drive prices up. It also advocated unlimited coinage of silver, which would have tended in the same direction, the government having recently stopped coining silver money. These were the days of "sockless" Jerry Simpson of Kansas, and Ellen Lease's slogan "Raise less corn and more hell," to which conservative young William Allen White of the *Emporia Gazette* replied with a famous editorial which advised: "Raise less hell and more wheat."

In 1891, the Populist Party came into being with a platform far to the left for its time: free coinage of silver, government ownership of railroads, a graduated income tax, an eight-hour day, old-age pensions, and direct election of senators, who at that time were chosen by the state legislatures. The Populist Party attracted wide support among the farmers and the people of the small towns who depended on the farmers for their livelihood, and it hoped to become the chief rival of the now dominant Republicans. But it was not to be; the Democrats in 1896 stole the Populists' chief plank by nominating William Jennings Bryan as their presidential candidate on a platform of unlimited coinage of silver in a ratio to gold of "sixteen to one," the phrase over which the campaign was fought. Bryan lost the election to the ultraconservative Republican William McKinley. But now the slump of a quarter century gradually ended, and with it the hopes of the Populists.

As for Emmetsburg, the Chicago, Milwaukee & St. Paul finally built the twenty-four miles from Algona on the east; it reached the town, amid great celebration, in 1878. A second railroad, the Burlington, Cedar Rapids & Northern, arrived four years later in 1882; the boys promptly translated the initials into Bums Can't Ride North. (Later this line was bought by the Rock Island.) In Emmetsburg the two lines crossed at right angles to each other, but a few miles to the north they were both racing to the town of Estherville, in a competition so bitter that it almost led to bloodshed. At one point where the lines crossed again, one road left an engine sitting squarely on the intersection and the other was forced to go to court to get it removed.

Iowa was by now a network of railroad branches, so many that a large proportion were soon bankrupt; towns henceforth would be established only on a line or directly in its path. New communities were created according to a simple rule: they had to be numerous enough so that the great majority of farmers could drive to town with a team and wagon and get home the same night to feed the stock. Usually the farmer's wife accompanied him, and guarded the vehicle while he was doing his errands; nobody thought of providing for the comfort of these poor women, who sat stoically on the high wagon seat, hour after hour, without complaint; in most places it was many years before it occurred to the towns to construct rest rooms and other facilities for them.

Palo Alto County was settled primarily by American farm stock from a few states farther east—Indiana, Ohio, western Pennsylvania, and western New York. Around Emmetsburg there were some Scottish immigrants, and a few Scots-Irish from Ulster, who had bought their land sight unseen before leaving home; some of them brought good breeding stock, both cattle and horses. The next wave was the Scandinavians; though they came from all three countries, the earlier settlers called them all "Swedes" or "Norskies." These immigrants were poor, and like all new ethnic groups moving into a settled community, were scorned and ridiculed. The Anglo-Saxon children imitated their dialect, which substituted "y" for "j," and mocked at their ignorance of American ways. Today, of course, the Americans of Scandinavian origin in the Middle West are among the area's best citizens, respected everywhere, as are the people of their homelands.

Another group that our Anglo-Saxons looked down upon, as I now recall with shame, was the Irish Catholic town dwellers. The C. M. & St. P. bisected the town, running east and west; the area north of the railroad was given over to what today are called "WASPS"—white Anglo-Saxon Protestants. The area south of the tracks was almost entirely Irish Catholic families, many of whom had settled there after working on the railroads, liking the town and its adjoining lake. There was strict segregation of churches: all the Protestant denominations on one side of the railroad, and the Catholic church on the other. Most of the Catholic children attended the parochial school. The town's wholesale and retail business and its banking were firmly in the hands of the Protestants. I am told that Populism appealed to some of the WASPS, but I had no knowledge of it as a boy. Almost everybody I knew when I was growing up was a Republican. One of my early memories is of watching a torchlight parade for McKinley in 1896, and smelling the pungent kerosene torches. I never saw a parade for Bryan and I am not sure I had heard of him.

None of my forebears were in Iowa when the Sioux were still dangerous, but if they had been, they presumably would have taken it in their stride. Both my father's and my mother's families had been fighting Indians off and on in New England since the seventeenth century. Perhaps it is time for a long parenthesis, which is all the subject deserves, about family history.

For some years after I was grown, I believed, on the basis of incorrect information, that the Blivens were of Dutch descent, and I could see in myself what are commonly believed to be Dutch characteristics, stubbornness, candor, a rough integrity. Then I learned that my family had come from Wales, and promptly my mental picture of myself changed; I was now volatile, emotional, and intuitive. All of this was of course ridiculous; I am in the eighth generation of the Bliven family in America, and my genetic inheritance from the first of the line is only one two-hundred-and-fifty-sixth of the total.

There seems little doubt about the Welsh origin of my father's family. The name, under various spellings, Blevin, Bleddyn, et cetera, is familiar in Welsh records back to the eleventh century. There was a Welsh ruler named Bleddyn who, at the time of the Norman invasion, held a precarious control of the area between Chester (near Liverpool) and Machynlleth, sixty miles to the southwest on Cardigan Bay. Jessie Weston, in her book about the legend of the Holy Grail, says that a Welshman of that name was responsible for passing on to the Normans the whole mass of the tales about King Arthur, the Round Table, Lancelot, and Guinevere. The Bleddyn just mentioned survived the Conquest by nine years, and could have been the teller of tales; so could any of his immediate descendants, who continued to hold their district in Wales for some little time. Naturally, the American Blivens have always claimed King Bleddyn as an ancestor, but for nine generations, nobody, so far as I know, has ever tried to trace any actual connection.

The firm family records begin with an Edward Bliven who came from the British Isles in 1684, landed at Oyster Bay, Long Island, and after a few years moved to Westerly, Rhode Island, where the family lived for several generations; the old cemeteries of the town have the graves of a number of Blivens, causing my small son to remark once when we walked among the headstones that it was obviously unhealthy to have this name.

About the year 1700, the family lived in its own blockhouse near the center of the town, surrounded by a high stockade. One stormy night a squaw came asking for shelter, and was allowed to stay. A male member of the family was suspicious, however, armed himself with an axe, and stayed up all night to watch. Sure enough, in the middle of the night the squaw rose, tiptoed to the barred gate, and opened it for the braves waiting outside. The watching Bliven gave the alarm, and, aided by other members of the family, beat off the Indians and got the gate closed again.

There was a second Edward Bliven, and then a third, who bore arms in the Revolution, first as "Captain of the Alarm Men" of Westerly, and then as Captain in the regular forces, where his son, Arnold, and also his brother, Major John Bliven, served. The family luck was not very good; Edward was captured early, and held on one of two British prison ships lying in the New York harbor, the *Jersey*. Like many others, he died of mistreatment on the ship; there is a monument in Brooklyn to these victims. His brother John was captured by the British at the battle of Oriskany, which was preliminary to the great American victory at Saratoga, and died of wounds received at that time.

Five generations of Blivens lived in New England, mostly in Westerly. Then my grandfather, Albert Bliven, moved west to Michigan, and married and settled down in the little community of Blissfield, not far from Detroit. My father, Charles Franklin, was born there in 1850; both his parents died when he was very young, of the great curse of those years, tuberculosis.

My mother's family, the Ormsbys, also arrived from England; the first members appeared in Saco, Maine, in 1641. They presumably came from Lincolnshire, where the name is common, and is supposed to derive from the family motto, "In Arms Be"; as with the Blivens, no one in ten generations, as far as I know, has been sufficiently interested to try to trace the family back before Saco.

The fifth generation in America produced a soldier in the Revolution, Nathaniel Ormsby, who, like Major John Bliven, was killed in the Saratoga campaign. The Ormsbys lived in various parts of New England for almost two centuries; some of them were for many years in Norwich, Connecticut, only about twenty miles from Westerly, where the Blivens were.

In 1839 my grandfather, Lysander Ormsby, moved to Deerfield, Michigan, and there my mother, Lilla Cordelia, was born in 1859. The town was so near Blissfield, and both were so small, that she must have known from an early age the orphan boy, Charles Franklin Bliven, nine years older than herself, who was being brought up by an uncle. He had a rough childhood, being forced to do hard farm work while much too young.

When I was growing up, my parents hardly ever talked of their early days, and I did not have wit enough to ask them for facts they would have been glad to report. I remember my father's once telling me how as a boy, weighing little, he waded fast-flowing streams by carrying a heavy stone that helped prevent his being swept away. Once, when he was a little older, he rounded a corner in a woods path and came face to face with a bear; they both scuttled away in opposite directions.

My father had almost no formal education, but he was an incessant reader; I never in my life heard him make a slip in grammar, or exhibit the least gaucherie in manners. He was a handsome man, better looking than my mother, whom I resemble.

Of her early days, I know only that she attended a female seminary, where she learned to play the piano. Lysander Ormsby was one of the leading citizens of Deerfield, not wealthy but universally liked and respected. The town probably felt that Lilla Cordelia married beneath her station when, in 1876, she cast her lot with a penniless twenty-six-year-old orphan. But they were in love, as they were for the rest of their lives; and Michigan in 1876 was close enough to the frontier to make differences in social status comparatively unimportant.

My mother had two much older brothers, both of whom fought for the Union in the Civil War, which broke out when she was two (and my father, eleven). Both brothers did well under fire; one of them was with Sherman on his march to the sea. Demobilized and back home, they suffered from soldiers' restlessness, and within a few years my Uncle Alvin headed west. How he hit upon Emmetsburg, I do not know, but he did, and soon sent for his brother Edwin. Both were there when Old Town was succeeded by Stake Town; both decided promptly to be bankers, not farmers. They started a bank and, presently, a mortgage and loan company; where they got the necessary capital I never learned.

Both brothers had left brides behind in Michigan, and as soon as possible, they sent for them. They arrived by stagecoach from the railhead, and tactfully concealed their notice of the sharp contrast between the miserable little town they saw and the glowing portraits of a coming metropolis their husbands had described in letters.

My parents went on their honeymoon to the 1876 Philadelphia Centennial Exposition and marveled at the new scientific wonders there displayed—the telephone, the Westinghouse air brake, and the novel barbed wire that was finally to end the bloody wars between sheep and cattle men on the Western plains. They returned to Deerfield, where my sister, Maude, was born in 1879, and some time later, my two uncles persuaded their sister and her husband to settle in Emmetsburg. I came into the world ten years after my sister, so that we were both brought up like only children—a fact that I believe had an important effect on our character development.

It has become a platitude to point out that the world has changed more since I was born than it had in all its previous history. To anticipate a little, I remember when there were only a dozen or so telephones in Emmetsburg and you told Central the name of the person you wanted to speak to. When I was ten, electric lights in the home were still a rare novelty, though arc lights were used for street illumination. Every few weeks somebody had to climb a ladder and push the carbon points closer together as the tips were burned off.

My boyhood saw the beginning of many things that are commonplace today. The town's first phonograph belonged to one of my uncles; it had the big horn, the fragile wax cylinder, and the handle to wind up the spring, that are well remembered today. Humorous monologues were more popular than music; the favorite with us, as it was everywhere, was "Cohen on the Telephone."

The town's first automobile was, I believe, a Winton, purchased by one of my rich cousins. You entered the high tonneau up a short flight of steps, in the middle of the rear; I remember the delicious terror of moving at such a height, and at twenty miles an hour, along the dusty roads. Most of the horses we met went into a panic; my cousin would pull off the road, stop the car, get out and lead the frightened animal past.

Our first motion picture was not *The Great Train Robbery*, which I never saw until it had become a treasured antique. To Emmetsburg came a traveling lecturer with a set of films which he narrated while cranking the projector. Folding chairs were set up in Masonic Hall, upstairs over the drugstore, and a thrilled audience saw such incredible spectacles as a train approaching down a track, looking as though it were about to leap off the screen, acrobats performing, and as a grand climax, a picture of the Niagara Rapids. The narrator told us that the night before he had shown his pictures in Algona, and that someone in the audience said: "That certainly *looks* like water; *golly*, that looks like water; *gosh*, it *is* water." No doubt this was a standard joke told every night and attributed to some nearby community.

We never got a movie house while I still lived in Emmetsburg, but a theater was finally built, in which touring companies occasionally played one-night stands. The first that I remember was a romantic comedy along the lines of *The Prisoner of Zenda;* no experience with drama in later life ever equaled the thrill of my first contact with live, professional actors.

From time to time a traveling medicine show came to town and performed in a vacant lot near the corner of Main Street and Broadway. I remember one pitchman, a large, placid gentleman who of course called himself "doctor"; this one sold soap as well as bottled medicine, and to prove its purity he calmly sliced off a good-sized hunk of a bar and ate it; I assume it was not real soap, but how this trick was performed, I still do not know. My chief admiration went to the perspiring young man, the doctor's assistant, who set up the platform and the kerosene torches, sang songs during the preliminary warm-up, accompanying himself on the banjo, did a trombone solo, walked on his hands, did back flips, and sold bottles of medicine at the end of the show, making change with great dexterity, and as far as I know, with complete honesty.

Once a year, the circus came to town, and performed in a vacant lot a block from our house. It traveled by road, in a series of huge red-and-gold wagons, drawn by two, four, or sometimes six horses; when they arrived, usually about four o'clock in the morning, hardy small boys were at the grounds to greet them and to listen to the occasional growls of wild animals from inside some of the boarded-up wagons. I never got a chance at the traditional task of carrying water to the elephants but my family always managed to scare up the price of admission. Since I lived so near, I saw the morning parade assemble for its journey through town, and break up after its return.

Almost as exciting as the circus was the tent show of *Uncle Tom's Cabin*, which played Emmetsburg now and then. For the scene in which Eliza is pursued by bloodhounds, the show carried several huge mastiffs —far more terrifying than real bloodhounds would have been. To my amazement, "Topsy" turned out to have gone to school with my mother in Deerfield, and she came to supper at our house. I found that the incredibly energetic, fourteen-year-old, kinky-haired, black-faced Topsy was a quiet white woman in her middle fifties, wife of the owner of the show. I realized that the theater is a place of illusion.

My uncles acted generously toward the Blivens. They gave my parents a farm, 160 acres of good land near the lake shore. My father was a competent, hardworking farmer, who raised wheat, corn, and oats; he had a dairy herd of sound Jersey stock, and a few fierce breeding bulls. These dangerous animals could be managed only by means of a six-foot pole with a snap on one end which engaged a ring in the bull's nose. When one of them got out of control, my father and a hired man were both gored, on separate occasions, neither very seriously. One of my earliest memories is the thrill of looking through the heavy barred gate at one of these monsters, who seemed constantly furious for reasons I did not comprehend.

Elderly people are notorious for looking back on their childhood as a golden age, and their memories are subject to heavy discount for this reason. Yet there is a formidable list of problems existing today that were unknown at the turn of the century, when I was eleven—overpopulation, destruction of natural resources, pollution of air and water, the Cold War with its threat of atomic annihilation of all mankind. To be sure, there are also areas in which great progress has been made in the past sixty or seventy years, progress that should be included in any balance sheet of our times; however, I am not trying to write a balance sheet, but to recall the distant past.

In those days nobody had ever heard of the population explosion (*Webster's Third* accuses me of having invented the phrase half a century later); while there was already crowding in some other parts of the world, such as India, we did not know it. Only a little to the west of us, the prairie and the high plains stood open and empty; both public and private agencies were working hard to persuade settlers to come. (I was dumbfounded, many years later, to learn from the calculations of Kenneth Boulding that probably about a quarter of all the people who have been born since the beginning of history are still alive, and are all younger than I.)

It is true that we hurt our soil with overuse, but there were still such huge quantities waiting for the plow that it did not seem to matter. In any case, before long, crop rotation, measures against erosion, and chemical fertilizers were to ameliorate the problem as far as Iowa was concerned.

American cities were not yet decaying at the heart; there were dreadful slums in the biggest ones, but the people who lived there usually agreed that the Lord had ordered things this way, and accepted their lot with resignation. The richer part of the community built a few settlement houses, indulged in a little charity work—especially at Thanksgiving and Christmas—and otherwise ignored the subject. As successive waves of immigration of various racial stocks came from the Old World, each in turn was subject to merciless economic exploitation, and was made the butt of racist jokes—at which theater audiences laughed with no inner sense of guilt.

Members of these races joined in poking fun at their own foibles; there were famous German, Italian, and Jewish comedians who carefully cultivated their native accents. For many years, traveling minstrel shows were highly popular, composed almost entirely of white men in black face, imitating the Negro accent and basing their humor largely on the stereotypes of Negro laziness, addiction to fried chicken, and so on.

The ministrel shows faded out, and were succeeded by Negro comedians—real or synthetic—using the same type of material. Although slavery had been abolished with the Emancipation Proclamation almost forty years earlier, most Negroes still lived in the South, in utter and unquestioned segregation. I can't remember one member of this race in Emmetsburg in 1900. There were a few Jews, accepted socially by the Protestant and Catholic communities. I can't recall anyone whose European origin was readily visible, beyond those I have already mentioned.

It is true that there seemed always to be some war going on somewhere in the world, but these were small-scale conflicts, far from the peace of the broad and quiet Iowa prairie. Nobody even discussed the possibility that there might some day be another conflict like our own Civil War, whose survivors in large numbers still put on their blue or gray uniforms and marched in annual celebrations.

In no country, so far as we knew, was there any Socialist movement of more than negligible importance. Reports occasionally came of political assassinations in some part of Europe, usually Russia, and usually the work of Anarchists, a sect that was already caricatured as bewhiskered individuals carrying smoking, grapefruit-sized bombs. We had just barely heard of the mild and gentle Fabian Socialists of England. Though Marx and Engels had hurled their first intellectual thunderbolt half a century earlier, and the Paris Commune was a memory of only thirty years ago, in Iowa the Marxist doctrine was ignored as thoroughly as Hitler's *Mein Kampf* was to be, universally, in the mid-1920's. The affair of the Chicago Anarchists in 1886 must have made a stir in Emmetsburg, but it was all forgotten by the turn of the century. I remember the news of the assassination of President McKinley when I was eleven, but I don't recall any talk about the fact that the man who killed him, Leon Czolgosz, was an Anarchist.

The proliferation of science that was to mark the twentieth century was just beginning. The principle of atomic radiation had been discovered by Becquerel when I was six; nobody dreamed either of its coming usefulness as a medical tool or, of course, of the horrors of atom and hydrogen bombs. Nobody had enough vision to foresee a time, only fifty years away, when the world would be so split between two economic and political systems that each half would be grimly intent on destroying the other.

At the turn of the century, we still lived in an orderly, disciplined, and authoritarian world. God was an old gentleman with a long beard, up in the sky, who watched every detail of the life of every one of us. The doctrine of evolution was beginning to find acceptance everywhere except among the Fundamentalists, but it was assumed to be a kindly device intended to make things better and better for mankind. God's vicar on earth was the father of the family, whose authority was unquestioned even when he ruled with a light hand as, in our town, he usually did.

There was practically no juvenile delinquency in Emmetsburg, perhaps partly because in our nonaffluent society nobody ever had cause to complain that he "had nothing to do." All children did some work from the age of ten or so; on the farm, the boys helped with the outdoor chores, and the girls learned the details of cooking and sewing, and aided their mothers. On Halloween a few high-spirited boys tipped over a few privies, or hoisted a buggy to a roof; usually the culprits were quickly identified and compelled to undo their damage. "Trick or treat" had not yet reached Iowa; the younger children stayed home and went to bed, or attended early parties at which there were bobbing for apples, jack-o'-lanterns carved from pumpkins, and comic masks.

For the few years of my youth, Palo Alto County was dry by local option. Until I left home at eighteen I had never seen a saloon, a drunken man in the street, or any kind of alcoholic beverage served on a dinner table—or for that matter, anywhere else.

No doubt there were goings on of which I was ignorant, but as far as I knew, we were still in the grip of the Puritan tradition as to sex. When my friends and I were turning adolescent, Freud's doctrines, which were eventually to crumble the foundations of so much of our philosophy, were still unheard of. So was birth control, and the whole idea of "planned parenthood." Yet I can remember only one girl in my generation who "got into trouble," and if there were some shotgun marriages I did not know of them. (I am speaking of the Protestant segment of town, but I doubt that things were much different among the Catholics or Jews.)

Discipline in school was good; rarely indeed did anybody need to be sent to the principal's office, the only form of punishment employed. The principal was a mild-mannered man (whose small daughter grew up to be editor of *The Ladies' Home Journal*); how he handled disciplinary problems I do not know, for neither I nor any of my close friends were ever sent to him.

In my case, my passion for reading (and doubtless some other factors) kept me from getting into any serious mischief. I was never punished physically, and I was not unique in this respect. My mother objected to my reading at the dinner table and once, goaded beyond endurance, she marched me to the bathroom and locked me in. But she had overlooked the book under my arm, and I promptly sat down and went on reading. Twenty minutes later, perhaps alarmed by my silence, she came and unlocked the door and announced through it, "Bruce, you can come out now." My reply became a family joke: "Thank you, Mother, I don't care to."

I don't know how my classmates and I compared in scholarship with children elsewhere. I do know that in the first grade we all memorized the alphabet and went on to pronounce syllables by phonics (a word not yet in use). I am told nowadays that the situation can't have been as good as I remember, but my recollection is that every child in town could soon read, with little or no trouble. Nobody to my knowledge dropped out of school, though the farm boys might be absent for a week or two now and then, to help with the spring plowing or at harvest time.

The greatest annual excitement of my early boyhood was the arrival of the threshing machine and its crew. The huge mechanism was drawn along the road by its own steam engine, like a locomotive miraculously escaped from the railroad, belching smoke and moving at a steady four or five miles an hour amid an uproar like doomsday, its steel wheels cleated for better traction and made broad to conquer the quagmires of mud sometimes encountered along the dirt roads. It was the first self-propelled road vehicle I had ever seen, and like the bulls, it induced an unforgettable alarm.

Our house was on the edge of town, close enough to the farm to permit the threshing machine to function in the yard near our huge barn. It was a small operation by today's standards, half a dozen men, only two or three of whom came with the rig; the others were recruited locally. The engine and the threshing machine were now connected by a long, wide, endless belt. Team after team drove up with shocks of wheat; into the hopper they went amid a fearful roar, and out came the wheat in a pile on the ground, with the straw in another, ten times as big.

The air was full of dust; the men shouted to one another above the noise, or to their horses. When the rig shut down for noon dinner, the silence was so sudden and so deep it was startling.

This was thirsty work, and the men drank water, when they could snatch a moment, from gallon crockery jugs; you removed the big cork, picked up the jug in one hand, swung it onto your shoulder, and lowered it to an almost horizontal position. Only a greenhorn would use both hands to bring the jug up to the level of his face.

The noon dinner was a hasty but epochal feast. All morning my mother and the hired girl worked furiously in the kitchen preparing vast platters of meat, mashed potatoes, baked beans, two or three other vegetables, apple and pumpkin pie, and, of course, big tin pots of coffee. The men sat around a sawhorse table and ate hugely; I don't remember much conversation. They were deeply sunburned except their foreheads; and when they took off their hats, these were a clammy white. Next day the rig and its crew had moved on to another job a few miles away and I felt that a holiday was over.

Not only did my uncles give my father a farm, they found a job for him in their new mortgage and loan company, at the staggering salary of $200 a month, more money than he had ever seen; he worked the farm in his spare time, with the aid of a hired man. He was now able to build a comfortable house. In addition to the barn there was a huge lawn, a vegetable garden, and a chicken house and yard. The barn included a carriage house big enough for three or four vehicles, box stalls for several horses, and a tack room, which Iowa sensibly called "the harness room." Upstairs there was a trunk room and a big haymow. The former, when I was ten or twelve, contained old trunks full of discarded clothing, some of it fancy-dress costumes. There was a wide ledge about six feet above the floor at one end, and naturally, my playmates and I improvised plays, and acted them out on this stage, wearing such parts of the discarded clothing as we could manage, with an audience of one or two younger children, or nobody at all.

In the haymow, small boys could climb the exposed studs and make a daring leap down onto the hay while small girls watched admiringly. My father loved gadgets, and installed a hay fork which came down outside one end of the barn, picked up a great mouthful of hay from a wagon, and carried it up and through a big double door. The fork traveled on a steel track under the ridgepole and released its load at any desired point.

On the day I was born, my father, by way of celebration, planted a tiny Colorado blue spruce in the middle of the largest sweep of our lawn, and when I was old enough to understand, I was told that it was just my age. It was one of the most beautiful specimens of its kind I have ever seen, and it grew mightily. The neighbors, and eventually the whole town, came to know of this as "Bruce's tree," and on one of my rare visits back home in later years, a local paper published a photograph of me standing beside it, and told the story of the planting. To this day, the sight of a Colorado blue spruce anywhere arrests my attention momentarily in a special way.

I am not superstitious, but I used to wonder sometimes which of us, the tree or I, would outlive the other. When I was about sixty a letter from Emmetsburg, received in New York, reported that a blight of some sort had struck "my tree" and it had to be cut down. I felt I had lost a friend.

There was a gay social life in Emmetsburg in the early days. Though Iowa was far from prosperous in the twenty years from 1873 to 1893, as I have recorded, my family was doing well; the mortgage and loan company was thriving, and the future looked bright.

We had a hired girl and a hired man, our table was laden with food, in the fashion of the day, and my parents entertained and were entertained. In winter my father drove a matched pair of horses, drawing a sleigh with flowers painted on the dashboard, and a big heavy buffalo robe for warmth (the temperature was often in the minus twenties and once got down to forty below). In summer the same horses pulled a two-seater surrey with a fringed top like the one celebrated in *Oklahoma*. We always had a dog or two, pointers and setters, and they went with the family on Sunday drives, ranging freely through the fields on either side until they were tired, when they trotted sedately behind. Another of my early memories is leaning over the rear of the surrey, watching the road shoot backward from the wheels, making me pleasurably dizzy.

Social life in those days included lawn suppers in summer, with Japanese lanterns tied in the trees, and card tables set out on the grass for the diners. In winter there were bobsled rides in a wagon equipped with runners, with plenty of hay and half a dozen buffalo robes. Christmas, Decoration Day, the Fourth of July, and Thanksgiving were celebrated as they were all over America.

Much of the social activity centered around the churches. One of my uncles was Episcopalian, the other Methodist, and my parents plumped for Methodism, I never knew why. Our church frowned on drinking, smoking, dancing, the theater, and card playing. My parents did not drink, my father did not smoke, and I don't remember their dancing, but they cheerfully ignored the other taboos. My mother staged amateur operettas among the town's young people, doing almost all the work herself, including playing the piano at the single performance. The Blivens belonged to a whist club that met regularly during the winter at the houses of the members in turn, and played until about eleven o'clock, after which ice cream, cake, and coffee were served.

My mother was also the town poet, writing a set of doggerel verses for every public occasion and many private ones. (She knew they were doggerel and did not take them seriously.) The town seemed to like them, and they were invariably printed in one of the local weeklies. She also wrote songs, words and music; one of them, "Little Overalls of Blue," was printed, I assume by some vanity publisher, with my photograph on the cover as a ten-year-old, wearing overalls and a broad-brimmed hat, and throwing a rubber ball in an impossibly awkward gesture. (When I protested that no boy ever threw like that, I was over-ruled on the ground that "it makes a better picture that way.")

One of my earliest vivid memories is my parents' return from a visit to the 1893 Columbian Exposition in Chicago, when I was not quite four. I remember the greeting from my parents and my fourteen-year-old sister, who had gone along. The hired girl, who had been left in charge of me, was hovering in the background, and there was a huge square trunk deposited by the expressman on the lawn near the front door. But most of all I remember the miraculous present I got—a rubber ball attached to an elastic cord so that I could bounce it and it would return into my hand.

The trip to Chicago must have been the last wholly carefree moment my parents were ever to have. The panic of 1893 was on, and a little later in the year the mortgage and loan company closed its doors. It had overextended itself, lending money on farms not only in Iowa but far out into the Dakotas; when the market for farm produce dwindled and prices dropped, the mortgages had to be foreclosed but the farms could rarely be sold for the sum of the loan.

My two uncles managed to escape with their personal fortunes intact; indeed, they got richer, by buying up quantities of land at forced sales, recognizing that eventually prices were bound to rise. But my father had no capital, only his $200 a month, which he spent as fast as he got it. He was in no way responsible for the debacle, but the harsh recriminations of the townspeople, some of whom had bought stock in the enterprise, extended to everybody connected with the company. My two uncles shrugged it off, but my father developed what would now be called a psychosomatic malady; he was unable thenceforth to endure working indoors, at a desk. He still had the farm, but a farm was now more a liability than an asset, and he sold it off, a few acres at a time, for money to live on. He was a wonderful person, loved by all who knew him, and he could do almost everything, but among the exceptions were making and saving money.

Gone now was the spirited team that pulled the surrey, gone were the hired girl and the hired man, gone were the costume parties and the suppers on the lawn with Japanese lanterns. My father tried a small dairy with a milk wagon, on each side of which was a beautiful painting of a pretty milkmaid leading a Jersey cow; this failed. He installed a dozen hives of bees, and tried to sell honey, but everybody in town either had bees of his own, or didn't like honey. From time to time Father got a little work in a general store, but in those hard days the wage was small and employment precarious.

Over the years, my mother did what she could to come to the rescue. She sold toilet and cosmetic supplies to her friends; while these

27

included almost everybody north of the tracks and a few from the south side, they didn't want many beauty preparations. She acted, with little success, as subscription agent for forthcoming books. Some of these were sets of classic authors, while others were journalistic enterprises. When an important event came along, like the death of Queen Victoria, or the Mt. Pelée disaster, a Chicago publisher would put together with fantastic speed a dummy volume, with a few sample pages of text and pictures. Copies of this were rushed to hundreds of agents in small towns, who then showed them to possible buyers. The agents promised delivery of the completed books within a few weeks, and this was in fact accomplished, with a speed equaled only by the mediocrity of the product. But very few in Emmetsburg wanted such books.

My mother by now was doing all her own housework, and hating every minute of it; she was so interested in public affairs, local and national, that she begrudged the time spent on routine tasks. The uncles helped us intermittently for a while, but in a few years one had died and the other (and both their families) had moved to southern California.

If you must be poor, plan to do so in a small Midwestern town in the 1890's. Even when things were at their worst, we always had a cow or two, pigs for slaughter, and chickens. We had a big vegetable garden, apple trees, grapevines, and did not need very much cash income. Transportation was a necessity, and instead of the surrey we now had a basket phaeton; our fat and lazy old horse, Chubb, was a town character.

Many other people were about as poor as we were and there was complete social equality. My parents kept up a brave front; I don't believe my mother ever uttered a word of recrimination as to my father's neurosis about office work. Only once in my life did I come upon her crying quietly alone, at a particularly difficult moment; the memory still hurts.

From an early age, reading was my chief passion. If our town had the rudiments of a public library, I did not know it, and I found books hard to come by. In their grand days, my parents had accumulated richly bound volumes of *The Century* for ten or twelve years, ending in 1892, and I read and reread these; I remember chiefly the almost endless reminiscences of Civil War generals and the story illustrations of E. W. Kemble, a famous illustrator of that day, who also worked on some of Mark Twain's books, and was a master at portraying violent action.

The Methodist Sunday School had a small library of stories for young people, designed to inculcate the highest moral principles; I read them all. Friends of mine tipped me off that the Congregational Sunday School had a similar library; I became temporarily a Congregational child, and went through that collection as well. A friend of the family gave me a tear-jerking story translated from the French, *Remi, the Boy Wanderer*, by Hector Malot, and I got it almost by heart. There was a wretched British series of dime novels about Jack Harkaway, and I accumulated half a dozen of them. I was also addicted to the books of G. A. Henty, which told many bits of history painlessly by having some teen-age boy involved in them.

For some unknown reason, my family had acquired G. Stanley Hall's big book, *Adolescence*, and I had waded through it before I myself had entered my teens. Many years later, when Dr. Hall was president emeritus of Clark University, I told him this story and he chuckled over it.

I can see that I am exaggerating the paucity of reading matter at this time. My Uncle Alvin had a library in which I was permitted to browse; he had complete sets of Dickens, Scott, and Robert Louis Stevenson, and I read them all straight through, going back to reread my favorites. My parents belonged to an informal book club whose members took turns buying the best sellers of the day, which were then passed around. My memory refreshed by Alice Hackett's *Sixty Years of Best Sellers*, I recall that while in high school I read *The Crossing*, by Winston Churchill (the American novelist, not the British statesman); *Beverly of Graustark*, by George Barr McCutcheon; *Rebecca of Sunnybrook Farm*, by Kate Douglas Wiggin; *The Garden of Allah*, by Robert Hichens; *The House of Mirth*, by Edith Wharton; *The Jungle*, by Upton Sinclair; and *The Spoilers*, by Rex Beach. Almost none of these books are still read today, except *Rebecca of Sunnybrook Farm.*

Somehow I got hold of Jerome K. Jerome's now almost forgotten *Three Men in a Boat*, which I thought and still think was a very funny book. I was enthralled by Kipling's *Plain Tales from the Hills*, quite unaware, at fifteen or sixteen, of the jingoism that was to cause people to look askance at him many years later.

I never saw *St. Nicholas* magazine, to which so many Eastern boys and girls of my generation were devoted. My paper was *The Youth's Companion*, which not only provided quantities of highly moral reading matter, but also premiums for peddling subscriptions to your friends. I never wanted anything so much as those premiums, pictured and described in a catalogue that I wore to tatters. I hounded my uncles and cousins into subscribing, and won a sled, the only one I ever had. The seat was high above the narrow, tubular, black iron runners, you steered by dragging a toe, and I adored it.

My family read two of the three local papers, *The Republican* and *The Tribune; The Democrat* circulated mainly south of the tracks. We took the weekly edition of a Chicago paper, I believe *The Inter-Ocean.* We should have read the excellent Des Moines paper, but the rail connections from Chicago were better and its papers came through faster.

Through my reading, I had acquired a vocabulary of some hundreds of words that nobody in Emmetsburg had ever spoken in my presence; the result, English being the illogical language it is, was that I mispronounced a large proportion of these. It took me years, after I had gone to college, to get them all straight, if indeed I ever have.

I assume it was my mother's example that got me interested in writing. At ten or eleven I won essay contests for children held by *The Woman's Home Companion* and *Success Magazine;* the rewards, aside from the thrill of seeing what I had written printed in national magazines, were books. I received as prizes Ida Tarbell's *Life of Lincoln,* and Captain Joshua Slocum's *Sailing Alone Around the World;* the latter I must have read forty or fifty times in the next half century.

In high school I started a paper; if my memory is correct, I wrote almost all of it myself, and I know I solicited all the advertising which made it financially possible; I also helped see it through the press in the job-printing department of one of the local weeklies. I learned to set type from the case; sixty-five years later I can still feel the "stick" held in my left hand, my right picking up the individual characters, and my thumb checking the little notch which told me each was right side up. But I never became good enough to be of much use to the professionals who set most of the type, made up the forms, and ran off the copies on a job press for me. The paper lasted four or five issues.

One of my friends and I invented a variation of thieves' jargon, as countless other children have done before and since. Ours consisted of removing the first letter or diphthong from a word and adding it at the end, followed by a meaningless "iker" or "aker," intended to confuse any eavesdropper. Thus "this is the way to do it" became "isthiker siker ethuker aywiker otoker odoker tiker." With practice we developed lightning speed and were able to tell each other secrets with impunity in front of our friends. A triumph came when the telephone operator, who naturally listened in, reported that Willie Morling and Bruce Bliven were talking "Russian or something" over the wire.

Our accomplishment became a wonderful morale builder for us. Neither of us had much physical prowess; Willie was lame, and I had flat feet and poor eyesight (I wore glasses from the age of seven or eight). Being athletic was, naturally, the chief characteristic of any importance among the children (to be bright in school was tolerated, if you weren't stuck up about it). The fact that we could talk this gibberish and understand each other was the solitary status symbol either of us had.

Our family finances never got any better while I was growing up, but there was no suggestion that I should drop out of school and go to work, and indeed, there were no jobs available to an adolescent in the small town that would have been of any real assistance. On one occasion, when I was about twelve, my mother popped some popcorn and told me to peddle it at a sandlot baseball game near our home. I did so, but I was so shy it was torture, and my mother could see that the few pennies I earned were not worth the misery.

On another occasion I caught a huge and beautiful butterfly. A neighbor of ours was an amateur lepidopterist, and my mother, who must have been really desperate that day, suggested I see whether he would buy it for twenty-five or fifty cents. I hated the errand; I wanted to give him the butterfly, as man to man. When he refused to pay anything at all, it was with a great feeling of relief that I made him a present of it and went home happily to tell my mother, with a clear conscience, that the sale had fallen through.

One of the uncles had a summer cottage on West Okoboji, and for years it was lent to us for a few weeks each summer, if no closer members of the family wanted it. Iowa roads follow the section lines; from Emmetsburg it was about forty miles to the lake, and my father and I made the journey with Chubb and the phaeton, while my mother took the train (my sister had by now married and moved away). We started about 4 A.M., so as to give the horse time to rest during the journey. The prairie was beautiful at that hour, so quiet and so fresh. Wherever the sod was unbroken, it was thick with dandelions, wild roses, and Indian paintbrush; when the sun rose, meadow larks saluted it, and if there was any wind, the telephone wires hummed, sliding up and down a few notes of the scale with the variations in the breeze.

Sometimes the road dipped down through a slough, with a few yards of thick mud, and on rare occasions we got stuck. When this happened, my father, swearing very mildly under his breath, took off his shoes and socks, rolled up his trousers, and got out into the muck. While I held the reins and urged old Chubb on, my father pushed from behind and got us across to the higher ground. These episodes were alarming, but pleasurable too, at least in retrospect; my father and I were Men without Women, undergoing strictly masculine adventures.

Nearly half a century later, when I was back home for a brief visit, my host at a dinner party discussed what to do for the evening's entertainment. They decided to drive to Okoboji and back, and we did. Nobody but me saw on the old dirt road paralleling the modern highway the ghost of an ancient white horse, a basket phaeton, and an anxious man and boy who had started before dawn and hoped to reach the lake by dark.

Another of the rare times my father and I were alone together was when we went hunting, an excursion of a few hours along the shore of the lake, or on our own farm property, while we still had some. Most of all I remember the times we went looking for small game, with heavy snow on the ground. It was a world of almost intolerable whiteness, the sun a smudged blur in the sky. I had a BB gun, a smaller imitation of my father's rifle, and I looked around fiercely for any prey as we tramped along on crusted snow or on frozen puddles, where the ice was flawed in every direction, with tips of vegetation visible beneath the surface. I can't remember that we ever killed anything, but we did a lot of walking, with no word uttered, and came home in contented comradeship.

By the turn of the century, the prairie was dotted with groves of cottonwoods and willows, usually planted just north of the farm houses as a windbreak; in town there were many buildings and trees to lessen the force of a storm. Old-timers told us that these were much less formidable than they had been thirty years earlier, but even so, our three or four blizzards each winter were terrifying. In the midst of one of them, my father left the house in late afternoon to feed and water the stock in the barn, a hundred yards away. The heavy snowfall was swirled in all directions by the full gale that was blowing; with every landmark obliterated, he got confused even on this short journey, and wandered back and forth for a long quarter of an hour, until he caught a glimpse of the lighted kerosene lamp in our kitchen.

The children of my day were a hardy lot. In my case, school was about a mile's walk from our house, and I can't remember more than half a dozen winter storms bad enough to keep me home. On very snowy days, I took my lunch, in an old lard pail with a wire handle; otherwise I walked, four times a day.

In winter we skated on the lake. There was only one iceboat, but a number of children, including myself, had skate sails, and got the thrill of tearing along under wind power, watching out for the tips of weeds sticking up through the ice, which could send you sprawling.

We had no "old swimming hole" for summer use by half-grown boys. The lake was unpleasantly muddy and weedy, and the river was several miles away, with transportation rarely available. My family swam daily during our visits to Okoboji and that was all.

Children don't appreciate natural beauty, or at least my generation didn't, except for an occasional sensational sunset, or a rainbow. It was not until many years later that I began to appreciate the wonderful great sweep of the gently rolling prairie, the mass of wild flowers in summer, the pristine whiteness of a winter day.

Normally, as I have noted, the rising generation in Emmetsburg was kept reasonably busy with odd jobs after school. We had no organized athletics, though we played Run, Sheep, Run, One Old Cat, and rudimentary football. (There were never enough boys at one spot at one time for two teams of nine or eleven.) Winter evenings we played checkers, dominoes, crokinole, Authors, another card game called Flinch, and, doubtless, others I have forgotten. On mild Sunday afternoons we walked down to the Milwaukee station to see the train from Chicago come in. We had, of course, no movies, no radio, no television, no cars for aimless driving around, but I can't remember ever feeling the restless malaise of the spirit that seems so conspicuous in the younger generation today.

In the long, hot summers, we lived under the threat of tornadoes, which we called cyclones. Like most other people, we had a cyclone cellar a few rods from the house, with a flight of wooden steps going down into a space of forty or fifty square feet, the roof of heavy sod, the room deep enough to let us stand upright. I can't remember that we ever actually took refuge in it; part of each year it was used to store root vegetables. But at least once I do remember seeing a cyclone passing a few miles away, from southwest to northeast, with its long, slender, evil funnel disappearing at the top into a roiled black cloud. On another occasion we drove out into the country to see a farmhouse that had been destroyed. It was almost perfectly flat, like a heap of trash that someone had carefully smoothed out over a large area.

Though I was kept in school in spite of the family poverty, when I was old enough I usually had a job in the summer at West Okoboji. One year I was employed by a "steam laundry" in the nearby town of Spirit Lake, picking up and returning linen for fifteen or twenty nearby cottagers. Another year I peddled *The Saturday Evening Post.* I had to buy my copies, but I got a credit if I tore off and sent in the covers of the unsold ones; I can still remember a few of the cover drawings, done by one of the Leyendecker brothers, popular artists of the day, as well as back-cover advertisements for Uneeda Biscuit, a boy dressed in bright yellow Down East oilskins—to emphasize the fact that the crackers did not get damp in the package.

For two high-school years I spent my summers acting as crew on a sailboat that carried passengers commercially; for fifty cents each, we would take a party of twenty or thirty people for a sail of an hour or two from Arnold's Park, where the one-day excursion trains brought their crowds; or we could be chartered at a fixed fee for a moonlight sail. Captain Lewis, who owned and sailed *The Golden Rule,* was a practicing dentist in Ottumwa, Iowa, who had hay fever and preferred to spend the summer on the water. He can't have made much money with his boat, but he didn't care. He paid me the entirely satisfactory wage of $10 a month, plus board and room, and supplied my sailor's blue uniforms, complete with a big square collar and a horrible number of buttons on the trousers. My duties were to help people on and off the boat, collect fares, tie up and cast off at docks ("Three half hitches will hold the devil," he told me), trim the jib sheet, and, rarely, have the thrill of taking the helm.

A few times, fouled halyards or some other problem required me to climb the mast, and I recall the excitement of swinging far to leeward while the boat was running close-hauled, looking down at the deck so suddenly diminished in size, and seeing from this fresh angle the modest "bone in her teeth" at the bow.

Captain Lewis was an intelligent and literate man; like me, he was devoted to reading, and when we were sailing with no passengers, we engaged in animated discussions of the popular novels of the day. Sometimes we went on quietly with these conversations even with passengers on board. If these were readers, which did not seem to happen very often, they would exchange startled glances, having taken it for granted that the captain and the crew of a commercial sailboat would be able to communicate only in grunts.

On a few occasions we were caught out in the middle of the lake by sudden, violent windstorms, and I learned how people act in unexpected peril. Most of them behaved well, but I remember one woman who in terror let her baby slip from her lap to the floor of the cockpit alongside the centerboard box, where it lay with the rain beating down on it. Another time, four big, stalwart men panicked and were less than useless as Captain Lewis and I got the sails down (we had only mainsail and jib) and got the anchor out. It didn't hold, and we were driven ashore on a pebbly beach, with little damage.

I had only one personal mishap in two summers. One dark night, in a mild breeze, I was walking aft along the deck when the mainsail jibed and knocked me overboard, the boat sailing off into the darkness. I was wearing heavy oxfords and a blue jacket (I was going to a dance later that evening), and since it was half a mile to shore, I was frightened. But Captain Lewis came about at once, found me in two or three minutes, and threw me a line. You may be sure I made the most of this adventure when I returned to high school in the fall.

When I was in high school my father and I carried on a running joke for a long time whose basis was the idea that Women Talk Too Much, and that we ought to get away to some small, deserted island somewhere. But instead, the whole family began to dream of migrating to California, away from Iowa's bitter winters and—I now suspect—away from the debacle of the mortgage and loan company. We sent to various towns for Chamber of Commerce "literature," and for some reason I have forgotten, we settled on Auburn, then a decaying foothill town north of Sacramento, as our ideal. When we finally did go west, we ended up, like almost all Iowans, in the Los Angeles area. None of us have ever seen Auburn; but for many months it represented a shining hope of the future.

I was sent to the Methodist Sunday School from an early age, and without being consulted as to whether I wanted to go. I don't remember much about it, with one exception. When I was very young, our teacher repeatedly showed us a large, vertical, colored poster called something like *The Drunkard's Downfall*, a series of pictures zigzagging down across the sheet. At the top left the protagonist, not yet an alcoholic, was a handsome young man, living in a nice house, with a pretty, well-dressed wife and two cute children, the boy a year older than the girl, as he ought to be.

In the second scene, a little down the sheet and to the right, he is persuaded against his better judgment to take one drink at a party. In successive zigzag scenes he becomes a compulsive imbiber, and loses his job, home, and family. In the last scene, the wretch lies in rags in the gutter, clutching an empty bottle. He now wears whiskers—not neat ones like those of President Grant, but wild and unkempt. It is obvious that if the poster had been a little longer we should have seen him in a pauper's grave.

This drawing made such an impression on me that seventy years later I can still recall most of it. We all abhor the amateur Freudian who generalizes from insufficient data, but it interests me that all my life I have never been able to take more than one drink without getting slightly nauseated. Even that single drink results in no pleasurable sensation— only a slight dizziness and a tendency to talk in long, complicated sentences. This defect of mine has been a serious handicap to my career as a journalist, as we shall see.

At about fourteen, soon after my voice had changed, I found myself to my astonishment singing tenor in the Methodist choir. The merit that acquired this honor for me was a simple one—nobody else was available. My voice was mediocre, but I could read music and could refrain from giggling at inappropriate times.

Actually, I should have preferred to spend the period of the church service, as I had been doing for some time, when I could get away with it, in the small room behind the pipe organ, where my friend, Charlie Milham, pumped the bellows by hand. Charlie had a wonderful collection of old magazines—mostly *The Argosy*—and on at least one occasion he got so engrossed in reading that he did not hear the buzzer telling him to start pumping, resulting in an embarrassing brief gap in the church service.

The director of the choir was a young man who seemed older than he was because he was prematurely bald; he, also, sang tenor. When we did anything more ambitious than lead the congregation in hymns, he always picked out a work that included a tenor solo. I knew I wasn't good enough for solos, and didn't really want to sing one; nevertheless, I was jealous.

The Methodists rarely held revival meetings; I remember only one with a special, imported preacher, during my three years or so in the choir; but that experience was memorable. This man was famous for his ability to get repentant sinners to rise and come forward to "the mourners' bench"—the first row of pews, left vacant for this purpose, where they would be talked to, in a state of hysterical emotion, by the revivalist, by our own minister, or by one or two especially helpful elder members of the congregation.

The revival meetings went on every night for a week, and at the climax of each session, after a sermon by the revivalist, all possible pressure was put on. He would chant over and over, at once the hypnotizer and the hynotized, "Come to the mourners' bench—come all ye who are weary and heavy-laden—come lay your burdens at the foot of the Cross," and much more of the same. Throughout his words, we in the choir sang softly and repeatedly as an obbligato in the background, the last stanza of an old Methodist revivalist hymn:

> *Almost persuaded,*
> *Harvest is past.*
> *Almost persuaded,*
> *Doom comes at last.*
> *Almost cannot avail;*
> *Almost is but to fail;*
> *Sad, sad, that bitter wail,*
> *Almost, but lost.*

Some of the congregation, smugly sure that they were among the saved, sang softly with us. One by one, a few others who believed they were in a state of sin would come down and kneel by the altar, or sit in the first row of pews, where they could be encouraged, *sotto voce,* by one of the little group waiting to receive them.

Nowadays it is fashionable to say that most of these highly emotional conversions are only temporary; at that time we all knew of a few chronic repeaters who came forward whenever there was an opportunity. But in general, the church and the whole community thought the revival meeting was a fine idea. The revivalist traveled a circuit, appearing in one town after another, in the fashion exemplified years later by such famous pulpit orators as Billy Sunday and Billy Graham.

I did not feel strongly involved in these proceedings; I thought I was doing my bit by standing in the choir loft each night and joining in the singing of "Almost Persuaded." I was therefore shocked when, one day, our own resident minister stopped me on the street and said, "Bruce, when are you coming down to the mourners' bench?" It had seemed to me that the members of the choir would not be expected to perform this rite; and if I had dropped my hymnal and climbed down (the choir loft was up a flight of steep steps behind the pulpit), what would become of my duet with Gretchen Schroeder, which was a part of most meetings? I stammered out that I would think about it, and managed to escape.

My dilemma was solved in a way I could never have expected. Only a few days later, the electrifying news ran around the town that our pastor had deserted his family and eloped with the wife of a leading member of the congregation! This was by far the most dramatic event of my boyhood years, outdistancing the time my Uncle Ed's barn, only a block from our house, burned down, killing several valuable horses.

A new pastor was hastily brought in from somewhere else, and there was no more discussion of having Bruce climb down from the choir loft to the mourners' bench.

Year by year, the boy grew older; in spite of our poverty, it was on the whole a happy childhood. I can't remember that I ever had a crush on a teacher, but at fifteen I was half in love simultaneously or in quick succession with some of my classmates, Gretchen, Lucy, Ruby, Jessie, and others whose names I have forgotten, though I remember their shining, soap-and-water faces. A shy boy, I adored them from a distance.

A few small triumphs of those years stand out. At about sixteen, I starred in an operetta put on by my mother, of which I remember only that I wore a white naval uniform, like Lieutenant Pinkerton in *Madame Butterfly;* I am sure I got the part by nepotism, though in fact, bad as I was as an actor or singer, I recall no other boy in town who was any better. I won a countywide oratorical contest with a speech I wrote and memorized, in praise of the sturdy inhabitants of the Mississippi Valley. A few short stories of mine were printed in one of the town newspapers —at the prompting, I am sure, of my mother—and got me more attention locally than did the prize-winning essays in national magazines, which were seen by few in Emmetsburg.

As my senior year in high school came to an end, the family began to discuss whether college was possible for me, and if so, which one. I was notified, out of a clear sky, that I had won a scholarship at Cornell College (the one in Iowa), but it paid only my tuition.

Then came the wonderful news that my cousin Scott, Uncle Alvin's son, would help see me through some university, to the extent of $40 a month—a fortune. Though there was a little talk of Harvard, it vanished almost at once in favor of Stanford, in California. The ostensible reason was that my health seemed a little frail; I had frequent tonsilitis and was underweight, and the family doctor agreed that the mild climate of Palo Alto would be good for me.

But the real reason was the one already mentioned: my family, like practically everybody else in Iowa, yearned to move to the Golden West. There was in those years, as there has been ever since, a tremendous migration to California from the Middle West, of which I shall have more to say a little later. With Bruce in Palo Alto to spy out the land, the move would be easier and simpler for my parents.

In those days college entrance was far from being the ordeal it is today. Application was made to Stanford, my high-school records were forwarded, and word came that I was accepted. There was only one hitch; American History was then required for admission, Emmetsburg High School had no such course, and I should have to pass an entrance examination in this subject. To anticipate a little, I bought a history of the United States, read it on the train, and was one of a minority who passed the test. I could hardly have missed; my head was full of facts I had read only a few days earlier.

The family was up at Okoboji at the beginning of August, when it was time for me to leave on the first long train journey of my life. My father came down with me to Emmetsburg to help with the final preparations; we crossed the lake by steamer to Arnold's Park, leaving my mother trying not to cry as she stood and waved on the pier. I was too excited to cry, which in any case would never do for a boy who had passed his eighteenth birthday a week or so earlier.

Father and I came down by train and stayed overnight in our house, strangely quiet with only "the men" there. We packed my suitcases for the trip, cooked our meals, and in the late afternoon of the second day we walked together to the Rock Island depot, only two or three blocks away. Though hardly a word had been spoken, I never felt closer to my father than I did in those twenty-four hours. As we heard the southbound train coming past the water tower, at the narrowest point on the lake, he made me a very short speech, which he had clearly been rehearsing in his mind for some time.

"Take care of your health," he said, "and improve your opportunities."

I said I would, and he helped lift my suitcases to the platform of the day coach (there was only one) that was to carry me to my connection with the San Francisco train. As we began to move, I went out to the rear platform to wave good-bye. Father waved back, a small and lonely figure among the gathering shadows. The train rounded a slight curve, and I went in and sat down. I had left home.

Chapter 2

THE RED TILES OF STANFORD

Before I was an hour out of Emmetsburg, trouble began. Heavy rains had flooded the whole state, and our train was unable to reach the town where I was to transfer to the express to California. We sat all night in a soggy meadow, the rain beating down, and next day, after backing up for many miles, traveled on half a dozen unscheduled lines, and arrived at the junction long after the through train had departed. I was supposed to go to California in a tourist (second-class) coach, at a reduced fare, but since I had missed the train through no fault of my own, I was put on board what was probably the swankiest train then operating west of the Mississippi, the Rocky Mountain Limited. I had not been on a long-distance train of any sort since I was old enough to remember, and I was overwhelmed by luxury such as I had never seen in my life.

After three days I arrived in Oakland, the loneliest eighteen-year-old in the state of California. Many years later, in an article written at the request of *The San Francisco Examiner,* I described my first contact with the city, doing so in the third person.

> *He had never been away from home before* [*I wrote*]. *He had never been anywhere near an ocean before, and he had never in his own memory seen a really big town.*
> *The Ferry Building at the foot of Market Street was itself enough to panic a small-town Midwestern boy, with its thousands of commuters*

rushing in and out, the flower stands, the coffee-and-doughnut shops, the newsboys underfoot and shouting.

But the eighteen-year-old braved it all and got into Market Street where the big electric streetcars were charging up and down, two abreast. With a little time to spare before college opened, he found a cheap hotel room and began to explore this fantastic city.

If the boy was only eighteen, most of San Francisco was for all practical purposes even younger, only sixteen months old. Yet so swiftly had the work of rebuilding been done that evidences of the 1906 earthquake and fire were amazingly few.

The boy walked up and down Van Ness Avenue, the temporary main street of the town, where famous old restaurants and stores were doing business on an emergency basis in painted wooden shacks. He got out to the Cliff House and saw his first ocean, staring west across an incredible seascape of misty gray water.

On lower Market Street he viewed the steel skeletons of the new buildings that would, everyone said, be fire-and-earthquakeproof. He felt the thrill of an indomitable, vital, and surging people who, when the ground shook beneath their feet, yelled "Let 'er buck!" and as soon as the earth had stopped trembling, began picking up the pieces.

On his last day, the boy had his great personal adventure. He had never seen a saloon until he left home, but San Francisco was full of them, all with stained glass fronts that shut out the light—and the stares of the curious.

Boldly he entered one near the railroad station at Third and Townsend streets, and found a place for himself along the bar. Those were easy-going days; though the boy probably looked even younger than he was, and some of the men glanced at him a little curiously, no one questioned his right to be there.

The coatlesss, aproned bartender finally reached him, adjusting his sleeve garters. "What'll it be, Bud?" he asked.

The boy was stumped, suddenly realizing he didn't know the name of a single stylish drink. Then up from his subconscious came a title and he grasped at it.

"I'll take a glass of crème de menthe," he said, pronouncing it as it had looked to him in print—cream dee menth.

The line along the bar grew silent at the words. The bartender looked dubious, but after some groping in the ranks of bottles in front of the big mirror, which had the items of the day's free lunch written on it in soap, he produced a dark-green square bottle and poured out a small glass. "That'll be fifteen cents," he said.

The boy pushed the money across the bar, and with everyone in the room now looking at him, he tasted the green liquid, astonished to find that it had a peppermint flavor.

He downed the rest of it in a few gulps, and set the glass back on the bar, impervious to the amused glances from up and down the room. A slow smile lit the corners of his face. Now he was a man, he felt, a regular crème-de-menthe-swigging adult. And what a time, and what a city, in which to be one!

When I came back to California to live nearly fifty years later, the city had changed tremendously, and mostly for the worse. It still had its glorious hills, its cable cars—saved only after a desperate struggle from the destroying hands of vandals with no sense of history—its sparkling blue bay, its days of brilliant sunshine, its gray afternoon fog rolling in from the ocean, its fine restaurants, its flower stands. But in addition it was now laced with ugly, monstrous freeways on stilts, it had two huge bridges spanning the bay to Oakland and to Marin County, some of the finest views were marred by skyscrapers along the very water's edge, and the city was a mass of parking lots which were still inadequate to handle the volume of traffic.

Gone were the beautiful ferry boats on which commuters could breakfast comfortably, walk the decks in the bracing salt air, and arrive in the city invigorated for a day's work. Now the suburban commuters were arriving one by one, each in his own automobile, choked with smog on many days, often infuriated by the traffic delays, and using almost as much time as the ferries had required. San Francisco's fate is probably no worse than that of most other American communities; some of its aspects cannot be ruined no matter how hard people try—and they try very hard indeed—but you do not need to be a nostalgic oldster to see how much of the charm of fifty years ago has departed.

My very first day at Stanford gave me a trauma that lasted for years. I had reserved a place in a boardinghouse in College Terrace, half a mile from the university buildings, and had been told to take a carriage from the Palo Alto railroad station to my destination. When I boarded the train in San Francisco, I chanced to sit beside a boy a little older than myself, and with the easy gregariousness of the West, we exchanged names and I discovered that he was a Stanford sophomore, and a fraternity man. In those relaxed days, fraternity "rushing" was not bound with the rigid rules found at the university today. Any likely prospect could be snatched by the first house to get its hands on him, pledged, initiated (often a cruel ordeal), and start living with his brothers immediately.

My seatmate persuaded me, instead of going at once to my boardinghouse, to come first and have lunch at his frat. I did so, and tried to hold up my end of the conversation with the eight or ten members who had arrived a few days before college opened. A carriage was ordered, to be used after lunch to show me around the campus, and I felt, rightly or wrongly, that the brothers were looking on me with favor.

But then I made what must have been a dreadful faux pas. Though I had my cousin's firm promise of $40 a month, and assumed this was all the money I would need, I thought it would be in the best Horatio Alger tradition to announce, just as lunch was ending, that I intended to work my way through, and I did so.

The frozen silence that descended on the table was so thick that even a small-town boy from Iowa noticed it. After a long, grim pause, the president of the chapter addressed me. He had discovered that the carriage ordered to show me the campus was not available. I had said I had a reservation at the Cardinal Club, in College Terrace? Well, it was down the road only about a mile, to the left. Firmly he handed me my two heavy suitcases and started me off on foot down the dusty road.

I am sure this fraternity was no worse than any other in that era. Houses did take in some boys without money, but almost always they were outstanding high-school athletes, or had some other claim to special attention. The humiliating experience left its mark on me; toward the end of my freshman year, when I showed signs of producing the whole contents of the several undergraduate magazines all by myself, I was invited to join another fraternity, reported to be at a higher intellectual level, and curtly refused.

No doubt I had a lucky escape; though presumably there were some literate men in every Greek-letter house, I'm sure I should have been miserable trying to accommodate myself to the average level of interest and activity. But for many others in my generation, both men and women, being passed over was a bitter experience. It was especially hard on the girls; I knew of one young woman who dropped out of college rather than continue with "Rejected" stamped, in imagination, on her forehead. For most men, being turned down meant that you had to hunt for a furnished room somewhere in nearby Palo Alto, and eat your meals in mediocre restaurants (there were no good ones, and few boarding-houses). President David Starr Jordan, an admirable man in many other respects, was completely indifferent to this problem, so acute for many of his charges.

Today the fraternity system is everywhere fighting with its back to the wall. Most of the fraternities were started long ago in the South, and were still operated, in the mid-1960's, on strictly segregationist principles. Several at Stanford and elsewhere have lost or relinquished their charters because of pledging Negroes or members of other minority groups.

In spite of the ordeal of carrying my suitcases that long mile, I was luckier in my living quarters than many other freshmen. The Cardinal Club, where I had my reservation, was a boardinghouse run by two upperclassmen who were working their way through school. It turned out to be a pleasant place with a dozen congenial occupants, most of them freshmen like myself. We paid $16 a month for room and board, both of which were more than adequate, and we protested bitterly when rising costs made the Tuttle brothers raise the price to $18.

I adjusted promptly and easily to the new way of life. My letters home recorded my recognition of the beauty of the Santa Clara Valley, and my amazement at living in a mild climate—no snow, flowers blooming all winter, no need for heavy clothing. My appreciation of the natural beauty of the area was well justified. The valley lies along the southern end of San Francisco Bay, with a low, wooded mountain range to the west, between the valley and the ocean, and another beyond the bay to the east. The swelling flanks of the foothills were golden brown in summer's clear air, laced with the vivid green of the live oaks up the steep canyons. When the rains came in late autumn, the meadows turned miraculously in a night to green; early in the new year great areas of yellow poppies and blue lupin appeared in such masses that the fields on the mountain flanks could be seen miles away.

In 1907 the valley was one vast fruit orchard of prunes, apricots, cherries, peaches, with many acres of vineyards supplying the wineries. For a few weeks in spring, the whole area, as seen from any hilltop, was an almost solid carpet of white blossoms, tinged here and there with pink.

Today, of course, this beauty has been all but destroyed. Only on a few days after winter rain can the mountains across the bay be seen clearly; usually they are shrouded in brown smog. Many of the orchards have been bulldozed away to make room for a proliferation of urban sprawl, little wooden houses on narrow lots, connected by a gridiron of blacktop roads. Nearly all the main arteries are what the British call ribbon slums. Palo Alto, a mile from the university, still has handsome residential areas, but its once beautiful El Camino Real, "the King's Highway," is now so desecrated that the author of a book on ugly America, wanting a horror picture of wayside spoliation, found it here.

The university, which, like my hometown, seemed to me to have been there forever, was actually younger than I was; it had opened its doors in 1891, to about five hundred freshmen, one of whom was Herbert Hoover. A few words about it will help explain the impact it made on me.

Leland Stanford, born in 1824, had come to California in the 1850's from upper New York State; he came twice, in fact, having gone back once to Albany, where he made a very mild success at running a general store. In the 1860's, a storekeeper again in Sacramento, he joined forces with three other men in modest circumstances, Mark Hopkins, Collis P. Huntington, and Charles Crocker, and all four of them became multimillionaires by building the Central Pacific Railroad, which in 1869 met the Union Pacific tracks at Promontory Point, Utah, to bridge the continent for the first time.

That same year, Stanford's only son, Leland, Jr., was born. Fifteen years later, when the family was making the Grand Tour of Europe, the boy caught typhoid in Athens; he was hurried to Italy for better medical care, but died in Florence. The university was his heartbroken parents' memorial to him; technically its name is still Leland Stanford Junior University, a title not now used in full because of the ambiguous meaning of "Junior" which, applied to a college, indicates a two-year course. The endowment, considered gigantic in those days, was about $30 million; in the mid-sixties Stanford was spending much more than that every year.

Whether by luck or sagacity, the Stanfords did well at the very beginning in two important matters: the choice of a president for the university, and of architects to build it. For the first, they chose Jordan, a distinguished young ichthyologist, trained at Cornell, who had recently been named head of the University of Indiana. Jordan was the first real scholar and famous personality I ever encountered, and he made a deep impression on me. He was a huge man, with a deep rumble of a voice, a scientist, humanist, and world citizen, with a good sense of humor and a real liking for people—even including freshmen.

For architects, the Stanfords chose the Boston firm of Shipley, Rutan and Coolidge, aided by the famous landscape architect Frederick Lee Olmstead. Since the climate of Palo Alto is semitropical, the architects explored the styles of building to be seen around the shores of the Mediterranean, and came up with an idea for what was then, and may still be, the most handsome single complex of buildings on any American campus. The design was two quadrangles, one inside the other, of one- and two-story buildings of rough tan sandstone capped by red-tiled roofs. Around the perimeters of both quadrangles ran covered promenades, supported by a series of longitudinal arches, providing protected access from every classroom to every other during the rainy season. A dormitory for men and one for women were set on opposite sides of the front of the outer quadrangle, each a block away, both carrying out the motif of buff sandstone and red tile.

Jordan had to start from nothing, and he naturally recruited his first faculty from Indiana and Cornell. His task was made harder by the general nationwide pessimism about whether a new university in the wilds of California was needed and would ever amount to anything. Some established professors in the East were reluctant to come, though others accepted the challenge with pleasure. A few years later William James, spending a few months on the campus as a visiting lecturer, wrote disparagingly to his friends about the place. He admitted the architecture was magnificent, but doubted that the faculty and students were up to it.

The scholars who had declined to come west probably felt justified when Stanford, now a United States senator, died unexpectedly in 1893.

His will was promptly attacked in the courts by his relatives, and the whole estate, including most of the bequest to the university, was locked up tight for several years. To make matters worse, the United States government also entered suit, for $15 million, in a dispute growing out of the building of the transcontinental railroad. Stanford had acted in all cases in consort with his three partners; Hopkins and Crocker were dead, Huntington still alive. Since the estates of these three men were ignored, partisans of Stanford decided the government's action was politically motivated.

Meanwhile, the university was desperately short of money. Of the $30 million bequest, only $2.5 million had been handed over, and Jordan was told he could have only $12,500 a month with which to pay salaries and all other running expenses—far short of what was considered a bare minimum. Salaries were cut, but even the reduced amounts sometimes could not be paid. A few outside suppliers of materials were willing to extend credit, for a limited time; most demanded cash.

Stanford's widow, Jane, emerging from his shadow after his death, unexpectedly revealed great fortitude and firmness of character—as well as an imperious determination always to have her own way, which made endless trouble for poor Jordan. But at the beginning she was magnificent. It was she who insisted against the advice of many counselors that the university should not close down, waiting until the suits were settled, but must go on.

At one time the institution was almost out of coal for heat and electric power. Mrs. Stanford told a companion, as they neared the campus on a return from San Francisco, "I can't bear to look and perhaps not see smoke coming from the big chimney, for I know the coal is almost used up." Her friend was able to reassure her.[1]

The faculty members kept going by a series of desperate expedients. A grocer in Palo Alto extended unreasonable amounts of credit, and was rewarded with lifelong patronage. Most of the faculty were very young, with no savings and with small children; friends in the East sent out cast-off clothing to be cut down for their use.

At one black moment, Mrs. Stanford managed to put her hands on $500 in $20 gold pieces. A college legend says that Jordan himself walked from house to house along "Faculty Row" and handed out the gold, one piece to a family, to those whom he knew to be in the most desperate straits.

The litigation against the Stanford estate dragged its tortuous way through one leisurely tribunal after another until it reached the most leisurely of all, the Supreme Court. When it threatened to rest there indefinitely, Jane Stanford scraped up a couple of hundred dollars and

[1]Edith R. Mirrielees, *Stanford: The Story of a University*, New York, Putnam, 1959.

went to Washington for a personal appeal to the President. It worked: the Court at last decided everything in Stanford's favor. When the news reached the campus, classes were suspended for a day, and students and faculty danced along the corridors of the inner quad.

The next few years saw a silent but sometimes bitter struggle between Jane Stanford and Dr. Jordan. With money still limited, she wanted to spend it on buildings (the outer quad was still not finished); he wanted to enlarge the faculty and increase salaries. The result was an uneasy compromise; the most badly needed buildings were finished, and the position of the faculty was improved, though for many years it was worse than in comparable institutions in the East.

Mrs. Stanford was responsible for the most notorious episode in the university's history, the dismissal of Professor Edward A. Ross. She had no academic background; she thought of her faculty as she did of her household servants, who could be dismissed out of hand when they displeased her. Ross, an outspoken young radical, incurred her displeasure by off-campus political activity, and—worst of sins in her eyes—by disagreeing with the views of her late husband on the question of Chinese immigration, then a matter of hot dispute in California. Finally she ordered Ross's dismissal, and Jordan, after many months of delaying tactics, was forced to obey, causing a nationwide uproar. There is some evidence that Ross deliberately sought the role of martyr. His career was not harmed; he went to the University of Wisconsin, where he served many years without any public commotion; he used to drop in on me in New York and would talk of old Stanford days with no bitterness.

Oddly enough, his attitude on Chinese immigration was what today would be considered conservative; he was against it. Mrs. Stanford knew nothing about it one way or the other, but her late husband had imported coolies by the thousand to build the railroad, and that was enough for her.

At the end of my freshman year the students who had been operating the Cardinal Club left, and I had to find a new place to live. The only dormitory for men, Encina Hall, was always full; you could obtain a room only if some departing senior pulled wires for you, or by bribing the janitor with a few dollars. I got in, by a means I refuse to divulge, and had room three on the ground floor, next to the front door. Mrs. Stanford had ordered the door locked and the lights turned off every night at midnight, and late-returning revelers invariably climbed in my window, a practice that interfered with sleep for my roommate and myself, but augmented the sociability of our nights.

At the girls' dormitory, Roble Hall, the rules were even stricter. The lights were turned off and the doors locked at ten o'clock; growing girls, Jane Stanford felt, needed plenty of sleep. A senior proctor lived in the room equivalent in position to mine. She would let a hapless female in after ten, but would normally report her name to the disciplinary committee; three such episodes and you were in bad trouble.

Mrs. Stanford had other eccentricities. Disliking automobiles, she ordered that there should be none on the campus, and this made trouble for the university doctor, young Ray Lyman Wilbur, who afterward became president of the institution, and secretary of the interior under Hoover. He lived on the campus, a mile or more from the Stanford home; he used a car, but came and went by a circuitous route, and Jane never discovered his transgression.

With more than sixty years of hindsight, I can see some things that were wrong with Stanford and with me in 1907. The university was operated on the elective system; there were very few required courses, and they were soon disposed of. The result was that a lazy student could take the easiest subjects, and get a degree having acquired a shockingly small amount of really useful knowledge.

I chose English as my major, for no special reason, and took the necessary number of courses, but few of them made any deep impression on me. I studied elementary French and German, but did not go far enough in either of them to read or converse with ease. I took no physics or chemistry or biology, and far too little history, political science, or economics. If I could do it over, I should dig hard at all these subjects. I have spent a lot of time in the reading room of the New York Public Library trying to patch the holes in my education left by the complacent attitude of Stanford sixty years ago.

In my day the university graded many courses with a mere plus or minus—passed or failed. This is a fine system for students pursuing knowledge for its own sake, but it does not seem to me to work very well in a hard, competitive culture where scholastic honors can have an immediate and important effect upon one's earning power and position.

Written examinations were miniature essays; I had facility as a writer, and could weave a web of words that usually concealed my fundamental ignorance. As a result I often got marks that were better than I deserved. The other day I looked at my grades for the first time in half a century. A quarter of them were scored only "pass" or "fail" and I passed them all. I passed all the others, with one exception, getting "A" or "B" in two-thirds of them.

The exception is the only reason I mention this not very distinguished record. The head of the English Department was a now-forgotten scholar, who let me, as a freshman, enroll in his course for seniors in Robert Browning. At one of the first meetings he observed that Browning's obscurity was a mark of his genius, that some of his thoughts were too deep for clarity. I spoke up brashly and said that, on the contrary, I believed if you were great enough, you could express *any* thought clearly. The argument went on intermittently through the term, and at last the professor, a pompous and irascible man, gave the annoying

47

freshman a failing mark. Since I had worked as hard in this course as in others for which I got an "A," this injustice rankled.

Like many another student before and since I found many college lectures and classroom discussions almost unendurably boring. The pace of the class was often painfully slow, and many lecturers labored the obvious to the point of agony for the listener. I found I could get the same facts out of a book in half the time, and I often escaped with a great sense of relief into the library stacks, where I felt like Aladdin in his cave. I reveled in having, for the first time in my life, more books available than I could possibly read. My tastes were conventional; I devoured Meredith, Hardy, Galsworthy, Bennett, Shaw, Ibsen, Wedekind, Hauptmann, and a dozen more. I was fascinated by H. G. Wells's early romances, which still seem to me the best science fiction ever written. I carried Housman's *Shropshire Lad* in my pocket for weeks, and later did the same for Logan Pearsall Smith's *Trivia*. I was about equally impressed by Edward Bellamy's optimistic picture of the future, *Looking Backward*, and Ignatius Donnelly's pessimistic one, *Caesar's Column.* My classroom work seemed pallid and remote compared to these vivid, authentic voices of the present, through whose books I could gallop at my own pace.

The most valuable experiences of my college life came, as they do for most people, outside the scholastic routine. A member of the English faculty, Henry David Gray, invited half a dozen aspiring writers among the undergraduates to meet once a month at his home, to read aloud and discuss their work. There was, of course, no college credit; you worked for love. The group included, at one time or another, Maxwell Anderson, the playwright; Robert L. Duffus, later assistant editor of *The New York Times;* Frank Hill, who was to be coauthor with Allan Nevins of the definitive biography of Henry Ford; and Ernest Hopkins, who wrote half a dozen books, was a celebrated newspaper reporter in San Francisco, and taught journalism at Arizona State University at Tempe.

An extracurricular activity I myself started was a "course" in contemporary fiction. The university offered instruction in nineteenth- and twentieth-century literature, but somehow, such courses, which began with Dickens and Thackeray, were always cut off by the ending of the school year about when the year 1900 had been reached. My friends and I were soaking ourselves in the writers I have mentioned above, people rarely mentioned in any classroom. Accordingly, a few of us got together, and on long sunny afternoons we would climb the hills behind the campus, sit in the shade of a live oak, and talk about the startling ideas of these new writers.

Without meaning to, I presently did Dr. Gray some damage. I wrote a short story, published in the college literary magazine, *The Sequoia*, on a theme popular in those days, dual or split personality. My heroine seemed to be of this type, but the reader was left wondering whether this was true, or whether she was only pretending, in order to discourage a suitor she didn't like, and encourage one she did. Dr. Gray, himself only a few years out of college, had ambitions as a dramatist. He asked me whether I should object if he based a play on my story, and I said not at all, to go ahead.

That miserable play almost ruined Gray's life for decades. He worked on it for many months, and at last achieved a production by an amateur group in Palo Alto, but this did not satisfy him, and he began trying to storm the producers' offices in New York. He persuaded several of them in succession to read it, and each, naturally, told him to rewrite it on quite different lines. This process took years; before it was over, I was myself in New York as chief editorial writer for a newspaper, *The Globe.*

Gray's annual trip to that city to show his latest version to some producer was always marked by the same ceremony. My wife and I would give a small dinner party for him in our apartment, attended by a few Stanford men of my generation interested in literature, and after dinner he would read the latest version aloud to us. Naturally, I was filled with guilt, having started this mad project, and I appointed myself a one-man claque to laugh at all the jokes. But the other alumni present did not share my sense of obligation; they responded only when the jokes were funny, which was not very often. Finally Gray asked pointedly why I laughed so much alone, and I had to moderate my transports.

After years of this, the hopeful playwright gave up. He devoted the rest of his life to scholarship, specializing, as I remember, in the Elizabethan poets, and I'm sure the English Department was pleased and relieved.

Before I had been in college long, I decided to make good on my unfortunate boast at the fraternity house, and try to earn some money. I registered at the student employment office, and was sent to wash windows at the home of Professor Green of the Mathematics Department, at the standard rate of fifty cents an hour.

Rarely in my life have I hated anything as much as my few hours at Professor Green's house. There were two pretty daughters of about my own age, and I felt they were laughing at me (many years later, they assured me this was not true). The soapy water ran up my arms, the stepladder seemed precarious, I got tired long before the job was done. I hated the whole thing; surely, I said to myself, there must be some easier way to earn money.

As it turned out, that was the last day in my life that I ever did manual labor for money. A short time later, the job of college correspondent for *The San Francisco Bulletin* came vacant, and I managed to land it. Though I didn't realize it, this led to one of the turning points in my life.

The Bulletin was an afternoon paper, poorly financed and far from prosperous, but it had as editor one of the towering figures of American journalism, Fremont Older, and he was engaged in what was probably the greatest crusade against municipal corruption in the nation's history. As a college correspondent, I knew little about it, but before long I was thrown into much more intimate contact with the paper and its editor.

As a correspondent, I was paid fifteen cents an inch for my articles. I pasted them together, one below another, a practice that has produced the widely used term "stringer." The *Bulletin* cashier measured the inches and paid me accordingly. I was supposed to omit headlines and to crowd the items reasonably close together, and like all stringers, I was in perpetual battle as to whether I had permitted too much "air" between stories.

I wrote my daily quota in the late afternoon, in the office of the student daily, and then walked to Palo Alto, about a mile away, and handed the bulky envelope to the mail clerk on the 6:30 train. My facility with words was now a valuable asset; I had many ideas for articles, and managed to pad the length of each without seeming to do so; I was able to earn $50 or $60 a month in this way, a huge sum in those days to an Emmetsburg boy.

Presently I was invited to spend a summer vacation as a cub reporter in the *Bulletin* office, at $15 a week; no invitation I have ever received has excited me more. Now for the first time I came into direct contact with the famous editor and learned some of the facts about him.

Older was born in 1856, in Wisconsin; his father and six uncles had been killed in the Civil War, the widow was desperately poor, and at ten, Fremont had to leave school and go to work. He had all sorts of jobs, finally becoming first a printer's devil and then a tramp printer. After many years of knocking around, always poor, he landed in San Francisco and was offered a job as managing editor of *The Bulletin*, a dying paper with only 9,000 circulation. Though he did not learn this until long afterward, the paper was kept alive largely by a secret monthly subvention from the Southern Pacific Railroad. That line was the most powerful political force in California, and it kept scores of papers subservient by handouts.

Older made an immediate success. He pioneered the use of big, black headlines, created news where there was none, splashed pictures all over the paper. Not having had his enthusiasm ruined by formal education, he got enormously excited about great writers, new and old, and did not hesitate to print on the front page in large type a poem by Kipling or Edwin Markham—or anything else that struck his fancy.

By the time I began doing summer vacation work in the office, Older was the most loved, most feared, most famous editor in the West. He was a giant of a man, with a bald head, a Western-sheriff mustache, piercing eyes above a prominent nose, and a deep bellow of a voice. When he was angry, his wrath was terrible to behold, yet every good piece of work by any reporter was swiftly recognized and appreciated.

He had a special place in his heart for the poor and afflicted, particularly those who had been in jail, deservedly or not. He once remarked, in turning away a charity fund-raiser, "I'll let you handle the deserving cases. My hands are busy with the undeserving."[2]

Older insisted on having a small and shabby office, so that the humblest visitor would not be overawed; I'm sure the penny-pinching owner of the paper had no objection. Miriam Allen de Ford, a well-known novelist and alumna of the *Bulletin* once wrote that

> *the editor's office was a confessional, an employment bureau, a loan office; everyone had access to him, and all day long a stream of visitors, mostly in trouble and needy, sat across from him at the desk marred by careless cigarette butts, while Fremont Older leaned back in his swivel chair, his head against the wall, his ears and his hands open.*[3]

Over the next few years I learned some of the favorite stories about Older that circulated in the city room. Perhaps the most famous was one showing how hard he worked to teach the rudiments of journalism to his cub reporters. One man seemed incapable of seeing and remembering any of the vivid details that are the lifeblood of good newspaper writing. Older sent him to live with the Salvation Army, day and night, for three weeks, but when he returned, his report was as lifeless as all his earlier writing had been.

"Don't you ever observe anything?" asked the editor in despair. "You lived with them for three weeks; when they reached the barracks at night, *where did they hang the bass drum?*"

The reporter could not answer, and Older had to advise him to follow some other career. But the story became famous, so much so that Niven Busch applied it to a fictional editor in his San Francisco novel, *The Californians.*

As noted, having come to the masterpieces of literature late in life, Older found them enormously exciting. Once he called up an editorial writer in the middle of the night, demanding that he come and see him at once. Fearful of some catastrophe, the man did so, to find the editor striding up and down with a book in his hand. "Listen to this wonderful stuff," he exclaimed, and proceeded to read aloud from Montaigne's *Essays,* on which he had just stumbled. "The odd part of it was," the editorial writer later explained, "that Older got *me* all worked up over it, too."

[2]Evelyn Wells, *Fremont Older,* New York, D. Appleton-Century, 1936.
[3]Miriam Allen de Ford, *They Were San Franciscans,* Caxton Printers, Caldwell, Idaho, 1941.

51

I had been in the office only two or three days when Older used me to indicate his dissatisfaction with the paper's star reporter, John Francis Neylan, who afterward studied law and became the millionaire counsel for all the far-flung enterprises of William Randolph Hearst. Neylan had written a story, Older didn't like it, and he came charging out of his office holding the manuscript up by two fingers, like carrying a dead rat by the tail.

It happened that Neylan and I were the only two men in the city room, Neylan at the first desk, the place of honor, I cowering as far in the rear as I could get. Older saw me and roared like the captain of a windjammer in a gale. "Bliven!" he shouted. "Take this stuff of Neylan's and make something printable out of it."

I had no choice but to try, and my rewrite made page one. I don't think Neylan ever forgave me for it.

One of my assignments showed Older's mischievous side. In those early days automobile insurance was more a racket than a business: the small type of the typical policy contained many escape clauses for the company. Older had me dress in my best clothes and go up and down Market Street insuring a mythical automobile. Then I wrote the story, reporting all the loopholes. The headline Carl Hoffman, the city editor, put on my piece said "Push Your Auto Off a Ferry Or Down a Volcano If You Want to Collect." The brokers protested loudly, but Older shrugged off their complaints.

If Older could be terrifying in his wrath, he could also be unexpectedly gentle when wrath might have been expected. On July 4, 1910, Jack Johnson, the Negro heavyweight world champion, fought Jim Jeffries, former champion attempting a comeback, in Reno, Nevada. As was the custom of the time, *The Bulletin* prepared, days in advance, alternate "extras" with one front page saying Johnson had won, and the other, Jeffries. The pages, below the huge headlines and a single sentence in each case about the victory, were filled with accounts of the fight, masterpieces of evasive writing, going in very heavily for (imaginary) local color. On the day of the contest, the pressroom crew in the basement stood ready to start printing one version or the other, and a group of newsboys waited to hurry them out into the street.

The flash came through to the city room on the fourth floor that Johnson had won, and a member of the staff phoned the news down to the press foreman. Either he gave the wrong message, or someone picked up the wrong plate; several thousand copies came off the press saying in huge type, "Jeffries Wins." By the time copies got upstairs and the mistake was discovered, the papers were in the hands of the newsboys and a few hundred were sold before they could be recovered.

The Bulletin's chief rival in the afternoon field was *The News*, which next day reprinted a copy of the erroneous headline, in reduced size, and made the charge that *The Bulletin* was so anti-Negro it would not even admit that a member of that race had won the championship! Since, however, *The Bulletin* had never shown the slightest sign of hostility to Negroes, this charge fizzled out.

Older might have been expected to tear the culprit in the office limb from limb, but on the contrary he passed the incident off casually. "Anyone can make a mistake," was all he said.

While I was a freshman at Stanford, Older's enemies, a corrupt gang who were looting the city, kidnapped him intending to kill him; his life was saved by an astonishing accident. His fight against corruption went on through my whole service on the paper; to indicate what it meant, I must go back to a time six years before I came to California.

In 1901, San Francisco experienced a bad waterfront strike, with strikers beaten up and some men killed; the strike was broken, and the workers were left bitterly angry. The political boss of the city was a brilliant young lawyer, Abe Ruef, and he saw a great opportunity. Taking control of the Union Labor Party, he picked a candidate for mayor, Eugene Schmitz, the orchestra leader in a theater, a big, handsome, bearded man. When Ruef first approached him, the musician protested that he knew nothing about politics, and Ruef assured him this did not matter. The important thing was his size, and Ruef proceeded to lay down a fundamental political law: "The psychology of the mass of voters," he told his pupil, "is like that of a crowd of small boys or primitive men. Other things being equal, of two candidates they will almost invariably follow the strong, finely-built man."

He proved to be right. With weak (and smaller) candidates on the Republican and Democratic tickets, the Union Labor Party won.

The problem now was to teach Schmitz the rudiments of municipal government in a hurry. Ruef hid him away in a hotel in the small town of Sonoma, and for several days hammered into him the chief points of the city charter. The cramming course must have been a success; after he was sworn in, no one complained of Schmitz's ignorance. He was triumphantly reelected in 1903 and in 1905, for a total of six years.

Now began an era of open, brazen corruption unparalleled in the history of American cities. Anybody who wanted anything from the city, legitimate or illegitimate, had to pay Ruef to get it, and millions of dollars were spent in bribes. Invariably, the little boss became "attorney" for the seeker of favors, and the bribes were officially described by him as "lawyer's fees." The corruption extended to the judiciary, right up to the State Supreme Court. (Some of this had begun years before Ruef came on the scene.)

Technically, San Francisco was governed by the Mayor and by a board of supervisors of eighteen men. Seventeen of them proved susceptible to bribery; the eighteenth, for some inexplicable reason, was honest.

When the seventeen showed signs of seeking to operate singly, under the free-enterprise system, Ruef called them together and read them the riot act. All monies were to be channeled through him, and him alone; he would destroy anyone who defied him. From then on, with few exceptions, nobody did.

A typical distribution was a bribe of $125,000 from the Home Telephone Company, which wanted to offer a competing service against the existing monopoly of the Pacific States Company. Ruef kept one-quarter of the money, gave Schmitz a quarter, and distributed the other half to the seventeen crooked supervisors.

San Francisco was in those days a wide-open town, as I learned when, during my summer *Bulletin* "internship," I covered the court beat for a while. There were rows of houses of prostitution along Jackson Street nearby. Tourists could and did come to dance halls like the "Thalia," where all the dancers were prostitutes engaged in drumming up trade. One very large house of prostitution was believed to be partly owned by Mayor Schmitz, and was universally known as "the municipal crib."

But if San Francisco was in general "corrupt and contented," in Lincoln Steffens' phrase, there was one man who chafed at the situation —Fremont Older. He had little help from the proprietors of *The Bulletin*, who, left to their own impulses, would doubtless have kept their eyes shut and continued to take the monthly subsidy from the Southern Pacific. But Older, by sheer force of character, compelled them to follow him. He began to expose the corruption in the city, beginning with the notorious French restaurants. These had ground-floor eating rooms that were entirely respectable, but the upper floors contained a series of private rooms which were nightly scenes of debauchery.

As long as *The Bulletin* fought only such matters as prostitution and the dope traffic, the "best people" of the city were approving, or at least neutral. But Older soon discovered that the trail of bribery led into the ranks of these "best people" themselves. Public-utility magnates like Patrick Calhoun of the street-railway system were paying Ruef large sums annually. In Calhoun's case, he was fending off an order to put his trolley wires underground, but all the utilities, and many other businesses, had some reason to buy Ruef's friendship.

When these facts were printed, there came an abrupt change in community sentiment; Older and his wife suddenly found themselves ostracized. Things were made so unpleasant for him at his club that he was forced to resign. Years later Mrs. Older wrote that

> *the minds of the well-to-do and wealthy seemed narcotized by the statement that "the graft prosecution hurts business." . . . Members of the prosecution were not bidden to entertainments where people of fashion*

gathered . . . [where] women reserved their sweetest smiles for the
candidates for state's prison . . . [and] to ask whether one believed in
looting the city became a delicate personal question.

Animosity to Older took a more direct form: efforts to kill him. A
skyscraper was being built across the street from the *Bulletin* building
where the editor sat daily in front of a fourth-floor window in plain view.
A gunman was hired to climb up the scaffolding, dressed like a workman,
and shoot him while the pneumatic riveting was going on to drown out
the noise. The Olders had a cabin at the beach, and two attempts at
assassination were planned there, one by shooting, one by dynamite
planted under the floor. All these plans fell through, chiefly because the
gunmen proved temperamental and exorbitant in their demands for
money.

During my freshman year in college came the most serious attempt
of all. A venal Justice of the Peace in Los Angeles, four hundred miles
away, was persuaded to sign arrest papers for Older on a trumped-up
charge of criminal libel, and two gangsters were sent to San Francisco
to get him, joined there by two local thugs in Calhoun's pay. By a false
telephone call offering him valuable information, he was lured some
distance away from his office, where the four men seized him and hustled
him into an automobile.

A few years later, they might have shot him in the car and then
thrown his body over a cliff, but this type of gangland operation had not
yet been invented. Instead, they drove a few miles down the San Francisco Peninsula to a railroad station, and, with a pistol in his ribs, got him
into a drawing room on the overnight train to Los Angeles, the Lark.
They afterward confessed that they planned to shoot him and throw his
body out the window as the train was on a bridge over a deep canyon
between Santa Barbara and Los Angeles. The story they intended to
tell was that they had left the train with Older at a way station in the
night, that he had tried to escape, they had shot at him, and he had disappeared.

As I have reported, his life was saved by an amazing accident. Secure
in their legal status as arresting officers, the gunmen actually took Older
with them into the dining car! There he was recognized by a young San
Francisco attorney who knew him by sight. This man became troubled
at seeing the famous editor in the company of four such hard-looking
individuals.

Although he had a ticket to Los Angeles, this man gathered up his
possessions and got off at the next stop, the little town of Paso Robles.
The only available telephone was in the locked railroad station, and the
stationmaster, who lived upstairs, had gone to bed. The young traveler
managed to rouse him, got admitted, and rang up the San Francisco

morning *Call*, knowing most other establishments would be closed at that late hour.

"Is Fremont Older missing, by any chance?" he asked.

"My God, yes," came the answer. "He has disappeared. The whole town is looking for him."

"Well, he's on the Lark, southbound, with several tough-looking characters," said the traveler.

While the young attorney tramped the streets of Paso Robles trying to find a place to sleep, Older's friends burned up the wires. A judge in Santa Barbara was awakened in the middle of the night, and asked to issue a writ of habeas corpus; a group of sheriff's deputies went down to the station to serve it. Somehow, word of what was happening spread through the town, and there was quite a crowd on the platform when the train arrived in the early morning. One of the kidnappers looked out the window and remarked that "there must be a wedding." He was wrong. A few minutes later, there was a knock on the door, and the gangsters and their victim were led away to a local courtroom. Older was set free, and the thugs were bound over for trial.

Of the four kidnappers, two turned state's evidence, and admitted they had planned to murder Older. One man jumped bail and was never recaptured. One man was tried in San Francisco for abducting the editor, and was acquitted, in a court where the jurors were wholehearted supporters of the graft ring.

Through my four undergraduate years Older and his few allies went on with their struggle against corruption; most of the time it seemed a hopeless fight. President Theodore Roosevelt had lent the graft prosecution an able lawyer from Washington, Francis J. Heney, who succeeded, in the beginning of my sophomore year, in bringing Abe Ruef into court. As Heney stood before the jury, a man rose from a seat in the rear of the room and shot him in the head with a revolver. The would-be assassin was seized and hustled into a jail cell, where next morning he was found dead, a small pistol beside him.

The natural assumption was that this man had been pressured by the grafters to kill Heney, and had then been killed to shut his mouth. In fact, however, he was an ex-convict who had been called for jury duty; Heney had learned of his record and had publicly confronted him with it in refusing to let him serve. He had brooded for months over this fact, and the shooting was presumably an attempt at revenge.

A new attorney for the prosecution was brought forward, and the trial ground on. Heney lay at death's door for many weeks, but at last he was convalescent, and sent word to Older that he planned to visit the courtroom (as a spectator) on a given day. By coincidence, that was the day the Ruef case went to the jury, which deliberated in a room just overhead, within easy earshot.

Older was a master showman, when he needed to be; he assembled a large group of his friends in the courtroom, and when Heney entered, they set up a great shout. The jurors deliberating upstairs heard the sound, and presumably thought it was angry citizens thirsting for their blood if they should set free the flagrantly guilty Ruef. They returned a verdict against him, and he was sentenced to fourteen years in San Quentin.

When I left the campus to work in the *Bulletin* office for the summer of 1910, I found the editorial staff sunk in gloom. Case after airtight case had been presented in the courts, only to result in hung juries, or acquittals, or reversals on appeal. With very few exceptions, judges dismissed indictments on flimsy pretexts. Ruef, the only one of the scores of guilty men to be sent to jail, was preparing an appeal to the State Supreme Court, and that body was expected to grant it; a new trial would probably produce an acquittal—in spite of the fact that Ruef some time earlier had made a complete written confession.[4]

Yet if we had known it, victory was soon to come. There was a gubernatorial election that fall, and the graft prosecution decided to run Hiram W. Johnson, the attorney who had taken Heney's place. The *Bulletin* staff, who knew him best, thought poorly of Johnson, an egotistical, humorless, and avaricious man (alone among all the lawyers connected with the fight against corruption, he demanded, and received, a large fee for his services). Nevertheless, the paper got behind him. Neylan was assigned to help write his speeches, the best he ever delivered, and the paper gave him daily warm support.

Though most of the rich and powerful people of San Francisco, and their followers, were still on the side of corruption, this was not true of the rest of the state, or of the nation, where Older's titanic struggle was watched with admiration. Thousands of Californians resented the merciless tactics of the Southern Pacific Railroad, and other corporations, which dominated the state legislature in Sacramento, and they welcomed Johnson's repeated promises that he would break the grip of the despoilers. In November of my senior year he was elected governor, and with him many reformist members of the State Senate and Assembly.

Ruef's confession, and other facts about wholesale bribery that got into the record during the various trials, had frightened off both the givers and receivers of bribes. Suddenly the fight was almost over.

Ruef's appeal for a new trial was rejected through a seemingly trivial mischance. The corruptionists controlled four of the seven members of the State Supreme Court, and the last of the four signed the order for a rehearing on the final day on which it was legally possible to do so. It

[4]The whole story of the graft prosecution is told in *Boss Ruef's San Francisco,* by Walton Bean, Berkeley, University of California Press, 1952.

happened, however, that another member of the court was out of the state that day, and a quirk of the law invalidated his previously written signature, reducing the required majority to a minority. Ruef's sentence had been reduced from fourteen years to nine, but appeals for his early release were rejected by the newly virtuous government, and he had to serve the legal minimum of four and a half years in prison before he could be paroled.

Ruef, indomitably buoyant, came back to San Francisco when set free, and practiced law there (honestly, as far as anyone knows), for many years, though when he died it was found that his liabilities exceeded his assets. Schmitz, who from first to last maintained his innocence in the face of irrefutable proof of his guilt, also lived on in San Francisco for some years. He had the gall to run again for mayor, and was defeated. Later, however, he was actually elected to several successive terms on the Board of Supervisors—by now probably the most painfully honest, because most closely watched, group of its kind in the United States.

Having worked so long and hard to put Ruef behind bars, Older now had a change of heart. He decided that the bribers and the bribed were both victims of the social system, and should not be punished individually for yielding to the pressure on them. He now began a struggle to get Ruef set free. But the community was not ready on such short notice to follow him into a new Tolstoyan attitude, and he made hardly any converts.

I had left Stanford and northern California before some of this happened, but I was kept informed by my friends on *The Bulletin*, and later by the published documentation of Evelyn Wells and others. Older's visits to San Quentin to see Ruef brought him into contact with many other prisoners, and he began helping them rehabilitate themselves when set free; some of them were actually paroled into his care. One of them, Donald Lowrie, had some talent as a writer; Older published his life story serially in *The Bulletin*, and it was a huge success. Another ex-convict was a redoubtable second-story man, Jack Black, whose autobiography, first in *The Bulletin* and then in book form, earned him many lecture engagements all over the country. In the midst of a speaking tour he wrote to Older:

> *This speaking is the softest and easiest racket in the world. Wish I had known it years ago. Chauncey Depew made 15,000 speeches and never got arrested once.*

Black, a small, soft-spoken man, came to dinner at my home (I was by now living in New York) and enthralled my other guests by his casual reports of desperate adventures, delivered in the mild tones of a college instructor. He told us that the surest way to fend off burglars is to crumple newspapers and strew them on the floor; nothing, he said, terrifies a second-story man like the discovery that he is making a noise.

Another enormously popular serial in *The Bulletin* was the (mostly ghostwritten) memoirs of "Alice Smith," a prostitute, who debunked the romantic aspects of her profession. To follow her story, Older sent a girl reporter to call on a number of San Francisco clergy pretending she was a fallen woman who wanted to go straight. They all gave her good advice, but not one lifted a finger to help her, financially or otherwise. There were some red faces when *The Bulletin* reported all these interviews.

Older also serialized, among others, Ruef's life story, in which the ex-boss, writing from his jail cell, carefully omitted any revelations not already on the record; and finally, the editor published his autobiography, *My Own Story.* His value as a newspaperman was shown by the fact that when he left *The Bulletin* for *The Call* (transformed from a morning paper to an evening one, and owned by William Randolph Hearst), the circulation of *The Bulletin* dropped by one-half. [5]

Many convicts, paroled or released, headed straight for Older's big country home in the foothills, some miles south of the city, where the editor put them to work, at least temporarily, around the place. Guests discovered, with mixed feelings, that the cook might be a confessed poisoner, and the "butler" who carved the roast at the sideboard could once have performed a similar operation on a girl friend. When the shutter on a high window broke loose one night in a windstorm, a second-story man climbed up easily and made repairs. Nobody ever misbehaved at the Older ranch, though a disturbing proportion of the men the editor helped eventually went back to crime and either disappeared or wound up in prison again. But he never regretted the help he had given.

During my years on *The Bulletin* I was living in two worlds. On the paper I saw, as few youngsters of my age have a chance to do, the forces of good and evil locked in violent struggle. On the campus, I lived the life of a normal adolescent, groping toward maturity. As a freshman, I was, like everybody else, mercilessly hazed; a group of sophomores dragged me one night into Encina Hall, the men's dormitory, and held me under water in a bathtub until I thought my lungs would burst. The fact that I had not yet been able to get a room for myself in Encina made the use of its facilities for this purpose seem ironic.

Before the annual football game with the traditional rival, the University of California at Berkeley, I stayed up all night for the first time in my life, as one of a group of men designated to guard the huge, centuries-old redwood at one corner of the campus, from which the town

---

[5] *The Bulletin* was soon taken over by *The Call*, and many years later, the third San Francisco evening paper, *The News*, was added to the amalgam. Finally all three of them disappeared when Hearst's *Examiner* switched to the evening field, leaving the town with only two papers, the (morning) *Chronicle* being the other.

of Palo Alto (tall tree) gets its name. We sat around a campfire on the edge of El Camino Real (there was no traffic after 11 P.M.) and looked belligerently into the dark for Berkeley invaders who never came.

In my sophomore year, either my roommate or myself got a letter from New York asking about starting a Stanford chapter of the Intercollegiate Socialist Society; we never knew where they got the name. Neither of us knew much about Socialism, though my roommate had some pamphlets of the Fabian Society in London, including, I believe, H. G. Wells's masterly *This Misery of Boots*. In those days, of course, the word "Socialism" did not carry the enormous burden of emotion, hostile or favorable, that it does today. It was about as respectable as Henry George's Single Tax, and some hardy souls embraced them both, along with vegetarianism, sleeping porches, Hindu philosophy, and loose-fitting clothes.

What we saw in the invitation was a chance for a letterhead, with which to lure outside speakers to the campus. Both of us had been surprised to find so little of current world problems, in the classroom or out of it, in this somewhat parochial university, and felt this should be remedied. A chapter of the I.S.S. therefore came into being, a letterhead was printed, and outside speakers from San Francisco and Oakland were sought. We had practically no money; my memory is that our visitors paid their own carfare, but that among us we managed to dig up fifty cents each time for the speaker's supper.

The meetings were held in our room in Encina, where there were two single beds in a curtained alcove for my roommate and me. Eight-thirty on Sunday evening was a favorite time for a meeting, and ten or eleven people was the maximum attendance, most sitting on the floor or the window ledges. And now I ran into a personal difficulty. I have always been one of the "day people," up with the sun, and showing a tendency to set when it does. Our speakers were one and all intolerably long-winded, and the subsequent discussions equally so, going on until the lights were turned off at midnight, and even longer if we had an (illegal) candle.

I solved my problem with a simple and direct attack. I would introduce the speaker, listen for a few minutes with ostentatious attention, and then leap up as though I had just remembered some urgent household task, and slip into the curtained alcove. Once there, I proceeded to undress and go to bed, leaving the speaker to take care of himself. While I slept, the meeting went on and on, and so far as I know, I was never particularly missed. If I seem to have been lacking in intellectual curiosity, the answer is that all these men had the same few and simple ideas, and when you had heard one, you had heard them all.

The Stanford I.S.S. continued for a year or two, with perhaps a dozen meetings, and then died of inanition, since we had run out of free speakers. Nationally, the organization presently changed its name to The League for Industrial Democracy, and under the devoted care of Harry W. Laidler, it kept going through the decades.

One well-known Socialist came to live in Palo Alto while I was an undergraduate: Upton Sinclair. Most of his enormous output of books was still ahead of him, but he had already become famous through the best-known of them all—*The Jungle,* a story of the Chicago meat-packing houses. Sinclair meant it to portray the sufferings of the exploited workers, but what caught the national attention was his vivid picture of a working man falling into the machinery and ending up as packaged sausage on the breakfast table. He made no attempt to proselyte for Socialism at Stanford, but several aspiring writers on the campus courted him, and copied his dietary idiosyncrasies.

This was harder to do than might appear. Upton was a food faddist, but one who changed his ideas rather rapidly. At one time he ate nothing but meat, and at another, no meat at all—both modes difficult to fit into the menu of a college boardinghouse, though we did our best.

Still harder to cope with was the idea, popular not only with Sinclair but with many other people at the time, that an occasional total fast of a few days is a fine thing for the health. We were growing boys with good appetites and while we believed in fasting, we found the flesh weak.

The climax, for me, came when I was invited to a Thanksgiving weekend in a cottage at Boulder Creek, a resort town in the heavy forest of the Santa Cruz mountains. Our hostess was an ardent Sinclairian, and when five or six guests arrived, we found it was to be a weekend of high thinking but plain living—plenty of drinking water but no food. However, our hostess had a ten-year-old son, and she felt it was unfair to ask one so young to refrain from eating, so she prepared a complete, conventional Thanksgiving dinner for him. We all sat famished around the table and saw him consume modest portions of turkey, chestnut dressing, mashed potatoes and gravy, and pumpkin pie.

The weekend was to continue foodless for the adults until Monday; but coward that I was, I couldn't take it. I got down into the village and telephoned to a friend on the campus, who sent me a telegram saying my presence was urgently needed there. With every show of regret, I caught the next train back to the outside world, and food.

A powerful influence on me during the latter part of my college years was the owner of a secondhand bookstore in nearby San Jose, N. L. Greist. Like Sinclair, he was in theory a Socialist, but he, also, refrained from proselyting. The back room of his store was headquarters for the intellectuals of San Jose, then a peaceful and pretty town of 50,000 (now about ten times larger). An argument was always in progress, on politics, economics, or religion—heady stuff for a boy from Emmetsburg. Greist's great heroes were Herbert Spencer, and the pioneer anthropologist Ales Hrdlicka, and he quoted them impartially on every occasion. He resented having the discussion interrupted by a customer, and his patrons must have sensed this, for he did not have many. Few outsiders ever joined the perennial debate in the back room, though I remember Big Bill Haywood of the I.W.W. on one or two occasions, glowering from a corner. He did not know that all his worst troubles were still ahead of him.

I had a few warm friends on the faculty, but I was too busy earning my living to have much time for social contact. One of them was Dr. Lewis Terman, who some years later was to shake the educational world by rewriting and vastly improving the intelligence tests developed by Simon and Binet in France.

Thorstein Veblen overlapped with me at Stanford but I wasn't eligible for his classes, and hadn't wit enough to try to weasel my way in. Edward Krehbiel, a vigorous and popular teacher of history, turned up a few years later running Black, Starr, Frost and Gorham in New York, and very well, too. Edith Mirrielees, who taught English at Stanford and later at the famous Breadloaf summer writing conferences, became a dear and lifelong friend. There were half a dozen others whom I liked very much, who influenced me in varying degrees, but I am sobered to realize their names would mean little today except to Stanford alumni of my generation.

In Palo Alto I made friends with a gentle, elderly theosophist whose two towheaded small sons always remained quietly in the background. They grew up to be Russell and Sigurd Varian, inventors of the Klystron tube, a foundation stone of electronics, and a powerful factor in winning the Second World War.

In my senior year a young English instructor came to Stanford who evoked my sympathy. He was fresh from Harvard, incurably shy, had a thick Boston accent, wore flowered vests at which the students laughed, and was hopelessly unable to control the young men who made his classes a shambles. Van Wyck Brooks had already published *The Wine of the Puritans*, but only a dozen of us had ever heard of it, or cared about the ideas of which he was a protagonist. After a year or so, he went back east; though his autobiography does not say so, I'm sure he must have been happy to get out of California.

A few other celebrities swam briefly through my skies. I remember a public dinner in Oakland with Jack London at the head table, smiling silently into space, his thoughts far away. George Sterling, the poet, came up from Carmel for some reason, and recalling his haunted eyes, I was not surprised to learn that he had killed himself not long afterward in the Bohemian Club in San Francisco.

He was far less known at the time than another poet, Joaquin Miller, an impious old fraud who modeled himself on Walt Whitman and lived in a shack on an Oakland hilltop. Two or three of us, counting our pennies, asked him to join us for dinner one night at a famous San Francisco restaurant which was still operating from a wooden shack on Van Ness Avenue, a refugee from the 1906 earthquake and fire.

The table d'hôte dinner was terribly expensive, a dollar; it consisted of five or six courses, beginning with breadsticks, olives, and radishes. We plied the old man with questions about his work, all of us nibbling the food meanwhile. Presently the waiter came in with thick china bowls of onion soup.

Miller looked down at his as if in surprise. "What's this?" he asked.

"That's the beginning of your dinner, sir," one of us answered.

"Dinner?" said the poet, as though he had never heard the word. "But I've had my dinner," indicating the bread crumbs and olive pits on his plate.

There was a stunned silence for a moment, but we were starving boys, and none of us cared to emulate his restraint. While the conversation went on, we worked our way through the soup, fish, roast chicken, salad, and cheese and fruit. On the train back to Palo Alto we noted that if we had only known in advance, we could have shared our breadsticks and olives with him, and saved the dollar.

In my senior year, a well-known journalist, Dr. Edwin E. Slosson of *The Independent*, spent a few days on the campus, writing one of a series of articles on ten or twelve American universities, and the president's office asked me to serve as cicerone. In his article he acknowledged my help, and after that issue of *The Independent* appeared, I was a campus celebrity to a dozen people or so, for a week.

In the same year, Wallace Irwin, who had attended Stanford a few years earlier, wrote a series in *Collier's, Letters of a Japanese Schoolboy,* commenting in fractured English on current events, like Mr. Dooley. I was by now editor of *The Chaparral*, the college humorous magazine, and I wrote some parodies on Irwin. Somebody on *Collier's* gave me a pat on the head in an editorial, and I was gratified. The club of Japanese students on campus voted me an honorary member.

That was a busy year for me. I still wrote daily for *The Bulletin;* I got a salary as an assistant in the English Department, and a token one as editor of *The Chaparral.* In all, I was taking in some $200 a month, the equivalent of about $600 today. This did not leave much time for study, but I managed.

A couple of weeks before the end of the year I woke up with a start to the fact that I owed one professor five or six essays on leading British writers of the nineteenth century. I sat up all night, for the second time in my life, and wrote them all, one after another. I got a "B" in the course, which was probably better than I deserved.

In 1910 I saw my first airplane flight. A barnstormer advertised that he would take off and land again on the infield of Tanforan racetrack, a few miles up the peninsula toward San Francisco. There was a high board fence around the entire track, and several thousand people, of whom I was one, paid fifty cents each to sit in the grandstand and see this marvel. The plane was of course the flimsy box-kite structure of that day. There was no cockpit; the aviator sat in front of the engine, his feet braced on the struts. It must have been ticklish work getting enough altitude in a short space to clear the fence, but he made it, circled a few times at an altitude of 400 or 500 feet, and came down safely.

So far as I know, I was the only person at Stanford interested enough to travel to Tanforan. However, I was asked to report on it in detail at a meeting of a debating club to which I belonged. No other member had ever seen an airplane in flight.

Sending Bruce to California to spy out the land worked pretty well for my family. Encouraged by my glowing reports of roses in January, my father sold our Emmetsburg home in the spring of 1908. It was so heavily mortgaged that he got hardly any cash, but at least he was able to leave town. My parents settled in Santa Cruz, on the northern shore of Monterey Bay, about two hours by train from Palo Alto. They set up a pattern they would follow the rest of their lives—renting an old house, larger than they needed, and getting two or three lodgers for a little cash income. My father raised pure-bred Rhode Island Red chickens and sold the eggs and young chicks to poultrymen up and down California. Before I was out of college I was earning enough to contribute to the family support.

My father died in 1921 of a complication of old men's diseases; his last words were, "Let me go, Lil," and I have wondered ever since what he meant by them. In his own terms, he was a strong man; but the vicissitudes of life had beaten him down, and in the final years, my mother played the major role in the family. It could be that by what he said he was in a way apologizing for being forced to abandon her after so many happy years together, but I think it is more likely that he was asking her permission to die.

Toward the end of my junior year occurred an event of great importance. At a college dance I met the girl I was to marry.

How does one write, in an extroverted, reportorial memoir like this, about one's life partner? I don't know, except to say that at frequent intervals in the past fifty-odd years someone meeting her for the first time has come up to me to ask, in effect, "Do you realize what a wonderful person your wife is?"

This, too, is a question I don't know how to answer.

Rose Frances Emery (named Frances for Grover Cleveland's popular wife) was living in San Jose with her widowed mother and two brothers, and was a freshman at Stanford during my senior year. Our really serious business that year was getting better acquainted with one another, and how either of us got any classroom work done, I still don't know. By the middle of the year, we were engaged; like nearly everybody else, we arrived at this situation by tacit agreement, with no formal proposal and acceptance. I managed to scrape up the money for an engagement ring; it had what must have been the smallest diamond in the world, but my fiancée loyally insisted that it was *huge*.

In fair weather, she often walked with me in the late afternoon a mile through the campus arboretum, to put my *Bulletin* story on the San Francisco train. This prevented her eating dinner at Roble dormitory, so I had to buy one in town. Usually we went to "the Greeks," where we got a substantial three-course dinner, a thick minestrone-type soup, meat and vegetables, dessert and coffee, for twenty-five cents each, and a twenty-percent tip of ten cents. The proprietor and his wife, who were waiter and cashier, became our friends and beamed at these so young Americans, so much in love.

My fiancée had a history far more dramatic than my own. Her father owned a prosperous limestone quarry in Indiana, but became infected with gold fever and sold his business and moved his family to California. He and a partner invested in a mine near Angels Camp, the town made famous by Mark Twain in "The Jumping Frog of Calaveras County." The mine was a failure, the father died not long thereafter, and the family moved to San Jose, a few miles from Stanford. As I have said, his daughter entered as a freshman as I began my senior year, we met, and promptly fell in love.

That I ever plucked up courage to get really engaged was noteworthy, for the shyness that had afflicted my childhood had clung to me in college, and continued even after I had learned the ominous deductions psychiatrists now draw from such a condition. I remember that at the age of four, I was given a birthday party, and when the children assembled on the lawn, I hung back. Thereupon my fourteen-year-old sister bundled me by main force into a toy wheelbarrow and trundled me back and forth through the group; the pain of the experience remains to this day. As a senior in college, the English Club, of which I was by now an officer, would meet in the evening at one or another of the sorority houses, and I would have to walk up and down the block two or three times before I could get up the courage to ring the bell.

In later life I have probably overcompensated for this weakness, as my friends kindly point out to me, by trying to dominate every conversation in which I take part.

I decided to stay on at Stanford for a fifth year, for no special reason except that my fiancée was now a sophomore, and I was earning more money than I seemed likely to get anywhere else. Yet I was far from being an enthusiastic Joe College; in my junior year I had expressed a desire to get out into the world, and was talked out of it by my father, who, with almost no schooling at all, perhaps overestimated the value of a college degree. But staying on for a fifth year was a mistake for me. The point was driven home by an English professor in the first week of the new term. He was giving a graduate seminar in *Hamlet,* and at the first meeting of the class, he assigned each of us a subject for a term paper. "You, Mr. Bliven," he said to me, "will write on the history of Denmark for the hundred years before Hamlet's father came to the throne."

I waited until the hour was ended, and approached the professor. "I'm terribly sorry," I said, "but I won't be able to take this course. I find I have a conflict." I did not explain that my conflict was spiritual, that it seemed absolutely idiotic for a man of twenty-two to spend half a year on such an arid enterprise, when the purpose of reading *Hamlet* or seeing it performed, is to enjoy Shakespeare's genius.

Unfortunately, the other graduate courses in which I was enrolled seemed equally remote from reality. I was fed up with the academic life, and within a few weeks I dropped the whole thing, packed my trunk, and was on the daylight train for Los Angeles, where most of my family were now living. I left behind my fiancée, many good friends, and the memory of four on the whole fairly happy years. In fact, I was repeating what I had done in 1907: I was again leaving home.

Chapter 3

LOS ANGELES BEFORE SMOG

It is hard nowadays to believe that in 1912 Los Angeles was a very pleasant place in which to live. There was no smog, no automobile traffic to speak of, and a leisurely pace of living, almost the only remaining trace of the Spanish culture of sixty years earlier.

The city had about 400,000 people, and there was a necklace of suburban towns small enough to make an Emmetsburg boy feel at home in them. We had a fine transportation system, a network of yellow trolleys in the city itself, and the wonderful big, red Pacific Electric interurban cars that went in all directions to the ocean and to the foothill towns, fast, clean, and quiet. There were very few commuters by automobile; you boarded the interurban with your morning newspaper and had time to read its comparatively few pages before you were delivered to the downtown area. Since this was only roughly three blocks wide and seven blocks long, walking to work from one of the interurban depots was no problem.

Los Angeles was a world capital for crackpots, though in fact they were only a small proportion of the population. All sorts of odd religious sects had their headquarters in or near the city, and these groups overlapped heavily with diet faddists, physical culturists, and dress reformers, among whom the men tended to dress like women, and vice versa—a commonplace half a century later, but disturbing to the proprieties at that time.

In addition to the religious groups, many of them based on various

Oriental philosophies, there were many types of faith healers, astrologers, and fortune-tellers. Individual religious cranks, usually male, could be seen walking the streets, dressed like the popular idea of the Apostles, in loose robes, with long hair and luxuriant beards, often carrying signs announcing the imminent end of the world.

On Hill Street there was a six- or seven-story building that was headquarters for many sects prosperous enough to pay modest rent for a room or two. The old-fashioned elevator was encased only in a lattice cage, and as it slowly rose you could read a fascinating list of names on the office doors.

The climate was chiefly responsible for bringing these odd groups to the city—and all the other migrants as well. During three or four months in winter it rained often, and sometimes hard; the rest of the year, the fog usually rolled in from the sea during the night and burned off in mid-forenoon. Thereafter as a rule we had a brilliant blue sky, a cool breeze off the ocean, very low humidity. You could plan a picnic any time from May to November with no fear of rain. Now and then there would be a day or two of temperatures at or over 100 degrees, but with little humidity such heat was nothing to worry about.

Even in 1912, so many people had come to southern California from the Middle West—chiefly Iowa, Minnesota, Illinois, Nebraska, and Kansas—that theirs was the dominant culture. They overlapped with another large group—semi-invalids, especially those with pulmonary tuberculosis. The climate, with its daily heavy fog, was not very good for this disease, and why they came in such numbers is still something of a mystery.

The typical Midwestern migrant of that time was elderly, with modest means, a devout Methodist or Baptist, with a grammar-school or at most a high-school education. Real-estate taxes were low, the income tax was still several years in the future, and government at any level hardly touched him. Sacramento seemed far away, Washington farther still, and the world overseas simply did not exist.

Some members of the immigrant tide had enough capital to live on their interest and dividends; others, like my parents, had almost none. But the typical couple had sufficient resources to make a down payment on a bungalow, and to plant flowers and a vegetable garden. Thereafter, they lived partly on capital and partly on odd jobs and on remittances from their children, who were usually still back in the Middle West and hard at work.

Somehow they made do. I remember the annual Iowa picnic, held in Bixby Park, in nearby Long Beach; a big area was laid out in the geographical pattern of the Iowa counties, each in its proper relation to the others, with a series of pennants on flagpoles carrying the names. The expatriates clustered around their own county standards, where they found old friends from home, or made new ones in the easy American fashion. Mountains of fried chicken, potato salad, and apple pie from box lunches were consumed, and the planning committee provided huge urns of fresh-made coffee. These old people seemed untroubled by financial or other worries. They were respectably if plainly dressed and told one another ceaselessly how wonderful it was to live where they did not need to shovel snow. The papers reported there were a hundred thousand people at one picnic I attended, and I believe it. Other Midwestern states held annual outings of their own, attended by equal numbers.

The Iowans and their neighbors were nearly all conservative Republicans; they took little part in the political revolution of 1910 which broke the grip of the big corporations on the state legislature. At first glance, it seems surprising that so many of these people should, two decades later, have embraced the crackpot scheme of Dr. Francis Townsend. In fact, however, with their limited understanding of economics, this weird plan seemed to them not at all radical. After all, it did not touch the sacred principle of private property. (Perhaps faint echoes of the Midwestern Populism of the 1890's may still have lingered in some of their heads.)

I do not mean to denigrate these people, with whose culture I am myself saturated. They had solid merits, which seem even more valuable as time passes. They married for life, worked hard, stayed solvent, kept out of trouble, and brought up their children successfully, each generation getting substantially more formal education than the one before. If their Puritanism seems a little old-fashioned nowadays, there are worse evils.

Though few knew it, many of them had come to California as the result of an artful selling campaign by the Los Angeles Chamber of Commerce and the railroads. Today, we look with dismay on any organized attempt to swell the number of migrants to any area, since there are now too many people practically everywhere; but at that time any such notion was far in the future. The rapid increase in the population of southern California, which even then was unparalleled in the history of the world, advantaged chiefly the landowners and the businessmen who served the local markets; but almost everybody was convinced it was a fine idea. The only conspicuous malcontent that I remember was Rob Wagner, a painter, who also taught wrestling at a local high school, and for some years published a sprightly local magazine, *Rob Wagner's Script.* Years ahead of his time in vision, Rob urged that the area stop encouraging immigrants, foreseeing the deadly overcrowding that would appear long after he was in his grave.

But in 1912, this was heresy. The chief factor in encouraging migration was, as I have said, the Los Angeles Chamber of Commerce. It flooded the whole country with advertising material planned to appeal to elderly people in small towns in the blizzard belt. It was ably seconded by *The Los Angeles Times*, whose Sunday edition was filled with editorial and advertising matter on the bliss of buying a little home in Paradise, for a small down payment and easy monthly installments. On January first of each year appeared its famous Midwinter Edition, which said the same thing in many more words, and was for sale all over town, ready wrapped for you to mail to Middle-Westerner friends who hadn't yet got the message.

Land was not expensive; suburbs which now sell business property at high prices per front foot were still vacant, or occupied by recently planted citrus groves. There was a real-estate boom, but it was of modest proportions. This had not always been true; a quarter of a century earlier, there had been a fantastic orgy of land speculation, almost on the scale of the Miami fever of the mid-1920's. When I arrived in southern California at the end of 1911, there were still leftover rudimentary streets and surveyors' stakes many miles out on the barren desert waste. Large sums had been lost by those who failed to get out before the bubble burst.

There was still a good deal of hoopla in the real-estate business. New developments were being opened in the San Fernando Valley, for instance, in a circus atmosphere. People were hauled in big buses from the heart of Los Angeles to visit the new tracts, where they got a rather skimpy free lunch in a big round tent. After they had walked over the property, a "spieler" told them of the millions to be made by those who rode up with the boom. A dozen "closers" circulated through the crowd, and in an atmosphere of artificial urgency got their victims to sign up.

Many of the sellers of real estate, I am sure, thought of themselves as confidence men; they did not believe the city would ever reach so far. But the joke was on them; while most of the high-pressured purchasers soon let their payments lapse, those who held on made a lot of money. If there is any land in California near a city that has not gone up five or ten times in value in half a century, I have not heard of it. When I came back to the state to live, after almost forty years in New York, I was struck by the fact that those of my college classmates who had been shrewd enough to buy land early and hang onto it were millionaires, or close to it.

Los Angeles was an open-shop town, as San Francisco was union-dominated. Wages were low, hours were long, fringe benefits were unheard of. One reason for this was the constant migration from the East by those in frail health; many of these people were strong enough to do light work, and their bargaining power was small. There were also drifters who came west under the impression that things were booming, and were shocked to find that business was not all that good, and that the labor market was overcrowded.

Leader in the anti-union crusade was General Harrison Gray Otis, editor and owner of *The Los Angeles Times*. He thought unions were wicked, and found willing supporters in the business community. Gossip said that fearing an attempt on his life, he carried a weapon in his car at all times. His apprehension seemed to be well justified, for in October, 1910, when I was a senior at Stanford, the *Times* plant was blown up with a bomb, with a loss of twenty lives. General Otis, naturally, assumed the bombers were men opposed to his anti-union policy.

About seven months later, three men were arrested for the crime, two of whom were brothers, James and Joseph McNamara. The third was Ortie McManigal, and all three were members, not of any printing union, but of the International Bridge and Structural Iron Workers. McManigal at once confessed that the union had embarked on a policy of bombing buildings all over the country that had been erected by anti-union contractors. The McNamara brothers swore they were innocent, and trade-unionists and liberals everywhere rallied to their defense. The famous Chicago attorney, Clarence Darrow, was engaged as their chief counsel.

Then came the shocking news that the brothers had also confessed. They were at once sentenced; James got life, Joseph fifteen years, and the liberal and labor elements who had been shouting that they had been framed were left looking very foolish indeed.

But the affair was not over. Bert Franklin, an employee of Darrow who had been investigating prospective jurors, was arrested for having paid a bribe to one of these. He confessed his guilt, and said he was acting under orders from Darrow, who was promptly arrested for this bribery case and for another alleged attempt to do the same thing.

I was by now in Los Angeles, and I remember the wild excitement in the city at these developments. Darrow was tried separately on the two counts; in one case he was acquitted, and in the other, the jury disagreed. The District Attorney, perhaps cowed by Darrow's formidable impact in a courtroom, decided not to try the case again.

I had come to Los Angeles partly because my sister was there. Her marriage to a brilliant pianist, who turned out to be an alcoholic, had ended in divorce, and she was working as a saleswoman to support two small children. She made room for me in her apartment, and I promptly started looking for a job in a market oversupplied with recent college graduates who had no special skills of any kind.

I soon got a place, by accident. I had been editor, in my senior year, of the college humor magazine, *The Chaparral*, and I tried to pick up some advertising for the paper; a large proportion of the Stanford student body came from Los Angeles. I dropped in one day at the old, conservative store of Harris & Frank, which sold clothing, shoes, and hats for all members of the family. The vice-president of the firm, Mr. Mel Adler, listened while I made my pitch for *The Chaparral*, and then told me their advertising man had quit and they had no one to write copy.

Naturally, I offered to write the ad myself, on speculation; if they didn't like it, well and good. Mr. Adler agreed, and I went home and wrote the copy—planned, of course, for a full page of *The Chaparral.* Next day, I brought it in; Mr. Adler read it, and approved it for publication.

"Do you know the advertising business?" he asked me. This was no time for truth-telling, and I assured him that I did.

"How would you like to be our advertising manager?" he asked. "Twenty-five dollars a week, and start Monday."

I told him that would be fine. Twenty-five dollars a week, the equivalent of about seventy-five today, seemed to me a fortune.

But my brashness had its limits. The day was a Friday, and I headed straight for the Los Angeles Public Library, a few blocks away. I had already made friends of the nice girls who handled the check-out desk, and I put my problem before them. I needed to take out *all* the books on advertising, simultaneously, breaking the rule which said only one book at a time.

In those benighted days, there were only four or five books on the technique of advertising, and I went home with all that were available. I sat up most of the next three nights and learned the rudiments of writing newspaper advertising—how to lay out an ad, place the illustrations, count the letters in copy in various sizes of type. I reported for work on Monday, started spending a very large sum annually, and nobody seemed to know the difference.

There were six daily papers in Los Angeles, and we used them all in varying degrees. Each had an advertising solicitor who called on me several times a week; they took pity on the green young man, and tactfully helped me to keep from making a conspicuous fool of myself. Los Angeles had a flourishing Advertising Club which I promptly joined. I doubt whether many of the members knew much more about advertising than I did; within a year or so, I was a vice-president of the organization, and could talk the patter of the trade with anybody.

With a lifelong predilection for moonlighting, I promptly looked about for extra jobs, and found them. There was a weekly local magazine, *The Outlook,* devoted to civic affairs, run as a hobby by a businessman, Meyer Lissner; it made no money, but it usually managed to break even. The owner-editor agreed to let me review books in its pages, for no remuneration except the books themselves, which I could keep for my library or sell second-hand.

I promptly invented what still seems to me an ingenious scheme to get publishers to send review copies to a small-circulation magazine in Los Angeles they had never heard of. I mailed a form letter to the leading book houses saying: "Please do not send us any review copies unless they are specifically requested. If we want to review a book of yours, we'll let you know."

The plan must have worked, because when I did request a copy, I usually got it. I assigned very few books to other people to review, at the standard rate of no money but you get to keep the book; I managed to write two or three reviews a week, and kept this up for a year or so, until the owner decided that publishing a magazine was less fun than he had thought, and discontinued it.

During my connection with the paper, I did a few other odd jobs for it. When celebrities visited Los Angeles, I interviewed them, in more space and a more leisurely style than the dailies could manage. Among them I remember Rabindranath Tagore, the famous Indian poet, mystic, and teacher; I was allergic to most of his philosophy, but I admired the quiet, dignified, warm personality of this great man.

Another visitor I talked to was Irvin S. Cobb, American newspaper-man and humorist. A few weeks earlier, Cobb had published an interview with Kaiser Wilhelm of Germany, who, as he often did, spoke recklessly, and then when the interview brought a bad reaction, blandly denied he had said the things he obviously had. I took the text of my interview to Cobb and explained, tongue in cheek, that to avoid a similar incident, I was asking him to initial each page. Cobb chuckled, and obliged.

One spare-time job of mine was teaching English composition at the Y.M.C.A., one of a number of courses given by various people in subjects like bookkeeping, typewriting, etc. Each student paid a few dollars to enroll in each course, and as I remember, the instructor got about half. With twenty or twenty-five students, I got a very small remuneration, but I felt useful in helping these young men whose formal education had been scant.

The University of Southern California was then a rather sleepy institution in an old building in the southwest section of town. It was heavily dominated by the Methodist Church; it had only two or three thousand students, and its football team was mediocre. I was invited to teach a course in English composition, on a part-time basis, and cheer-fully accepted. (Not all these extra activities were simultaneous, though some of them overlapped.)

One day a man in his mid-forties came into my office at Harris & Frank, rather sloppily dressed; he wore a Windsor tie, and had keen, intelligent eyes behind thick spectacles. He was looking for H. W. Frank, president of the firm, whose office was next to mine; he was a well-known civic leader, head of the Board of Education.

When the caller found Mr. Frank was out, he cheerfully dropped into a chair in my room and began to talk. Lincoln Steffens had been in Los Angeles when the storm over the McNamaras was at its height.

73

According to his own account, published nearly two decades later,[1] he had been the key figure in a plan to get the dynamiters to confess in return for a promise that they would receive only nominal punishment. He claimed he got all the main figures on both sides to agree to this, but was betrayed at the last moment.

Now, with the affair ended, he had returned to try once more to get capital and labor in Los Angeles to accept the Golden Rule, or "Christian principles," in their relations with each other. But it did not work; he came back to see me a few days later to report ruefully that he had got nowhere in his talks with employers, and that there was no one really empowered to speak for labor. He departed again for New York.

Writing advertising was for a while an exciting adventure for a boy just out of college. Every day, like a newspaper reporter, I made the rounds of the departments, to see what they wanted to advertise in next day's papers; often the size and shape of the advertisement would depend on what they wished to push, and their degree of enthusiasm about their special offerings. Today, record-keeping is scientific; each department is charged with its proportionate share of the cost of advertising, and this cost is checked against sales, but we were much more hit-or-miss. Los Angeles was growing, and our business kept increasing—a development for which I naturally tried to take credit. Usually I was allowed to lay out ads according to my own judgment of what was interesting and exciting in the day's offerings; there were, of course, occasions when a department head felt he had been too cavalierly treated, but I was able to smooth these over. The store was honestly run, most markups were moderate, dissatisfied customers were treated generously as to refunds or exchanges, and they were correspondingly loyal to the firm.

Seeking to augment my salary, I began free-lancing in trade and technical publications—*Men's Wear, System* (a magazine devoted to advancing business organization), and especially, *Printers' Ink*, the pocket-sized "bible" of advertising, which was far ahead of its few halfhearted competitors. Before long, I was its ex-officio southern California correspondent.

Another paper I wrote for regularly and voluminously was *The Christian Science Monitor*. I was not a Christian Scientist, but since I dealt strictly in facts ("hard news," in the language of the business), this did not seem to matter. My material for *The Monitor* all went in by mail, and was written so that a few days' delay in publication did no harm.

Nearly all this free-lance activity was performed at night or on weekends, and I am reasonably sure it had no adverse effect on the quality of my work for Harris & Frank.

In 1913 came the most important fact of my life, between birth and

[1] *The Autobiography of Lincoln Steffens*, New York, Harcourt, Brace and Company, 1931.

death: I got married. My fiancée was going through college on sparse financial resources, and had written me that she would have to work in the library next year; it seemed to me only sensible for us to wed and let me underwrite the rest of her education.

In May, she came south to visit me (carefully chaperoned, in those puritanical days, by my sister). She traveled on one of two very good twin coastal steamers, the *Yale* and the *Harvard*, which ran between San Francisco and San Pedro. I met her boat, and on the hour-long interurban ride back to Los Angeles, I outlined the advantages of getting married now, instead of waiting another year or more. By the end of the ride, she had agreed; long afterward she told me she might have done so a lot sooner if I had only stopped talking to give her a chance.

The ceremony took place a day or two later, in the basement of the Congregational Church, the single room in the building available at the moment. We had brought only one friend with us, my cousin by marriage, Grace Ormsby, not knowing two witnesses were required. The minister pressed the janitor into service as the other; he changed from overalls to trousers, put on a jacket, and stood up with us; in the golden haze of that day, we couldn't have cared less.

Our honeymoon was spent at a hotel on top of Mount Lowe, behind Pasadena, reached by funicular railway. I had asked Mr. Adler for Saturday off, explaining that I planned to get married. Not only did he agree, but he gave me Monday off as well, and on the spot, he raised my salary from $25 a week to $30! No bridegroom in history was ever showered with so many blessings, all at once.

My wife wore her blond hair long—so long that she could "sit on it," in the expression of the time. With her pink-and-white complexion, inherited from her English ancestors, she looked even younger than the college senior she was about to become. We were too poor to do much traveling, but on one occasion we ventured down the coast as far as La Jolla, where I had a hard time convincing a hotel clerk I was not eloping with a high-school girl.

We rented a furnished apartment a block from the University of Southern California, and less than a month later my wife was back in college, attending the summer session to pick up a few extra credits needed in transferring from one institution to another. To save time for her, we took our evening meal with the family next door, transplanted from a Midwestern farm; they served the solid country food with which I was familiar, pounded flank steak, boiled potatoes, apple pie.

About this time, the Southern Pacific Railroad asked me to write their official booklet about Riverside County. Accompanied by a representative of the line I toured the county (one of the largest in the United States) from end to end. My wife and I spent the best part of a week (on an expense account) in the beautiful Mission Inn in Riverside, more like

75

a museum of religious statuary and painting than a hotel. Neither of us had ever been in such a grand establishment before. What I remember most clearly is that the table d'hôte breakfast was a dollar. For this sum, you could have everything on the giant menu if you wished, and the temptation to kill yourself with overeating was almost irresistible.

My booklet about Riverside County slighted the west end, where the town of that name was already surrounded by thickly clustered orange and lemon groves. I also passed over the moribund little community of Palm Springs, which we were sure had no future, to emphasize the hamlets of the arid Coachella Valley, where the date industry, highly prosperous today, was just beginning. The railroad printed, I was told, a million copies of my brochure, and I probably helped the huge increase in population in the area that has since taken place. I was invited to do a similar booklet on neighboring San Bernardino County, but I was too hard pressed at the moment, and turned the job over to a college classmate who was momentarily out of work.

A few months later, my wife and I moved to a rustic cabin clinging to a hillside high above the Eagle Rock Valley, in the northwest corner of Los Angeles. The district was sparsely settled; our address was simple: corner of Avoca and Wildwood Trail. At night we could sometimes hear the coyotes howling in the wilder area across the valley, one of the loneliest sounds in the world. We had a three-room furnished house with a fireplace and a big sleeping porch embowered in roses, where we woke every morning to see the hummingbirds at work. We looked across the valley to Eagle Rock, where part of each day, the sun created the shadow of a huge bird with outstretched wings. For this Elysium we paid $17 a month, a modest charge even in those days.

While we were engrossed in our private affairs, the First World War started. But in 1914, Europe seemed very far away; America was overwhelmingly isolationist, at least on the Pacific Coast, and the war touched us hardly at all.

After a couple of years of writing advertising, I began to get bored with it, and looked around for a new field. Departments of Journalism were just beginning to be established in American colleges, and it occurred to me that the University of Southern California ought to have one. Accordingly, I prepared what advertising men call a "presentation." I bought a big loose-leaf book, and on page after page I described a possible department. I gave the names of friends of mine employed in Los Angeles who might be willing to teach one course each, for nominal pay, in various aspects of newspaper work and advertising. I would be the only full-time teacher, and I laid out several courses for myself, in writing news and headlines, editing copy, and the history of journalism.

Armed with this prospectus I sought an appointment with President George Bovard of U.S.C., an amiable, easygoing gentleman presiding over a poorly financed private institution that was growing at unparalleled speed. I sat down across the desk from him, put down my big book, and turned the pages as I talked, pointing out that he could acquire a complete Department of Journalism for less than two full salaries. He had every right to think I was crazy, but on the contrary, he agreed then and there to the whole plan. My salary would be $2,000 a year and he swore me to secrecy about the sum, since he assured me this was more than any other member of the faculty was receiving.

I parted amicably with Harris & Frank, and proceeded to negotiate with several friends about teaching one course each, succeeding in signing up enough of them to make a respectable array in the college catalogue. The university had bought a private house half a block from the college building and this was turned over to me for classrooms.

That autumn my department started off full blast with about a hundred enrollments in one course or another, and even a handful of hardy souls who proposed to get an A.B. degree in Journalism. Luckily, I had sense enough to set up heavy requirements for these in history, political science, economics, and language. Whatever they did or did not learn about journalism, they would be graduated with some knowledge of the world about them.

My favorite among the subjects I myself taught was a two-hour laboratory course in news writing. We had scrounged up a dozen typewriters, which were set up in rows, with a copy desk for three or four people at the front of the room. I would open the class by announcing I was H. G. Wells or Lloyd George or Theodore Roosevelt, and demand that I be interviewed as though I had just arrived in the city. After twenty minutes of questions, each student wrote his story and they then copyread one another's work, before turning it in to me. On other days I would announce a dramatic (fictitious) development in the world war, and have them prepare, first a wire-service flash and then a full story. The students seemed to appreciate assignments with such an air of immediacy about them.

When real celebrities, and especially those in publishing, visited Los Angeles, I did what many other teachers do, and tried to lure them out to address my students. One such that I remember was S. S. McClure, then still going strong, though his great days as a muckraking magazine publisher were now some years in the past.

Having pinned him down to a day and hour, the next problem was transportation. He was staying at the then-fashionable downtown hotel, the Alexandria, and the university was far away. I had no car, and neither did any possibly helpful friend; such things as expense accounts of course did not exist. I decided I would have to pay for a taxi both ways, regardless of cost.

I met McClure in the hotel lobby, got a cab, and we drove to the university. As we alighted, he spoke four words that stabbed me to the heart: "Just wait, please, driver." His listeners afterward assured me he had made a good talk, but all I could think of was that taxi meter ticking away, out in the street. At the end of his address I wrestled him away from the students and got him back into the taxi. The episode cost me $9 or $10, and my wife and I economized hard for some weeks.

Years later I read McClure's biography and learned that he had always lived in lordly style. I could well believe it.

Another outside speaker I brought in was a man in an angry mood. He was a well-known foreign correspondent who had been engaged by William Randolph Hearst to report the civil war then raging in Mexico. The guerrillas of Carranza, Villa, and Zapata were fighting one another as well as the organized armed forces of the government, and the country was in chaos.

The correspondent, at some personal risk, went out into the field with the insurrectionists, sometimes sending an Indian runner many miles to file his stories at the nearest telegraph office. After about a month of this, he emerged for the first time and came back across the border to a spot where a file of the Hearst papers was available. To his amazement, he found in the papers day after day long articles signed with his name, not a word of which he had written. He had become convinced that the revolutionaries had the best interests of the half-starved peasants at heart, and had said so; but Mr. Hearst, in New York, took a contrary view. The publisher was very anti-Mexican at this stage, and wanted nothing printed in his pages showing any of the citizens in a favorable light. (I have no way of knowing whether he had ordered this particular job done, or was even aware of it.)

The correspondent resigned in an outraged telegram and came to Los Angeles to tell his troubles to me, and to my students. Today, of course, the Hearst papers are solid, conservative, and respectable, and would never undertake such high-handed procedures.

In the summer of 1915, my wife and I learned with the usual combination of excitement, happiness, and apprehension that we would have a baby about the end of January. Since our hillside eyrie was remote from transportation—to say nothing of doctors—we reluctantly moved to a spic-and-span new five-room bungalow near the university, and a staggering increase in rent, from $17 to $25 a month.

About the same time I was made a delegate to the World Congress of Journalists, to be held at the Panama-Pacific Exposition in San Francisco, my credentials including an unlimited free pass for two to the Exposition. The university was not in session, and we emptied our savings account and went. The Congress of Journalists did not amount to very much, but we were enchanted by the Exposition, built on filled-in tidal marshland by the bay, and in many ways one of the most beautiful ever held anywhere. We heard Sousa's band in daily concerts and dutifully tramped through the buildings of various states and nations and the horticulture and machinery halls. We admired Rodin's *The Thinker*, the impressive Court of the Universe, and Bernard Maybeck's baroque Palace of Fine Arts, so beautiful that half a century later millions were spent to rebuild it on the same spot, this time in concrete instead of stucco. We enjoyed the landscaping done by John McLaren, father of San Francisco's fabled Golden Gate Park.

It was at night that the Exposition came to life. Many people have heard of the famous Tower of Jewels, which seemed, when spotlights played on it, to be encrusted with diamonds, sapphires, rubies, and emeralds. On the edge of the bay stood a powerful locomotive, painted white; at night it emitted huge clouds of steam on which there shone a rainbow of colored spotlights. Today the result would be called "camp," but in that beautiful setting it was effective, or seemed so to my untutored taste.

The most exciting thing at the Exposition was the nightly show of aerial acrobatics by one or two pilots seemingly bent on suicide. They had fireworks attached to the fuselage, and set these off as they did climbs, loops, and dives over the water. Their canvas-and-wood biplanes were hardly more sturdy than the one I had seen a few years earlier at Tanforan, and we agonized over them each night until the show was over. Soon after we had returned to southern California we heard with no surprise that one of the best of these young pilots, Lincoln Beachey, had been killed.

Before I had been at U.S.C. very long, I discovered that President Bovard, a shy man and an awkward speaker, hated to make public appearances. I on the other hand did not mind such chores, and he happily began turning them over to me. I began showing up in various odd places as official spokesman for the university.

One of the oddest was the Panama-California Exposition of 1915–16 at San Diego. The university was asked to send someone to serve on the art jury, and (in desperation, I assume) I was nominated. The Exposition was tiny compared to San Francisco's, the exhibits were meager, but it was laid in beautiful Balboa Park, the commercial aspects were held to a minimum, and the result was handsome. I was of course grossly incompetent to act as a judge of painting, but there were two other highly qualified people on the jury, the art editor of *The Los Angeles Times*, and a well-known local painter. We awarded gold medals and honorable mentions right and left, and I never heard that anybody protested our decisions.

Early in our married life, my wife and I made the acquaintance of a brilliant, locally famous psychiatrist, Dr. Josephine Jackson, who a few years later was to write the hugely successful book *Outwitting Our Nerves*. Though neither of us was ever a patient of hers, we spent a lot of time at her sanitarium in Altadena, a foothill town behind Pasadena.

Dr. Jackson, a tiny, determined woman of Irish-American origin and temperament, was a Freudian, but she did little work with her patients individually. Instead, every morning at ten o'clock the whole group—usually ten to twenty—assembled in her living room for a free-ranging discussion of psychological problems and their cure. Sometimes the doctor read aloud from Freud, from his biographer, Ernest Jones, or from some other psychoanalyst; sometimes she told stories of her past patients, omitting their names; often there was an animated general discussion, out of which each person present got what he could. She took no patients who did not come and live in her house; one weekly fee covered everything. She was sought by some famous men from all over the country, including the U.S. Senate, and she had a record of sensational cures—a combination, I surmise, of some Freudian philosophy, a few weeks in a calm, relaxed atmosphere, and Dr. Jackson's powerful personality—so powerful that her patients were afraid not to get well.

As trusted friends, my wife and I were nominated to act as volunteer aides when we happened to be present. I remember some long walks with a distinguished corporation president, an alcoholic, my presence being required to see that he did not get hold of a bottle.

A standard neurotic symptom is being allergic to foods that other people ingest without difficulty; there were some slightly comic scenes at the dinner table when the doctor quietly insisted that somebody, perhaps with a famous name, eat his cucumbers or his hard-boiled egg. He ate.

I remember one patient who had such indecision that he would lower himself halfway into a chair and then be unable to complete or to abandon the action; Dr. Jackson cured him, at least for a while.

Naturally, my wife and I, in our mid-twenties, became enthusiastic Freudians, at a fairly low level of comprehension, and remained so for decades.

Soon after I arrived in Los Angeles I was invited to teach writing at the Cumnock School of Expression, a finishing school for daughters of the rich. The word "Expression" conveyed a vague interest in the drama, though I never heard that any student actually became an actress.

Before I had been teaching long, I got an agitated telephone call early one morning. The head of the school had died suddenly in the night, and I had been chosen to take over her famous course in Shakespeare, starting two or three days after the funeral. I agreed, and began in the middle of *As You Like It*, having been coached by the class as to how far they had already gone. Anything is possible if you are sufficiently young and brash.

When I was married, the Los Angeles newspapers carried a small news story, and a couple of days later, as I started to enter the room at

Cumnock for my weekly Shakespeare class, I found the rostrum decorated with a huge bow of white satin. It was a friendly gesture from the girls, and I wish now I had accepted it in that spirit, but I panicked and asked one of the regular staff to go in ahead of me and remove the decoration.

Los Angeles had a morning newspaper, *The Tribune*, now long defunct, and I noticed that it had no music critic. Accordingly, I asked the city editor whether I might cover the winter season of the Los Angeles Philharmonic, without remuneration. The paper agreed, and for a year or two I performed this function. I knew as little about music as I did about painting; my taste was about at the level of Liszt's Second Hungarian Rhapsody. But I had sense enough to report the concerts as news, rarely attempting any criticism. To some performances I took a musician friend, and he helped (I hope) to keep me from noticeably making a fool of myself.

The only time my life was ever in danger (except from illness) occurred about now. I was one of three men who started before dawn one summer morning to drive by car to a ranch far out on the Mojave Desert, northeast of the sleepy, decaying (as we thought) little village of Palm Springs. One of the party, my friend, was an experienced desert man, but the other, a stranger, was even more a greenhorn than myself. When we were miles from anywhere, on a road consisting of two ruts in the sand, our engine temperature suddenly shot up. Our radiator was out of water.

The tenderfoot, before anyone could stop him, picked up our precious canteen and poured its contents into the radiator; there was a broken line, and the contents promptly ran out into the sand. We were without water at ten o'clock on a summer morning, on a road where it might be days before another car came by.

Two or three miles away there was a line of low hills, with a thin haze of green vegetation along the base. We struck out in that direction, as the sun beat down and the temperature mounted. When we got there, we found evidence of a spring in a clump of bushes, but it had dried up. We dug with our bare hands, and a couple of feet below the surface we found wet sand, from each handful of which a few drops of water could be squeezed into the canteen.

All day long, we dug and squeezed; our composure was not improved by the discovery of a rattlesnake coiled on a ledge, a few feet away. He was shedding his skin, a period at which rattlers are supposed to be blind and to strike at any sound; we killed him with a dry stick.

After nightfall, we struck back again to the road and started walking toward Palm Springs, many miles away, feeling for the ruts with our feet in the moonless night. About ten o'clock we saw what we had no right to expect, the lights of a car heading our way. The driver, a lone rancher, picked us up.

Years later I learned how serious our plight could have been. Scientists now know that with a high level of dry heat, dehydration can occur with great rapidity, and affects the brain almost at once. This explains why men are sometimes found dead "of thirst" with a canteen of water beside them.

My friend and I never went out with that particular tenderfoot again. To this day I am not sure he realized what a fool he had been.

On the last day of January, 1916, our son was born, a day or two earlier than we had expected. We had spent the day visiting Dr. Jackson, about ninety minutes away by streetcar (it would be years before we had an automobile of our own). She had examined my wife and assured us the accouchement was not imminent, but she was wrong. Back home, at almost midnight, the warning signals started, and we called a taxi to take us to the Methodist Hospital, a few blocks distant. When we arrived, the doctors took one look and rushed my wife into the delivery room. When the baby was born, just after midnight, she was still wearing most of her clothes, including a very stylish small black hat. As very rarely happens, the birth was completely painless.

Like all young parents, we fluctuated between bliss at the presence of the most remarkable baby ever born, and terror that any slightest ailment should prove fatal. But our doctor was reassuring, and our fears gradually abated.

Early in 1916 I was teaching a writing course at the university, open both to students and to older unregistered individuals. One day as I was sitting in my office, one of these special students came to see me, a handsome, fading woman with a warm personality, perhaps in her early fifties. After the customary few preliminary words she plunged into her errand.

"Mr. Bliven," she said, "you know me as Mrs. Mary Hulbert. But I am better known under another name." She paused dramatically. "I am the 'notorious Mrs. Peck,' supposed to have had an affair with President Wilson."

Her news not only surprised me, but worried me as well. All the members of the English Department had offices in a row, tiny cubicles whose walls did not rise all the way to the ceiling. Anything said in one of them could be overheard by faculty members in the cubicles on either side. The university was a highly puritanical, church-dominated institution, and I did not know what my colleagues would think if they overheard my caller. I don't know what I said in reply, but Mrs. Hulbert plunged ahead.

"The stories about the President and me are completely false," she said. "We were never anything but good friends. But he wrote me a large number of letters. What I fear is that these letters will be stolen and selections from them published in garbled form to give a wrong impression and hurt the President when he runs for reelection this summer."

I must have made sounds indicating incredulity, for she went on:

"Already, my house has been ransacked while there was no one at home, but nothing was stolen. Also, two gentlemen unknown to me, though they had letters of introduction, have called on me and talked vaguely of very large sums of money. Apparently they thought I would stoop so low as to sell the letters from my friend.[2]

"What I want you to do," she went on, "is to read President Wilson's letters to me. Then if there is any trouble, you could make a public statement that you had read them and found nothing improper in them. Would you be willing to do this?"

Would I!

Apparently it did not occur to either of us that her letters should long ago have been placed in a safe-deposit vault. Moreover, I was so naïve that it was some days before I realized that I had only her word that these were *all* the letters Dr. Wilson had written her. I hastily agreed to her suggestion, and opening her handbag, she handed me a fat sheaf of letters tied in the conventional blue ribbon.

I sat up most of that night reading them, fascinated by their contents and by the assurance that I was the only person ever to have seen them, except the author and the recipient. They were all neatly typewritten on small folded stationery. Years later I learned that he had kept carbons of many of these letters, which were found, with some from Mrs. Hulbert, in his files after his death; he must have used small pieces of carbon paper and slipped them skillfully between the folded pages of the notepaper.

My own excitement at being plunged suddenly into dramatic affairs on the national level, at age twenty-six, may be imagined. These were the first original letters from a world-famous individual that I had ever seen, and I was doubly enthralled and alarmed by the thought that enemies of the President might even now be seeking to get possession of them. I returned them to Mrs. Hulbert as soon as possible, and, I believe, the very next day.

They were indeed charming letters, beautifully expressed, and often using poetic imagery. Their friendship had begun in Bermuda in 1908, when he was president of Princeton, and many of the letters referred to scenes and incidents during various vacations when they had both been in that enchanted isle. Once he wrote of walking along the seashore early in the morning, accompanied by sand-pipers running on the wet

---

[2] I am paraphrasing from memory many years later but the conversation was substantially as I have recorded it. In 1933 Mrs. Hulbert published her own autobiography, *The Story of Mrs. Peck*, New York, Minton, Balch & Company, in which she repeats these statements.

83

strand; he recalled similar walks he had taken with her.

She was an established vacationer in Bermuda before Dr. Wilson had ever seen the place. Shortly before they met, he had commented in his diary that Mark Twain had arrived in Bermuda and "Mrs. P. at once took possession of him. . . She seems to know everybody that is worth knowing." This was the last even faintly hostile reference he was to make to her. Very soon they were friends, and he was writing her on his little portable typewriter, almost every Sunday, as he did for many years.

As early as 1908, the presidential bug had bitten him, since he began, as is customary, by repudiating any thought of the office for himself. "Certainly, I do not want the Presidency! The more closely I see it, the less I covet it"[3] He was looking forward to retiring in 1910 with a Carnegie pension of $4,000 and a private income of $2,000 (with a total purchasing power of about $18,000 today).

The most interesting letters came after he was elected governor of New Jersey in 1910. He accomplished some notable achievements, forcing through a reluctant state legislature the direct primary, a Corrupt Practices Act, and employers' liability, and revitalizing the State Public Utilities Commission, but his letters to his friend were mostly concerned with the impact of public life on the cloistered scholar he considered himself to be. He was dismayed by the spotlight of publicity that beat down upon him every hour of every day. He disliked many of the professional politicians with whom he was now thrown into contact, yet he believed he had to function at their level; he tells of an evening spent with a group of them, in which some of them drank to excess, an evening that ended with a spectacle I would have given worlds to see—the Governor of New Jersey doing a cakewalk around the dinner table arm-in-arm with a politician of whom he privately thought very poorly indeed.

He was always able to laugh at himself. He drew a comical word picture of himself at Sea Girt, the official seaside summer home for New Jersey governors, reviewing the New Jersey National Guard on horseback, while wearing a frock coat and silk hat. He was shocked at the readiness of his enemies to circulate what they must have known were lies about him, but he was philosophical about this burden. Wryly he wrote of making a speech when John Grier Hibben was inaugurated as president of Princeton; he disliked Hibben bitterly, but he had to take part in the ceremony—especially since President Taft was to be present.

On the eve of the Democratic National Convention in 1912, he wrote that he was confident he had no chance of obtaining the nomination. (In fact, he got it when his friend, Colonel Edward M. House,

---

[3]I made no notes on these letters at the time. Many years later Mrs. Hulbert permitted Ray Stannard Baker, Wilson's biographer, to see them, and they are quoted extensively in several volumes of his eight-volume *Woodrow Wilson: Life and Letters*, Doran & Company, New York, 1931.

whom he afterward treated so cavalierly, persuaded William Jennings Bryan to throw his influence behind the "scholar in politics.") He was exhausted by the ordeal of campaigning, in those days before television, the radio, or even the microphone, had been invented, traveling from town to town, speaking a dozen or a score of times in a day. He was shrewd enough to predict that the real contest would be between himself and Theodore Roosevelt's Progressive ("Bull Moose") Party, and that President Taft, the nominee of the Republicans, would run a poor third. He was a good prophet; Taft got 3,483,000 votes, Roosevelt 4,216,000, and Wilson was elected with fewer than 6,300,000, but an overwhelming majority in the electoral college.

When he was in the White House, the sense of drama in his letters increased. He was enormously impressed by the way in which masses of people trusted him to take the right decision on matters they did not understand.

The death of his first wife, in September, 1914, was a heavy blow, and he poured out his anguish in his letters—a fact that itself showed he was in love with no one else. He threw himself into his work to forget his loss, not very successfully. In his desolation, he was cynical about the value of being president. "For the moment," he wrote,

> *I am approved of and trusted by the party and the country, and am popular. But I am not deceived. I know by what tenure a man holds popularity. It is only a tenancy at will, and may be terminated without notice. . . The place has brought me no personal blessing, but only irreparable loss and desperate suffering.*

With the beginning of the world war, the strain and pressure were of course worse than ever. Only his belief in God kept him going, he wrote, when "the world itself seems gone mad." In those early days England and Germany appeared to him to be acting with equal contempt for the rights of neutral nations. He felt he was working each day beyond his powers of recuperation, drawing on his reserves of physical and nervous energy.

The letters stopped in 1915; in December of that year, President Wilson married for the second time.

Was there in fact anything improper in the relationship between Mrs. Peck and Woodrow Wilson? At the time many thousands of people seemed to think so, with the perverse eagerness so many of us have to believe the worst of a popular public figure. The Republican National Committee, of course, had too much sense to lend itself to the dissemination of scandal, even in a whispering campaign. There may have been some individuals who did so, but there is no record that they influenced the outcome of the election. Wilson was reelected for a congeries of reasons, important among them being that on a swing through California his opponent, Charles Evans Hughes, snubbed the liberal Republican followers of Hiram Johnson, who proceeded to knife him.

The commonest charge was that Mrs. Peck was blackmailing the President over a long period of time, and that he had bought her silence with huge payments. The cause of these stories was the fact that she borrowed $7,500 from him, an indiscreet act in view of all the circumstances, but just the sort of thing that would be done by a woman conspicuously innocent in the ways of the world.

Her son wanted money to buy an avocado ranch in the San Fernando Valley near Los Angeles. Apparently as gullible as his mother, he was told that a great bargain was available only for immediate action. The young man owned two mortgages on property in the Bronx, in New York City, and his mother, according to her own account, thought there was not time to sell the mortgages on the open market. She wrote the President asking him either to buy them or to lend her one-half of the face value. He did the latter, sending her $7,500 and taking both mortgages as collateral for the loan. The avocado ranch was a failure, the Hulberts could not repay the money, and the President recouped himself out of the collateral. Says Mrs. Hulbert in her book:

> *It would seem that we were the ones who lost, for I have always believed that this transaction was the basis of the story current at the time of the* "huge sums *of money paid to 'Mrs. Peck',"* [*Emphasis in the original. —B.B.*] *There were many, it was said, who had* "seen the check" *and* "know it was true." *This lie belongs really in a chapter of horrors to be written of a scandalous persecution.*

I do not believe that Mrs. Peck and President Wilson ever had any sort of improper relationship. While she could have withheld incriminating letters from my inspection, it would not have been humanly possible for him to write so many others completely innocent in tone. Nobody could have displayed the profound anguish he showed at the death of his first wife in a communication to a woman who was his paramour.

Woodrow Wilson loved the attention of women. During the whole time of his friendship with Mrs. Peck he was writing in much the same friendly tone to several other ladies.

Mrs. Hulbert and the President met once more, during Wilson's last desperate nationwide speaking tour on behalf of American entry into the League of Nations. He and his wife visited Los Angeles, and invited Mrs. Hulbert to have lunch with them at his hotel. Jonathan Daniels, in his book *The Time between the Wars* (Garden City, New York, Doubleday & Company, 1966), says that the two women "clawed each other"; Mrs. Hulbert in her autobiography gives a completely opposite report. She says both the President and his wife were as friendly as possible. They spent the afternoon in desultory conversation, interrupted from time to time when the President had to excuse himself to step into another room to receive visitors. Mrs. Hulbert was in severe financial straits—all her money had been lost in unhappy business ventures by her son. She reports that President Wilson "laid his hand on his wife's shoulder and said to her: 'Isn't there something we can do?' "

Mrs. Hulbert broke in before she could answer, saying, "Not for me; not for my sake. I am quite all right."

When Mrs. Wilson had left the room for a moment, the President again asked, "Mary, is there nothing we can do?" She again refused but suggested that her son in New York might need help. The President wrote down his address, and as Mrs. Hulbert says, "The elevator quickly dropped me out of the life of my friend Woodrow Wilson—forever." A few days later, the President suffered the stroke from which he never fully recovered.

A few weeks after Mrs. Hulbert came to see me, I had another office caller, a lady who had made an appointment by telephone. She was in her late fifties, I should guess, dressed with the utmost dignity and decorum; more than half a century later, I remember a dark suit, a white jabot at her throat, and gray hair freshly coiffed. She told me her name —Mrs. Fiske—in cultured accents, and stated her business.

A few days earlier, I had made a public address somewhere, and had remarked in passing that writing is excellent mental discipline. Mrs. Fiske had been in my audience, and was impressed by this observation. She felt that her own mental powers were declining, and wondered whether trying to write would do her any good.

I made the conventional reply, that if you feel your mind is giving way, the chances are that it isn't; people who are really in trouble rarely feel this is true. However, if she wanted to try writing, I saw no reason why she shouldn't. If she wished me to read some of her work, I'd be glad to.

Would it be expensive, she wanted to know. I explained that this was part of the university service: no charge.

Several people had come to me wanting to get started writing, and I had developed a standard formula. Why not describe some episode of her past life, if she had had experiences worth reporting.

"I think I have," said Mrs. Fiske. "I was a prostitute for many years, and for some time I was the madam of the best-run brothel in Winnipeg."

I gulped, again having visions of my fellow faculty members rising out of their chairs in the cubicles next door to catch every word. In that case, I suggested, Mrs. Fiske certainly ought to tell the story of her life. I proposed that she write a chapter a week, mail it to me, give me a few days to read it, and then come in for my comments.

I thought it possible I should never hear from her again; a good many people who talk about wanting to write have no intention of sitting down and going to work. But I was wrong; a few days later I got the first chapter of her autobiography, written in a clear hand, properly punctuated, and using an impressively wide vocabulary. She was a natural storyteller, who needed almost no help from anybody.

For about a year, she sent me a chapter, or a good part of one, every week. It was a horror story, told with calm understatement that made it all the more effective. She had been brought up in deep poverty in a small town in Illinois; her father was an intellectual but an alcoholic, who favored her above his several other children when he was sober, but picked her out for savage beatings when he was drunk.

At seventeen, she had been seduced and became pregnant; this was the only part of her story about which she was reticent. Not knowing her condition, she left home to work in a St. Louis garment factory for five dollars a week. When her pregnancy became evident to the other workers, she was so ashamed that she quit her job. Her small savings were quickly gone, and one midnight, walking the streets without money or shelter, she accepted a man's invitation to go to his room. Prostitutes are famous for inventing sad tales of their downfall, but Mrs. Fiske's story seemed to me utterly convincing, and still does.

For the next twenty years or so, she practiced the oldest and most repulsive profession. She loathed every minute of it, she said, adding that most prostitutes feel the same way, but overcome their feelings for the sake of the lazy, luxurious life they lead—for a while. In Mrs. Fiske's case, her father had by now deserted her family, the other children were about to be scattered among various orphanages—this was about 1880—and she sent money regularly to her mother, earned in the only way she knew.

Her attitude was old-fashioned even in 1916, and seems archaic half a century later. She accepted most of the ideas of Victorian morality, even though she protested her sufferings under them. She was bitter against society for making almost no efforts at rehabilitation of prostitutes, and especially angry at "respectable women" as a class. She complained that they showed no interest in the reasons for vice, which she said were mostly poverty and low intelligence.

She had belonged, she was careful to point out, to the highest of the four grades of prostitutes—those who lived and worked in "parlor houses." Next lower were call girls, below them free-lance streetwalkers, and lowest of all the pitiable occupants of cribs, who were especially common in rough pioneer towns in the West; these women sat in the windows of one-room shacks, soliciting all passersby.

In her experience, girls in parlor houses were rarely supporting pimps. The madam of the house charged room and board—in the 1880's about $25 a week—and in addition took half of each girl's earnings. She in turn had to buy her own wardrobe and jewelry, and large sums were invested in expensive evening gowns, which seemed to be of great importance to the customers. In the half dozen cities where Mrs. Fiske had worked, in the United States and Canada, bribes were paid regularly to the local police, but she brushed off this aspect casually as just one of the facts of life.

At seventeen, she had, in many things, standard middle-class morality. She would not touch liquor, and drew back in horror when offered a cigarette. Her parents had taught her good grammar and the excellent diction I noticed the first day she came to see me. She reported that her refined speech was a severe handicap in her calling—potential customers thought she was affected. She was also unpopular with the other girls because she was an omnivorous reader, with a tenacious memory. Her standards of taste, especially in poetry, seemed to me banal, but the girls were not very good judges of this and her habit of quoting bits of verse now and then was deemed "stuck-up."

Her puritanical outlook finally disappeared, as was to be expected. Eventually she became both an alcoholic and a compulsive gambler, letting thousands of dollars slip through her fingers. For many years she carried on an intermittent love affair with a Montana businessman who repeatedly asked her to marry him, but she never quite got around to doing so—though she reported that some other "fallen women" she knew made fine marriages and became model wives. She traveled all over the world, for business or pleasure, met a great many people—nearly all men—and accumulated a large store of useless, disorganized information.

The Winnipeg interlude came in her early thirties, and by accident. Western Canada was being opened up rapidly, the country was teeming with bachelors or men away from their wives, and the supply of prostitutes fell far short of the demand. Mrs. Fiske sold several thousand dollars' worth of her jewelry, and bought a house on the prairie on the edge of town. In her narrative she told proudly how clean and "respectable" it was, and how carefully she repressed loud and boisterous conduct on the part of her girls or their customers.

Finally, for reasons she herself never quite seemed to understand, she suddenly stopped drinking and gambling, gave her brothel as a present to a girl who was more or less her second in command, and came to southern California. She had lived there for some years before she called on me, but she never gave me any details, except to say she had not gone back to the underworld.

When her book was finished, I queried Harper & Brothers (now Harper & Row) as to whether they would be willing to read it. The reply was affirmative, we sent it off, and acceptance followed promptly. It was published anonymously as *Madeleine: An Autobiography*, and I was later told that sales at the beginning were excellent.

But then came disaster. There was at that time an organization called

The New York Society for the Suppression of Vice, established in 1873 by a redoubtable antagonist of sin named Anthony Comstock. As far as I know, he never made any attempt to help prostitutes rehabilitate themselves; his sole idea was to suppress pornography. He had written the New York State law on this subject, and rewritten the U.S. Postal Code.

By the time *Madeleine* appeared, Comstock was dead, but he had a worthy successor named John S. Sumner. No book could possibly lend less encouragement to lubricity than Mrs. Fiske's, which made illicit sex seem totally repugnant; but Sumner, guided by who knows what obscure psychological quirk, decided it must be suppressed. He went to Harper & Brothers, threatened to drag them through the courts on a charge of publishing obscene matter, and the firm hastily stopped publishing the book. Secondhand copies soared in value, but the author got no royalties on such sales, and suffered a heavy loss on her reasonable expectations. She lived some years longer, and once came to dinner with my wife and me, on a visit to New York where we were now living, looking as always the quintessence of respectability.

One evening in 1916, my wife and I dropped in at Los Angeles' new Little Theater, just established by Aline Barnsdall. The play, *Nju*, by Ossip Dimov, did not amount to much, but the stage set—six screens in three sections each—was stunning. Lights were thrown on them from several sources in succession to mark the change from scene to scene, giving a remarkably varied and beautiful effect.

Following my notorious habit of getting unpaid jobs in journalism, I was now theater critic for *The Los Angeles Daily News*; I wrote a tepid review of the play but a rave notice for the sets. Next day their creator called me up, stammering his thanks in a high, squeaky voice, and then came to see me. Thus began a friendship with Norman Bel-Geddes, which ended only with his death from a heart attack in 1958, at age sixty-five.

Norman was the most abundantly talented man with whom I have ever been in close contact. As he reports in his autobiography,[4] written in the last year of his life, he had held a variety of jobs at a very early age, including touring in his mid-teens as a professional magician, playing second-rate vaudeville houses in cities near his native home in Michigan. He was brilliantly successful as a painter, writer, stage designer, architect, industrial designer, city planner, and a dozen other things, and all with seemingly little effort.

Not many people know the origin of his exotic-sounding name. His first wife was Belle Schneider, and to symbolize the closeness of their

[4] *Miracle in the Evening*, by Norman Bel-Geddes, Garden City, New York, Doubleday & Company, 1960.

union, he abbreviated her name to Bel and added it to his own: Norman-Bel Geddes. (Another friend of mine, Raymond Swing, the broadcaster, followed the same plan when he incorporated his wife's last name into his own and for some years was Raymond Gram Swing.) But in Norman's case the hyphenated first name was too much for the general public; they insisted on calling him Bel-Geddes, and after a long struggle, he gave up and accepted the change.

Though later in his life Norman earned very large sums of money, in those early days he lived like most people in the theater, swinging between affluence and bankruptcy. On one occasion he asked the Blivens and another couple to dinner, and we took the long streetcar ride to his home west of Los Angeles, in what is now Beverly Hills. We arrived on time, and sat in the living room with Norman and Bel for several hours, with the animated conversation that Norman always inspired. After this interval, with no signs that any dinner was in preparation, we said a friendly good-night, caught the streetcar back to Los Angeles, and dived into the nearest restaurant for a tardy meal. Later we learned that the grocer that day had cut off their credit without warning, and the Geddeses were too proud to admit their predicament.

Their policy was the opposite of that of a young writer whom we also knew, Myron Stearns, who afterward became a successful free-lance magazine contributor in New York. Myron and his wife lived near the ocean, at the mouth of Santa Monica Canyon, and they, too, invited several couples, including the Blivens, to dinner. When an expected check failed to arrive and they had no money to buy food, they cheerfully improvised. Myron gathered a lot of mussels along the shore, and popped a huge bowl of popcorn. He had accumulated many empty beer bottles, and traded them to the flinty-hearted grocer for a much smaller number of full ones. His guests dined on mussels, popcorn, beer, and a magnificent flow of good talk, one of the happiest social occasions of my life.

Of Norman's later brilliant success in New York I shall speak at its proper place in my narrative.

Our social life in Los Angeles was modest but pleasant. We joined the Sierra Club, which organized a hike every Sunday except during the rainy season, most of them into the canyons running up into the hills north of Los Angeles. Today these are jammed with concrete roads and houses; in 1913 they were wild and empty, usually with only a footpath. We carried our lunches, walked in five or six miles from the nearest public transportation, and came out before sunset. When my wife and I moved to New York we joined the Green Mountain Club, which organized similar Sunday outings, and came to know the countryside around the metropolis better than we ever could have done on our own.

In 1913 we met W. J. Ghent and his wife. He was an old-time New York Socialist, exiled to the mild southern California climate because of an (arrested) case of pulmonary tuberculosis. He was the author of a widely known book of the time, *Benevolent Feudalism.* When other Socialists were predicting the breakdown of capitalism, Ghent came far closer to the truth by saying the big corporations would develop a sort of welfare state of their own, treating their employees so well that these would lose all interest in drastic change in the economic system. The Ghents had known a dozen New York writers whom we had read and admired, and gave us a feeling of vicarious contact with the great Eastern world of ideas.

He had been a member of a New York informal club that, like thousands of others everywhere, met at frequent intervals for lunch or dinner and a session of good talk. He and I started a similar group in Los Angeles, and it continued as long as I lived in that city. When I came to New York, I carried the idea back where it had originated, and a few friends and I started the Dinner Club—known as the Monday Opera Club, since it did not meet on Monday and had nothing to do with opera; we dined together eight or nine times a year for forty years. It had a roster of about thirty distinguished members, mostly lawyers, writers, or college professors, remarkably faithful in attendance.

My friend Rob Wagner was fascinated by the movies, then still a very modest enterprise. Production crews were likely to turn up in any part of town, setting up their lights, reflectors, and cameras in the streets or on people's front lawns; a few years later a friend of mine accumulated a small fortune by allowing his house to be used month after month for the exterior shots of the *Andy Hardy* series.

Since he was so interested, I suggested that Rob try his hand at a magazine article about Hollywood. He sent it to *The Saturday Evening Post* and was dumbfounded when they accepted it and asked for more. His articles were finally published in book form by the Century Company, and enjoyed a substantial success.

In those days workers in the movies were boycotted by all the respectable people of the community. There was in fact a fly-by-night atmosphere around the studios; even third-rate hotels were reluctant to take in film people, and when they did, they sometimes had reason to regret it. As late as 1913, nobody foresaw the multibillion-dollar industry that lay ahead.

All my life I have had a weakness for second-rate vaudeville: the actors try so hard to please, and so often fail to do so. I dropped in one day at such a place on Main Street, then more or less Los Angeles' Skid Row, and saw a skit called "A Night in an English Music Hall." Most of it was rowdy knockabout farce, but I was impressed by one actor who, pretending to be very drunk indeed, wore full evening dress, sat in a box as though he were part of the audience, and only in the last seconds of the show climbed out onto the stage and joined the pandemonium there.

I was so delighted by him that I asked two or three friends to join me in a second visit. The actor was, of course, Charlie Chaplin, and this was his last appearance in vaudeville; his movie career started at once.

As correspondent of *The Christian Science Monitor* I occasionally visited a studio while a picture was being shot (as a rule, visitors were still excluded). Long before the days of the talkies, there was often a violinist, or two or three musicians, who played "mood music" while the cameras were rolling, to help a star get into the right frame of mind.

On one occasion the studio press agent suggested I come and interview Sir Herbert Beerbohm Tree, brother of Max Beerbohm, who was making a film of *Macbeth*—Shakespeare without words, except for subtitles. On another occasion I remember Douglas Fairbanks, Sr., in a gigantic birdcage, doing acrobatics on swings and bars; I have forgotten the name of the picture, and I never saw it in a theater.

Several years after I had gone to New York, some errand brought me back to Los Angeles, and I went with Rob Wagner to a studio where he was working on an article for *The Saturday Evening Post*. There we saw a young actress just imported from Sweden do a highly emotional love scene. It was the first film, and almost the first scene, ever done in Hollywood by Greta Garbo; none of the studio crew seemed much impressed by her.

Rob Wagner had become a good friend of Charlie Chaplin, and told me how he had persuaded the actor not to leave large sums of cash lying around the house. He noticed one day that Charlie was putting a fat roll of bills into a desk drawer, and discovered that all his by now substantial fortune was being handled the same way. Rob suggested it would be safer in a bank.

"I don't like banks," said Chaplin. "You stand there in front of a set of bars and feel like a prisoner." He was astonished to learn that for a deposit of a large amount, the bank would probably be willing to send a man to his home. The matter was so arranged.

Charlie had spent much of his boyhood in an English orphanage, little better than the terrible institutions of Dickens' day, and was marked for life by the cruel treatment he received there. The one great occasion for the orphans was Christmas, when each child received a whole orange. Charlie, perhaps excited by the occasion, had wet his bed the night before. He told Rob, with wonderful pantomime, how he had stood, trembling with anticipation, in the long line waiting for the Christmas treat. Just as he was reaching for his orange, a matron snatched him back out of line by the collar. "You'll wet your bed, will you?" she snarled. "No orange for you!" Remembering it years later, a millionaire and the best-known actor in the world, Charlie wept real tears for that lost orange.

I remember only one visit to Charlie's studio when he was making a picture. (He was especially fussy about visitors.) Rob and I chatted with him during a lull before the shooting of a scene in which a teen-age girl, dressed like an angel, was to float across the set on wires. He was enthusiastic about the acting ability of the girl, Lita Grey, who afterward became one of his series of wives.

My wife and I started a lifelong friendship with Thyra Samter Winslow, who went to New York about the same time we did. Thyra, born in Little Rock, Arkansas, had gone to Chicago in her teens and became a chorus girl there; she attributed her ravaged complexion to too much stage makeup. She was already writing her brief, powerful short stories which were to cause her one day to be compared, quite reasonably, to de Maupassant. Over the years she wrote scores of these, collected into several volumes. Then she developed a writing block as to fiction, and spent the rest of her working life in journalism, mostly dramatic criticism.

Like the characters in her most famous story, "A Cycle of Manhattan," Thyra moved often from one part of New York to another. With a flair for designing, she decorated apartment after apartment, only to move on in a few months. She made my wife and me, who changed our habitat only five times in a third of a century, and always for some compelling reason, feel we were old fogies indeed. Thyra, like so many others, died much too young.

In the summer of 1916 the Associated Advertising Clubs of the World (an organization which changed its name soon thereafter) held its annual convention in Philadelphia. Though I was no longer in the business, I was invited to be a delegate, and agreed; I had only once been east of the Mississippi, and then only to Michigan, at the age of five.

The Los Angeles contingent all wore identical white flannel suits, white shoes, and flat straw hats; we carried whitish canes, and marched in a big parade in Philadelphia, distributing California oranges to the crowds along the way; the suits, hats, and canes we had to pay for ourselves, but the oranges were supplied by the Los Angeles Chamber of Commerce.

The advertising business in 1916 was trying to shake off its disreputable past; national advertising at the turn of the century was dominated by patent medicines, each of which was supposed to cure a long list of diseases, often including cancer. Many of these medicines were mostly alcohol, innocently and avidly consumed by Prohibitionist Methodists and Baptists. The keynote of the 1916 convention was "Truth in Advertising," and the speakers all pointed out that honesty is good business. At the climax of the convention a huge electrically lighted floral wreath was carried on stage, with the word "Truth" emblazoned across it on a wide diagonal ribbon. I'm sure the delegates got the idea.

President Wilson came to Philadelphia to address our convention, seeming bored and ill at ease as he read his speech to us. I have forgotten what he said, but I remember thinking how surprised he would be if he knew that the white-suited young man in the twentieth row had read all his letters to Mrs. Peck.

After the convention, I visited Washington and New York, and in the latter city I dropped by the office of *Printers' Ink*, in a skyscraper at Thirty-fourth Street and Madison Avenue. Harry Wright, the managing editor, received his Los Angeles correspondent in friendly fashion, and we chatted for a few minutes. I had been in town for a day or so, and had picked up a few items of information about what was going on in the advertising business. I mentioned one of these; Mr. Wright hadn't heard of it.

"Lend me a typewriter and I'll write it for you," I said, and this was done. It turned out that a couple of my other pieces of information were also new, so I wrote them out as well, said good-bye to Mr. Wright, and departed for Los Angeles.

I had been home only a short time when I got a letter from *Printers' Ink* asking me to come to New York as a member of the editorial staff. I had told Mr. Wright my salary at the university and he offered me a 50 percent increase, or $3,000 a year, about the same as $7,500 in the 1960's.

I was inclined to reject the offer; I loved college teaching, and the Los Angeles climate. I had a comfortable home near the campus, and some spare time for writing. It was my wife who made the decision for me. She pointed out that unless I tried my wings in the Big Town I should never know whether I could fly or not. This may not have been the figure of speech she used; she might have said something about "a small frog in a small puddle." At any rate, after exchanging a few more letters as to what my duties would be, the cost of living in New York, and similar matters, I told Mr. Wright that I would come, as soon as I had solved the problem of disengaging myself from the university. By now we were in the second (and final) semester of the year.

Shaking in my boots, I told President Bovard of the offer from New York, and he was so amenable as almost to hurt my feelings, since I was half hoping he would say I was indispensable. On the contrary, he wished me God speed, adding only that of course I should have to find someone to take over the Journalism Department.

This proved easier than I had at first feared. A Stanford classmate, Ernest Hopkins, had become a reporter on *The Bulletin* in San Francisco, and had done brilliantly well. But he had been working hard, was getting restless, and I felt he might consider a change. I was right; he agreed to come south and take over my classes. He arrived in February, and over-lapped with me for a week or two. Without knowing it, I had started him on a career. Though he afterward worked as a reporter in other places, including *PM* in New York, he finally settled down as head of Journalism at Arizona State University at Tempe, a highly respected member of the faculty there.

My wife and I agreed that I should go to New York alone and find a place for our little family of three, while she stayed on a couple of months to dispose of loose ends in Los Angeles. We gave up our house and presented nearly all our furniture to my sister or to my parents, who were now living in the city. On March 1, 1917, I set off for New York in a welter of confused emotions—fear I should fail, gratification at being invited, regret at being separated even temporarily from my family, and well-justified doubt that I was competent to set up housekeeping in New York by myself.

Chapter 4

PRINTERS' INK

I demonstrated my naïveté on the day I arrived in New York. Seeking an inexpensive, temporary place while I searched for an apartment, I looked in a daily paper for rooms to rent and found one in an apartment house at Ninety-seventh Street and Riverside Drive that suited my needs. My landlady was an attractive young woman, living alone in an apartment larger than she seemed to need. I saw little of her as I came and went, and it took me several days to realize that she was a call girl.

When the truth dawned on me, I was unable to move out, as an ex-professor from a Methodist university should do, for a reason that seems comical now, but didn't at the time: I was down with measles. Feeling much out of sorts, I called up my friend Charlton Edholm, a free-lance writer from Los Angeles who had preceded me to New York by a few months, to ask him for the name of a doctor. Charlton lived a few blocks away, he knew a general practitioner in the neighborhood, and I went to see him. Before I entered his inner office, I could have diagnosed myself, for as I sat in his waiting room reading a magazine, I burst out with measles spots. The doctor took one look at me, and ordered me home to bed. He assured me it was a light case, warned me not to overuse my eyes, and charged me five dollars.

I now had a problem: I was reasonably sure that if my landlady discovered I had measles, she would turn me out into the street. While she was away from the house, which was a great deal, at odd hours, I used her phone to consult Charlton; he agreed with me about the probability of eviction, and we worked out a plan together. Every day he and his wife, Lizette, came over and smuggled in a quart of milk, a box or two of Uneeda Biscuits, and newspapers and magazines. The measles lasted a few days; what my landlady thought of my remaining in such seclusion, I never knew.

I had a week or so before I needed to report to *Printers' Ink*, and once I was on my feet again, I spent my time getting acquainted with the city, and house hunting. One of my first acts was to search out the Henry Street Settlement, in the heart of the Lower East Side slums, and to stand a long time looking at it from the sidewalk. In California I had been greatly moved by Lillian Wald's book, *The House on Henry Street*, an account of her many years of heroic struggle as head of the settlement there. The area was then almost entirely inhabited by half-starved Jews, murderously exploited by employers in the garment trade; David Dubinsky and Sidney Hillman had not yet come along to fight through their respective unions, the International Ladies' Garment Workers' Union and the Amalgamated Clothing Workers.

Years later, when Miss Wald and I had become friends, I told her of my pilgrimage, and she asked me why I hadn't come in; but I had been too shy.

I had never seen anything like the East Side ghetto, the streets packed with people day and night, the bedlam of noise, the clotted pushcart peddlers, the parade of small wagons, each drawn by an emaciated horse who looked as though any step would be his last.

Only three years later there was an enormous hegira of these people into new walk-up apartments in the Bronx, a development in which I played an important part, as I shall tell.

Almost at once, I was lucky enough to find an apartment where Californians would not feel too lost. It was four unfurnished rooms in a new building on tree-shaded Loring Place, in the Bronx, only a block from New York University with its big, green lawns and the long corridor of the Hall of Fame on the hillside. The University Heights station of the New York Central was nearby, on the bank of the Harlem River, at the foot of the steep hill, and at the other end of the trip, the office of *Printers' Ink* was only eight short blocks from Grand Central Station. In those days the commuting trains were fast, clean, comfortable, not over-crowded, and the fares were low. In more than a third of a century in New York, I never again had such ideal transport between home and office.

Like Los Angeles, the city was a far more pleasant place in which to live then than now. Traffic on the avenues was almost never congested and there was no smog. People whom I met one by one were as friendly as anyone could ask, but I found it hard at first to get used to the reluctance of people in a crowd to "get involved," as they were to call it many years later.

I moved into the new apartment, buying, as my wife had adjured me, only the barest minimum of equipment until she arrived. I struck up an acquaintance with a number of people in the neighborhood, including one elderly gentleman who told me a horror story of an experience a few months earlier, that proved the point just mentioned. One winter afternoon, walking up the hill from the University Heights station, he slipped on the ice and broke his leg. He was well dressed and sober, and yet one commuter after another ignored his pleas for help, presumably with the idea that he was a drunk who had fallen down. Not until a friend came by who recognized him did he get aid.

I expressed my own emotions about the aloofness of the city in a scrap of mediocre free verse, making myself, for literary purposes, more of a desert rat than was the case. I quote from memory fifty years later, perhaps not word for word but nearly so.

> When I got off the train at University Heights
> It was raining.
> But no one offered to share an umbrella,
> Or even asked, Are you getting wet?
>
> Out on the Mojave, whence I came,
> You cannot pass a ranch house
> Without a friendly hail,
> And an offered glass of water.
> And the rancher stands by the door
> To watch you ride away.
> . . . I think I'm a little homesick tonight.

In those days Franklin P. Adams was conducting his famous column in *The World*, to which the city's gifted writers were eager to contribute —without payment, and often under a pseudonym. A few months later, I should have been too intimidated to try to contribute, but as a green Westerner, I cheerfully sent along my piece, and F.P.A., as he was universally known, printed it, over my signature.

I was shocked by the violence of the reaction I received. A dozen people wrote, in purple anger, to invite me, if I didn't like New York, to go back to the sticks. I got only one or two friendly letters, and these were from ex-Californians who sympathized, but assured me New Yorkers were like everybody else—when you got to know them.

One other impression of the streets of New York in 1917 has remained with me. I was staggered by the awful epithets the taxi drivers used against each other over a dented fender. Even in my mild and urban West, you couldn't call a man names like that without a fist fight, and in cowboy country guns might have been used. The first dozen times I witnessed such an altercation, I instinctively ducked, until I learned that in New York you could call a man anything, and he would merely reply in kind.

In the office of *Printers' Ink*, people went out of their way to be kind to a Western greenhorn. Most of the stock was owned by John Irving Romer, the working editor, who had bought the magazine years earlier, and had built it up into what many people called it, the bible of the advertising business. It was pocket-sized, fat with advertising, and the weekly issues were almost entirely written by a staff of four or five people. Our chief articles were cast in the mold that *Fortune* was to use years later, stories of advertising campaigns that had succeeded or (very rarely) failed. We interviewed participants in such campaigns, and reported the results in sober prose.

The magazine also printed the routine news of the business, and campaigned editorially for the things you might expect—honesty in copy, careful identification of potential customers, and consideration for aesthetics, in a day when many advertisers used ugly black boxcar type, and scorned handsome layouts.

Mr. Romer was almost pathologically shy and inarticulate, qualities that had not prevented his becoming a millionaire in a brief space of time. Like Dr. Bovard at U.S.C., he hated public speaking, and was relieved to find I did not mind it, and was willing to represent the magazine on formal occasions. He was also a shrewd psychologist; he began raising my salary every couple of months, but he did so five or ten dollars at a time, keeping me in a steady state of gratitude. Within two years I had gone from $60 a week to $125, worth about $300 in the dollars of the late 1960's.

I had been in New York only a few weeks when my loyalty to Stanford was summoned into action. President David Starr Jordan was a lifelong pacifist; quite apart from other considerations, he argued, as a student of biology, that in war, the best human stock gets killed off, leaving inferior men, genetically speaking, to become the fathers of the next generation. He thought he had proved this by studies of European areas where wars had been frequent for millennia. When I was an undergraduate he taught overflowing classes on the subject of peace, and as the 1914 war grew nearer, he resigned as president of Stanford to work in the cause, through such groups as the World Peace Foundation and the Anti-Imperialist League. By the early spring of 1917, he was touring the country urging an isolationist policy.

This went pretty well in the West, which mostly agreed with him. But the Eastern seaboard was much more interventionist, and he began to meet stiff opposition. The climax came when he tried to speak in Baltimore; the audience shouted him down, threw eggs and vegetables, and some members started to climb on the stage. His life perhaps in real danger, he was rescued by the police and hustled out the back door.

A university president usually moves in an atmosphere of great respect and friendliness, and when the news of what had happened reached New York, I realized what a dreadful shock and humiliation he must have experienced. Two or three alumni who were in the city conferred by telephone, and agreed to do what little we could to set the balance straight. With some difficulty we reached Dr. Jordan in Baltimore; would he come to New York and be the guest of honor at a small dinner of Stanford men and women? He agreed (I think he was coming anyway). Several of us met him at the train and escorted him, first to a hotel and then to the banquet room. There we took turns telling him that he was a great man, and that regardless of how one felt about the war (we differed on this among ourselves), the Baltimoreans had acted disgracefully. His drooping countenance lifted visibly in the course of the evening, and we took him back to his hotel feeling we had done our Boy Scout good deed for the day.

Two months after I had come to New York, my wife arrived with our sixteen-month-old son. She approved of the apartment, and proceeded to buy the most urgently needed equipment; we had no money for luxuries. With no trouble we found almost at once, for a nominal wage, a part-time household assistant; Mrs. Frantz was the wife of an apartment superintendent a couple of blocks away, with half-grown children of her own. She made time to come over daily, cook our evening meal, and baby-sit when needed. She was of German origin and spoke both languages with facility; for a year or two our son was bilingual. She was our warm friend until her death, decades later.

I was meeting new people through *Printers' Ink*, and making acquaintances among my fellow commuters from University Heights; but my uprooted California wife had almost no contacts in New York, and was lonely. I had told her of a nice young man whom I saw on the train, who lived on the floor below us, and one day my wife, with her baby on her hip, went downstairs, rang the bell, and told Hilda Perry who she was, and that if she didn't get someone to speak to during the long days she would go crazy. Hilda, bless her, took Rosie in and the Reginald Perrys and the Blivens became lifelong friends. Their blonde daughter Jane played in the park daily with young Bruce for several years, until we both moved away; she grew up to be Mrs. John Gunther, who accompanied her husband on many thousands of miles of travel, leaving behind her everywhere remembrance of her beauty, charm, and devotion to John's welfare.

I have mentioned that when the war began in Europe in 1914, it seemed very remote from sunny, self-absorbed California. But as time passed, it impinged more and more strongly on our consciousness.

In the beginning, opinion may have been almost evenly divided between Germany and her enemies. (There were no public-opinion polls in those days to check people's sentiments.) But as time passed, Americans swung more and more behind the Allies, for several reasons. America was still dominated by people of British extraction. Great Britain did a lot of highly effective propaganda in the United States, whereas Germany had few means for presenting her side of the case. The British controlled the surface of the Atlantic, and Germany could only operate with submarines sinking Allied ships—always an unpopular operation, no matter how desirable from a military point of view.

Nineteen-fifteen was an especially bad year for Germany's reputation in America. In April she used poison gas for the first time in history, with dreadful consequences to its totally unprotected victims. In May, she sank, seemingly without warning, the British liner *Lusitania*, with the loss of more than 1,100 lives, including 124 Americans. It did Germany little good to insist that the *Lusitania* carried war materials, and that the government *had* given warning, by a newspaper advertisement, before the ship left New York. In October, British nurse Edith Cavell was executed in Belgium for helping smuggle people out of the country. German saboteurs were active in the United States. With unrestricted submarine warfare, more American lives were lost, and some American ships were sunk. A few days before I arrived in New York in 1917, German Foreign Secretary Arthur Zimmermann wrote his fatuous note to his Minister in Mexico, urging that that country be persuaded to enter the war to recover her lost territories north of the Rio Grande; it was intercepted by the Allies and published.

There was certainly still plenty of isolationist sentiment; early in 1917, Congress refused to arm American merchant ships as President Wilson had asked, and he was forced to accomplish this by executive order. But the anti-German tide was rising, and most people seemed to approve when, on April 6, he asked Congress to begin formal hostilities. It was a month and two days after he had been inaugurated for his second term, having run on a platform of "he kept us out of war."

Conscription followed promptly, and two months later, all men twenty-one to thirty were registered. A lottery system was used to determine in what order they would be called up, and if there was dissatisfaction with this procedure, we heard little of it. In due course, I was called before my draft board and promptly deferred; I had a wife and child, and I also had flat feet and bad eyesight. I sat out the war on Madison Avenue.

Printers' Ink was of course greatly changed in character, as we reported the impact of hostilities on advertising and merchandising. The President had set up a Committee on Public Information, headed by George Creel, a fairly capable San Francisco newspaperman, of whom

I have always remembered with some envy that he was said to be an amateur gymnast who could walk on his hands. I was assigned to be liaison man between his committee and the magazine, reporting constantly for our readers what the government expected of business. I also wrote articles about "Reconstruction," the wonderful things that were to happen to our economy when peace had been restored. (None of them took place.)

In those days, as now, most institutions in the field of advertising demanded of their workers a spiritual commitment, or at least ardent lip service, to the theory that it is a great source for social development, and responsible in large degree for the high level of American civilization. Mr. Romer made no such demand of his staff, and I was never asked to write a word that I did not honestly believe. The radicals were saying that all advertising is a dead waste, a drag on the economy, but I already knew that this idea was far too simplistic. Some advertising is wasteful, as when dairies in a single city spend money competing in the sale of milk, and neither increases the volume of activity enough to reduce the unit cost of service, but in most cases the social and economic results of advertising are a highly complicated and sophisticated question with good and bad sides.

Half a century later, advertising, and the merchandising of which it is a part, are enormously more skillful than in those clumsy rule-of-thumb days. Color was yet to come, except on billboards and in some aspects of direct mail. The average degree of skill in layouts and typography has greatly increased, though they are no better than the best of 1917 (they couldn't be).

In some ways there has been a great deterioration, from the point of view of the public welfare. John B. Watson, father of behaviorism, was then just moving over from being a college professor of psychology to an agency executive, a move I always regretted, and suspected that he did too. Disciples of his produced the appalling new idea that advertising should be as irritating and obnoxious as possible, on the ground that the infuriated customer will have the name of the product stamped indelibly on his unconscious, but will forget his annoyance. This philosophy was applied to radio, and later to television, with dreadful results. Certainly no other great nation would put up with the huge quantity of commercialism heard and seen on American radio and TV today, or the low quality of much of it. In the late 1960's students of this subject were blaming commercials for increasing the desire of the poor for a wide range of material possessions they cannot buy, and thereby helping to cause the orgies of looting that accompanied ghetto riots.

With my incorrigible habit of moonlighting, I accepted an invitation to teach writing in the evening session at the Washington Square branch of New York University. The contrast with U.S.C. was startling. In

California my students had been the big, good-looking sons and daughters of the orange growers or others of the prosperous middle class. They were relaxed and easygoing; while some of them worked hard, there were many others who leaned back and, in effect, challenged the teacher to intrude on their equanimity.

At N.Y.U., in the evening session, I dealt mostly with the children of the very poor, from the Lower East Side, who were attending college at heaven knows what sacrifice on the part of their families. They worked frenetically hard, actually demanding that I push them more than I was at first inclined to do; their sharp, abrasive intelligence was a most pleasurable challenge to me as a teacher. It was with reluctance that I gave up this work after a couple of years, when other duties came crowding in on me.

Most of my work on *Printers' Ink* was routine, but a few episodes stand out in my memory. In June, 1917, Lord Northcliffe came to America as head of the British War Mission and I managed with some difficulty to be allowed to interview him. Most people have forgotten today that he was the inventor of modern popular journalism in Great Britain, and owner of the largest publishing house in the world, with many magazines and newspapers, including the august *Times*. He was accompanied to America by Hamilton Fyfe, his best-known writer, whom he treated, I noticed, as though he were the humblest of stenographers. Northcliffe reminded me, in his animal vitality and single-mindedness, of the angry bulls of my childhood in Iowa. He answered my questions with courteous impatience until he thought the interview had gone on long enough. On a table within arm's reach, there was a pile of copies of a biography of himself, and he now autographed one for me to indicate that the interview was over.

Following a lifelong custom of mine, I sent the manuscript of the interview to his lordship to check before it was printed. (I included mention of the device to get rid of a caller by giving him a book.) I got it back with a warm letter of approval—from Hamilton Fyfe.

About this time, Mr. Romer asked me to talk to a young novelist who was planning to write a book about the advertising business. He was a tall, gangling redhead with a pockmarked complexion and I was not much impressed by him. Sinclair Lewis was still about three years away from his first great success, *Main Street*, and his serials in *The Saturday Evening Post* had attracted little attention. (He never wrote the novel about advertising, though he played with the idea for many years.) In the midst of our conversation I mispronounced a foreign phrase; I knew instantly that I had done so, but I was too embarrassed to correct myself. Not a flicker of emotion passed over his face, but a few years later that exact mistake turned up in one of his books, in the mouth of a young man pretending to be better educated than he was.

Among the friends I had made in New York was a man of my own age who was editor of a modest little magazine selling, as I remember, for three cents. It had been started in order to take up some slack on the presses of a big printing firm but was not doing too well, and presently came the news that it was to be discontinued. A day or so later, I met the editor on the street, and paused to chat. He was in a bitter mood. This was, he said, the third or fourth editorial job he had lost in quick succession through no fault of his own, and he was sick of it. "I'm going into the other end of the business," he told me. "My friend, Roy Durstine, and I are going to start an advertising agency. Nobody can fire me when I am my own boss." Bruce Barton's agency went on to become the hugely successful Batten, Barton, Durstine and Osborn, and he to be a member of Congress and author of the best-selling *The Man Nobody Knows*, presenting Jesus as an early exponent of skilled merchandising principles. We ended up far apart politically, but remained on a basis of casual friendliness until his death half a century later.

Norman Geddes arrived in New York not long after the Blivens. We had moved a block or so down the street to a seven-room apartment in a five-story walk-up, and the one on the floor below being vacant, Norman and Belle moved in with their daughter Joan, about the age of Bruce, Jr. The two families explored together the fascinating, seemingly infinite resources of New York as Norman moved rapidly up the ladder of success as a designer of sets and costumes for play after play.

His recreations were as unusual as his career. He designed a marvelous little nine-hole golf course that fitted on a ping-pong table, the contours of the land built up out of painted papier-mâché, the balls steel bearings, the "clubs" shutter mechanisms from cameras. Trees and shrubs were made to scale from sponge rubber, the water hazards were pieces of mirror, the greens billiard cloth. A good player went around in seventy-two, a duffer never broke a hundred. Dozens of famous people from the theater flocked to Norman's apartment to play.

He went on to an elaborate war game, many years before anyone had heard of the theory of games, John von Neumann, or the Rand Corporation. These contests were played on huge maps, laid down flat, the rules being based on the facts of logistics and strategy. A single game sometimes went on, in leisure hours, for weeks, and finally officers from the War College in Washington were sent up to be participants.

Of the young people I met at Norman's I remember most vividly George Kaufman, with a shock of black hair standing up above a white, unsmiling face, and Howard Dietz, neat and businesslike, who could beat us all at ping-pong. Howard was just out of the navy. Both these men were only beginning their brilliant careers, George as playwright and Howard as musical-comedy lyricist, librettist for the Metropolitan Opera, and publicist in the motion-picture industry.

Norman himself went on from triumph to triumph. He is best remembered, perhaps, for his "Futurama," the most popular feature of the New York World's Fair of 1939-40, where the spectators traveled on a moving platform above a model city of the twenty-first century, with widely spaced skyscrapers looking down on separated pedestrian malls and vehicular roadways. Years earlier, for Max Reinhardt's *The Miracle*, he turned a theater into a medieval cathedral, sheathing the whole interior in imitation stone, with "stained glass" windows lighted from behind. Rosamond Pinchot as the heroine, running with infinite grace across the flagged floor, was the talk of New York for months.

As architect, Norman planned theaters and other buildings; as industrial designer, he created scores of commercial products—autos, yachts, refrigerators; as typographer, he planned books and remade several magazines and newspapers, including *The New York Post*. He redid the Ringling Brothers and Barnum and Bailey Circus. Turning city planner, he created a new and brilliant scheme for the central core of Toledo, Ohio. At the peak of his success, he had hundreds of employees, working on a bewildering variety of projects. Through it all he remained the same squeaky-voiced, homely, small-town boy from Michigan, with ideas tumbling out so fast he could hardly enunciate them.

The world war ended, as far as New York was concerned, on November 7, 1918, when Roy Howard, the pint-sized journalistic Napoleon, head of the United Press, flashed the erroneous news that an armistice had been signed. As the report spread through the city, people dropped whatever they were doing and poured out into the streets to celebrate. I wandered for hours, with a couple of other *Printers' Ink* people, on the fringes of Times Square amid the celebrants, who sang and cheered themselves voiceless. We were all sure, as President Wilson had promised, that there would never be another war.

When the conflict really ended, four days later, it seemed an anticlimax, and there was little celebrating. Friends of mine on the United Press observed that it was lucky the boss had made this monumental goof; if it had been anyone else, Howard would have boiled him in oil. Roy had a good alibi: An American admiral had told him the war was over and had not forbidden him to spread the news. Within a few months the historic mistake was forgotten.

Toward the end of November, my wife and I and our baby were all laid low simultaneously by the influenza epidemic which killed 500,000 in the United States and twenty million throughout the world. By some miracle, our doctor managed to find a nurse who was willing to come and care for us (our part-time housekeeper, Mrs. Frantz, was also a victim of the epidemic). We all had light cases, and were back on our feet in a few days.

Beginning soon after we reached New York, my wife and I established a routine for ourselves parts of which endured for a third of a century. Every pleasant Sunday, except in winter, we traveled by train or bus to a designated spot a few miles out of New York and did an all-day hike of five or ten miles with the Green Mountain Club, eating a cold lunch out of doors around a small campfire, built to heat the coffee. In this way we explored scores of areas on both banks of the Hudson, both shores of Long Island, and many areas of New Jersey.

Each Saturday afternoon from September to June we went to a theater matinee; we saw almost every important production for three decades, attending the first and every subsequent important Broadway appearance of Katharine Cornell, Helen Hayes, Alfred Lunt and Lynn Fontanne, Margaret Sullavan, Mary Martin, Ethel Merman, Barbara Bel-Geddes (Norman's daughter), Dorothy McGuire, Gertrude Lawrence, Noel Coward, and many more. We attended every play of Eugene O'Neill, Sidney Howard, Robert Sherwood, George Kaufman, Moss Hart, Marc Connally, John Van Druten, Richard Rodgers and his succession of collaborators, Thornton Wilder, Elmer Rice, Howard Lindsay and Russel Crouse, Lillian Hellman, Sidney Kingsley, Ben Hecht. We began with seats in the highest gallery, and worked our way down to the orchestra floor as our income rose. Sometimes we waited until a hit show neared the end of its run and got half-price tickets at Joe Leblang's bargain basement at Forty-third Street and Broadway. For years, of course, we had many of the free seats that go to a working journalist.

We watched the whole career of the Neighborhood Playhouse, an offshoot of the Henry Street Settlement. We were excited by the one-act dramas of the Washington Square Players, and more so by the Theater Guild, their successor, with some of whose chief figures we had a nodding acquaintance—Theresa Helburn, Lee Simonson, the stage designer, and Lawrence Langner, who combined his activities in the theater with a highly successful career as a patent attorney. Our best and lifelong friend in the group was Warren Munsell, its business manager for many years, the sturdy, solid individual who kept the soaring artistic temperaments from losing all touch with reality. Our bond with the Munsells was not the Guild, but the fact that Bruce, Jr., was a classmate and close friend of Warren, Jr., from kindergarten until the Munsells were saddened by his death in young manhood.

I have total recall for a lot of useless information, and I suppress with a struggle a long list of brilliant plays, scenes from which rise in my mind as I write. If you saw them, you probably remember; if you didn't, the names would evoke no images.

I was as assiduous in going to movies as to the theater; from 1908 to the mid-century mark when my health became a handicap, I saw every good film—and a lot of bad ones. Over the years we wallowed in the luxury of New York's riches, the opera, the symphony, the Metropolitan

Museum, the Museum of Modern Art, the American Museum of Natural History, the New York Zoological Gardens, known always as the "Bronx Zoo."

In summer we took the sightseeing boats around Manhattan, and to Coney Island and Sandy Hook, or the big white steamers up the Hudson to Albany. When I had business in New England I went by the overnight boat to Boston and once or twice we tried the water trip to Norfolk, Virginia. For several happy summers we spent time on Martha's Vineyard or Nantucket, going up overnight on the New Bedford line, and then crossing the pier in the morning for the Nantucket boat, which made intermediate stops at Woods Hole and Martha's Vineyard. Most of these delightful water passages except the last have now been put out of business by the all-devouring automobile.

My wife was more ambitious scholastically than I. As soon as our son was old enough, she enrolled herself in Teachers College and him in the connected, and now departed, Horace Mann Kindergarten that was used for demonstrations and practice teaching. She deposited him in the kindergarten at 9 a.m., proceeded to her classes in another part of the building, and picked him up at the allotted hour for the return home. In nice weather they rode most of the way on the Fifth Avenue buses, in those days double-deckers with an open top. The choice seats were those in front, and young Bruce, at four or five, kept a sharp eye out for Indians or pirates. When my wife got her Master of Arts degree in educational psychology, her husband and son applauded in the audience as she stood up for it in cap and gown. She then went on to do most of the work for a Ph.D. but life crowded in on her, and she stopped just short of getting her hood.

We were now prosperous enough to afford a live-in housekeeper, and had no trouble in acquiring one. In fact, we had several in three or four years; we liked them all, and parted company with regret when they decided, variously, to leave New York or to take up another line of work. Then in 1926, Miss Ida Morstadt came to us, to remain more than a quarter of a century, until in 1953 my doctor exiled me to a warm climate and she decided to return to the Germany she had left before Hitler was even heard of. She had come to America with half a dozen young women whom she knew, nearly all of whom ended up in or near New York, and I was fascinated to see how, by sheer force of character, she had become the unquestioned leader of her group, not one of whom fell victim to the Nazi madness that for a time afflicted so many other German-Americans.

When my wife and I arrived in New York, Greenwich Village was still a great tourist attraction. Not only out-of-towners but middle-class couples from other parts of the city journeyed there to dine in dimly lit cellars and speculate whether the oddly dressed man at the corner table might not be Floyd Dell or Max Eastman (he was probably a Wall Street

clerk from Brooklyn). We went there often, though like the other trippers we were never more than onlookers at the real Bohemian life of the
place.

Most of our favorite restaurants are, I believe, long gone—Romany
Marie's, The Mad Hatter, the Pepper Pot, Alice McCollister's on Eighth
Street, which, with a minimum of "atmosphere," served good plain food
at astonishingly low prices. A survivor when I last checked was Lee
Chumley's on Bedford Street, whose walls were decorated with the
paper jackets of scores of books written by his patrons.

Very few of these places could be called tourist traps; their prices
were not high, their food was usually good. In some of them "Tiny Tim"
wandered from table to table selling his "soul candy," (mostly plain
vanilla fudge, as far as I could see) with an amusing line of prattle. Bobby
Edwards sang to his own ukulele accompaniment songs commenting on
current events, in calypso fashion. One or two rejected poets peddled
their manuscripts for twenty-five or fifty cents, the theory being that
there were no other copies of the work you were purchasing. Don
Dickerman's Pirates' Den, more fancy than most, had waiters dressed
like buccaneers. When we wanted to splurge we went to the Brevoort
or the Lafayette, very good French eating places, one on lower Fifth
Avenue, one a little farther east. Gonfarone's on Eighth Street served
multicourse big dinners for very little, as did a dozen other Italian places.

I don't remember the first production by the Provincetown Players,
but like every other patron I have never forgotten one a little later,
Eugene O'Neill's *The Emperor Jones*, with its feeling of brooding tropic
jungle and terror. Christine's restaurant, nearby, was almost a Provincetown Players boardinghouse; we ate there once or twice with our friend
Nina Moise, a backstage member of the Players, later a highly successful
Hollywood speech coach, and saw Gene O'Neill sitting motionless and
silent over a plate of minestrone. Whether he was sober I do not know;
it was a time when he was drinking heavily.

The struggling writers and artists of Greenwich Village ate in all
these places, when they could afford it, but as uptown trippers, we knew
few of them. One friend we saw often at Romany Marie's and other
places was Vilhjalmur Stefansson, the Arctic explorer, an agreeable man
unless someone challenged his thesis that humans can thrive on a diet of
meat, and meat alone. (He had done this for many months in the Arctic.)
We knew Floyd Dell casually, because he had married B. Marie Gage,
formerly a student of mine at U.S.C. Howard Scott, the brooding, angry
young inventor of Technocracy, courted me a little because I could get
publicity for his idea, which in fact I did, a few years later. We had a
casual acquaintance with Harry Kemp, the Village poet laureate, who
had been a friend of Upton Sinclair, and with Maxwell Bodenheim, the
alcoholic novelist who wrote obscene books a generation too soon and

therefore got into trouble with the law over things that wouldn't lift an eyebrow fifty years later. Like many other people, we knew slightly playwright Susan Glaspell, who seemed a placid homemaker but was in fact the mainspring of the Provincetown Players, and her big, easygoing husband, George Cram Cook.

Mabel Dodge Luhan was operating her famous salon on lower Fifth Avenue at this time, but I never met her until many years later when Witter Bynner introduced us in Taos, at a party also attended by her great rival, D. H. Lawrence's widow, Frieda. I have no mental image of Mabel, but I remember Frieda, a plump hausfrau, who asked me whether I had known D. H., and lost interest when I had to answer no.

Prohibition went into effect in 1920, and was a blow to the Village restaurant life of earlier years. The places we had known and loved either went out of business or became speakeasies requiring, at least at the beginning, some sort of special introduction. The Bohemians couldn't afford to pay high prices for (supposedly) good liquor, and the bootleggers supplied only gin and whiskey, not wine.

Within a few years, prosperous middle-class people began moving into the Village, occupying big, new apartment houses or renovating old brownstones as the artists and writers could never afford to do. A few of these who struck it rich departed for uptown, or for Westchester; the unsuccessful ones were pushed far over toward the Hudson or the East River. The Village remained a pleasant place—I lived there myself my last twenty years in New York—but the old charm had vanished by then. And so had my youth.

Very early in 1919, I got a routine assignment from *Printers' Ink* to interview Jason Rogers, publisher of *The Globe*, one of New York's half dozen evening papers. I talked to him, wrote my story, mailed it to him for his approval, and got it back promptly with his O.K. I was surprised, a few days later, to get a telephone message from him. Would I be interested in coming to *The Globe* as chief editorial writer, for $225 a week? This was $100 more than *Printers' Ink* was paying me, and worth in 1970 dollars perhaps $400.

Although I took a few days to think it over, after a rather perfunctory meeting with H. J. Wright, the editor, there was never any doubt in my mind that I would accept. While I had enjoyed writing for a trade paper, the mainstream of news and public affairs had always been my first love.

At this moment, Harry Wright, the managing editor of *Printers' Ink*, unexpectedly died of pneumonia. I drove to his funeral in the limousine of Mr. Romer, who tried hard to get me to reverse my decision; I was shocked that he used this solemn occasion to talk business. He asked me to be managing editor, offered to exceed the salary *The Globe* was promising, and even spoke of some stock (in days when letting executives share in ownership was very rare indeed). Looking back, I can see that I might have become wealthy (*Printers' Ink* went on to years of great success), but I declined his offer, and have never regretted it. Whether I became rich or not, I should surely have become bored. Two years to a day after I had arrived in New York, I cleaned out my desk and reported to my new boss.

Chapter 5

THE GLOBE

The postwar decade, 1919 to 1929, has been called various names—the Jazz Age, the Roaring Twenties, the Era of Wonderful Nonsense. The impression the popular historians give us is of wild youth, speakeasies, fantastic murder trials, and toward the end of the decade, universal stock-market gambling on margin, with everybody getting rich overnight—on paper.

All these things existed, but they did not engulf us as the historians suggest. I spent that decade working hard, and so did most of the people I knew. My wife and I never went to a speakeasy except a few times to meet someone there at his suggestion, and I'm sure this was true of millions of others. We never made bathtub gin, or bought any liquor that I can remember from any bootlegger. The wife of a member of the diplomatic corps in Washington once gave me a large bottle of champagne, and I kept it in a desk drawer at the office waiting for some reason to celebrate, until it turned flat. Somebody else gave us a couple of quarts of illicit gin, and in the course of several years, we drank about half of it, throwing away the rest when Prohibition was repealed. I didn't gamble on the stock market, and I can't remember anyone else in my circle of close friends who did, or at least, who ever mentioned it.

It is true that there were some gaudy murders and other sensational happenings exploited in the popular press, the Hall-Mills and Snyder-Gray killings, Peaches Browning and her sugar daddy, and Aimee Semple McPherson, the evangelist whose story of being kidnapped from the surf at Santa Monica and escaping days later in the desert on the Mexican border finally appeared to be a clumsy fabrication to cover up a tryst with a man. I doubt whether these happenings were any more spectacular than in earlier or later decades, but in the 1920's tabloid newspapers had just come into being in New York, and they gave a vehicle for vulgar journalism that had a great impact. The image of wild youth was largely the invention of a popular magazine illustrator, Johnny Held, whose drawings of flappers with rolled stockings doing the Charleston were enormously popular for a while. But the great majority of the population struggled as the great majority always does, to make ends meet, to bring up their children, and to behave themselves.

In 1919, *The Globe* was a mediocre evening paper, with a circulation of about 150,000. It was located in a three-story former tobacco warehouse on Dey Street, far downtown, and inside and outside the building was rough and plain. The ground floor was devoted to the presses, and the second floor was about equally divided between the news and composing rooms. On the third floor were the offices of the editor and publisher, the business department, and a few feature writers who rated cubbyholes of their own.

The Globe was one of fourteen English-language papers of general circulation in New York, a city which in 1968 had been reduced to three, two of them tabloids. In the morning there were *The Times, The Herald, The Tribune, The American, The World, The Sun,* and *The Telegraph,* the last named devoted to show business and horse racing. In the evening, in addition to *The Globe,* there were *The Evening World, The Telegram, The Evening Sun, The Journal, The Mail,* and *The Evening Post. The American* and *The Journal* were Hearst papers, with the usual strengths and weaknesses of his dailies. *The World* and *The Evening World* were the Pulitzer papers, liberal in policy, popular in tone. *The Sun* and *The Evening Sun* were in the Dana tradition, well written, somewhat conservative, catering chiefly to the financial district. *The Herald* and *The Telegram* were the Bennett papers, in a decline since the death of the younger Bennett. *The Times* was Adolph Ochs's paper, serious, packed with information, not very lively, already started on the upward climb that was to make it the preeminent daily of the United States, and one of the three or four most important in the world.

The Mail, nominally owned by Dr. Henry Stoddard, was dying. Control of it had been secretly purchased during the war by the German government, and while this fact had not yet been officially confirmed, the paper's pro-German attitude had proved ruinous.

The Globe, under its earlier title, *The Commercial Advertiser,* went back about a hundred years, second in age only to *The Evening Post.* It had had a checkered career, and in recent times a curious one.

I have already identified Mark Hopkins, the San Franciscan, one of the "Big Four," who had made huge fortunes out of building what was finally named the Southern Pacific Railroad. When he was middle aged, by the standards of the day, he met and fell in love with a cousin only half his age, Mary Frances Sherwood. There is no evidence that she cared for him particularly, and it is a legitimate inference that the marriage was in good part a pecuniary arrangement on her part. But instead of dying promptly and leaving her the money, he lingered on a quarter of a century. When she became what was commonly called "the richest widow in the United States," she was, again by the standards of the day, herself a somewhat embittered, middle-aged woman.

She developed a passion for building huge houses in various parts of the country, and one of her architects was a young man, twenty-two years her junior, named Edward Searles. He had no intention of ever marrying anyone, but the widow fell wildly in love with him, and he finally, with every show of reluctance, became a bridegroom. The earlier pattern was now repeated; she lingered on for some years before she died, leaving him a disillusioned widower, possessor of her whole estate, with an annual income of more than half a million dollars (and no income tax).

Searles was still alive in 1919, when I took my new job, living in seclusion in one of the castles his wife had built, this one in Methuen, Massachusetts. Somewhere along the way, the Hopkins estate had picked up *The Globe*, and Searles, who had no real interest in the paper, had never got around to disposing of it. He was said never to read a book or a newspaper, and to spend much of his time rearranging the furniture in his house. In other ways as well he was eccentric; he had a passion for building stone walls, and erected quantities of them on his estate. He was reported to dress his servants in footmen's knee breeches and powdered wigs, and if he took it into his head to play his fine pipe organ at three o'clock in the morning, as he often did, he roused the household and marched to the organ room accompanied by a retinue of linkmen carrying flaming torches.

In the four years that *The Globe* was still to survive, he interfered in its operations only twice, and not in any serious way. When Senator Henry Cabot Lodge, the grandfather of the diplomat of the 1960's of the same name, was fighting ratification of the Treaty of Versailles by the U.S. Senate, *The Globe* fought back vigorously and in our enthusiasm we got pretty personal. Mr. Searles sent a messenger to ask us please to attack Senator Lodge on public grounds only. He lived not far away and Searles was embarrassed to meet him socially with our excoriations reverberating in the room. The other message was a similar one in regard to Vice-President Calvin Coolidge, of whom we tended to take a dim view.

Jason Rogers, whom I had interviewed for *Printers' Ink*, was a happy

extrovert, who had written several small books on the business side of
newspaper publishing, and loved to talk to college students on this subject. He interfered not at all with the editorial side of the paper, in the
hands of Mr. Wright, a man in middle age who had learned his business
under the famous E. L. Godkin of *The Evening Post*. Wright was a
scholarly, reflective individual, a good writer in the British newspaper
tradition, but not the driving force to make *The Globe* a success against
heavy competition.

Twenty years earlier, Lincoln Steffens had been city editor of the
paper (then still called *The Commercial Advertiser*), having worked earlier
for Wright when the latter was city editor of *The Evening Post*. Steffens
in his autobiography writes at length of this experience; he says the paper
had only "two or three thousand" readers, a statement hard to believe.
Although he could pay reporters only "twelve or twenty dollars a week,"
he assembled a remarkable staff, including Norman Hapgood, later editor of *Collier's Weekly*; Eugene Walter, the playwright; Abraham Cahan,
who was to become editor of *The Jewish Daily Forward*; and (part time)
the famous literary figure, Harry Thurston Peck, professor at Columbia
and editor of *The Bookman*.

Now, in 1919, Wright and Rogers were determined to make the
paper, renamed *The Globe*, something distinctive, and proposed to do so
by way of the editorial page. This had been a weak feature; there was one
rather conservative editorial writer, and the editor himself did some
"leaders" when he had time. The editorial writer had departed for a job
on *The Tribune*, with whose right-wing views he felt at home, and Rogers
and Wright had decided to try to create a page with a real impact. I was
asked to find two other editorial writers as soon as possible, to work with
me and with Mr. Wright, to produce two columns a day of material (set
column-and-a-half measure, actually three standard columns of type).

In this emergency I did what everyone used to do under similar
circumstances before the days of trade unions and the union shop: I
turned to men I knew, in this case two members of my generation at
college. (Later I was to add four more Stanford men.) Robert Duffus, who
had done fine work as the sole editorial writer on *The Bulletin* in San
Francisco, had come to New York, and was available. Frank Hill had
been trained as an aviator during the world war, and with its end, he, also,
was open to an invitation. Within a short time we were ready to go.

Students of journalism may be interested to know how we produced
the editorial page. We began with an editorial conference with Mr.
Wright at about 8:30 A.M.; each of us was supposed to have read *The Times*
carefully before that, and to have skimmed some of the other papers.
Under a good deal of time pressure, we discussed the leading topics of
the day, each man putting forth his views, if any. By about 9 A.M. we had
decided on what each of us would write, and the general line to be taken.

Never, in the four years the paper lasted, did Mr. Wright ask anyone to write against his convictions; with only one exception that I can recall, he accepted the group judgment as to what our policy ought to be.

That single exception was the terms of the Treaty of Versailles in 1919. When these were published, Duffus, Hill, and I were outraged by their harshness toward defeated Germany. (We were for the League of Nations but against the other terms of the Treaty.) Mr. Wright maintained the contrary view, and when he found us adamant, he wrote the editorial himself, calling the treaty "wise and just." Fifty years later, history has certainly proved him wrong.

Normally, we broke up with each of us having about ninety minutes in which to write an editorial of three or four hundred words. When necessary, we got reference material from the paper's "morgue"; but often this was not needed. Many subjects ran on from day to day, and usually, once a man was assigned to a given topic, it was his baby from then on.

When our articles were finished, we handed them in to Mr. Wright. He read them quickly, sometimes changed a word or two, and sent them down to the composing room. Proof came up within a half hour, was read as fast as possible, and sent down again. The second edition was locked up by noon, and the paper was soon on the streets.

After lunch, each man wrote a second editorial for the first edition of next day's paper. Duffus and Hill checked with me or Mr. Wright to avoid duplication, and our three articles were usually approved, edited, and in type by half-past three or four. Sometimes these were on important themes left over from the morning conference, sometimes pieces in a lighter vein produced out of the writer's head, or from his current reading. Next day's first edition would contain these three articles and no more. Sometimes they survived all day, sometimes not, depending on the amount of space required for the next morning's work.

As can be seen, my title of chief editorial writer did not imply that I wrote the most important editorial every day. That might be written by any one of us, depending on how the news broke, or there might be two or three subjects of equal importance. As part of my duties, I sat in for Mr. Wright when he was absent for any reason. I solicited extra copy from other members of the staff, such as the book and music critics, when it seemed desirable, and I took care of personnel problems when we were short-handed for any reason. I also worked out the vacation schedule so that not more than one man would be away at any given time.

While the bright stars Lincoln Steffens had brought into the paper were long gone, in the interim there had been some other unusual figures in the office. One of these was Philip Littell, who had left the paper some years before I came and had become one of the founding group of *The New Republic*. He was a member of the family which many years earlier had owned *Littell's Living Age*, a successful magazine that translated and reprinted material from magazines and newspapers all over the world.

Once while he was doing editorials for *The Globe* there was a bad earthquake in Japan, and Mr. Wright assigned him to write a comment on it. Phil was so fascinated by the details that he produced a brilliant little summary of the facts. When he turned it in, Mr. Wright read it, and said, "Phil, this is fine, but it is all just news. You haven't made any editorial comment at all."

"I can fix that," Phil promised. He took the editorial back to his desk and almost instantly reappeared, having added at the end:

"This is deplorable."

During his tenure occurred the death of a popular lecturer on literature who was noted for his prudishness even in an era when Victorian notions of propriety still reigned in the Anglo-Saxon world. Phil was asked to write an obituary editorial about this man, and agreed to do so. The minutes raced by while he sat looking out the window, but when Mr. Wright inquired, he was assured the deadline would be met. Finally, with only seconds left, Phil turned in his piece, consisting of a single sentence:

"Hamilton Wright Mabie was a man who spent a lifetime conducting young ladies into the suburbs of literature, and leaving them there."

Writing two editorials a day was far from exhausting my energies, or the list of topics on which I wanted to say something. With Mr. Wright's approval, I began writing one or two long signed pieces a week on the editorial page. They stood farther back from the news than was possible in a brief editorial, and tried to put things into perspective. Though they were 90 percent factual, they were also slanted, in that I did not hesitate to include my opinions when it seemed desirable. These pieces were given fancy headlines of several banks, and were usually accompanied by a boxed paragraph emphasizing the reason for writing on this subject at this time. Mr. Wright and Mr. Rogers seemed intrigued by these pieces, and presently, for the first (and last) time in my life, I saw my name advertised in big letters, on the sides of *The Globe*'s delivery trucks.

Within a couple of months, one of these articles produced the greatest immediate impact of anything I ever wrote in my life.

As happens after all wars, New York was in the midst of a severe housing shortage. People evicted from their apartments had nowhere to go, and some were being housed temporarily in armories and even in a few churches with compassionate pastors. Builders claimed that because of high taxes and costs of labor and materials they could not afford to erect new apartment houses except for the rich (for whom, of course, construction went on as usual).

I have always had keen interest in urban and regional planning, and had made some friends in this field. One day I was having lunch with several of them, and among us we hammered out a possible solution to the problem; I promptly wrote a signed piece on the idea for the editorial page.

The real-estate tax was at that time about 3 percent on the actual value of the property. I suggested that the state should exempt new apartment buildings of a specified character from taxation for a period of ten years, which would mean a subsidy of 30 percent. I stipulated that such new buildings should be of good quality, and should be rented at not more than a set price per month per room. The land would be taxed as usual, so that city and state revenues would not be reduced on what were then vacant lots.

My article attracted a good deal of attention, but no immediate action. I therefore got an appointment with Governor Alfred E. Smith in Albany, and went up to see him. Smith had just begun the first of his four highly successful terms as New York's governor. A gravelly voiced man who grew up in poverty in New York's slums, he had little formal education, spoke with a pronounced East Side accent, and was one of the ablest political leaders of his time.

As he sat behind his desk in the Governor's Mansion, I handed him a clipping of my article, and while he glanced over it, I explained the idea in a few words. He asked me several abrasive questions, and then astonished me by saying, "If it's legal, I'll do it."

He picked up the telephone and got the state Attorney General on the line. Clearly and succinctly, he outlined my scheme, of which he had grasped every detail. In a few minutes he said thanks, and turned to me. "He says it's not unconstitutional, but will need some legislation," he told me. "I'll try to get it through." A few minutes later, I found myself out on the street, stunned by my success, and the speed with which it had been accomplished.

Governor Smith was as good as his word. He summoned the legislature into special session, and bullied and persuaded it into passing the necessary legislation, framed in such a way that it applied almost exclusively to New York City, where the shortage was at its worst. The city immediately adopted a necessary supplementary ordinance, signed by Mayor John F. Hylan.

The results surprised everyone and astounded me. With this 30 percent subsidy, speculative builders ran up a huge quantity of five-story walk-up apartment houses in the Bronx, where there was then plenty of vacant land; their total value amounted to many millions of dollars. Now began the great hegira from the Lower East Side, already mentioned. The slum dwellings thus vacated did not, of course, stand idle; these flats were filled by new European immigrants, who poured into the country until successive restrictive laws of the 1920's reduced the flood to a trickle. No doubt many of these new houses would have been built eventually in any case, but my article set in motion a chain of events that speeded up the process.

On *The Globe* I had my first real contact with reader reaction as expressed in letters to the editor. I speedily learned what every editor discovers: that most letter writers are cranks, or are angry, or both. I also learned that it is dangerous to rely on the public's sense of humor.

These were the days of the very first attempts to fly the Atlantic, employing flying boats which could survive at least briefly if forced down on the water. Lindbergh's feat eight years later thrilled the world because he made it in one hop, Long Island to Paris, and because he used a land plane; if he had been forced down it would have meant almost certain death.

In May, 1919, two men, Harry Hawker and McKenzie Grieve, tried the west-east flight, and when they became long overdue, were given up for lost. Many days later came the electrifying news that they had in fact been rescued from their downed plane, by a small Irish fishing vessel. It had no radio, and did not make port for some time.

The world rejoiced at the happy outcome of this air and sea drama, and one of the writers on *The Globe*—I think it was Bob Duffus—wrote a whimsical editorial about it. The whole episode was of course pure fantasy, he said; no such two men as Hawker and Grieve had ever existed. The chance that their plane would plummet down into the vast watery waste near enough to a fishing boat for a rescue was so remote that it must be dismissed as implausible fiction.

Promptly we got a barrage of furious letters. Hawker and Grieve did too exist, our correspondents stated. They enclosed clippings of news stories from our own columns, and suggested that any editorial writer too lazy to read his own paper should be fired.

I remember another parallel incident. All through the summer of 1919 the U.S. Senate fought over approving the League of Nations. Repeatedly we wrote editorials answering the hostile arguments of Senator Lodge and his friends. Finally, when it seemed to us that everything anyone could possibly say had been uttered many times, we printed a blank space in the editorial column, about the size of our customary article, heading it, "The Senate and the Treaty."

Again we got angry letters from our readers. What incompetent makeup man had omitted an entire editorial, leaving a hole in the paper?

I recall one other case of an unexpected reader reaction. One of us one day wrote a light piece commenting on the fact that no matter what an editorial said, someone was sure to object. In fact, our writer commented, there was nothing safe to denounce except the man-eating shark, and proceeded to say a few harsh words about such creatures. Promptly we got a furious letter from Dr. William Beebe, a famous ichthyologist of the New York Zoological Society. How dare we attack the so-called man-eating shark, he wanted to know? Sharks abhor human flesh and are really very affectionate and docile fellows.

I was spending so much time writing my long signed pieces that about now we decided to add another editorial writer to our group. Accordingly, I hired Maxwell Anderson, who had spent a year at Stanford getting an M.A. just after I had left.

Max had gone from Stanford to the staff of *The San Francisco Call,* then a morning paper, now defunct. One day he wrote a brilliant article about censorship on newspapers, which he called "The Blue Pencil." His sensible point was that owners don't need to set down a list of the men and institutions that must always be damned, or always praised; the staff knows the situation almost by osmosis; the writers conform to the publisher's wishes by a process that may even be unconscious, or partly so.

Max sent his piece to *The New Republic,* whose editor, Herbert Croly, was delighted with it, and bought and published it, paying the standard rate of two cents a word. He then did something almost unforgivable; on the strength of this one article, never having laid eyes on the author, he wrote to Max and invited him to come to New York and join the *New Republic* staff. The paper was then the most exciting journalistic enterprise in the country, and it is not surprising that Max threw up his safe job, and with his wife and two small children—and no bank account —made the trek to New York.

Unfortunately, when he and Croly met face to face, they did not hit it off. Croly, of whom I shall have a lot to say later, was a formidable and intimidating man; Max was shy and inarticulate (except with his pen). In a few months, antagonism between them had deepened so far that Croly fired the young man from the West. It was just at this moment that we decided to add a man to the editorial group; the Stanford tie brought Max and me together, and I hired him.

As a writer for a liberal daily, which *The Globe* had now become, more or less in spite of itself, he was something of a problem. We soon discovered that Max was a philosophical anarchist, with the utter pessimism about reform and reformers appropriate to that attitude. I never knew whether his position was genuine, or was a pose he had carried so long he himself was no longer sure how much of it was sincere. At any rate, we soon learned it was not safe to ask him to write on any subject when optimism was in order; he was sure to argue, with Mercutio, "a plague o' both your houses." (Significantly, years later he made part of that phrase the title of one of his plays.) However, it was not hard to find subjects for him outside the mainstream of the news, and he did very well with them—so well, in fact, that Frank Cobb, then editor of *The World,* offered him a place there, which he accepted.

Laurence Stallings, who had lost a leg in the world war, was doing a literary column on *The World*'s famous "opposite editorial" page, graced by Franklin P. Adams, Heywood Broun, and Alexander Woollcott. One night Stallings and Max went on *World* tickets to the opening of a bad play. As they left the theater Stallings said to Max, "That was awful. I could write a better one myself."

"Why don't you?" said Max. "Or why not collaborate with me?"

Stallings was agreeable, and they went to work. They found a satisfactory place for their activity in the huge main reading room of the New York Public Library, where they sat side by side conferring in whispers over a pad of yellow foolscap. The result was *What Price Glory*, the smash hit of the season, which set a new style in war plays, frank and bawdy by the standards of the day, tough and realistic.

Though they collaborated on a few more plays, *What Price Glory* was the greatest success either of them ever had. Stallings went to Hollywood and became a highly paid scenario writer. Max, working alone, produced his notable series of thirty or more dramas, including *Elizabeth the Queen*, *Both Your Houses*, and *High Tor*. *Winterset* was a poetic interpretation of the Sacco-Vanzetti case. *Knickerbocker Holiday* and *Lost in the Stars* were musicals done in collaboration with the composer Kurt Weill.

Though few people know it, *What Price Glory* was not Max's first play. He had done a poetic drama, *White Desert*, about a housewife trapped in a desolate winter scene in North Dakota (where he himself was brought up), which was produced and ran a week or two on Broadway. But it was fledgling work, containing little indication of the power of his later plays.

Early in 1920, Mr. Wright and Mr. Rogers asked me to become managing editor, and I had no choice but to agree. I preferred writing to being an executive, but I had no legitimate way to refuse. The paper had a managing editor, but he was getting old, and had little interest in the news; he dabbled in Wall Street, had quite a lot of money, and seemed willing to retire. (Pensions were unknown in newspaper work in those days.)

The city editor was also an easygoing, older man, likewise a stock-market player, who left the news department to run itself. This it did quite well, under the head of the copydesk, Raymond McCaw. Quiet, modest, highly competent, he was a dedicated professional; when *The Globe* went under in 1923, he went to *The New York Times*, where he served for thirty years, rising to night managing editor before he retired to Arizona.

The Globe was a ramshackle paper which had several unusual features, each designed to attract some special group of readers. On certain days, it published many columns of school news in its first edition only; thousands of school teachers bought that edition, and looked on the school editor, Tristram W. Metcalfe, as their friend and counselor. We gave Wall Street closing prices in another edition, planned to reach the newsstands as quickly as possible. In those days, stock tables were kept standing in type, and a special crew of expert typographers made the last-minute changes by hand at high speed. In spite of all our efforts, most of the financial community preferred *The Evening Sun.*

We had a Broadway reporter, S. Jay Kaufman, who worked out of his own office in the Metropolitan Opera building, and never came near our office. It was generally assumed that he had "special arrangements" with the plays, nightclubs, and performers whom he praised so warmly in his column, for his *Globe* salary could not have covered more than a fraction of his expenses. In those easygoing days, nobody cared very much. Our sports department was also a law unto itself. There would be an exposé from time to time of the fact that most of the city's sports writers, on most of the papers, were on the payrolls of prizefighter, baseball, and other sports managers, and they would turn briefly virtuous.

Our star special reporter was Alfred W. McCann, a wild Irishman who wrote about food. Highly excitable, he was always furious about inferior products or ecstatic about good ones; he could be heard all over the building as he dictated his daily article in thunderous tones to a cowering stenographer. Meat prices were very high in the postwar period; Mac imported a whole shipload of New Zealand mutton, sold to (presumably) grateful *Globe* readers at cost. The office was always being invaded by furious men in the food business looking for a fight with Mac, but his joyous acceptance of the challenge usually disheartened them.

At one time he had harsh words for a food chain with some three hundred outlets across the country. Each of them solemnly sued *The Globe* for a huge sum, the aggregate being many millions of dollars. My memory is that we managed to consolidate the suits into one, and settled for a trifling sum, rather than go through the nuisance of a trial.

Mac taught me a tactic I afterward found very useful. When he attacked a man, he usually held back some of his damaging material, and when the angry individual promised a libel suit, Mac in turn threatened to publish the rest of what he knew.

Before I had been managing editor very long, I arrived at the office early one morning to find among the mass of proofs of the matter set overnight an article by Mac attacking me by name! A day or so earlier I had written a signed favorable review of a book on evolution. Mac was a loyal, highly conservative Roman Catholic, and in those days the church was rigidly intolerant of "Darwinism." I proposed to print the column and answer it, but Mr. Wright decided a running internal feud in the paper was not a good idea, and killed the piece.

The last episode I remember about Mac was a tragic one. He lived in Yonkers, on a street that had become a throughway for trucks, which often exceeded the speed limit. One of Mac's small sons ran out into the street one day and was killed by a fast-moving vehicle. A few days later, we got word that Mac was sitting on his front porch with a loaded rifle; he had sworn that he would shoot the next speeding driver to pass his house. Mr. Wright, who had been his friend for many years, hastily went to Yonkers and talked him out of it.

I moved into the newsroom as managing editor amid some hostility from the local staff. The three editorial writers on the third floor, old friends from Stanford, were considered rather clannish and snooty, and now one of them was being brought down from "highbrow heaven" to run the paper. It was soon evident that I was not "one of the boys." I was not an easy mixer; instead of hanging around a nearby saloon after the day's work, I went home. Somebody in the news department some time earlier had packed the city room with clannish alumni of *The Kansas City Star*, and they resented an outsider.

I promptly made matters worse by having a small office erected for my use in the far corner of the big, cluttered city room. Like most newspapermen I could write anywhere, any time; but as managing editor, I had a succession of callers, some of them important people, who did not like a roomful of reporters staring at their backs. To make matters worse, I installed in my office a Dictaphone, an unheard-of gadget, and a secretary—Miss Nadine Rosewater, who stayed with me through various peregrinations for thirty years. The former managing editor, who sat at a desk out in the open like everybody else, had no secretary and never wrote anything; he did all his business face to face or on the telephone. Most of the reporters and copy editors were older than I was, at thirty, some of them by many years. An uneasy truce was the best I could manage for the first few weeks.

My Dictaphone figured in a mildly amusing incident. Somebody in Hollywood was about to make a newspaper movie and, a stickler for accuracy, he sent a scout to New York to observe what the working area for a daily was like. This man picked out *The Globe* as his field of study, and apparently wrote down that all managing editors use dictating machines. When the movie came out, the fictional m.e. had one. His and mine were the only two I ever heard of; the typical managing editor of my day was like the first mate of a sailing ship, and liked to do most of his work on his feet.

By far the most decorative member of the *Globe* staff was Alison Smith, the drama editor, a golden-haired, blue-eyed young woman from California. She looked like a candy-box blonde until she opened her mouth, when you discovered she had high intelligence and a corrosive wit. Most of the male members of the staff were half in love with her, hoping earnestly that our wives would understand.

Alison worked in the newsroom; in theory, anybody could use any of the six or eight typewriters available, but as usually happens, she had come to claim one as her special property. She was annoyed one day, returning from an assignment, to find a newly hired reporter sitting at her desk. This young man had a genius for sleep, and was exercising it now, his head on his folded arms, on top of the typewriter. Alison promptly shook him awake. "Go somewhere else," she admonished him. "This is my desk."

After such an introduction, there was nothing for Russel Crouse to do but fall in love with her, which he promptly did. Alison reciprocated his passion, but she was a free soul, a generation ahead of her time. Words uttered by a minister seemed to her an intrusion upon private sentiments, and matters were arranged accordingly.

Russel was our ship-news reporter, and presently Italy launched a new luxury liner and offered him (as was and is very common), a free round-trip to Naples in an elegant stateroom, for two. However, the press agent for the line knew about Alison, and added the condition that of course the stateroom could only be used by man and wife; he wanted no trouble with puritanical officials (or the press) at either end of the voyage. It was a hard choice, but Alison wanted to see Naples, and so they were married. Back in America, with the glories of Italy fading in memory, she was restive, and finally returned to the happy status quo ante, by way of divorce.

"Buck" Crouse went on from *The Globe*'s meager wage to affluence as a press agent, and then to fabulous success as a playwright, collaborating with Howard Lindsay on *Life With Father* and twenty other plays; their percentage of successes broke all records. They earned it. For years, while Russel had a hard nine-to-five job, they did their writing in the evening (if his collaborator was not working as an actor), in Howard's Greenwich Village home. Night after night, Russel sat at the typewriter, Howard paced, and they tried successive lines of dialogue until they agreed that one was right. They usually broke off at midnight, exhausted.

When *The Globe* disappeared in 1923, Alison got a berth as assistant critic on *The World*. One year the paper imported a visiting critic, an Irish playwright who, like a lot of other people, found Alison attractive. Both of them once came back to the office toward midnight, with reviews to write. The Irishman finished his first, in their deserted cubbyhole, and proceeded to "make advances" to Alison, who was busily pecking away at her typewriter. Finally she snapped at him: "Look, I can fight for my honor, or I can finish this review. Take your choice!" The review was done on time.

Alison died much too young, and Russel eventually made a second and thoroughly happy marriage to Anna Erskine, the attractive daughter of John Erskine. Her father was a professor of English at Columbia, who casually one summer had tossed off a smash best-selling novel, *The Pri-*

vate Life of Helen of Troy. Russel, the only man on Broadway I ever knew who didn't have a single enemy, had always been a family man at heart, and he luxuriated in his wife and children during the years that were left to him.

Though the world war ended on November 11, 1918, many months later there were still numbers of American soldiers in Europe; they had little to do, and discipline was a problem. There were several military prisons to which transgressors were sent for varying terms.

Soon after I became managing editor, two or three men recently discharged from the Army came to see me, with tales of shocking cruelty practiced at one of these camps, just outside Paris. The officer in charge, Major F. H. Smith, was so rough on the prisoners in his charge that he was universally known as "Hard-boiled" Smith. Men were gravely punished for minor infractions of prison regulations; some were beaten, or put on bread and water, or forced to stand at attention for hours. Some were pegged down, on their backs, on the grass, arms and legs spread-eagled, and kept a long time gazing up into the very hot sun.

I checked the stories of these men against each other, got verification from a correspondent in Paris, and then wrote several articles telling the whole story. (I had been in newpaper work long enough to know that a series has far greater impact than the same material told all on one day.) I had them all set into type and then took a set of proofs down to Washington, where I had obtained an appointment with Wilson's Secretary of War, Newton D. Baker.

Baker was an odd choice for the job; he was an avowed pacifist, so much so that he was actually investigated by Congress for this reason during his term in office. He had been an outstanding municipal reformer in Cleveland, a protégé of the famous Tom L. Johnson; Wilson owed him a political debt, and had fitted him into the Cabinet in 1916 in the only job available. What I had not realized was that, perhaps feeling guilty about his pacifism, he was leaning over backward to curry favor with the military establishment.

I handed him proofs of my articles, and explained the story while he skimmed them. Then I made him a short speech. "Mr. Secretary," I said, "there are many thousands of American boys still in Europe. Their parents will be greatly worried at the news of what's going on. If you will give me your word that you'll investigate and stop this kind of thing, I'll kill my series."

Baker drew himself up to his full height of, as I remember, about five feet six. "I'll make no bargain with you," he said firmly, "which implies any wrongdoing on the part of the American Army."

For probably the only time in my life, I answered like a movie hero. "Very well, Mr. Secretary," I said. "The first article will appear tomorrow."

It did, too, and the series, which Mr. Rogers syndicated to other leading papers, created a national sensation. It was reprinted in *The Congressional Record*, and there were indignant speeches in the House and Senate. Major Smith was promptly recalled from France, and tried and convicted for some of his more outrageous acts of cruelty.

I don't know the situation today, but in those times the army high brass always clustered in support of any officer accused of abusing a private. The public was so aroused that the generals did not dare let Hard-boiled Smith go free, but they gave him only eighteen months in Leavenworth, a very mild sentence indeed. By now some ex-inmates of his military prison were themselves in Leavenworth; Smith had to be isolated from the other prisoners lest they kill him.

Four months later, when the public furore had abated, the brass had its way, and he was quietly paroled.

One other time I engaged in mild heroics; it was the only occasion I recall personally on which an advertiser tried to dictate to the editorial department, which Upton Sinclair and other critics have reported as being so common. While I was managing editor, an elevator in Gimbel's department store fell a few feet, slightly injuring a couple of the passengers. The accident was so insignificant it deserved only a few lines, if anything; but somebody in the store panicked and called up Mr. Rogers to say that Gimbel's, a heavy user of space, of course expected us not to report the affair. Mr. Rogers referred the call to me, and I was annoyed, since I had been warned for so many years to expect this kind of thing. I put the story on page one with a prominent headline, and then sat back waiting for Gimbel's to cancel its advertising, or at least to get me fired. Neither thing happened; in fact, we never heard of it again.

In May, 1920, I did something that a few years later would have been surprising; I wrote an article in *The Independent*, a mildly intellectual weekly, long since defunct, suggesting Herbert Hoover for President, on either the Democratic or the Republican ticket.

People today have forgotten that young Hoover was then our chief national hero. He had kept the Belgians from starving, and he was a Great Engineer in a time when people thought engineering principles would save the nation. During the war he had been the highly successful Food Administrator, and the Washington propaganda machine had worked hard to identify his personality with economy in this field. Millions of copies of a handsome four-color picture of him were distributed with "Food Will Win the War" imprinted on the bottom; housewives hung the picture in their kitchens and mooned over it as they poured extra fat into a tin can. I remember only Lindbergh and Eisenhower as objects of such widespread devotion. (Admiral George Dewey was similarly worshiped during the Spanish-American war but I had been too young to recall it.)

Nobody knew whether Hoover was a Republican or a Democrat, and nobody much cared; engineering was above partisanship. I believed then and still do, that if he had kept still, the Republicans might have nominated him in fear that if they didn't the Democrats would, and that this might well have happened. He could have beaten anybody then in sight.

But just after my article appeared, the bubble burst; Mr. Hoover announced that he was a Republican. The pressure was now off; the G.O.P. knew the Democrats could not choose him, and they happily selected an appalling mediocrity from Marion, Ohio, Senator Warren G. Harding. Mr. Hoover, who could have swept the convention, received a few complimentary votes on the first ballot or two, and after the election Harding made him secretary of commerce.

I knew Mr. Hoover casually—Stanford was a bond between us—and a year or so later I asked him one day why he had so suddenly announced that he was a Republican, repeating the argument made above.

"I didn't have any choice," he told me. "Some friends of mine in California had entered my name in the primary there as a Republican, and I couldn't let them down."

This absurd statement revealed his political naïveté; what his friends wanted was for him to become president, and they would have agreed happily to any plan that would have brought this about.

One of the disagreeable parts of my job as managing editor was seeing applicants for employment and turning them down, no matter how well qualified they might be. I had no choice; our staff was as large as we could afford, and rarely did anyone quit. One young man who walked in unannounced was a recent Cornell graduate who said his name was E. B. White. "Andy" White, who went on to be one of the stars of *The New Yorker* and probably the most distinguished American essayist of his time, took his rebuff harder than most. For many years afterward, whenever I ran into him, he would remind me that "you turned me down for a job on *The Globe.*" I finally persuaded him that I had been rejecting a dozen applicants a week, and that my action in regard to him did not constitute discrimination.

We did get an occasional vacancy on the staff for special reasons. In those days every paper was supposed to have a sports cartoonist, and *The Globe* was no exception. One snowy winter day, shortly before I became managing editor, there seemed nothing in the world worth a sports cartoon. Our man dropped by the desk of my predecessor and said so, adding, "I've done a cartoon of another kind, and I hope you can use it." He showed the drawing, which was based on four or five unusual happenings or achievements from all over the world. The artist explained that he had a habit of clipping and filing news items of a striking character, and thought a drawing showing a few of them might be an interesting occasional piece of filler.

The editor agreed, and he and the artist cooked up a title together: "Believe It or Not." The drawing ran next day, and aroused enough comment to justify more like it from time to time. Within a month or two, the decision was made to abandon sports and print only drawings of this special kind, if the cartoonist could dig up enough material, as he assured us he could. Robert L. Ripley was soon taken over by a syndicate, appeared for many years in hundreds of papers, and became a millionaire.

While I was managing editor, a youthful copy editor from the rim of the desk came into my office one day and laid a manuscript on my desk. "I've written some light stuff," he said, "and I wonder whether you could use it?"

I read his piece, a series of disconnected paragraphs on various subjects, and found some of them enormously funny. I told him so, and asked the author, "Could you do a column like this every day?"

"I'm sure I could," was the answer, and a few days later the first installment of "The Globe Trotter," by H. I. Phillips, appeared on the editorial page, and was an instantaneous success. We raised Hi's salary, and told him to spend all his time on the column.

He objected strenuously, proposing to keep on editing copy and do the column in his spare time. "What if I run out of material?" he wanted to know. "Then I'd be out of work." We assured him if this happened he could have his old job back. When *The Globe* went under, *The Sun* snapped him up, and for many years his "Sun Dial" was a widely syndicated, highly popular feature.

Another competent rewrite man came in one day to tell me he was leaving. In his spare time he had been moonlighting doing rewrite for *The Saturday Evening Post,* and they had offered him a staff job in Philadelphia, where the paper was then edited. We said good-bye with regret; Wesley Stout, one of the *Kansas City Star* alumni on our staff, was a skilled master of his trade.

Only a short time later, we learned that he had been made editor-in-chief of *The Post.* He held the job for some time, until the Curtis Publishing Company, under the stress of competition in the weekly field, decided the paper needed a more liberal slant; rightly or wrongly, Wesley was identified in the public mind with extremely conservative politics, and he was replaced.

As Wesley learned, the top editor of a magazine, if he is fired for any reason, finds it almost impossible to get a similar place (as is true of any high executive in industry). Other editors fear to hire him lest he covet their jobs, and a humble place is considered beneath his dignity. His only recourse is usually free-lance writing, and when he starts this he suddenly becomes acutely aware of the hardships of this phase of the business.

The Globe had no foreign correspondents of its own; we used the

Associated Press, and the overseas service of *The Chicago Daily News*. This was and is a highly successful afternoon paper; in those days it was owned by Victor Lawson, the managing editor was Charles H. Dennis, and the city editor the much-loved Henry Justin Smith. *The News* had an excellent group of men abroad—John Gunther, Paul Scott Mowrer and his brother Edgar, Isaac Don Levine, M. W. Fodor, and half a dozen more. The service was syndicated but the gossip of the trade was that it lost a lot of money every year, and was maintained by Mr. Lawson as a matter of pride. *The Globe* was its New York outlet.

The men working abroad were treated with consideration except for one thing: Chicago rarely answered their letters and telegrams. Months would go by with no communication from the home office except their salary checks. Their pieces were printed, and that was all.

I was an eager young beaver, and I soon stepped out of line by firing off telegrams to the men in the field, making suggestions for stories or commending good jobs. I had no business to do this, and Mr. Dennis, out in Chicago, might have taken umbrage at my actions, but like his correspondents, I never had a word from him. The men abroad expressed gratitude that *somebody* in America took an interest in their work; they followed up my suggestions, when they were on home leave they came to see me, and when I went abroad (some years later) I met those who had not come to New York.

One of the most enterprising and valuable of this group was Isaac Don Levine. Of Russian parentage, he spoke the language fluently; when the fighting stopped in 1918, he was one of the first correspondents to get inside that country.

The importance of his articles sent to *The Chicago Daily News* at this time, all of which *The Globe* printed, was great. Most American correspondents were in Riga or other points outside Russia, and were sending back to America a weird mass of nonsense picked up from refugees, or invented. These were the days of the reported "nationalization of women," at a time when the Soviet government was repeatedly said to be on the brink of collapse. Regularly on Tuesdays Trotsky was said to have killed Lenin; on Thursdays the reverse was true.

Twice in 1919, in May and September, at serious personal risk, in the midst of the civil war raging between Reds and Whites, Levine entered the Soviet Union. He traveled many hundreds of miles by cattle car, troop train, and otherwise, and reported what he saw. He was the first correspondent to insist that the Soviet government was not on the point of collapse, and that the Allied blockade only strengthened the hand of the Communists.

One of his sensational scoops was the revelation that in March, 1919, the Allies had offered to make peace with Russia. The terms were severe: The Soviet government must pay off the Tsarist foreign debts, it must stop fomenting revolutions abroad, and it must let the hostile Whites retain the territory they then controlled. Moscow, in desperate straits, was prepared to accept these drastic proposals, but now the Allies took a new tack. At the instigation of Winston Churchill they gave vast quantities of munitions and other supplies to the White armies. When these were defeated in the field by Red forces directed by Trotsky, relations between East and West were, not surprisingly, embittered for decades. The course of history would have been changed for the better if Levine's factual statements had been accepted in Washington and London, his warnings heeded.

In the early days of the Revolution, the Bolshevists had opened all the archives of the Tsarist regime, and freely handed out documents of great historic interest. Levine was presented with an extraordinary set of letters—the private correspondence of the deposed Tsar, Nicholas II, with his cousin, the German Kaiser, Wilhelm II, who, with the German defeat, had abdicated and fled to the Netherlands. The letters had a mass of interesting material; they showed the cousins scheming together when their governments were supposed to be hostile. The "Willy-Nicky Letters" were published in the papers taking *The Chicago Daily News* service, and were successful in book form, edited by Levine. He left *The News* not long afterward to pursue an independent career as an author; most of his many widely read books have dealt with the Soviet Union.

While *The Globe* had no salaried foreign correspondents of its own, we bought occasional pieces from abroad that came in over the transom. One of these writers was a young man who had been sent to Europe by President Wilson to gather material for a history of the war. He loved action, soon abandoned history to see some fighting, and presently got into the Middle East. Here he spent a good deal of time with T. E. Lawrence, the legendary desert fighter, who played a great part in the uprising of the Arabs led by Feisal I against the Turks. In a classic example of guerrilla warfare, Lawrence's men harassed the Turks, broke their rail lines, and tied down forces many times larger than their own. Lawrence thought he had a promise from the Allies that after the war independent Arab states would be created, and felt he was betrayed when no such action was taken at the Paris conference.

Our young correspondent was not only a good reporter but a photographer as well. After he came back to New York, he dropped in to see me one day, in a mild state of panic. He had acquired an agent, who had rented Carnegie Hall for an illustrated lecture, "With Lawrence in Arabia," and the correspondent was alarmed at facing such a big audience, though he had often lectured in the past to smaller groups, like college classes. I did my best to cheer him up. Lowell Thomas's lecture was a great success, he repeated it all over the country, and went on to become, as author, explorer, and radio, television, and film personality, one of the best-known commentators in the world.

Among the few reporters I hired was young John T. Flynn, who had worked on a New Haven newspaper and now wanted to try his wings in New York. We needed a real-estate editor, and he filled the post acceptably. With my support, he succeeded in smashing a petty racket among confidence men who bought for almost nothing a quantity of unusable, marshy land out near the end of Long Island, valueless for any purpose except perhaps hunting. These men would call up somebody picked at random from the telephone book, and tell him that he had won a piece of land in a lottery, neglecting to mention that it was mostly unreachable except by rowboat at high tide. The only payment required was a nominal $50 for transfer of title—nearly all of which, of course, went into the pockets of the swindlers. The operation was quasi-legal, since the land really existed; very few of the victims troubled to go to look at it until after they had paid the money. Flynn hammered away at the crooks day after day, until the publicity put them out of business. He stayed with *The Globe* until it went under; years later, his path crossed mine again, as I shall tell in its proper place.

As the presidential primaries of 1920 drew nearer, I felt the urge to get out into the field as a reporter, and worked up an idea for a series of interviews with all the candidates of both major parties. By asking each man the same questions, I could get replies that would compare their views on all the leading issues of the day. Mr. Rogers distributed the series to the newspapers that were in his informal coalition, *The Chicago Daily News, San Francisco Chronicle, Los Angeles Times,* and a few others. Of the interviews I remember most vividly the one with Senator Harding, who assured me that "what this country needs is a tariff policy that will aid the struggling industries of Europe." I was so surprised that I asked him to repeat it, to make sure I had not misunderstood him. I hadn't.

I journeyed to Miami to interview former Governor James M. Cox of Ohio, who, like Harding, was a newspaper publisher; I got a strong impression that he was sure the Republicans would win and was only going through the motions of seeking the Democratic nomination because the Party expected it of him. In Illinois I was impressed by General Leonard Wood and by Governor Frank O. Lowden, two Republicans who seemed to me the ablest of this mixed bag.

The Democratic Convention was held in San Francisco, and I assigned myself to report it. The city offered its usual warm hospitality; Henry Mencken, who also covered the proceedings, remarked on the high quality and abundance of the free liquor, in spite of the fact that Prohibition had gone into effect a few months earlier. The Democrats nominated Cox, and for the vice-presidential candidate they chose a tall, slim, athletic-looking young man, not very well known but a member of a familiar family—Franklin D. Roosevelt.

On election night the *Globe* news staff sat up late putting together the summary of the returns for next day's early extra. Our building was a firetrap and normally, smoking was strictly forbidden, especially in the city room which toward the end of every working day was heavily littered with paper. Traditionally, however, this rule was broken on election night. Having had the custom explained to me, I came in after dinner and lighted a ceremonial cigar, the signal for everyone else to do likewise.

As we expected, the election was a Harding landslide, 16 million votes to nine. Cox had inherited all the antagonisms the Democrats had incurred during the hardships and deprivations of the war, and the ugly feelings aroused by the fact that President Wilson, a helpless invalid in the White House, had refused to step aside and was letting the country be run, apparently, by his wife and his doctor.

Early in 1920, I had the pleasure of turning down an offer of a job by William Randolph Hearst, whose papers I disliked more and more as the years went by. I had written in *The Globe* an open letter to a witch-hunting politician in Albany, suggesting that instead of punishing people for being discontented, it would be better to ameliorate the causes of that discontent. In 1920 Hearst was still something of a radical, and he apparently liked this piece. At any rate, a day or two later Bradford Merrill, editor of Hearst's morning *American,* telephoned that he would like to see me, and came over. Hearst, of course, should never have sent a man as important as Merrill on a recruiting errand, and both of us were embarrassed by it.

Merrill, who seemed to me a cowed and beaten man, asked me what I was earning, and I told him my salary: $11,500 a year. Clearly acting under instruction, he offered me $23,000 and annual increases which in two years would bring the figure to $25,000.

I waited a day, for the sake of courtesy to Merrill, and then telephoned him my refusal; he seemed to expect it. I had heard too many horror stories of Hearst's treatment of his men when they tried to think for themselves to put my head into the trap. I have never regretted the decision; I might have ended up a rich man, but I should surely have ended up a miserable one.

About this time, Hearst also offered a job to Heywood Broun, the brilliant columnist of *The World.* Broun was more important than I; the messenger in his case was Arthur Brisbane, Hearst's best-known writer, who outranked Merrill. He asked Broun to dinner in his luxurious apartment, and after dinner, sitting over coffee and brandy, made his pitch, offering complete freedom and a huge salary. Stalling for time, Broun admired a large portrait hanging on the wall—Arthur's father, Albert

Brisbane, a utopian Socialist of forty years earlier, the chief American disciple of Charles Fourier.

Arthur identified the subject, and then suddenly and inexplicably added: "He was a wonderful man. *He* wouldn't have worked for Hearst."

Broun declined the offer.

H. G. Wells's most successful book was *The Outline of History;* professional historians were cold to it, but the public loved it, and it sold two million copies. I read it as soon as it appeared, and got excited over the possibilities of making a motion picture of it, using animated cartoon techniques. I visualized moving maps that would show empires expanding and contracting, the deployment of troops in historic battles, the migrations of peoples, and other aspects of history that could be presented graphically.

I wrote Wells making this suggestion in a long, enthusiastic letter, and was astonished to get back one from him which seemed to give me the motion-picture rights to the book, though I had not asked for, and did not want, them; my thought had been that Wells himself should carry out the project. However, armed with his letter, I tried in succession all the leading motion-picture companies, only to be turned down by each. Try as I would, I couldn't get anyone to see the possibilities in cartoon treatment, which I felt would be priceless in the schoolroom, as well as in theaters. One and all persisted in regarding the project as just another historical drama, presumably to be produced with live actors.

It happened that Hearst, in his long, unsuccessful campaign to make Marion Davies a movie star, had just paid for a terribly expensive film featuring her in a pre-Revolutionary story of New York; like nearly all her other pictures, it had failed. Hollywood thereupon decided historical drama was no good—a verdict that would be canceled as soon as somebody produced a successful example of that genre. I remember especially one lone-wolf producer (still alive and active in 1970), sitting behind a big desk, chewing tobacco and expectorating with virtuosity into a spittoon at an incredible distance, who assured me that "there's nuthin' in that costume stuff."

I still think my idea was good, and that some day it will be done, but I had to write Wells regretfully that the American motion-picture industry was not interested.

When I became managing editor of *The Globe,* I found myself in the odd position of being a good deal more liberal politically than the news staff I had inherited. These professional reporters were either indifferent to politics, or inclined to be conservative. We had a strike on the waterfront, and one reporter was assigned to cover the story, day after day; he did a competent job of telling all developments. After the strike had gone on for several weeks, I asked him once what were his personal views; were the strikers right or wrong?

He looked at me in bewilderment. "I don't know," he said. "I never thought about it."

I adopted a policy in regard to labor troubles that the staff didn't like. In really important strikes, I published two articles side by side, every day when the news justified it, one giving the strikers' side of the story, the other the employers'. In those days, when almost all papers as a matter of course sided with the owners on all occasions, this was deemed an outrageous innovation.

A few other new features I introduced got some attention. Today, when a story runs a number of days in succession, most papers are careful to repeat each time the main facts in dispute, but in the early 1920's this was rarely done. Accordingly, I demanded of the copydesk that when a story went on for some time they add each day a "shirttail," under a three-em dash, indented on both sides to indicate its character, summarizing *all* the information anyone needed about the situation.

The whole office fought me on this. The shirttails took up a lot of space, they said (though in fact there were rarely more than two or three a day, and each occupied only a column inch or two). Anybody who had read yesterday's paper didn't need this material, I was told. Moreover, it was a nuisance to prepare.

I felt I was vindicated by an incident not long afterward. In 1920, the troubles between England and Ireland, struggling for her independence, were at their height. The Irish Republican Army conducted an underground guerrilla warfare; the British "Black and Tans" responded with terrible acts of cruelty. Terence MacSwiney, the Lord Mayor of Cork, was in prison, as were most Irish leaders, and he resolved to fast to death, if necessary, in protest against British policy. It took him about fifty days to die, and we carried a story about him every day on the front page. Every day I insisted on a shirttail on the story telling who he was, and why he was fasting. As the days went on, the news room was in revolt, but I stuck to it.

On about the fortieth day, Norman Geddes happened to catch the same commuting train that I did, and dropped into the seat beside me. He had a copy of that day's *Globe*, and as he unfolded it, the top head about MacSwiney caught his eye. "Who is this fellow MacSwiney?" he asked me, "and what's he done?"

"Norman, I've been waiting for you," I said, and showed him the shirttail.

Years later, my friend Glenn Frank, who had gone from editor of *The Century* to be president of the University of Wisconsin, made what seemed to me a sensible observation. "Never underestimate the intelligence of the public," he said, "but never overestimate its information."

I inherited a Washington correspondent who had been with the paper for some years. He was a good man, but he suffered from a disease common among newspapermen in the national capital: he was on terms of warm personal friendship with many men high in the government, who kept telling him important facts as confidential information, one friend to another, pledging him to secrecy.

I solved this problem in a way that seems ludicrous now, but it worked. Every few weeks I sent a hard-boiled police reporter down to Washington for a day to interview our correspondent; then he came back to New York to write the stories. The correspondent could tell his friends with a clear conscience that he had not written this material, and we got the news into the paper.

Another innovation I worked out was simple, effective, and cheap. In those days there were outstanding English-language dailies in various parts of the world, and I picked out four of them for an experiment, the papers in Calcutta, Cairo, Capetown, and Sydney. I wrote to each of them suggesting that once a month or so we exchange background articles on what was going on in our respective countries, leisurely reports of a couple of thousand words each, telling what people were doing and thinking. (I have always had a weakness for this sort of reporting, believing that hard news that comes by instantaneous means suffers from too much "day-to-dayness.")

All these papers accepted my proposal, and each of us presently began to receive about one article a week, on the average, of unusual quality, at no cost except a few hours of the time of one good reporter, and the trouble of making and mailing four carbon copies. Since the articles were not highly topical they could be held over if the news hole was especially crowded. We kept the scheme going as long as *The Globe* lasted; whether the other papers went on longer I do not know.

Our last edition each day was devoted to sports, and making over the first page for final scores was a constant headache. I finally worked out a system whereby, with a good deal of juggling of material, page one of the earlier editions became page three of the last one, with a four-page "wrap around" of sporting news. This enabled me to keep in the paper the valuable general news that had previously been slaughtered for sporting results, in most of which I had little personal interest.

Like all managing editors, I had season passes to all the home games of the New York major-league teams, the Yankees, Giants, and Dodgers. Night baseball had not yet been invented, and although I loved baseball (and still do), I was almost never able to get away early enough in the afternoon to go. The office boys, passionate fans, were well aware of the passes lying unused in my desk drawer, and suffered accordingly.

Nearly all afternoon dailies in those times lost money on their Saturday editions. Advertising was at a minimum, with the department stores saving their money for the big Sunday papers. Though the five-and-a-half-day working week was now quite common, Saturday circulation was also at a low ebb. About this time someone in our office (not I) had a brilliant idea that helped us greatly. Radio broadcasting for the home was just beginning and many thousands of mechanically minded men and boys were building their own sets. They bought their supplies from stores nearly all of which were concentrated into a couple of blocks of one street, far downtown. *The Globe* began publishing a tabloid supplement on Saturdays, giving instructions on how to build a receiver and carrying advertising of retailers selling the necessary equipment. A few years later, everyone was buying ready-made sets, but in the meantime this supplement relieved our Saturday problem substantially.

When I came to *The Globe* the cultural side of the paper was uneven. Our book editor, Mrs. Nell Dawson, produced a Saturday page with four or five reviews, most of which she wrote herself, the others being done by staff people for no additional remuneration. We never succeeded in getting more than a minuscule amount of publishers' advertising.

Our music critic, Pitts Sanborn, was sound but not very exciting; he had modest financial resources of his own, and usually spent the summer months, a musical vacuum in New York, in Europe. One day in June of my first year as managing editor, he appeared in my office to announce that he planned to sail the following week, if the paper had no objection. I assured him that we did not.

"I shall have to go tourist," he said. "I can't afford to go first class." He waited for me to speak, and when I did not, he went on. "I don't know whether *The Globe* would care to have it known that its music critic has to travel tourist."

I assured him that we would try to live down this ignominy, and he departed.

When I became managing editor *The Globe* had no regular dramatic critic. The custom was to give first-night tickets to any of half a dozen reporters, to write an anonymous report on a new play, mostly just the news of its arrival. I engaged as play reviewer a man whom I had met some time earlier, Kenneth Macgowan, a 1911 graduate of Harvard. He was a recovered victim of pulmonary tuberculosis, his normally sunny nature augmented, as is often the case, by this fact. Kenneth had a lifelong passion for the theater, in every form, and did brilliant reviews. He was so engrossed in thoughts of the playwright's problems and how he met them that his reviews often became little essays on the drama, good in themselves, but not always helpful to the playgoer who wanted to know whether he should or shouldn't buy tickets. I solved this problem by another "shirttail": I asked Kenneth to add at the end of every review three or four italicized lines, indented one em on each side, telling people whether to attend; our readers seemed to like the innovation.

When *The Globe* disappeared, Kenneth went on to a distinguished career. He was associated with Eugene O'Neill and Robert Edmond Jones, the theatrical designer, in the Provincetown Playhouse, and then he and Jones did a number of productions of their own in another theater on lower Seventh Avenue. Next he became a Hollywood motion-picture producer, doing fifty films, including *Young Mr. Lincoln, Lifeboat,* and *Little Women.* The University of California at Los Angeles lured him away to become head of its newly created Department of Theater Arts, and when he became emeritus, shortly before his death, it named its new theater in his honor.

The Globe was also lacking a motion-picture reviewer, and rushing in to a fill a vacuum, I began reviewing a few exceptional films myself; the others were mostly ignored. I reported, among others, on *The Covered Wagon,* and *Broken Blossoms,* and I was ecstatic about a documentary film of Eskimo life, *Nanook of the North,* done by a newcomer, Robert Flaherty. Few other reviewers liked it, Flaherty came to see me to express his gratitude, and we were friends for many years, until he died, like so many others, too young.

I once did him what was probably a disservice. He was about to go off on a long expedition to film *Moana of the South Seas,* on a schooner which would be out of touch with civilization for months. He planned to carry no doctor, and since I had recently had an appendectomy, I was conscious of this matter. "What will you do," I asked him, "if your appendix gives you trouble?"

He looked at me in alarm, and then asked me to tell him all about my operation. A few weeks later, I saw him again, and he told me he had solved the problem. "I went and had it out," he explained. I never learned what provision he had made for a similar difficulty among other members of the expedition, or what he planned to do about any other medical matters.

In addition to our own features, we bought the work of syndicated writers and artists. A highly successful author of a daily "inspirational" column was Dr. Frank Crane, a former minister, who wrote eloquently of the joys of an austere existence, devoted to contemplation of truth and beauty. When he asked me to dinner at his home, I discovered that his private life was slightly different. He lived in luxury, had a handsome apartment, and smoked Havana cigars at a dollar each; when he gave me one it was so strong it nearly killed me. He wanted me to write a monthly article in a now-forgotten magazine, of which he was a part owner, and I did so for a while. The pay he offered was not large by today's standards, but he talked as though it were a fortune. I can still hear his voice pronouncing the word "money" like the name of his beloved.

Another daily column we bought had just been started by a hard-working, idealistic young Washington journalist, a deep admirer of Woodrow Wilson. *The Globe* was the first paper to sign up for it, and he was correspondingly grateful. A few years later David Lawrence, with help from Bernard Baruch and others, started a daily paper in Washington, intended for a nationwide audience and dealing solely with government affairs. It was a smashing failure, but out of the wreckage he pulled the highly successful weekly *U.S. News and World Report.* Dave has grown more conservative since those early days, or as he would say, the world has grown more radical. I remember being impressed by the fact that he composed his daily column on a mimeograph stencil, not having time to do a rough draft.

Our best-known syndicated cartoonist was Fontaine Fox, creator of "The Toonerville Trolley," "The Powerful Katrinka," and "The Terrible-Tempered Mr. Bang." On rare occasions, he dropped into the office, a shy man with a quick, warm smile, who perched birdlike on a chair for a few moments and then was gone again.

About this time, two or three of us saved *The Nation* from extinction. It belonged to Oswald Garrison Villard, who had inherited it, and *The New York Evening Post,* of which it had been a weekly supplement, from his father, Henry Villard, a railroad mogul. *The Nation* had gone on for decades as a stuffy but sound literary magazine, and when Villard sold *The Post* in 1918, he retained the weekly, and turned it into a liberal magazine commenting on current affairs.

Unluckily, once it was detached from *The Post, The Nation* began losing money at an alarming rate, even for the millionaire son of a millionaire father. After the war, Villard made a trip to Germany, the home of his ancestors, and came back much depressed. He told his friends, including me, that he didn't see how he could continue to pay *The Nation*'s annual deficit.

Several of us got together and talked over the situation. We decided that Villard felt he was not adequately appreciated, and we therefore engineered a big testimonial dinner for him in a leading New York hotel. A few of us made short talks emphasizing what a useful citizen he was, and the good influence *The Nation* exerted. With tears in his eyes, Villard rose to reply, and his first words were, *"The Nation* will go on."

He remained as editor, publisher, and angel for another twelve years, after which he sold the paper to a consortium of liberals. He was a regular contributor, however, until the eve of the Second World War; he was an ardent pacifist, *The Nation*'s editor, Freda Kirchwey, was no longer one, and he felt he could not condone her new policy, which approved America's entering the war. He and I remained good friends, in spite of political differences, until his death in 1949.

When my health forced me to return to California in 1953, I was pleased to find Oswald, Jr., whom I had known as a small boy living in the Villard mansion up the Hudson, a member of the Stanford faculty, a highly respected engineer and astronomer.

Though Searles owned most of *The Globe,* there was a minority stockholder, an elderly man named William Shillaber. He had an office in the building, and came to it daily, though what he did there was a mystery. I don't think he was very happy with what the cabal of young Californians was doing to the paper, but it was gaining in circulation and prestige, and if he ever protested, I never heard of it.

In 1921, I had a (probably unnecessary) appendectomy, and it was decided I should have a few weeks' recuperation in the Adirondacks. While I was gone, Shillaber came to Mr. Wright and urged him to fire me while I was still away. "A man who has had his appendix out is never any good afterward," he said, with more enthusiasm than expertise. "Bliven will only be a drag on the paper if you let him come back."

Mr. Wright refused the suggestion, and I did not hear of it until some time later. So far as I know my operation never had the slightest adverse effect on my health.

I presently added two more Stanford men to the staff. Frank Taylor and Earl Hadley were both, consecutively, assistant managing editor. Taylor, some years younger than I, I knew because his attractive wife, Katherine, had been one of my best students of journalism at U.S.C. As a junior in college, Frank had found the war in Europe irresistibly exciting, and went to France with the American Ambulance Field Service, seeing front-line activity in Greece and Albania.

Back in Paris convalescing from dysentery, he joined the United Press as a correspondent with the American Army. He was the first American reporter to get to Berlin, and soon thereafter he struck out for Moscow. Both the German and the Russian forces were still in the field, in a haphazard and chaotic way, and Frank was picked up by the Germans in no-man's-land in Lithuania. Since he wanted to go to Russia, it was assumed he must be of some value to the Bolshevists, and a thrifty German general traded him off for about ninety German prisoners of war! The Russians put him into a boxcar which wandered the rail lines for about a week before it got to Moscow.

As the United States still had armed forces in Archangel and Siberia, presumed to be anti-Communist, the Russians decided to keep an eye on Frank, and they put him under a luxurious type of house arrest in the Hotel Metropole. Among his hardships was being taken out to dinner and to see the ballet from the Tsar's box, by Maxim Litvinov, with whom he had made friends.

The Bolshevists, who were having trouble getting their story told in the hostile press of the capitalist world, also arranged interviews for him with various dignitaries, and let him send out dispatches. However, in a few weeks they concluded an American correspondent was not a very desirable "prisoner" and deported him to Finland, putting him in charge of five American soldiers they had picked up somewhere, and wanted to get rid of.

In Finland, anyone arriving from Russia was of course suspect, and Frank was promptly interned again. However, the only other Americans the Finns had seen lately were representatives of Herbert Hoover's omnipresent relief organization, and reasoning that Frank must be one of these, they turned him loose. By now he had had enough wandering around Eastern Europe for a while, so he came back to America to marry my ex-student, and go on with his newspaper career.

Frank served *The Globe* ably for some time, but like many another good reporter, he preferred to be out on the firing line, and with regret I let him return to the Scripps-Howard organization in Washington. A year or two later, he dropped in to see me and announced that having sold a few magazine articles, he proposed to return to California and become a free-lance writer.

"You can't do that," I told him. "It's hard enough to make a living as a free-lance anywhere, but in California it's impossible."

He listened politely but indicated that he intended to go ahead anyhow. My skill as a prophet was up to my usual standard; in the next forty years he made a record as one of the most successful magazine writers in the country, selling hundreds of articles to *The Reader's Digest, The Saturday Evening Post,* and other periodicals—all written from his hilltop home in Los Altos, next door to the Stanford campus.

Earl Hadley had been editor of *The Chaparral,* the college humor magazine, when I was a freshman, and his friendly receptivity to my work was a great help to me. When I lured him to *The Globe* he was city editor of *The New York Evening Sun.* He worked ably with us until the paper went under, and then made a successful career in finance.

I quickly observed on *The Globe* what every newspaperman learns, that it is important to know some well-placed people in public life who can tell you, usually for background use only, some of the facts behind the headlines, including those that never get into the headlines at all.

My first acquisition of this type came with no effort on my part. Almost my first long signed article in *The Globe* brought me an appreciative letter from Ivy Lee, who was, I believe, the founder of the modern art of public relations. (Later I learned that he showered many new writers with such notes.) His greatest coup had been to change the public "image"—a word not then in use in its present meaning—of John D. Rockefeller, Sr., founder of the Standard Oil Company. Although John D. had begun to give away his millions as early as 1902, and had retired from business in 1911, people still thought of him as a ruthless monopolist who crushed all opposition and gouged oil producers and users alike. Ivy Lee, with great skill, had gradually changed the public picture of John

D. to a harmless old golf player giving away shiny new dimes to children at every opportunity.

When I began work on *The Globe*, the head of the dynasty was John D., Jr., a mild, deeply religious man, with a profound sense of public responsibility. He was in trouble; in a labor dispute some time earlier, between miners and the Colorado Fuel and Iron Company, private police of the company—and to their shame, some state militia—had machine-gunned tents in the Ludlow colony in which were the wives and children of the evicted strikers, causing about twenty deaths. The Rockefellers were part owners of the company, and although John D., Jr., had nothing whatever to do with the incident, and deplored it as much as anyone, the nationwide wave of anger did not distinguish between individuals, and Ivy Lee saw all his long and patient work going down the drain.

At his suggestion, I interviewed John D., Jr. As I entered his office I remarked that he must have a child in a progressive kindergarten. He said he did—it was his son, David—and asked how I knew. It was simple: he had a roughly shaped, baked clay ashtray on his desk, like the one on my own; every father of a five- or six-year-old in a New York progressive school had one of these, made at school and presented to the parent whether he smoked or not.

My interview reported his views, very advanced for the time, on labor-management relations; whether it had any effect I do not know.

Another V.I.P. with whom I made contact was Judge Elbert Gary, head of the United States Steel Corporation. Judge Gary asked me to lunch in his office high in a downtown skyscraper, which had a restaurant in the basement from which food was sent up. The Judge, a wary little bald man with apprehensive eyes which belied the truculence of his business career, said nothing in any way remarkable. What I remember about the interview is the fact that a white-jacketed waiter handed me a menu with four or five choices of entrees and desserts, from which I made my selection. Judge Gary did the same, and the waiter instantly brought our food from the next room. This magical feat was now explained to me; to save time, the Judge had ordered two of every dish to be brought up from the restaurant, and kept at the right temperature so there would be no delay. I was only thirteen years away from a life of poverty in Iowa, and this waste of good food shocked me. It still does.

My best source of information about the American merchant marine was a soft-spoken young man who seemed to have no other interest in life, though he was the multimillionaire son of a famous railroad tycoon. Averell Harriman was less than thirty, but I found him an inexhaustible source of facts and ideas about how to keep American ships on the high seas in the face of heavily government-subsidized foreign competition. I had no notion that he would go on to his distinguished career as secretary of commerce, governor of New York, ambassador to Russia and Great Britain, and the chief troubleshooter for more than one president. My main personal memory of him was noting that he wore beautiful custom-made silk shirts; I didn't really want one, but I felt a twinge of envy for the man who had been rich all his life.

On financial matters, I used to get word-of-mouth information from a brilliant "Wall Street lawyer," Russell Leffingwell. When he was invited to become a partner in J. P. Morgan and Company, which meant automatic great wealth for him, I wrote him a forked-tongue letter of congratulation on his joining a "nest of robbers," and he replied that my letter had made him laugh out loud, which was more than any of the others he received had done.

One man whom I visited from time to time as a courtesy and not because I could get current information from him was Colonel Edward M. House, who had been President Wilson's alter ego for eight crowded years. He had helped get Wilson the Democratic nomination in 1912, and thereafter performed some difficult assignments for the President—a trip to Europe to try to prevent the 1914 war, another to try to end it, a job on the council which in 1917 coordinated Allied war activities, and an important role in the 1919 Paris peace conference. Then Wilson had suddenly discarded him, he never knew why. In 1920, an old man at sixty-two, he was living in an apartment on the Upper East Side, as frail and delicate as the beautiful china with which he surrounded himself. His voice was hardly above a whisper; though he had come from Texas, as I had done from Iowa, he made me feel gauche and clumsy. He had no inside information on anything any more, and I mustered up all the scraps of political gossip I could for him; he seemed grateful.

One of my best sources was a tall, garrulous Southerner, William G. McAdoo, who had been practicing law in New York intermittently since 1892. In the interstices of this occupation he had built the Hudson Tubes from lower Manhattan to New Jersey, had married President Wilson's daughter, and had been secretary of the treasury during the difficult war years. We used to lunch together in the Bankers' Club on top of 120 Broadway, then the largest office building in the world. While I tried to pick his brains he tried to pick mine: I believe I had better luck. He once suggested we go around the world together, each man to pay his own expenses. I was momentarily flattered until I realized that he would be the subject of great journalistic attention at every port of call, and that I would be serving as an unpaid publicity man, if not, indeed, a social secretary. In any case, I could not leave my job.

One hot July when we were both summer bachelors, McAdoo suggested we go together to *The Ziegfeld Follies* that evening, and I agreed. He knew Will Rogers, at that time the star of the show, sent his name back when we came in, and got an invitation for us to visit him in his dressing room between the acts. We went back, and pushed through a swarm of chorus girls painted like Petrouchka dolls, to find the famous cowboy humorist in his tiny room. Nobody said anything of any importance, but I was interested to see a portable typewriter, with a sheet of paper in it, on a small shelf fastened to the wall at about breast height. While McAdoo and Rogers chatted aimlessly, I took a look at the paper. On it were five or six successive versions of the same joke. I have forgotten what it was, but I remember well how, in the second act, Will shambled on stage, chewing gum, and dangling the lariat which at that time he still carried. Halfway through his monologue, a new thought visibly struck him, and he ad-libbed (so it seemed) the last version of the joke I had just read in his dressing room.

McAdoo's unsatisfied political ambition was written all over him. He sought the Democratic presidential nomination in 1920, and again in 1924, when his struggle with Al Smith lasted for scores of ballots, until success was handed to an astonished third man, John W. Davis. McAdoo left New York for California, where he finally succeeded in becoming United States senator for one term, 1933 to 1939.

The most important of my journalistic friendships was with Bernard M. Baruch. In the early 1920's, with American farmers suffering a severe postwar depression, he had worked out a scheme to help them. *The Globe* printed an editorial critical of his plan, and I was surprised, one Sunday morning, to get a telephone call from him at my home, saying mildly that he felt we had been unfair. I hadn't written the editorial, knew very little on the subject, but followed my standard practice when a V.I.P. complained, and suggested I come to see him.

He agreed, proposed the time as that afternoon, and told me what train to take to his summer home on Long Island. A car met me at the station and took me to a big rambling wooden house on the South Shore. Baruch, a tall man of fifty, with a brown face, both long and rather plump, received me politely, and started to defend his agricultural scheme. He was enormously well informed, and in five minutes I was floundering beyond my depth. I went back to New York, did a lot of intensive homework, and wrote a new piece setting the record straight.

Baruch and I began a friendship of almost fifty years, until his death. On scores of occasions he gave me useful inside information, almost always as background, not for attribution. Having become a millionaire by Stock Exchange speculation before he was thirty, he gave up money-making in middle life; he was an adviser to every president from Woodrow Wilson to John Kennedy, sometimes spending hundreds of thousands of dollars of his own money, never reimbursed, to get needed information on which to base action.

He was a tremendous egoist, as perhaps you have to be to accomplish all that he did; yet he also performed many fine and generous acts

FIVE MILLION WORDS LATER

and tried to keep them secret. He paid the college expenses of dozens of boys and girls, including many Negroes from South Carolina, where he had a winter home on a huge plantation. He was chairman of the War Industries Board in the First World War, and in that role played a vital part in the victory of the Allies. When the struggle ended, the War Industries Board was suddenly abolished, and hundreds of young girls, secretaries or clerks, were caught with no jobs, no prospects, and little or no savings. Most of them had come from other cities, and out of his own pocket Baruch paid every girl's expenses to get back home. The only condition he made was that each girl write him a letter after arrival, to prove that she had really done what she had promised she would.

Of his many other public services perhaps the most important was the famous plan for atomic energy that he developed in 1946 as United States representative on the United Nations Atomic Energy Commission. America at that time had—or believed it had—a monopoly of the atomic secrets, and it certainly possessed all the fissionable material in the world. After, with enormous difficulty, getting the agreement of the American government, Baruch offered to share our atomic monopoly with all countries, with a proviso that every nation would use atomic power for peaceful purposes only.

Russia refused; Stalin's spies had already stolen the atomic secrets, and with his paranoid fear of the West, he preferred to develop bombs of his own. It is staggering to think of the changed world we might have had if Baruch's plan had gone through.

"Bernie" was famous because of his predilection for conducting interviews on a park bench. He actually got some mail addressed to "Bench No. 6, Lafayette Park, Washington, D.C." I never happened to sit with him there, but I used to talk to him on a bench in New York's Central Park, behind the Metropolitan Museum, near Cleopatra's Needle. His chauffeur drove him close to the bench and then parked nearby and waited. He had a passion for fresh-roasted peanuts, and he used to share a ten-cent bag with me, gathering up the shells carefully for the nearest trash box. His doctor had firmly ordered him to eat no peanuts, and as we talked and munched, he would look apprehensively over his shoulder as though fearing the medico might be approaching.

I once asked him why he conducted business conferences on park benches, and I got the answer:

> *Remember, I have carried out many delicate missions for various Presidents, dealing with important men. If I were to go see one of them, or if he came to see me, the reporters would not let us rest until they had found out what was in the wind. But a meeting on a park bench, with all the world looking on, dispels any idea of secret negotiations . . . Besides, I like to sit on park benches.*

About this time, two men who were starting new magazines came within a few months of each other to tell me about them. This did not necessarily mean that they valued my advice; the visits might result in useful publicity in the paper, and in any case there was no harm in having the managing editor of a New York daily know what was in the wind.

One of these was DeWitt Wallace, just about to launch *The Reader's Digest*. He was tall, pleasant, and shy; though he did not tell me so, he was working with the slimmest possible finances. He had sent out circulars advertising the magazine, promising refunds to subscribers who after receiving the first copy did not like it. With his own savings, and a borrowed $1,300, he mailed the first issue to 1,500 subscribers from his home in Minetta Lane, New York City, he and his wife doing nearly all the work. About this time he was so hard pressed for funds that he spent hours in the periodical room of the New York Public Library, copying in longhand articles from other periodicals, condensing them as he went.

He was almost exactly my age, having been born a couple of months later, and in a Minnesota town a few miles from Emmetsburg. I found him hard to talk to, but with a warm and cordial personality.

Today, of course, *The Reader's Digest* is one of the greatest publishing successes in history; in 1969 it had some 17 million subscribers in the United States and another 11 million in more than thirty other countries all over the world—except in Communist nations. Its condensed-book club has several million members, and it has other hugely profitable enterprises, ranging from new hard-cover books to phonograph records.

The heart of the magazine's success, now as in the beginning, is probably the idea that by buying this one periodical you can get the best articles from scores of others; but this idea alone did not guarantee popularity, as witness the scores of imitators in several countries, almost all of which have failed. Wallace has a real genius for knowing what middle-brow, middle-class people are worrying about, and what they want to read. In these particulars, and in some others, he is the most successful editor of his generation, and amply deserves the many millions of dollars that have rolled in on him.

The other new magazine editor who called on me was Briton Hadden, cofounder, with Henry Luce, of *Time;* I remember him as a pale, intense young man whose face lit up as he spoke of the need for such a weekly as his. Later I learned that he lived at a furious pace, both in work and in play; some people thought that exhaustion contributed to his death in 1929. He was popularly reported to be abler than his youthful partner, Henry Luce; but after Hadden's death, Luce created the huge publishing empire that includes *Time, Life, Fortune,* and *Sports Illustrated.* Empires are rarely accidental.

I spoke words of encouragement to both Wallace and Hadden. I believed both ideas were excellent, and I have always been of a sanguine temperament, more likely to expect success than failure. I don't suppose my encouragement was of the slightest importance, though Hadden told me only one other man in the business was optimistic about their venture, Henry Seidel Canby of the Yale English Department and the magazine then called *The Saturday Review of Literature.*

Though the founders of *Time* were trying hard to sell stock, I was not asked to buy any, and if I had, I probably should not have had brains enough to accept. Each $30 share of that day was worth $22,000 in 1968. More than one radical thinker of later years was then working for *Time*, and was being paid partly in stock because cash was not available; these men got out at various later times with comfortable fortunes, which put them in a position to attack with impunity Luce and all his works.

The Stanford contingent on *The Globe* usually lunched together, at a nearby restaurant, and a few people joined us with some regularity. One of these was a shy young man of twenty-five, with a hawklike nose and intent but friendly eyes, beneath a great cloud of fine hair. Lewis Mumford was working on his first book, *The Story of Utopia*, to be published in 1922. We knew he was brilliant and widely informed, but none of us foresaw the great career that lay ahead of him as a critic of architecture and city planning, marked by such milestone books as *Technics and Civilization*, *The Culture of Cities*, and *The City in History.*

Another member of our informal luncheon club was a man of about my age, whose strenuous daily program put us all to shame. He was an editorial writer on *The New York Evening Post*, but he was already determined to become a historian. Allan Nevins lived with his wife Mary on Staten Island, with a long and arduous daily trip to the office of *The Evening Post* on Vesey Street. He got up every morning at half past four or so, snatched a hasty breakfast, and then wrote on a book until about eight, when it was time to depart for the trolley and the ferry. At *The Post* he kept roughly the same hours we did on *The Globe.* Normally he was home again by four-thirty or five, where before and after dinner he got in two or three hours more of authorship.

All this industry would of course have been of little avail without the talent that helped produce his notable career, embracing many books and years of teaching in several universities, mainly Columbia.

A young woman who called on me one day had a letter of introduction from her father, whom I have already mentioned as principal of the high school in Emmetsburg. Beatrice Blackmar was a very pretty girl, just out of the University of Iowa, and hoping for a career in journalism. Since she arrived just before lunch time, I promptly asked her out. My memory is that I had her join the informal editorial luncheon club, but in her autobiography, written with her husband, *An American Story*, she says I took her out alone, and who am I to argue with a lady?

I do remember that after a leisurely lunch, we walked back to the

Globe office, and as we approached, a tall young man leaning against the wall stood up straighter and waited for us. Beatrice introduced me to "my fiancé, Bruce Gould." She had made a phone call from my office to tell him of the lunch, and he had been waiting for some time to pick her up. He didn't hit me, but I'm not sure the thought didn't cross his mind.

Beatrice and Bruce Gould went on to highly successful joint careers, with published short stories, literary journalism, a play on Broadway, and twenty-seven years of solid achievement as joint editors of *The Ladies' Home Journal.* They can look back with pride to saving millions of lives with a campaign for lower maternal mortality rates in child birth; to fighting for racial integration before most people had even heard the phrase; to breaking the neurotic taboo against public mention of venereal disease; to elevating standards of taste in dress and home decoration; and incidentally, to making the magazine for a time the most widely read periodical in the world.

With my unbreakable habit of holding several jobs at once, I was already fitting into my schedule work for other employers. One item was teaching an evening class at the Labor Temple on Fourteenth Street, on journalism as a social and cultural force. The Temple charged the students almost nothing, its own finances were miserable, I was paid a pittance, but I enjoyed the contact with poor young trade-unionists from the Lower East Side, very like my students at New York University. The director of the Temple was an agreeable young man who tried to make himself look older with a trim Vandyke beard.

He was in contact with a friend of mine, a labor journalist from Los Angeles named Emanuel Julius. Julius had drifted as far east as Girard, Kansas, the home of a once-successful Socialist newspaper, *The Appeal to Reason.* There he married the publisher's daughter, and added her name to his with a hyphen. *The Appeal to Reason* was dying, but Haldeman-Julius had developed in its place a hugely successful enterprise, "The Little Blue Books," which sold by mail, a dozen or two in each order, for the unbelievable price of five cents apiece. Each contained a few thousand words, mostly on philosophy, history, or economics, though almost every subject was included in the hundreds of titles in print.

The head of the Labor Temple was interested in philosophy, and he had written "Little Blue Books" on a number of men, ranging from Socrates and Plato to Descartes, Berkeley, Hume, and Locke. They had been well received, and he told me one day he was thinking of expanding these sketches and making them into a book. He did, too, and Will Durant's *The Story of Philosophy* was a huge success; people to whom these recondite scholars were only names burned to get some closer acquaintance with them. Will went on to write, with his devoted wife Ariel, over the next forty years, the massive *Story of Civilization,* whose ten big volumes tell all anyone needs to know about the life of homo sapiens, from primitive man down to the French Revolution.

Another of my sidelines was writing articles for *Physical Culture*, a magazine devoted to biceps and a fruit-and-nut diet. A mild hypochondriac from childhood, I loved telling people how to remain healthy though chair-bound. The publisher was an elderly eccentric, Bernarr Macfadden, who looked younger than he was, and attributed this to daily exercise and never touching such poisons as meat, alcohol, coffee, or tea. I noticed, however, that when we lunched together to plan my next article, he ate a big steak, washed down with a pot of coffee.

Macfadden seemed intrigued with the number of editorial ideas I was able to produce, and he once offered me $5,000 a year to lunch with him once a week and propose subjects to him. I declined, and I'm sure I was wise. While in theory the lunch would have taken only ninety minutes a week, in fact I should have spent many hours trying to dig up enough good ideas to earn my keep.

During the next few years I engaged in other sidelines. *The Jewish Daily Forward* was trying to convert itself from a Yiddish paper to English, since young Jews brought up in New York scorned any other tongue; for a year or two I wrote a weekly article for it. Later, I did a weekly column for *The Brooklyn Eagle* and *The Boston Transcript;* my friends, in the kindly way that friends have, pointed out that shortly after taking me on, both these papers suspended publication, and suggested cause and effect, an idea I repudiated.

By far my most important form of moonlighting was writing for *The New Republic;* in three years I submitted at least seventeen articles to the magazine, all of which were accepted and published. I had read and admired the magazine from the time of its first issue in November, 1914, when I was teaching at U.S.C. I also had a slim personal contact: Alvin Johnson, one of the editors, had taught economics at Stanford in my day. My first article, however, was submitted over the transom, with no previous correspondence. It was a sociological study of the attraction Atlantic City had for vacationing members of the American middle class.

I either invented, or copied from some now-forgotten source, a framework for such articles that seemed to me well suited to their mood. I wrote in the present tense, and in the first person plural. This format had the immediacy that I wanted; it simulated the relaxed air of fiction while retaining the authenticity of truth; and it was flexible, for use at various levels of emotion. I went on using it for fifty years, and still do. I employed this form for sociological reports on Coney Island, small towns in Vermont, Maine, and Iowa, a famous horse race, the Dempsey-Firpo fight, Miami, a New York nightclub, Havana, Bermuda, and many other places and events.

In February, 1922, I wrote the earliest article in a national magazine about a radio broadcasting station; I visited the first of these to be established in the New York area, an almost-amateur, primitive studio, broad-casting records for a few thousand listeners at most, from a room over a boathouse on the bank of the Harlem River not far from University Heights, and I called my piece "The Ether Will Now Oblige." (Bruce Barton once claimed he had written the first such article, but when we checked we found I had preceded him by a couple of months.)

In June, 1921, I had tired myself out with a bout of hard work, and took ten days off to recuperate at Freddie Welsh's health farm in New Jersey. Freddie had been the world champion lightweight boxer, 1914-1917, and his guests went through part of a fighter's training routine—up at 6 A.M., drink a pint of hot water, walk and run, alternately, a couple of miles wearing a heavy sweater. Later in the day, more road work, and a few calisthenics.

To my surprise, when I got to Freddie's place I found Jack Dempsey there training for his championship bout with Georges Carpentier on July second at "Boyle's Thirty Acres," a temporary, circular outdoor arena in Jersey City. This was before the days when training camps were turned into circuses, with people paying stiff admission to see a fighter working out with his sparring partners; the general idea then was to keep the public out so that training could proceed unhampered. There were only one or two other paying guests, and we shared in some of Jack's roadwork, as far as we were able—which wasn't very far. I found Jack a mild and friendly person, outside the ring, with a strong tendency to call me "Professor."

In those days, only one or two sportswriters were covering Jack's training full time. One of these was a shy, monosyllabic young man of twenty-six, named Westbrook Pegler; I was struck by the fact that he seemed to have no views on any public question.

I attended the fight, in which Jack with no trouble knocked out Carpentier in the fourth round. Carpentier was really a light heavy-weight, never in Jack's class, and only managerial greed caused the match to take place at all.

Twelve years later my path and Peg's crossed again. In 1933 there was a brutal kidnapping and senseless murder of the victim in San Jose, California; the two guilty kidnappers were caught and lodged in the San Jose jail. An angry crowd broke in, took the two men out, and hanged them in St. James's Park, across the street, where my wife and I used to sit in our courting days, almost a quarter of a century earlier. That very week, Pegler was switching from a syndicated column on sports to one on things in general, and he wrote a piece warmly approving of the lynching. A group of outraged journalists in New York met, and were prepared to issue a joint statement blasting him for his irresponsible attitude.

I was present at this meeting, and at first I was, I believe, the only person present to advise against the statement. I pointed out that to attack him now might only harden him in a reactionary position that, if left alone, he himself might come to regret. (How wrong I was!) I also pointed out that his employers (*The Chicago Daily News* and in New York, *The World Telegram*) would probably rally to the support of an employee under attack. I won the day, and the statement was never published.

When Peg died, in 1969, an embittered old man, he had become so extreme and so reckless in his writing that in his last years nobody would print his material.

In the autumn of 1921 the great Naval Disarmament Conference began in Washington, and I assigned myself to cover it for *The Globe*. *The New Republic* asked me to write a weekly reportorial piece for them in addition, and I agreed. Herbert Croly, the editor, went down with me for a few weeks, to produce on the spot his long leading editorial for each issue. We were house guests of Gifford Pinchot, the famous conservationist and friend of Theodore Roosevelt, and his wife, in their big, rambling home. I liked the Pinchots, but I have always squirmed a little at being a house guest and especially with the rich.

As I have said, people were naïve enough in those days (and some still are) to believe that the nations will reduce their armament while still feeling their security is imperiled. For centuries Britain had ruled the seas, but after the First World War the United States and Japan were both coming up fast. The bumbling President Warren Harding knew nothing about such matters, but he had a remarkably able secretary of state, Charles Evans Hughes. Hughes had been told in secrecy that Great Britain would be satisfied to be equal with the United States in naval tonnage and armament, and believed he could coerce the other naval powers, Japan and (lagging far behind) France and Italy. (Soviet Russia demanded to be included, but was summarily rejected.)

Britain and America decided, behind locked doors, on a ratio of vessels for the five powers—roughly 500,000 tons each for the two of them, 300,000 tons for Japan, 175,000 tons each for France and Italy, with corresponding limits on the size and number of guns. At the first working session of the conference, with no advance warning, Hughes sprung this proposal on the three lesser powers. I was present in the room, and watching the faces of the Japanese delegates. Caught completely by surprise, as we all were, they turned purple; I thought some of them were going to die on the spot. The French and Italians, brutally relegated to third-class powers, were almost equally agitated. But none of the three had any choice, and a series of treaties were signed, after months of wrangling, guaranteeing the Pacific colonies of those powers that had any, and reaffirming the "Open Door" policy toward China—meaning that all the Great Powers were to have equal rights to loot her, and that the looting should be orderly.

Within a few years, of course, the nations represented at Washington, beginning with Japan, tore up the seven treaties they had signed, and were back to the status quo ante.

Two incidents of the conference stand out in my memory. President Harding was, I believe, the first president to hold press conferences and to answer spontaneously the questions the correspondents threw at him. I was present one day when a reporter asked him whether the treaty regarding possessions in the Pacific covered also the "home island" of the Japanese archipelago. He said that it did.

When this news was printed, it caused a worldwide storm (the statement was of course false). Secretary Hughes proceeded to treat the President like a naughty schoolboy, and Harding meekly took it. Hughes issued an order that for the duration of the conference, all questions to the President must be submitted in writing, well in advance; they were screened by a State Department representative, and poor Harding was told what he was to say.

The other incident concerned a mammoth Sunday party given by Van Lear Black, one of the chief owners of *The Baltimore Sun*, for the foreign writers covering the conference, who included such famous names as the French "Pertinax," and H. G. Wells. I was one of the few Americans included, I forget just why. The party must have cost Black many thousands of dollars; it took place on his big, luxurious estate outside Baltimore. The guests were picked up in Washington by a fleet of sixty or seventy rented limousines, which drove us to Baltimore, waited all day, and then took us back. This was in the early days of Prohibition when bootleggers had not yet hit their stride, and good liquor was notoriously hard to come by, yet the refreshment tent had a long bar and a row of white-jacketed bartenders who cheerfully offered to provide any drink anyone could think of.

Black, wishing to show the Europeans a little of what America is like, had found a Wild West show in winter quarters in Atlanta, and had imported tents, horses, riders, and even cattle for bulldogging. One of the Negro colleges, Tuskegee or Hampton, had a famous choir; Black brought its scores of members to Baltimore, dressed them in overalls, checked shirts, and straw hats, and set them to singing their heavenly harmonies while ostensibly trimming shrubs and doing other light yard work around the estate.

The few Americans present were enormously impressed by all this but the Europeans not at all. They didn't realize the enormous difficulties that had been surmounted to assemble the stock of liquor. They took it for granted that cowboys and cowgirls doing highly skilled trick riding and roping were a normal feature of any Baltimore suburban home, and so were bands of Negro "field hands" singing as no plantation crew had ever sung.

In addition to my stay in Washington for the first two or three months of the Naval Disarmament Conference, during which I left Raymond McCaw and George Hughes, the city editor, to get out *The Globe,* I used to visit the capital frequently, mending journalistic fences that are always in need of repair. On some of these occasions I dropped in on my casual acquaintance, Herbert Hoover, then secretary of commerce under Harding; he liked to spend quiet Sunday mornings in his office, accompanied sometimes by his special assistant, a bright young man from Boston named Christian Herter, who was to go on to service in Congress, as governor of Massachusetts, and as secretary of state for Eisenhower. Frank Taylor and I would join the two of them for leisurely talk on many aspects of the state of American public opinion.

On one occasion Hoover sought our advice on a problem. In the early 1920's, postwar Germany was in desperate financial and economic straits; France had taken away huge quantities of her machinery in the guise of reparations, and her credit was at low ebb for the purchase of goods abroad. Medical and other supplies were desperately short; newborn babies were being wrapped in paper because no linen or cotton cloth was available. Some people were starving.

Hoover told us that the American Relief Commission, which he had headed, still had huge stocks of nonperishable food stuffs in storage all over Europe. But feeling against the Germans was still very high in the United States; he wondered how the Americans would react if some of these supplies, not urgently needed anywhere else, were used to aid the Germans.

That one was easy. Frank and I pointed out that the Americans were the most generous people on earth; that they did not make war on women and children; that they would applaud this action.

I don't know how much we had to do with his decision, if anything, but soon thereafter the Relief Commission food began to be distributed in Germany, where it was a godsend.

With me downstairs as managing editor, and Max Anderson going to *The World,* we were short a man in the editorial-writing group, and in 1921 we brought in for Mr. Wright's approval a recent arrival in New York whom Bob Duffus and I both knew, William L. Chenery. He and several siblings had been brought up in Virginia, and he retained through a lifetime in the North a touch of soft Southern accent. (A brother, Christopher, became one of the leading public-utility magnates of the country.)

Bill had been a reporter, editorial writer, and columnist in Chicago and Denver. He was working on *The Rocky Mountain News* in the latter city at the time of the Ludlow Massacre, mentioned above. He wrote a furious editorial, "The Massacre of the Innocents," that got nationwide attention, and helped to get federal troops sent to Ludlow to keep order. During the war he worked with George Creel's Committee on Public Information, and then he had come to New York, where he free-lanced and worked part time for *The Survey*, a magazine whose primary audience was social workers.

On *The Globe*, with nothing going for him but personality and talent, Bill promptly went to the top of the pecking order of the writing staff, next to Mr. Wright himself.

By the end of 1922, I was finding the job of managing editor, with its mass of petty routine and endless personnel problems, more and more irksome, giving me less and less time to write. I therefore asked Mr. Wright to relieve me of these duties, and to replace me with John T. Flynn, who had some time before risen to the post of city editor. Mr. Wright agreed, and I went back to writing full time. In newspaper career terms, this would have been a mistake if the paper had survived; but it didn't.

A little later, we received news that Mr. Searles had died, and left his whole estate to the man who had been his secretary for many years. I don't know whether he had followed the pattern of Mark Hopkins and of his widow, holding out the expectation years earlier that he would die soon and make the secretary his heir; at any rate, New York gossip said that he had given his employee a hard life. He would send a telegram from Methuen to the secretary in New York, saying "Arriving Thursday; meet me," but failing to mention what train he was taking. The secretary had to camp in Grand Central Station all day until he saw Mr. Searles come up the ramp.

We now realized that the future of *The Globe* under its present management was more precarious than ever. The newly enriched secretary had no more interest in journalism than had Mr. Searles, and a paper is a volatile and uncertain property, lacking the solidity of government bonds. Accordingly, we began a rather frantic search for a possible buyer who would retain the paper's present policy and staff. Mr. Wright sent me to Chicago to confer with one of the great meat-packers of that city, who had seemed interested, and I spent an uneasy twenty-four hours as his house guest before he decided against us.

I had better luck with my friend, Bernard Baruch. When I explained the situation to him, he thought a minute and then said, "How much is the paper worth?"

I told him the newspaper brokers put a rough valuation on it of $2 million.

"All right," Baruch said. "Keep my name out of it for the present, but you may offer $2 million for the paper." He also assured me that as owner he would make no changes in policies or staff.

The heir was in a panic over the responsibilities suddenly thrust upon him. He had, however, financial and legal advisers, and I went to them with my offer to buy the paper for $2 million. They were courteous, but said they thought the price should be $2,200,000; how they arrived at this figure I never knew. When I went back to Mr. Baruch with this proposal, he refused to meet it. He thought they were just horse-trading, and would finally come down to our figure.

I thought so, too. Moreover, the spokesman for the heir said that if they decided to sell at $2 million, we should have the first chance to buy, since our plan would keep the paper going, and save the jobs of hundreds of people. But we were double-crossed; only a few days later came the news that *The Globe* had been sold to Frank A. Munsey, for $2 million. Although Baruch's offer, like most of his business operations, was for cash, Munsey paid chiefly in long-term notes.

The heir was advised at that time by a reactionary Wall Street lawyer, Lewis Delafield. I was told, though I have no proof, that Delafield advised the sale to Munsey on the ground that "the men now running *The Globe* are a bunch of radicals; Munsey is a safe, solid conservative."

The safe, solid conservative was famous at the time for buying and selling papers right and left. He had been a poor boy from Maine, who started two successful magazines, *The Argosy* and *Munsey's*, on a shoe-string, and even wrote for them himself in the early years. He owed his fortune, however, chiefly to the fact that when the United States Steel Corporation was formed, he managed to get control of a big block of stock at a low price; he was for a long time the largest single shareholder.

Munsey was a bad editor of newspapers, in spite of his success in the magazine field. He seemed to believe that if he bought two dailies, and consolidated them, "retaining the best features of each," to use a phrase he made famous, he could cut operating costs in half while retaining full circulation and advertising revenue. But it did not work that way; people did not like his papers, and much of the circulation usually dwindled away, and the advertising with it.

Men who knew him say he had one of the coldest, hardest personalities of his time. If he had any real friends, I never heard of one. Chenery in his autobiography, *So It Seemed* (Harcourt Brace, 1952), calls him "the most conspicuous eliminator of newspapers in American history." When he died, he had no one to whom to leave his fortune, and presented it to the Metropolitan Museum of Art, though he had not previously been known to have any interest in painting. William Allen White of *The Emporia Gazette* summed him up in a famous sentence: "He found journalism a profession and left it a business."

The news he had bought *The Globe* came on a Friday morning; the word spread that next day's issue was to be the last. The death of a healthy, growing newspaper is a terrible thing; the staff got out that day's issue, and the next, and the product was up to standard, but whenever the men had a moment free, they gathered in small groups to discuss the calamity, speaking in hushed voices as though at a funeral. Newspaper jobs were scarce in the spring of 1923; some of the older men never did get work again in their chosen profession. There was no Newspaper Guild to protect the employees, no such thing as severance pay. The rank and file were given a couple of weeks' salary, and that was all.

Mr. Wright was too old to hope for another editorial chair comparable to the one he was losing, and the death of *The Globe* probably hit him harder than anyone else. The buoyant Jason Rogers came into his office to tell him that maybe something could somehow be worked out, that perhaps, for instance, Munsey would keep the paper going, unchanged. Mr. Wright listened to a few words, and then interrupted. "Jason, you're only making it worse," he said, and for a moment he put his head down on his folded arms on his desk. For the proud, taciturn Scot, it was as sensational an action as if he had burst into tears.

Munsey "combined" *The Globe* with *The Evening Sun,* retaining few of its features except, as already noted, Hi Phillips' column, rechristened "The Sun Dial." He then combined *The Mail* and *The Telegram,* and presently all four papers were but one. In the early 1930's the Pulitzer family sold *The World* to Roy Howard of the Scripps-Howard papers, who had already bought *The Telegram,* and now the ghosts of six papers hid wanly behind a single logotype. By 1968, as I have said, all the evening papers in New York were gone, except the tabloid *Post.*

Wright, Chenery, Duffus, and Hill were taken into the Munsey organization, where they endured life until, a year or two later, they one by one escaped. Chenery became editor and then publisher of *Collier's Weekly,* where he served with distinction for many years. Duffus became assistant editor of *The New York Times* and author of a heavy armload of books. Hill had a radio show of his own on the Columbia Broadcasting System for years, and was also an author of many books, collaborating, as I have said, with Allan Nevins to write the first full-scale biography of Henry Ford. Wright, after some lean years, joined the publicity department of the A & P grocery chain.

Munsey offered me my choice of several jobs, including that of London correspondent of *The Herald;* but luckily, I did not have to accept. At the critical moment the job of managing editor of *The New Republic* opened up, was offered to me, and I thankfully accepted, feeling like a cavalryman in battle who finds a fresh steed ready just as his horse is shot from under him.

The previous occupant of the post had been Charles Merz, who afterward went on to serve for many years as editor of *The New York Times.* Merz had been offered a free, leisurely trip around the world, and a salary, serving as tutor to the two half-grown sons of Mrs. Seymour Cromwell, widow of the late head of the New York Stock Exchange. It was a tempting proposal and Merz asked the *New Republic* editor, Herbert Croly, if he could have a leave of absence for a few months.

But Croly, fiercely loyal to the paper, would never tolerate anyone's leaving, even temporarily. (I later saw him dismiss Francis Hackett, literary editor and a brilliant critic, when Francis asked for a few months off to write a popular history of Ireland for which he had been offered a large fee.) He told Charles he could go, but he need not bother to return, and the young man, justifiably angered by Croly's attitude, left without ceremony.

Thereupon the job was offered to me, and I jumped at the chance. The standard *New Republic* salary was $7,500, but Croly received $9,000, and since I was coming down from $11,500, he gave me the same as himself.

On March 1, 1923, I gathered up the sparse contents of my desk and moved. It was four years to the day since I had come to *The Globe*, six years to the day since I had started work in New York, a coincidence without meaning. I settled down in my new quarters, where, although I did not know it, I was to spend the next thirty years.

Chapter 6

THE NEW REPUBLIC

The New Republic came into being because a U.S. vice-consul in Tientsin, China, was assigned to show the sights of the city to an American girl on a world tour.

The girl was Dorothy Whitney, daughter of the very wealthy William C. Whitney, who had made a fortune in municipal streetcar lines and had been in Cleveland's Cabinet. The vice-consul was Willard Straight, who came from a family of ministers and missionaries, had studied architecture at Cornell, and had worked for the government of China and in journalism before joining the U.S. Foreign Service, assigned to Tientsin. Acting as a guide to a visiting daughter of a V.I.P. was a standard part of the chores of any young man in a consulate; what was not so standard was the fact that they instantly fell in love, and were soon married.

The young couple stayed in China briefly, and then came back to the United States. Straight joined J. P. Morgan and Company, where his expertise on China was extremely useful in the days of the banking consortium, in which capitalists from several countries pooled their resources to make massive investments in the Far East.

But his family had a tradition of public service, and while he performed a valuable function in protecting China somewhat from merciless gouging by the Western bankers, he wanted to do more than merely add to the large fortune his wife had inherited from her father (who had died some years earlier). The Straights toyed with the idea of buying or starting a daily paper in New York, but were soon diverted from this idea by one of their consultants, an unusual man, Herbert Croly.

He was the son of two New York newspaper people: His father was undistinguished but his mother was a famous sob sister, whose byline was "Jennie June." She did the things expected of a female journalist in those days—trips in balloons, interviews with condemned murderers just before their execution, talks with prostitutes rounded up for night court, and so on. In my years of close association with him, Croly never mentioned his mother, and I had a feeling he was ashamed of her career in popular journalism. Certainly he bent over backward in the opposite direction.

He attended Harvard intermittently; it took him many years to get his degree, dropping out to do magazine work in New York, first on *The Real Estate and Builders' Guide*, then on *The Architectural Record.* He had a modest inheritance from his parents, and with inside information from his job, he purchased a piece of land on Seventh Avenue at about Twenty-eighth Street. It gained greatly in value, and gave him a comfortable income the rest of his life.

In 1909, he published his widely known book, *The Promise of American Life*, dealing with political prospects and possibilities for the United States in the twentieth century. It sold only 7,500 copies in the original edition (it was reprinted by the Harvard University Press in 1965 with an introduction by Arthur Schlesinger, Jr.), but it had an enormous influence. Walter Lippmann, twenty years later, was to call it "a political classic, which announced the end of the Age of Innocence, with its romantic faith in American destiny, and inaugurated a process of self-examination," and described Croly as "the most important political philosopher who appeared in America in the twentieth century."

In a matter of weeks the author became famous. Many "movers and shakers," including Theodore Roosevelt, then barely out of the White House, were impressed by the book and entered into correspondence with the author. Perhaps the most important aspect of the work was that it was one of the first to take American politics and politicians seriously, and envisaged a new kind of America to be achieved at the ballot box.

In 1909, class divisions in this country were deep, a situation that most prosperous people viewed with equanimity if not with satisfaction. Industrial and service-trade workers were terribly exploited; wages were low and the work day long; the abolition of the twelve-hour day in steel, for example, was still more than a decade away. Unions were few, and were fighting with their backs to the wall; "yellow dog" contracts were common, in which the workers agreed in advance never to join a union. Strikebreakers were freely employed, and when violence occurred the police were on the side of the employer.

The businessman who clawed his way to the top, whether by mistreating his workers, suppressing competition, or ravaging natural resources, was almost universally admired. The courts generally upheld the rights of property over those of the individual, and the Supreme Court, in particular, was nearly sure to do so. Theodore Roosevelt was called the "trust buster," and denounced in the Union League Club as a radical, though when the smoke of his battles cleared away, it was always surprising to see how little he had accomplished, and how firmly rooted special privilege still was.

Croly was no radical, then or later. He did not argue for the abolition of classes, but hoped to see them brought into some sort of rough balance. This of course meant greater curbs on capital than then existed, and he discussed ways of bringing this about. Since he rejected laissez-faire, and demanded strong controls by the federal government, someone (I think it was Lippmann) once said shrewdly that "he sought Jeffersonian ends by Hamiltonian means." In fact, he preferred Hamilton and was critical of Jefferson (in my view, unfairly so). He felt that Hamilton exerted power while Jefferson just drifted.

He professed to be skeptical of changing people by moral exhortation, leaning somewhat toward economic determinism; yet I always sensed in him a yearning for a self-sacrificing group of elite rulers, something like H. G. Wells's "order of Samurai." Though he did more than previous writers to view the United States as a world power, he was still rather parochial; as Schlesinger pointed out, he almost ignored the Middle Western Progressives who should have been his natural allies. He differed from them in one particular; the Middle Westerners were usually isolationists, and Croly wanted the United States to play an important role in world affairs.

The Straights had read his book while still in China, and had been much impressed by it. When they returned to New York they sought his advice on several things, including the idea of a daily newspaper. But Croly had already been brooding over the possibility of a journal of opinion like the British weeklies, one that would "raise insurrections in men's minds." The Straights were attracted, agreed to underwrite the enterprise, and in 1914, *The New Republic* was born. It sent a thrill of excitement through many people, including me, as a twenty-five-year-old teacher in a California university.

There is a persistent myth that the first issue was planned to appear on August 1, 1914, the day the world war broke out in Europe, and that the paper was postponed three months while the editors took stock of the new situation. But the story is false; while the editorial office did open on August 1, the first issue was always planned for early November, and appeared on time. But the war of course altered the magazine's character, profoundly and forever.

Office legend says that the first style sheet had only two items on it, which read: "*The New Republic* will spell 'God' with a small 'g' and 'Negro' with a capital 'N.' " If there ever was such a rule, it survived only a short while. Though the paper always spelled Negro with a capital, I never saw the name of the Deity without one.

Croly assembled perhaps the most brilliant group of editors ever brought together for the beginning of any American periodical. First on the list was Lippmann, just outgrowing his youthful enthusiasm for Socialism which had caused him to become, briefly, secretary to a mayor in upstate New York, who had been elected on that ticket. He had published a year earlier the first of his long series of notable books, *A Preface to Politics,* and the second, *Drift and Mastery,* appeared in 1914.

Walter Weyl was another able writer on political and social affairs. Francis Hackett, a young Irishman, had made a reputation for himself as a literary critic in Chicago. Philip Littell, who had preceded me on *The Globe,* was a critic and light essayist who wrote an informal weekly column, "Books and Things."

An early business manager of the paper was Robert Hallowell, a painter and as hopelessly unbusinesslike as can be imagined. It was he who invented the *New Republic* symbol, a square-rigged ship of the period of the Spanish Armada. It was coupled to verses of Walt Whitman:

> *To sail to sea in a ship!*
> *Passage to more than India,*
> *Passage to you,*
> *To mastership of you,*
> *Ye strangling problems.*

Hallowell, like Somerset Maugham's hero (in turn based on Gauguin), wanted to be only a painter (his portrait of John Reed hangs at Harvard), and he finally gave up his position at *The New Republic* to go live in the Caribbean. I liked his work—brilliant tropical scenes in gay water color—but few people bought them. He and his family lived in poverty, and after his early death his wife's position was even harder.

In the beginning days of the war, *The New Republic* was close to Woodrow Wilson; he took his famous phrase "peace without victory" from an editorial in the magazine. Colonel House, at the time Wilson's alter ego, already had an apartment in New York; Croly and Lippmann visited him there regularly. They were not alarmed as America's active participation in the war grew nearer, but other members of the *New Republic* group were, especially Weyl, Hackett, and a brilliant young salaried contributor, Randolph Bourne. They were, in varying degrees, pacifists. Offsetting them were two Englishmen who were close to the paper in those days—Harold Laski, a talented youthful Socialist, and Norman Angell, who had written a book shortly before 1914, generally interpreted as saying there could never be another big war because the international ties of capitalism were too strong. (He later denied this interpretation of his work.) These men helped to push the paper toward the side of the Allies, where it would certainly have gone in any case.

With America's declaration of war, Lippmann departed for Washington, where he performed valuable services in planning the war and the peace. He is generally credited with the main authorship of Wilson's famous "Fourteen Points," though I believe he has never admitted this.

Because of Lippmann's presence in Washington, and perhaps because of the ties with Colonel House, people in Wall Street came to believe *The New Republic* was an unofficial organ of the Wilson Administration. The paper sold out instantly every Thursday morning when it went on sale in the financial district. It is comical to think of tough, uneducated speculators struggling with Croly's turgid, Latinized prose for tips on which way the market would go. The story was of course nonsense; the paper never had any secret information from Washington.

As the war went on, and as civil liberties in the United States were trampled in the drive for victory, Croly was aghast. His strong protests alienated him from Colonel House, and from Theodore Roosevelt, now a ferocious militarist, who spewed out his furious scorn for the paper and the editor he had once admired.

Worse was to come. Croly was shocked by the Carthaginian peace terms hammered out at Paris in 1919, even though these terms were fully consonant with the secret bargains the Allies had written early in the war. (They tried to tell Wilson the details of these agreements, but he refused to hear them, perhaps the worst mistake of his whole life.)

When the Treaty of Versailles came up for ratification in the American Senate, Croly opposed it. But a part of the Treaty was the League of Nations, and most *New Republic* readers were in favor of the League. (The editors of *The Globe* agreed with these readers; we thought the League could be used to moderate the harsh terms of Versailles and the other peace treaties.) Croly stubbornly refused to listen to such arguments and a large proportion of the paper's readers canceled their subscriptions in a fury. If it had not had the Straights' financial support, it would have gone under.

Willard Straight, in Paris to help on the peace conference, died in the great influenza epidemic of 1918; his friends believed he might have survived if he had not been exhausted at the moment with overwork. A little later, Weyl and Littell also died, and Hackett departed under circumstances I have described elsewhere. Lippmann was soon to go to *The World* as assistant to its editor, Frank Cobb. Only Croly was still active of the original group.

But new men came in, as new men always do. Alvin Johnson, an economist who wrote so excitingly that he made the dullest subject sparkle, had come from teaching at Stanford. Robert Morss Lovett came, a half year at a time, from the English Department at the University of Chicago. Charles Merz, from Yale and *Harper's Weekly*, was first Washington correspondent and then managing editor.

Almost from the beginning, Croly had insisted that all the editors be listed in alphabetical order, with no indication of where power actually lay. Nobody knew from any printed evidence that he was in command, or that Merz was next in line. We continued this plan for many years after Croly had died and I had become editor.

With the election of Warren Harding as president in 1920, the paper faced a serious dilemma. The progressive movement in America seemed to have come to a halt. Harding had been elected on a promise to return the country to "normalcy," which really meant stagnation. The young idealists who had flocked to Washington to share in Wilson's "New Freedom" were out of office, older, some of them badly disillusioned. A magazine of ideas cannot stand still, waiting for the pendulum to swing in its direction again. What should *The New Republic* do?

It was Alvin Johnson who came to the rescue. In a long memorandum to Croly, he urged that the paper should now put its emphasis on cultural matters. There were brilliant writers, most of them in England, on art, music, belles lettres. Many of them were already contributors to the paper—Lytton Strachey, Virginia Woolf, Clive Bell, George Bernard Shaw, Rebecca West. Johnson urged that they be used even more, and Croly took his advice. In America, Stark Young began his long career as the paper's dramatic critic, and Paul Rosenfeld, Lewis Mumford, Waldo Frank, John Dewey, Elsie Clews Parsons, and many more, discussed music, architecture, education, and American civilization in general.

The new direction for the paper achieved a modest success. Croly went abroad and got firm commitments from some British writers, paying them at rates far higher than they could get at home. In their private correspondence, published many years later, these writers displayed little enthusiasm for the magazine or its editor, but they were gleeful about the price per word they were to get. These rates were small by today's standards, $100 or $150 for an article of two or three thousand words, but they seemed generous to the beneficiaries. They also seemed high to me, accustomed to newspaper payments of a few dollars a column.

When I came to the paper, I quickly discovered that most people were frightened by Croly, an experience I did not share. Extremely shy, and devoid of small talk, he would let a conversation lapse into silence while his caller sat and perspired. His manner of expression was so curt as sometimes to seem brutal, and he rarely bothered to be tactful when he rejected an idea.

In spite of his long editorial experience I found him naïve in dealing with would-be contributors. He might like everything about a submitted manuscript very much except a sentence or two; but if he found these were displeasing he would reject the whole work. Often the phrases he disliked were peripheral to the main idea, and I would suggest that the author might be willing to alter them—an idea that never failed to astonish him. (I was usually right.) He had rarely written for any editor but himself, he strongly resisted suggestions for alterations in his own copy, and perhaps he assumed others would be equally intransigent.

While Croly was often gruff and seemingly callous, he was also capable of an occasional sudden emotional burst of generosity. I remember one episode when this quality of his was almost disastrous.

Waldo Frank, a literary journalist of the 1920's and later, wrote book after book, the main theme of which was that people should live by their unconscious impulses, not by cerebral rationalization. He found the quality he admired in the Latin peoples, both in Spain and the Americas, and was forever reproaching his fellow countrymen for letting the head rule the heart. He produced one book-length manuscript which was then called, as I remember, *The Rediscovery of the Whole.* It was read around the office, and we all agreed that it was unsuited for serialization, and could not under any circumstances be used. Croly agreed with this, with some reluctance. He said, however, that Frank was an important man, and that we should give him a dinner and break the bad news to him there. Accordingly, a dinner was arranged, and when the coffee was served, Croly turned to the author and said, "Waldo, I want you to know that we'll be happy to print your book."

It was the generous impulse of the moment, but it cost the paper dear. The serialization went on forever, amid scores of letters of complaint from the readers, and canceled subscriptions. When the opus came out in hard covers, it sank without a trace.

When an article came into the office, a "jacket" was attached to it, giving the author's name and address, the title if there was one, and a series of spaces for the editors to write their comments. This jacket was always removed before a rejected article went back to the author, and a good thing this was, since the editors were often savage in their comments. On one occasion Clarence Ayres, later a respected professor of economics at the University of Texas, was spending a few months in the office, and wanted to see what criticism an article of his would get if the authorship were not known. He therefore mailed it in under the name and address of a friend. Clarence was at the bottom of the pecking order of editors, and the piece came to him last, with the harsh verdicts of the other men already on it. When it reached him, he came to me, his face crimson, not knowing whether to laugh or cry. "I wrote this piece," he confessed. I pointed out to him that at least he had verified his well-justified suspicion that the editors were normally more tender toward one another than to outsiders.

It was part of my duties as managing editor to send back the bulk of the submitted material; nearly all of it had to be returned, since we got fifty or sixty articles a week, and we could print only two or three at most, in view of the volume of material written within the office. We had a printed rejection slip, but I used it only rarely, for several reasons. A lot of our would-be contributors were also subscribers, and I didn't want to offend them. Also, I had done enough free-lancing myself to know how wounding a rejection is. While my letters were short, I tried to make them as friendly as I could. In traveling around the United States in later years, on scores of occasions after I had lectured somewhere somebody would come up and remark that I had rejected an article of his on a given date (and he often knew the month and year), and had written him "a nice letter." Sometimes he had a scrapbook to prove it, with my letter pasted in.

But I have no illusions about the emotions my letters really drew forth. As the French say of farewell, to be rejected is to die a little. In thirty years I wrote thousands of letters saying we could not print what had been offered. I am sure that a large number of people hated me warmly—a gloomy thought to ponder in the middle of an insomniac night.

In 1923 the paper was still in its original home, two old brownstone houses on West Twenty-first Street between Ninth and Tenth Avenues. It was across the street from the (Protestant Episcopal) General Seminary, whose late-afternoon carillon concert could be heard for blocks around. It bothered me, since it always seemed to start just as I was engaged in a hard piece of writing or editing that had to go to the press that day. I knew one of the faculty at the Seminary, and once mentioned my problem mildly. He was shocked; he felt the carillon was God's music and nobody should criticize.

The business department occupied one house, the editors the other. Croly's office was the front bedroom on the second floor, mine the one in the rear, with an always open door between us. The literary editor had the room above mine, while the makeup editor, secretaries, and one or two other editors, were squeezed into cubbyholes on the second and third floors. My room looked out upon a garden where in summer we had a couple of umbrella tables and occasionally served iced tea on hot afternoons.

The main floor of the editorial house had a reception room, elegantly furnished in Victorian decor, and behind it, the famous *New Republic* dining room with a big circular mahogany table topped by a lazy susan, and surrounded by eight or ten black Windsor chairs. We had a resident couple from the South of France, Lucy and Etienne, who lived in the basement and cooked and served wonderful lunches for the editors and their guests three or four days a week. Lucy was the talented cook and white-jacketed Etienne was a model butler. The food was so good some of us, including me, fought a losing battle with overweight.

The *New Republic* luncheon table was often called "the best club in New York," and it was a highly selective one. Rarely was anyone invited merely because he was a friend of an editor, or was an amusing talker; he had to have something to contribute on a serious subject. Through our elegant dining room there passed in the almost forty years before the paper moved to Washington a long series of distinguished figures in journalism, authorship, the arts, and politics, most of them American or British, but with an occasional visitor from some other part of the world.

On rare occasions someone came along who rated a dinner, and these affairs had a special style of their own. Usually they were "dry," but once in a while Croly felt some guest deserved an aperitif and a bottle of wine.With the after-dinner coffee, cigars were passed, in a handsome mahogany humidor, with the *New Republic* ship in silver silhouette on the cover.

I remember one such occasion when the poet, Amy Lowell, thickset and masculine in jaw, was one of the guests. After dinner Etienne passed the cigars to the men but skipped Miss Lowell (there were cigarettes on the lazy susan). The rest of us knew her lifelong addiction to cigars, but Etienne didn't. No shrinking violet, she spoke up in a strong baritone. "Herbert!" she said, "your man went by me with the cigars."

"Give Miss Lowell a cigar, Etienne," Herbert said. I thought the butler would die on the spot, but he complied.

I was now back to the rhythm of a weekly, far different from five or six daily editions of an afternoon newspaper. On Wednesdays we had a rather casual editorial conference, in which, instead of discussing affairs of state, we spent our time deciding most of the contents of the next issue. On broad matters of policy, we were usually in substantial agreement, without need for elaborate argument. When we were not, Croly was *primus inter pares*, and his view prevailed. Other editors who disagreed with him wrote signed communications to the paper, which were punctiliously published.

On Thursday and Friday we put into type and made up the contents of the magazine, except the first few pages of unsigned editorials. Of these there were usually two or three long ones, a thousand words or so, and from six to ten brief notes, never more than one paragraph in length, about two or three hundred words each. The first few years, Alvin Johnson and I did the bulk of all the unsigned matter.

Croly wrote only one editorial a week, almost always the leading one. He stayed at home every morning to do it, arriving at the office just in time for one o'clock lunch. Wednesday noon he came in with the first draft of next week's article, started before the editorial conference. He wrote with a pen on yellow foolscap in his difficult script. During the afternoon his secretary copied his piece, and he took the typescript home with him and rewrote it. Next day the process was repeated, and every weekday until the final deadline on Tuesday, when he came in a little earlier. There was always a struggle to get his last draft into type, proofread, and final corrections telephoned to the printer. There were often errors in the printed copy, and Herbert was indignant at these; it never seemed to occur to him that the fault was chiefly his.

The rest of us wrote our editorials over the weekend or on Mondays. I also read proof Saturday and Sunday on most of the magazine, at my home, checking for typographical errors, mistakes of fact, and—an unending worry for me—possible libel.

Always a man for fact rather than theory, I changed the character of the short paragraphs with which the magazine opened. Instead of commenting only on a few subjects of special interest to liberals, I began making them brief summaries of the five or six most important happenings of the past seven days all over the world. To keep abreast of the news, I developed, in addition to other sources, the habit of dictating or typing a summary of all the important material in *The New York Times*, seven days a week; on Saturdays and Sundays, when no secretary was available, I did it myself, or dragooned into service my endlessly patient and cooperative wife. In those days, a digest of all the important news in *The Times*, for my purposes, usually took one page a day of typewriter paper, single spaced, in elite type.

My editorials were, of course, not mere recitals of the facts, but included opinion; I viewed with alarm or (more rarely) pointed with pride, on a host of questions. In the next quarter century I wrote, at a conservative guess, five or six thousand of these short editorials.

Someone on *Time* magazine once heard about my routine, but got it wrong, believing that I read every word of *The Times* every day, which would have taken many hours, and been a fearful waste. One of *Time*'s bright girl checkers from Vassar called me up to ask why I did this, how long it took, and so on. I explained the error, but never did succeed in getting *Time*'s morgue corrected; every few years I was called again, with the same set of questions.

There was a distinct aura of smart society around *The New Republic* in those days. Herbert had connections with the rich, and Mrs. Straight was of course a member of a leading American family. With surprise and a little uneasiness I found my wife and myself being asked to dine, or to spend the weekend, at the homes of wealthy people. My agrarian Populist background caused me to bridle slightly; but I soon found that the kind of wealthy people who were attracted by *The New Republic* were usually at least as radical in their views as I was, and generally better educated and as smart, or smarter. The ones the editors saw most of turned out to be chiefly ladies, often towing amiable husbands in their wake, when they were not widows or spinsters.

One lady I knew well was Princess Elizabeth Bibesco, wife of Prince Antoine Bibesco, the Rumanian minister in Washington, daughter of the noted British statesman, Lord Asquith, and a prolific author of verse, short stories, and novels. She was on my visiting list on my frequent visits to Washington, and exchanged with me the gossip of the capital. She was beautiful and brilliant, and, like Alice Roosevelt Longworth, something of a character.

I'm sorry to say that I inadvertently caused the Prince to be declared *persona non grata* by Washington and sent home. The Princess took a keen interest in American politics, and in an election year in the mid-twenties she sent me a most indiscreet letter intended for publication, making some disagreeable comments on a politician then running for office. She and I both knew that foreign diplomats must not comment on domestic politics, but both of us had inexplicable lapses of memory. I printed her letter, and her husband was recalled.

In 1920, Mrs. Straight met a young English agricultural economist of about her own age, Leonard Elmhirst, who had come to Cornell after taking a degree at Cambridge, and in 1925 they were married. Leonard Elmhirst was as remarkable a human being as she was, and they were to have a long and happy life together. He was enormously interested in *The New Republic*, and followed its activities for the next quarter of a century with close attention.

Soon after their marriage, the Elmhirsts bought Dartington Hall, a large estate in Devonshire, and turned it into a center for many experimental activities, all with the common aim of developing information with which to better man's relation to his environment. Best known of these is the Dartington School, now one of the leading educational institutions in England, with special emphasis on the arts. Every aspect of farming, including raising purebred cattle, and "tree farming," has also been practiced, as well as rural industry—furniture making, textile weaving, and a long list of allied activities. The impact of Dartington on British rural life, while impossible to express statistically, has undoubtedly been great.

Equally important in the long view has been Leonard's work in the field of international agricultural economics. For thirty years he was president of an association in this field; at its meetings at regular intervals over the years, experts in agriculture from the most advanced countries rubbed shoulders with those from the backward ones, with incalculable benefits.

This work was supplemented by his activity as chairman for fifteen years of a British organization called Political and Economic Planning—

"P.E.P."—which put forward the ideas its title implies, at a time when for governments to take thought for the long-range future was novel indeed.

While the Elmhirsts necessarily spent most of their time in England, their interest in *The New Republic* was not lessened. At least once a year, and sometimes oftener, they came to the United States for a leisurely working vacation, of which several days were always devoted to a non-stop discussion of the paper, its successes and failures. These were always held away from New York, on Long Island, Cape Cod, or the huge baronial Whitney estate of many thousands of acres in the Adirondacks.

For thirty years I was forced to engage in a running debate on many occasions with all sorts of people as to whether a subsidized paper like *The New Republic* deserved to exist at all. The short answer seems to me to be that if the editors—and the owners—are good enough, it does; if not, not. A subsidy—in my time, as I have said, it was usually only a few thousand dollars a year—gives the editors a freedom not otherwise available. Each copy of a large-circulation magazine costs far more to produce than the reader pays—often five or six times more, and the difference, and all the profits, come from the sale of advertising. The notion that, in America, individual advertisers pressure editors to advocate specified policies is, as I have indicated, largely a myth; but the whole atmosphere of such a paper is usually one of commercialism, big money, satisfaction with the status quo, "don't rock the boat." The editor lives in a milieu of conformity which is bound to affect him, even if only unconsciously. Such periodicals often do carry on fine crusades, and perform valuable services, but these are almost always in areas where the commercial world is involved little or not at all.

For example, in the late 1920's very few periodicals would have argued, as *The New Republic* did repeatedly, that the great prosperity of the United States was erected on an unhealthy and dangerously vulnerable foundation, with farmers and workers badly underpaid and capital overpaid. (One reader of the paper told me he heeded our warning and saved his considerable fortune by getting out of the market before the crash in 1929.) Few papers in those days were interested in the plight of sharecroppers and migrant farm workers, to which we repeatedly called attention.

Almost all the ideas of the New Deal had been threshed out in our pages—and in very few other places—years before Roosevelt became President. The paper had worked for two decades for the right of workers to organize, before the passage of legislation empowering them to do so. We pointed out the skulduggery of Wall Street well in advance of the Securities and Exchange Commission.

A characteristic recurring item in our editorial mail was a letter from a reporter on a daily, typically in a middle-sized city somewhere in America, exposing some bad situation in his town, a story which his own editor was afraid to print, or at least, to cover adequately. After checking, we published such stories, and sometimes with useful results. Two of them that I remember reported the existence of a small epidemic of bubonic plague in San Francisco, and the contamination of Denver's drinking water by manure used as fertilizer by nearby growers of vegetables.

We also got letters from time to time from college professors who claimed they were being penalized in their careers for holding unpopular views. We learned to handle these cases with care, since investigation sometimes showed that the individual was in other ways a hopeless misfit. (Mary McCarthy's brilliant novel *Groves of Academe* is based on this situation.) The American Association of University Professors, with its special committee on infringement of academic freedom, was in later years a great help to us on these cases.

It was interesting to see how a new idea, expressed in our pages, would soon be reflected in the editorials in daily papers across the country. The writers rarely gave us credit, which was quite all right with us.

We instigated one important project that none of the purely commercial magazines would ever have started. I had lunch one day with Stuart Chase, the talented philosopher-journalist, and we got to talking about the shoddiness of many consumer goods, the dishonesty of their advertising, and the fact that the purchaser had no way of finding out in advance whether what he bought was any good. I promptly said that the *N.R.* ought to expose these facts, and we did. The article was "100,-000,000 Guinea Pigs," signed by one of Stuart's collaborators, F. J. Schlink, and by Arthur Kallet. It created a strong response from our readers, and out of it eventually came Consumer's Research, an organization that tested all sorts of consumer goods and reported on their quality, by name, in a monthly magazine sent to subscribers. A few years later, internal dissension caused some of its staff to break away and start Consumer's Union; both organizations are still flourishing as I write. It took great courage in those days to name a manufacturer in print, and say his product was meretricious; today, thanks to the pioneering work that started in our pages, it is easier. In hundreds of cases, poor quality has been remedied after this public criticism.

Our circulation, in the 1920's and 1930's, usually hovered around 40,000 a week; the break-even point would have been more than twice that. There are several explanations for this situation. One, of course, could be that if the editors had done a better job, the number of readers would have been larger. Against this argument is the fact that none of the other papers like ours in this country did any better and some of them did much worse; if we were inadequate, we had a lot of company.

The chief obstacle, I believe, aside from the fact that some parts of the paper were always hard to read, was the charge of "radicalism" hurled against the paper from the very beginning. Witch-hunting began in the United States with the First World War, when real or suspected pro-Germans were treated with incredible cruelty. The Bolshevist revolution in Russia caused an enormous increase in such activities, which still go on, more than a half century later. Many of those who had benefited most richly from private capitalism seemed to have little faith in it, since they feared it could be toppled with such ease.

True, as they did everywhere, the Russians plotted revolution in this country, with never the slightest chance of success. Public opinion overreacted to the danger. Anyone who failed to conform to the prevailing conservative opinion was labeled "Communist," and the label did great damage, not only to the guilty but to the innocent, who were enormously more numerous.

The actual witch-hunters were few in number, but excessively vocal, free of any addiction to truth or justice. *The New Republic* was sometimes thrown out of school libraries on totally unfair and dishonest grounds. Here and there we found defenders who believed in old-fashioned American principles, but in most cases even those who knew better were afraid to speak out—or did not want to bother.

It didn't take much courage to be a liberal in a huge metropolis like New York; but it often needed immense stamina to play such a role in smaller cities—Houston, Des Moines, Los Angeles, and dozens more. As I have said elsewhere, I have only admiration for the hundreds of non-Communist progressives in those places who, often at heavy sacrifice, urged the counsels of reason when unreason was in the saddle.

The most successful single feature *The New Republic* ever had was started in 1926. Herbert and I decided that we needed a regular weekly column of Washington news, rather lightly written, and that to give the correspondent greater freedom, it should be pseudonymous. I went to the capital, checked several possible writers, and finally settled on Frank Kent, chief Washington correspondent of *The Baltimore Sun*. Long afterward, he became a rich and conservative stockholder in his paper, but at that time he was in modest circumstances, agreed in general with our policies, and was glad to do our column for $50 a week.

I rarely went to the press to close the paper, but the week Kent's first column appeared, I did so, for some reason I have now forgotten. At the last minute the foreman of the composing room came to me with a proof of Kent's piece, headed then and for years afterward, "Washington Notes." "This page is one line short," he observed.

This was true; I had cut the proof to allow a line for a pseudonymous signature, but Herbert and I had unaccountably forgotten to invent one.

With the presses waiting for me, I had to dig up a name in a hurry. I had come to the plant in lower Manhattan by a subway then called the Brooklyn Rapid Transit, so I turned the initials backward and signed the piece "T.R.B."

The new column caught on, and over the next forty years there was endless speculation as to the identity of the author. We wisely refused to reveal it, and this fact of course whetted curiosity all the more. When I went around the country lecturing, and invited questions at the end of my remarks, one of the first was always, "Who is T.R.B.?" I usually turned the inquiry off with a joke: "If his identity became known, he would have to resign from the Cabinet."

Over the decades, several men held the post. Kent was succeeded by Jonathan Mitchell, a young man of independent means, whose well-known wife was Doris Stevens, of the National Women's Party, devoted to removing all laws involving discrimination between the sexes. Mitchell was replaced by Ernest Lindley, followed by Richard Lee Strout of *The Christian Science Monitor*, who in 1968 celebrated his twenty-fifth year of producing the freshest, most courageous and forward-looking weekly article in American journalism.

When one "T.R.B." was succeeded by another, no reader ever seemed to notice the change in style. (All, of course, tried to write in the same vein.) On a few occasions when the copy failed to arrive in the first mail on Monday, I rattled off the necessary 1,200 words for a twelve o'clock deadline—and again no reader ever mentioned any difference.

Once the T.R.B. of the moment happened to mention that he had been publisher of a small-town paper in Arizona with an Associated Press franchise, and went on to make some adverse remarks about the A.P. The head of that organization in New York, Frederick Roy Martin, a man without much sense of humor, was furious. He set his secretary to reading the list of all Arizona publishers, seeking to find one whose initials were T.R.B., and by a remarkable coincidence she discovered one. Thereupon Martin dashed off an angry letter to this man, denouncing him for "fouling his own nest," by writing about the A.P. in *The New Republic*.

The victim wrote to me in bewilderment. "What is all this?" he demanded. "I don't even read your sheet, much less write for it." I sent a note to Martin telling him to call off his dogs, that the initials were fictitious.

When I came to *The New Republic* in 1923, my own political and social convictions were of course on the side of liberalism, as they had always been, and as they are now. I believed in putting an end to all discrimination between human beings as to race, religion, or sex. I was strongly opposed to war, at a time when many people still talked of its "ennobling" characteristics. I opposed restrictions on free speech, and as a newspaperman I knew better than most people how many and how sometimes subtle are the pressures on that freedom. I hated injustice, and had an unusually good vantage point from which to see how much of it there was—and is—in the world.

I believed in national planning in cases where it seemed obviously desirable, but only in such cases. In short, I was pragmatic about this and many other matters—a somewhat lonely position between the fanatic supporters and opponents of any given course.

A few years later, Professor Goodwin Watson of Teachers College, Columbia, circulated a questionnaire to several hundred people known to be left of center on various problems. I was pleased but not surprised to learn later that my answer turned out to have the highest "liberalism quotient" of all those who replied. I had been thinking of these matters for a long time.

The New Republic has always been a critic of the performance of American daily newspapers, and I hope it may have contributed modestly to the enormous improvement in the press during the past half century. Its most notable single achievement came before I had anything to do with the paper.

The Russian Revolution, as I have said, sent a shock wave of apprehension through American conservatives, who feared that by some application of the "domino theory," private capitalism would be destroyed in one country after another. They wanted the Russian experiment to fail, and most American newspapers obligingly reported that it *was* failing, and filled their pages with fantastic reports of dreadful conditions inside the U.S.S.R.

Charles Merz and Walter Lippmann collaborated on a notable *New Republic* special supplement, "A Test of the News." Since *The New York Times* was then, as it is now, the leading American newspaper, they analyzed its reporting on the U.S.S.R. over a substantial period of time, and marshaled the evidence that had later become available showing how false, and even absurd, many of its reports had been.

The supplement had a shattering impact, reinforced by a similar study soon after by Evans Clark, published in pamphlet form. The immediate response of *The Times* was to send Walter Duranty to Moscow (foreign journalists now being allowed to enter the Soviet Union). Duranty, an Englishman who had led an adventurous life in various parts of the world, accepted the new assignment eagerly. It is the fashion now to say that he went too far in his praise of the Russian experiment, but at the time he furnished a valuable antidote to the stream of hostile material that still formed the bulk of the American comment.

A few broad simple themes dominated *New Republic* editorial policy in the early 1920's. The paper fought invasions of civil liberties, of which there were many. It reported the misdeeds of Harding's cronies, who regarded his elevation to the White House as a license to steal. It attacked gunboat diplomacy in the Caribbean and Central America. It pointed out repeatedly the harm being done by the Draconian peace terms imposed on Germany. While Croly had moved the magazine somewhat farther toward cultural affairs, this was a matter of proportion only; there had been plenty of articles about the arts before, and there were plenty on social and economic matters now, including those from British contributors like H. N. Brailsford, Graham Wallas, J. M. Keynes, and Harold Laski.

For several years the paper paid John Dewey a retainer of $50 a week with the understanding that for this sum he would write as much or as little as he pleased, on any subject that interested him. He composed on the typewriter, double-spacing but changing as he went along, with so many interlineations that his copy was hard to unscramble. He was a murky writer, but what he had to say was so valuable as to make the difficulty of his prose relatively unimportant. It fell to me to edit his pieces for publication, and my changes were often drastic, but I never had a word of complaint from him. I learned, as all editors do, that with some exceptions, the greater the man, the less he is inclined to quibble over language, always provided his thought is not altered.

I knew, both from his writings and from private conversations with him, that he was dismayed by the excesses committed in the name of progressive education by some of his lunatic-fringe followers. He never intended his philosophy to be interpreted as justifying the abolition of all discipline. What he wanted was schoolroom activities that would engage the child's genuine interests, and that he should then be allowed to pursue these. While in recent years there has been a reaction against the worst excesses of Dewey's disciples, his real philosophy has had permanent and valuable effect.

Because of my own interest in this subject, and some writing on it, I was for several years in close contact with the Progressive Education Association, and a member of its School and College Committee. We got a large grant from a foundation and published an elaborate study, following the college careers of a number of students from progressive schools, matching them with about an equal number whose secondary education had been more orthodox. We were somewhat disconcerted to learn that both groups did about equally well in college. The progressive-school graduates seemed to show somewhat more creative imagination and a fresher way of looking at things, but they had no startling superiority.

A few years later, when the American Communists were infiltrating every possible organization, they managed to get control of the Progressive Education Association, changed its name, and proceeded to use it as another vehicle for propaganda. As often happened, they were so heavy-handed that the organization did not long survive.

Both on *The Globe* and *The New Republic* I spent much time, year after year, investigating and reporting the terrible scandals of the Harding era, centered around what was called "the Ohio Gang," though not all the members came from Ohio.

Later overwhelming events have dimmed the memory of these scandals, probably the worst in American history. They are often compared with those of the Grant Administration, but the latter involved only a few million dollars, and nobody went to jail. The Harding era cost the country, according to careful estimate, at least $2 billion in graft and waste, some people did go to jail, and two men committed suicide when exposure seemed imminent.

In Washington I sat for days in committee hearing rooms while Senators Thomas J. Walsh and Burton K. Wheeler, both by coincidence from Montana, patiently and with great skill unraveled the intricate story of men in high office being bribed to let private citizens act against the public interest. In New York I listened in the courtroom while Harry M. Daugherty, Harding's attorney general, and Thomas W. Miller, his custodian of German assets in the United States seized during the world war, were tried for bribery. The German owners of the American Metals Company, trying to get back their property, had set up a dummy Swiss corporation, and put aside $441,000 with which to bribe American officials; of this sum Miller and Daugherty received about a quarter; where the rest went is not known.

The most notorious of the scandals had to do with oil leases. The ships of the American Navy by 1921 were fueled by oil, and fearing a shortage in time of war, Congress had set aside some oil fields as a reserve, including two large ones—Elk Hills, near Bakersfield, California, and Teapot Dome, near Casper, Wyoming.

Harding had named as secretary of the interior a crony of his, Senator Albert B. Fall of New Mexico. Fall first got the oil transferred from the Navy to the Interior Department, and then leased Elk Hills to Edward L. Doheny and Teapot Dome to Harry F. Sinclair. Those two multimillionaire oilmen had virtually a free hand; if the deal had stood, each could have made at least $100 million for himself.

The first clue that something might be wrong came with the signs of sudden inexplicable prosperity on Fall's ranch at Three Rivers, New Mexico, at a time when prices were down and all other ranchers were having a hard time. Little by little the truth was pried loose, in the face of persistent lying not only by the crooks, but by wealthy friends not involved in any way, who shielded the grafters out of some sort of misguided sense of friendship.

The story is too long and complicated to be repeated here, but in barest summary, Doheny had bribed Fall with $100,000 in cash. Sinclair created a dummy corporation which sold oil to his own company, and those of three of his friends, at inflated prices, with a profit of about $3 million—at the expense of the stockholders. At least $304,000 of this was used to bribe Fall, but most of the rest was divided among the millionaire oilmen who had set up the dummy corporation.

When detectives for a Senate committee unearthed this shocking story, all four of the principals fled the country. Two of them, Harry M. Blackmer of the Midwest Oil Company and James E. O'Neil of the Prairie Oil Company, went to Europe and stayed there. Colonel Robert W. Stewart of the Standard Oil Company of Indiana went to Cuba, but finally came back. After a total refusal to help the investigation, he was tried twice, for contempt of the Senate and for perjury, and acquitted both times by juries which, in the lax moral atmosphere of the 1920's, sympathized more with millionaire crooks than with the prosecutors who were trying to expose their misdeeds.

Sinclair had also fled to Europe, under an assumed name, but urgent business problems in America finally forced him, also, to return. He was likewise tried; his agents bribed a member of the jury, but the prosecution by good luck uncovered this fact, and Sinclair at last went to jail for a few months, and paid a fine of $500.

After almost a decade of adroit legal maneuvering, Fall was finally found guilty of accepting one of his bribes, and sentenced to a year and a day in prison.

Shocking as were the oil scandals, they were only a mild forerunner to the whole story of what the Ohio Gang did. Daugherty and his pals had rented "the little green house on K Street"—No. 1625—and it was a center for wholesale corruption, as well as on-premises debauchery. Bootleggers and other malefactors paid the Ohio Gang huge sums to let them stay out of jail—or to be released if they were already in. Contractors and others seeking favors from the government found their way to K Street. So did tax offenders, people wanting to buy surplus supplies from the world war, and a host of others.

On a jaunt to Hawaii when he was still a senator, Harding had met a hard-drinking good-time Charlie with a shady past, Charles R. Forbes, and made him head of the Veterans' Administration. Forbes built veterans' hospitals around the country, buying the land at cost plus a standard bribe of $150,000 in each case, of which $100,000 went to the local contractors—to keep them quiet. For payments that were part of the padded cost, he purchased vast quantities of supplies—including, for example, enough floor wax to last a hundred years. He bought huge amounts of various items at the going price, and then declared them surplus and sold them to his "friends" at a heavy discount.

At Perryville, Maryland, there was a large warehouse with big doors at each end and a clear path between them, so that a truck could enter one end and exit at the other without stopping, its cargo being declared surplus in the process. But proper decorum was preserved: The trucks went through at only moderate speed. Forbes' short career cost the country at least $200 million.

I am aware of no evidence that at the time Harding knew what was going on. It seems certain, however, that before his death in August, 1923, he had learned something about it. Though he drank whiskey in the White House, and had earlier fathered an illegitimate daughter, he was not himself a crook. Like President Grant he was an appallingly bad judge of character, with a strong sense of misplaced loyalty to his associates who so cruelly abused his confidence.

A popular myth says that he died in a San Francisco hotel of heartbreak—or alternatively, that he was poisoned by members of the Ohio Gang who feared he was about to crack down on them. But Dr. Ray Lyman Wilbur, who was the Stanford physician when I was an undergraduate, and went on to be president of Stanford and Hoover's secretary of the interior, attended Harding in his last illness, and certified that he died of a cerebral hemorrhage.

Unearthing all these scandals and trying to get the malefactors punished took almost a decade. The sickly moral atmosphere of the times is suggested by the fact that in the face of overwhelming evidence of wrongdoing it was almost impossible to get a conviction. Over and over, juries, even when not bribed, acquitted wealthy men who had stolen millions, apparently because the jurors would gladly have done the same if they had the chance. The bribed juror in the Harry Sinclair case boasted to a friend that he was to receive "a car a block long." Famous figures in politics and finance took the witness stand and either lied outright or withheld vital information when not asked the right questions.

The senators who unearthed this mass of evildoing were subjected to persecution that went on for years. Their offices were broken into, their files rifled, and their telephones tapped. Detectives were sent to Montana to try to "get something on" Senators Walsh and Wheeler that could be used to blackmail them into stopping their investigation. Senator Walsh's daughter was threatened with physical harm if she did not persuade her father to drop the investigation.

Croly was disillusioned by the corruption and conservatism of Harding, the do-nothing politics of Coolidge. In the middle of the decade he returned to an interest in mysticism that had been dormant for many years. A. R. Orage, a British journalist, visited New York and recruited Croly, to my amazement, into an odd quasi-Oriental cult led by a queer character, George Gurdjieff, who believed like many before him that by mortifying the flesh one can gain spiritual insights. Gurdjieff had a colony outside Paris where Katherine Mansfield, the novelist, lived for a while, and endured hardships that may have hastened her early death.

The New York disciples met from time to time in various people's homes and Orage expounded the Master's philosophy. Croly tried to get me interested in joining the group, but all my life I have been highly allergic to mysticism of every kind, and I resisted. (Today, when all the visions of the saints can be duplicated by taking LSD, I feel somehow vindicated in my lifelong attitude.)

In the early autumn of 1928, I got a telephone call early one morning with shocking news. Herbert Croly had suffered a stroke in the night; he had lain for some hours on the bathroom floor, unable to move, until his wife discovered him there in the morning. Though he lingered on until the spring of 1930, he never made any real recovery, though toward the end he was well enough to be taken to Santa Barbara, California, where he died.

The eighteen months or so of his illness were terribly difficult for me. He assumed that he would recover, and had no thought of relinquishing his editorship. Yet there were important decisions that had to be made on the instant. I went to see him on his sickbed every week or two, and had to maneuver him into agreement with decisions which in some cases had already been made, and in others must be made, in the light of knowledge it was almost impossible for him to possess.

When he died, the Elmhirsts asked me to become editor, and while I was enormously complimented, I was also frightened. I didn't know whether I possessed the qualities needed to steer what I felt was in many ways the most important magazine in America. I talked the problem over with my friend Felix Frankfurter, and suggested that perhaps there should be an advisory committee of four or five leading liberals, friends of the paper, to whom I could go for guidance when I needed it.

Felix was strongly against the idea. A committee, he pointed out, would either be a nuisance if it tried to give advice, or so much deadwood if, as was more probable, it did nothing. I could see this, and therefore, with great trepidation, I started out on my own.

Chapter 7

LOST CAUSES

This seems a good moment to pause briefly and look backward and forward at some of the campaigns in which the magazine participated, which failed. There were plenty of these; we always felt it was our duty to work for what we believed to be right, even if the odds were hopelessly against success.

I was not on the paper in 1920, but I was in sympathy with its friendly attitude toward the Farmer-Labor Party, which held its national convention in Chicago that summer. The editors knew there was no hope of its winning a national election in the near future, or perhaps ever, but the organization offered a sounding board for ideas neither of the two old parties would tolerate.

I got a chuckle out of the way in which the party's presidential candidate was chosen. The summer of 1920 was terribly hot in Chicago, long before air-conditioning, and the delegates from all parts of the country wrangled day after day, as liberals always will. Tempers grew short and men grew weary. One delegate was Parley P. Christensen of Salt Lake, a big man who always wore white suits; by some miracle, he managed to appear every morning in one that was crisp and freshly pressed. When the delegates had hammered out the usual progressive platform, the problem arose of selecting a presidential candidate. Irresistibly all eyes turned to the big man clad in pristine white, and he was nominated. He probably ran as well as any other potential candidate could have done.

In 1924, when I had been on the paper a little more than a year, there was nothing inspiring in the program of either of the two major parties. The Republican candidate was Calvin Coolidge, who had been vice-president when his predecessor, Warren Harding, died in office. We disagreed with him on almost every public issue.

The Democrats, out of office since 1920, were divided and confused. Their two chief candidates for the presidential nomination were McAdoo and New York's Governor Smith. The Ku Klux Klan was by now a powerful force in America, and a burning question was whether the Democrats would have the courage, in their platform, to denounce the Klan by name, or would satisfy themselves with a general statement against "private groups that take the law into their own hands."

Another very hot issue was Prohibition, which had been in effect for four years. The corruption it was bringing was by now all too apparent, and everyone wondered whether the convention would have the courage to say so. Smith was the candidate of the big-city machines of the North, who opposed both Prohibition and the Klan. McAdoo was the spokesman for the other wing of the party, whose heart was the small town and rural South. His followers believed in Prohibition as a principle, no matter how much drinking they themselves might do in private. While they were certainly not all Klansmen, the Klan had enough influence among their leaders to make them reluctant to attack it openly.

I covered the convention for *The New Republic*, sitting hour after hour at the press table in Madison Square Garden, the original one situated, oddly enough, on Madison Square. The forces of Smith and McAdoo were so evenly matched that the convention dragged on for more than a hundred ballots, while the delegates ran out of money and clean linen. Each roll call began with the resonant voice of a delegate announcing that "Alabama casts twenty-four votes for Oscar W. Underwood."

The most dramatic moment of the convention came when the aging William Jennings Bryan appeared, to urge that in their platform the Democrats should be loyal to Prohibition, in which he was a sincere believer. The old man had been up all night arguing for this cause in the platform committee itself, and he was exhausted; rarely have I seen any man so tired. He started to argue the Prohibition cause, and faltered because of fatigue. I got a strong impression that he slipped off the subject, and introduced a few paragraphs from his famous Chautauqua oration, which he had given year after year in hundreds of small towns. He was the star performer in this cultural tent show; he could always attract, as one of the Chautauqua managers once said to me, "forty acres of parked Fords." He could have given his standard speech almost in his sleep, and on this occasion I had a feeling that that is what he very nearly did. If I am right, having rested himself for a few minutes in this way, he skillfully came back to the question of Prohibition.

The convention was in no mood to take a firm stand on anything; it evaded as best it could flat statements on both Prohibition and the Klan. When McAdoo and Smith had finally proved that neither could win, a compromise was sought, in the person of John W. Davis, a big, impressive New York attorney with a Wall Street clientele. By rights he should have been a Republican, and nobody quite understood why he was not.

When a newspaperman reached him at his summer home on Long Island to say that the wind seemed to be setting in his direction, and to ask whether he would head the ticket, Davis snorted in disbelief. "The Democrats are not going to be fools enough to name J. P. Morgan's lawyer," he remarked. But when they did, he took the nomination, made the best race he could, and was overwhelmed by Coolidge.

I saw Bryan once more, under sad circumstances. The great Florida real-estate boom was on, and a company selling lots in a Miami suburb hired him to act as a shill for the suckers. A big tent was erected on the shore of Biscayne Bay, and Bryan spoke several times a day on the glories of Florida to gaping crowds of elderly Middle Westerners. These were then packed into big buses and hurried off to "the property," to sign up for lots before the hypnotic spell had worn off.

A few months later, Bryan was dead of a stroke, in Dayton, Tennessee, less than a week after the ending of the famous Scopes trial, which had been to some degree another lost cause for liberalism. I was too hard pressed in New York to go myself and cover this trial, a fact I have always regretted. The Fundamentalists who dominated the Tennessee legislature had passed a law a few months earlier forbidding the teaching in the public schools of any doctrine (such as Darwinism) that contradicted the Bible story of the origin of man. John Scopes, a young high-school biology teacher, agreed to test the law, and the American Civil Liberties Union engaged Clarence Darrow to defend him. The case, which created worldwide attention, was later the basis for a highly successful Broadway play and a motion picture.

Scopes was found guilty, as everyone expected he would be, but was set free on a technicality by the State Supreme Court. The high spot of the trial came when Bryan agreed to take the witness chair and be cross-examined by Darrow; on the stand he swore that he believed every word of the Bible. Sophisticated Americans were amused, but in fact, biology teachers throughout the South were muzzled for many years by laws similar to that in Tennessee. It was more than forty years later that the U.S. Supreme Court struck down the last of the antievolution state statutes.

In 1924, *The New Republic* rejected both Coolidge and Davis, and supported Senator Robert M. La Follette of Wisconsin and his Progressive Party. We knew his cause was hopeless, and so did he; but we felt it was important that liberals should have someone for whom to vote.

The leaders of the La Follette movement were nominally Republicans from the Middle-Western farm states; they had attended the Republican convention at Cleveland which nominated Coolidge for his first term. When both the platform and the candidate proved highly conservative, the La Follette group bolted, and formed the Conference for Progressive Political Action, which became the Progressive Party, with La Follette as its presidential candidate and Senator Burton K. Wheeler of Montana for vice-president. It advocated public ownership of railroads, control of national resources, and lower tariffs.

The Republican strategists, shrewdly ignoring the Democratic candidate, revived the Red scare of 1920, directed at the La Follette-Wheeler ticket. Even so, the Progressives rolled up the respectable total of 4.8 million votes out of a total of 28.8 million, Coolidge winning with 15.7 million, and Davis coming in a poor second with 8.3 million. In the electoral college, Coolidge had a landslide—328 votes to Davis's 136. La Follette, with thirteen votes, carried only his home state of Wisconsin.

In 1928, when the choice was between Herbert Hoover and Al Smith, *The New Republic* saw no alternative but to support the latter. Hoover had become steadily more conservative during the eight years since 1920, and as a candidate he endorsed almost all the reactionary policies of the dominant bloc in the Republican Party. Smith had been a good liberal for four terms as governor of New York, and we agreed with him that the "Great Experiment" of Prohibition was an obvious and almost total failure. He was a loyal Roman Catholic, and we objected to some of the political activities of that church, but we objected even more to the rejection of any candidate on the basis of his religion.

Smith was a difficult candidate for the rank-and-file Democrats of the Middle West and South to accept. He had a strong New York accent, which sounded even stronger on the radio (which by some weird mischance he pronounced "rad-dio") than face to face. He was addicted to hard hats—a brown derby in winter, a flat straw sailor in summer, and he wore them at an excessively jaunty angle on the side of his head. (One of his political advisers once suggested that this habit was "bad for his image," as we would say today. Smith replied, "To wear my hat level hurts my head; If I can't wear it as I please, I'll get out of politics.")

In 1928 presidential candidates campaigned chiefly by special train, and I spent a few days on Smith's, touring the Midwestern states. In nearly every town the newspapermen, leaving the train to go to the meeting hall where Smith was to speak, were instantly jammed immovably up against the side of the car by unruly crowds eager to view the candidate. Since each of us was carrying a portable typewriter, and usually a briefcase as well, these episodes were sometimes terrifying.

Presidential candidates usually move in an aura of wild applause, even from crowds that have no intention of voting for them. Smith was cheered hysterically in town after town where, as it afterward turned out, almost nobody really approved of him. When I talked privately with him on the train I got a strong impression that he was sure he would lose, but like a good soldier was going through the motions of a candidacy.

In fact, his defeat by Herbert Hoover was not all that bad, 21.3 million to 15 million; with the increase in population, Smith got more votes than any Democratic candidate had ever done. In the electoral college, he was slaughtered—444 to 87.

Politically, Smith's later years seemed to me sad. He broke with Franklin Roosevelt, who had nominated him in 1924 and 1928, and growing ever more conservative, he voted for Landon in 1936 and Willkie in 1940.

One of our lost causes, which began before I had left California, continued for more than twenty years. In July, 1916, San Francisco, like other cities, held a "Preparedness Day Parade," as a public display of the citizens' belief that the United States should improve its military strength in view of the world war raging in Europe.

As the parade was coming up Market Street a bomb exploded, killing ten and wounding many more. Not long afterward two left-wing labor agitators, Tom Mooney and Warren Billings, were arrested and charged with the crime. There was no evidence whatever of their guilt, but they were tough customers who had engaged in violence in the course of various labor disputes and were highly unpopular with employers and with the friends of employers in the local government.

There was in fact irrefutable evidence that Mooney, at least, was innocent. He and his wife, Rena, had an apartment many blocks up Market Street, and like thousands of others, they had gone up to the roof of the building to see the parade go by. A friend had snapped a photograph of Mooney standing at the parapet, and by a great coincidence the picture included an outdoor clock across the street. When the picture was enlarged, its hands pointed to a time only a few minutes before the explosion. It would have been a physical impossibility for Mooney to get from the scene of the photograph to the scene of the explosion in the time remaining. Evidence was introduced that the clock was operating and was keeping good time. But in those days San Francisco juries were not much interested in facts when radical saboteurs were concerned. Billings got life imprisonment and Mooney was sentenced to death.

The case caused a storm of agitation around the world by radicals and by many others who felt that this was a transparent miscarriage of justice. When the United States entered the world war less than a year later, it became of great importance to the American war effort to do something about the Mooney case, over which there was great agitation in England, Russia, France, and Italy, all of whom were at that time our allies. President Wilson sent a Federal Mediation Commission to California to investigate the case. Its secretary and counsel was Professor Felix Frankfurter of Harvard Law School, who had taken a leave of absence to serve in Washington as assistant to the secretary of war.

By now, there was another important piece of evidence that Mooney and Billings had not had a fair trial. A letter was unearthed from a leading prosecution witness who had identified the defendants as being at the scene of the crime, inviting a friend of his to come and give perjured testimony, as he had done. He said he had been liberally rewarded and his friend could share the bounty.

This should have been conclusive, but it was not. President Wilson had to bring the greatest possible pressure on the governor of California to get Mooney's death sentence changed to life imprisonment. Successive governors over the years refused to do anything about the case, until in 1939 a man with humanitarian views, Culbert Olson, was elected and gave him an unconditional pardon. He died in 1942.

Mooney had a genius for publicity; Billings had none, and was almost forgotten, over the years—a fact that caused a bitter, never-healed quarrel between the two men. Though there was no more evidence against one man than the other, Billings stayed in prison a long time after Mooney had been freed. Finally the absurdity of the situation penetrated the heads of the California authorities; he was released, and went to work as a watchmaker in San Francisco.

Though the Mooney-Billings case was a lost cause for more than twenty years, while *The Globe, The New Republic,* other periodicals, and many individuals sought to have these men freed, it did produce some good results. Several changes in the law have been made both at the state and the national level, to safeguard the rights of defendants; so far as the judicial system is concerned, a repetition of the case seems unlikely.

The most serious of all the lost causes fifty years ago was, of course, the Sacco-Vanzetti case, which for believers in the democratic process cast a blight over the 1920's that did not end when the defendants were put to death in 1927. When I came to *The New Republic* in 1923, I had already been writing about the case for three years and I—and many others—went on doing everything we could think of to help these two men, until the end.

The case grew out of a holdup in South Braintree, Massachusetts, in April, 1920. The paymaster for a local factory, and a guard, were killed, and the robbers escaped with a payroll of about $15,000. Not long afterward, two men who lived not far away, Nicola Sacco, who worked in a shoe factory, and Bartolomeo Vanzetti, a fish peddler, were arrested and charged with the crime.

Both these men had bad reputations with the local authorities. They were long-time, dedicated, Italian-born anarchists, and fifty years ago the United States was badly frightened of this sect. As early as 1903, a federal law was passed excluding foreign anarchists from this country and authorizing deportation of those already here. This law was strengthened in 1918 (and again in 1952), and in the great Red scare of 1919-1920, some people were deported under its provisions.

Democracies have short memories; few nowadays remember the hysteria of those years and the many cases when innocent men were railroaded to jail. The Attorney General, one of the worst in our history, was A. Mitchell Palmer. He had presidential ambitions, and called himself "the Fighting Quaker." (Irreverent newspapermen amused themselves making up variations on that slogan—"The Faking Quitter," "the Quaking Faker," etc.) Palmer and lesser authorities sent people to prison on flimsy pretexts if they opposed the war efforts. Eugene Debs, a Socialist who was as near to being a saint as any man I ever knew, went to Atlanta Prison for ten years for publicly affirming his belief in pacifism. Victor Berger, a moderate Socialist member of the House of Representatives, from Wisconsin, was solemnly tried and found guilty under the Espionage Act. Newspapers and magazines had their mailing privilege denied. One man was jailed for trying to read the Sermon on the Mount in public. Among those charged with violating the laws against espionage or sedition—charges that might mean anything or nothing—twenty-four got twenty years each, six got fifteen years, and eleven got ten. A group of Socialists were expelled from the New York State Assembly.

In this atmosphere, Sacco and Vanzetti, and many other anarchists, were marked men. As such, Vanzetti had been charged with an earlier unsuccessful holdup attempt, and Sacco might have been similarly accused except for his successful alibi—the time-clock record of the shoe factory where he worked. Both men had at one time fled to Mexico in fear of being drafted into the United States Army.

The trial was conducted with what today seem shocking irregularities. There had been an eyewitness to the crime, but the prosecution did not call him, and concealed his existence from the defense. The presiding judge was a superpatriot, Judge Webster Thayer of the Massachusetts Superior Court, whose charge to the jury practically ordered them to find the defendants guilty. He remarked to a golf-club acquaintance after the trial, "Did you see what I did to those anarchistic bastards?" and then, when Robert Benchley, the humorist, quoted a similar statement publicly, tried to deny it.

Much was made of the fact that one of the holdup gang left a cap at the scene of the crime, and that Sacco had possessed a similar cap, but nobody ever proved that they were the same. Emphasis was also laid on the fact that when first arrested, both defendants had made false statements—not very surprising, in view of the fact that they feared deportation, or worse. (Not long before, an anarchist who was being kept a prisoner secretly by the Department of Justice leaped to his death from the fourteenth floor of a New York skyscraper, for reasons the government never deigned to set forth.)

Before the trial had gone very far, world public opinion began to rally to the support of Sacco and Vanzetti, as it had done for Tom Mooney. Not only anarchists, but Communists, who are always seeking a martyr, came to their aid. So did many old-fashioned Americans who believed that justice should be done even to people with obnoxious political views. Important new evidence was brought forward; a man named Celestino Madeiros, who was now in prison for another crime, stated that the murders had been committed by the Joe Morelli gang of Providence, of which he had been a member. Unfortunately, Massachusetts law at that time did not permit the review of a case by the higher courts on the basis of new evidence, no matter how important, but only on a charge that the trial was improperly conducted; the Massachusetts Supreme Court, acting solely on the written record of the trial, decided Judge Thayer had fulfilled his duties.

By now the case had become a worldwide cause célèbre. A dozen American liberals had gone to Boston to work full time on the case and hundreds more contributed money and moral support to the effort, not on the ground that the defendants were assuredly innocent, but that they had not had a fair trial. William G. Thompson, an outstanding Boston lawyer, undertook to act as chief counsel for the men, and saw his law practice ruined as his prosperous clients broke relations with a man who would stoop so low as to defend anarchists.

Governor Alvan T. Fuller finally recognized the worldwide clamor, by setting up a three-man committee to review the whole case and tell him whether he should exercise clemency. It consisted of A. Lawrence Lowell, president of Harvard; Samuel W. Stratton, president of the Massachusetts Institute of Technology, and former Judge Robert Grant. These three men were just as much members of the Massachusetts Establishment as Judge Thayer and Governor Fuller. They made what supporters of Sacco and Vanzetti considered a painfully inadequate and hasty inquiry, did not recommend clemency, and the men were put to death in August, 1927.

I interviewed Sacco and Vanzetti in prison shortly before their execution, and wrote a *New Republic* article about them. Vanzetti, with a big Western-sheriff mustache, was the talker; Sacco, clean-shaven, with a small round head, said little but what he did say was acute. They were both intelligent men, who had read widely in the philosophy of radicalism; their English was not perfect, but entirely adequate.

I stupidly tried to be optimistic. They had one more appeal to the Governor pending; perhaps, I said, he would at last see the merit of their plea. Vanzetti stopped me politely but firmly. "Please, Mr. Bliven," he said, "I know you mean to be kind, but it is useless. We are dead men."

He then went on to say something that affected me profoundly, and still does when I remember it. He pleaded with me to do all I could for Tom Mooney, now under a life sentence in San Quentin, in California. Here was a man who was to be put to death in a short time, and he was spending his time urging that I help another! He told me he had been writing letters about Mooney to a lot of people, asking them to see what they could do. "I may not be able to help much longer," he said with a twisted smile—not one of self-pity, but recognizing an obvious fact. "He needs help, Tom Mooney," he explained. "He's a sick man. If they don't look after him, he'll die."

I said I would do what I could, as indeed I had been doing for the past eleven years, and the conversation dwindled away to discussion of places in Italy that we both knew, and to favorite wines of theirs. I now learned quite by accident, and not from them, that I was keeping them from their dinner, and that if I did not leave they might have to go hungry until supper time. We all stood up and shook hands, and they walked away down the steel-barred corridor. I never saw them again.

Vanzetti wrote me a few days later that he had made me a penholder and was mailing it to me, but it never reached me. I think it is fair to assume that one of the prison guards stole it.

The night of the execution was an agony for me as it was for thousands of others. With one or two of my colleagues on the paper, I walked the streets of New York for hours, until I was exhausted and could go to bed and sleep.

Some time later, I went out to California, and visited Tom Mooney in prison, where I told him of this conversation. Mooney was a cross-grained, rough individual, but as we sat in the warden's office talking, he was deeply affected, as I was.

This lost cause, like the others, was not wholly in vain. The laws have been changed, and it is unlikely that another such gross miscarriage of justice could take place in Massachusetts.

Forty years after this famous case, several books have been published arguing that Sacco was in fact guilty of participating in the South Braintree holdup. I have read some of these books, but I am not convinced by them. It seems to me overwhelmingly likely that neither of these men was guilty, but this is not really the point. The point is that the majestic Commonwealth of Massachusetts put them to death without a fair trial because they were foreigners and radicals.

On the eve of the execution, Vanzetti made a statement that got printed around the world.

If it had not been for this thing [he said, referring to the trial], I might have live out my life talking at street corners to scorning men. I might have die, unmarked, unknown, a failure. Now we are not a failure. This is our career and our triumph. Never in our full life can we hope to do so much work for tolerance, for justice, for man's understanding of man, as now we do by an accident. Our words—our lives— our pains—nothing! The taking of our lives—lives of a good shoemaker and a poor fish peddler—all! That last moment belongs to us—that agony is our triumph.

Years later it was rumored that Vanzetti had not written this, but that it had been ghosted by an obliging Communist Party hack. To this I can only say that Vanzetti was I am sure perfectly capable of writing it, and in the absence of any proof to the contrary, I choose to believe he did.

My relation to one of the lost causes of this period was to some extent a personal affair. Early in 1928 the Sixth Pan-American Conference was held in Havana, and I persuaded Herbert Croly to let me go and cover it. Five years had passed since the Fifth Conference, at Santiago, Chile, and relations throughout the hemisphere were tense. The United States had been sending marines into several Caribbean and Central American countries "to preserve order," and keeping them there a long time. Latin America did not like this, but was usually afraid to say so. The United States was enormously stronger than all the Latin republics put together; even its population exceeded theirs by one-sixth. They were all exporters of raw materials, and we were their best customer; most of them urgently needed foreign capital, and again ours was their best source.

Europe sold them the lion's share of their imports, partly because they resented the United States, and partly because American exporters, with few exceptions, didn't take the trouble to study the market and find out what was wanted. In those innocent days American salesmen usually spoke only English, and they omitted all the delicate formalities of social intercourse so dear to the Latins' hearts. American machinery was often shipped with operating instructions in English only, and sometimes the manufacturers ignored the fact that their product might be used in tropical territory where it could be damaged by great heat and humidity.

Most of the Latin countries were members of the League of Nations, which the United States had refused to join; but a majority of them were not working at it very hard. For a variety of reasons, some had withdrawn "temporarily" from the Geneva organization, and others were badly in arrears as to their dues. They wanted the Pan-American Union to be turned into a Western Hemisphere League, less susceptible to domination by the United States, which naturally objected to any such development.

The delegation from "the Colossus of the North" was headed by Charles Evans Hughes, on temporary leave of absence from the World Court at The Hague. He made a speech of historic importance, promising that the United States would withdraw its armed forces from all countries where they still remained. It happened that I had an appointment for a private interview with Hughes a few hours before he was scheduled to speak, and I saw a demonstration of his remarkable memory. When I arrived, he was about to dictate his brief speech to a secretary, and he asked me to wait in the room until he had done so. Later I sat in the press section with a mimeographed copy of the speech before me, and heard him deliver it without a note of any kind, almost word for word as the printed text read. His speech did something to assuage the feelings of the Latin Americans, but not a great deal, and the conference ended in the atmosphere of an uneasy truce in which it had begun.

I enjoyed the easy life in Havana in January, while New York was sleet-bound. Lewis Gannett of *The Nation*, Raymond Leslie Buell of the Foreign Policy Association, and I took a house together in a nearby suburb; it came equipped with a servant or two at a very low fee. My chief memory of the lighter side of things was a long evening in the basement bar of Havana's leading hotel, sitting at a table with Henry L. Mencken and Will Rogers. Mencken was teasing Rogers about his famous saying that "I never met a man I didn't like," pointing out that in his long public career he must have met a lot of stinkers, and that it was ridiculous to like them. Rogers, whose wit was much gentler, appeared unable to think of any reply except to reproach Mencken for appearing in only one newspaper (*The Baltimore Sun*). Will was then in about five hundred papers, as I remember, and seemed to think that mentioning this fact was an adequate rebuttal.

Long before the conference ended, I was spending most of my time on another story. Members of the underground opposition to the government had cautiously made contact with me, and began to tell me the real story of what was happening in Cuba.

The president at that time was General Gerardo Machado y Morales, who had been elected as a Conservative in 1924 for a term of four years. He was as bloody-handed a dictator as the hemisphere had seen in a long time, suppressing all civil liberties and relentlessly rooting out every opponent, and especially liberals, radicals, and trade-union leaders. My informants, who met me under conditions of elaborate secrecy, supplied me with solid testimony about what was happening, and I wrote a series of articles in *The New Republic*. Rereading them more than forty years later, I marvel that I had the audacity to write them, and that I ever escaped from Cuba alive, since the first of them appeared before I left Havana. I charged Machado with the murder of several editors of opposition newspapers, and named them. I reported how freedom of speech, of the press, and of assembly had been halted. Several hundred of his opponents, some of whom I listed, had disappeared overnight without a trace. My informants believed that these had been taken to old Morro Castle, at the entrance to the harbor; it was known that there were dungeons near the waterline, with chutes down which bodies could be slid into the bay, swarming with sharks.

Like Mussolini in Italy, Machado had the warm approval of American capitalists, who owned two-thirds of the island's productive wealth. The United States ambassador was a close personal friend, which made it harder for protests from the United States to be heard. Under the Platt Amendment of 1901, the United States had the right to intervene in Cuba whenever it deemed this desirable, but Washington showed no signs of doing so in 1928.

The delegates to the Pan-American Conference met in the handsome white buildings of the University of Havana, and seemed to show no interest in why they were standing empty and available in the middle of the school year. As I reported in an article, Machado had prepared a plaque glorifying himself, and had installed it at the university. This was too much for the students, who tore it down, and a duplicate underwent the same fate. The furious dictator ordered the university closed; the ringleaders of the students, who knew what was happening to other opponents of the regime, took to the hills—as Castro did thirty years later.

As far as I know, I was the first journalist to tell the truth about Machado in any American periodical of general circulation. My articles got quite a lot of attention in left-wing circles, but if they had any effect in Washington, I am not aware of it.

After I returned to New York, spokesmen for the Cuban underground visited me from time to time to report how things were going, and I published brief follow-up comment when it was justified. They warned me not to go back to Cuba while Machado was in power; they said I would be severely beaten, with an immediate apology to the American Embassy about "an unfortunate case of mistaken identity." They told me wryly that the apology would probably be written out before the beating took place. Naturally, I was flattered at the idea a *New Republic* writer could be taken so seriously.

My best informant, first in Cuba and afterward in New York, was a pleasant, slight young man, Octavio Seigle. He would call on me from time to time, bring me up to date on what was happening, and then with a bow and a "But I must not take more of your valuable time," would slip away again.

After five years, Machado's misdeeds finally caught up with him; he had aroused so much and such bitter opposition that he was forced to flee the country. He was succeeded by a couple of puppet presidents, but a new strong man soon emerged—Fulgencio Batista y Zaldivar, who repeated all Machado's dreary round of acts of suppression. My friend Seigle had returned to Cuba at the risk of his life, and in 1936 Batista's men captured him. He and a friend were trapped in their automobile on the outskirts of Havana, were tortured and killed, and their bodies were then put back into the car which was set afire. The murderers may have hoped to make the whole thing look like an accidental fire but the torture had been so severe that it was still evident on the burned corpses.

Another member of the underground brought me the news in New York. For the sake of the record, I reported why and how he had died, in a *New Republic* article I called "They Have Murdered My Friend." It got some attention in the United States, but nothing happened in Cuba. Twenty-three years later Fidel Castro came down out of the mountains and Batista, like Machado before him, had to flee.

There were many other lost causes for which we fought during my thirty years on *The New Republic.* One that stands out in memory is that of the Scottsboro boys.

One day in March, 1931, a freight train halted on a siding not far from the little town of Scottsboro, Alabama. There were perhaps a hundred men stealing rides on the train, as was common all over the country in the Great Depression. Some of them were white, some were Negroes, and there was bad blood between the two groups, leading to scuffling in which Negroes were sometimes victorious.

There were also two girls among the itinerants, which was unusual. They had got off the train and were sitting on the ground; when some railroad police came along, they charged that nine nearby Negroes had submitted them to mass rape. The nine, ranging in age from twenty down to thirteen, denied that they were guilty, but they were all taken to Scottsboro, where they were promptly tried and, as was almost universal in Alabama in those days when a Negro was brought into court, were found guilty. Eight of them were sentenced to death; the thirteen-year-old was given a long prison sentence.

Thus far, nobody outside Scottsboro had paid much attention to the story, but it began to get more attention. The nine boys had steadfastly denied the charge of rape; they said they had never seen the two girls, and for that matter they did not even know one another—on a long train consisting mostly of gondolas filled with coal.

With outside help, chiefly from the International Labor Defense, the case now went all the way up to the United States Supreme Court, where the verdict was set aside on the ground that the defendants had not had proper assistance in court.

Alabama prepared to try the boys again, but in the meantime there was an important new development.One of the two girls—only sixteen years of age—wrote a letter to a friend, admitting that the nine Negroes were not guilty. She and her friend were prostitutes, temporarily down on their luck; they were traveling with their pimps, and feared they would be picked up for having crossed a state line for immoral purposes, illegal under the federal Mann Act. When confronted with her letter, she agreed to tell the truth in court, and did so. But the Alabama white jury was not swayed by it; it reaffirmed the first verdict. This was such an obvious miscarriage of justice that the presiding judge, James Horton, set it aside. His career was ruined by vengeful rednecks who at the next election voted him off the bench.

A third trial was held, with the same result as before. This one, also, went to the Supreme Court, which overturned the verdict on the ground that there had been no Negroes on the jury. Promptly Scottsboro put an obliging Uncle Tom or two on the panel, and found the defendants guilty for a fourth time.

By now, the affair was creating a worldwide uproar almost like that of the Mooney and Sacco-Vanzetti cases, and Alabama was hurting. Accordingly, a secret deal was made with the governor of the state: if the I.L.D. would relax its pressure, all the boys would be set free in one year. Then the other side brought renewed pressure to bear, and the governor broke his promise.

But with the heat back on, the state had had enough of the affair. Four of the defendants were set free. Another was given twenty years because, in a moment of blind rage, he had attacked a deputy sheriff with a knife. Three were given life, on the standard theory used in the Mooney case, that if you are innocent but are charged with a capital offense, life imprisonment is a fifty-fifty compromise. Gradually, they were all released, the last being set free in 1950, after nineteen years in an Alabama prison for a crime of which he was innocent.

The American Communist Party was enormously active in the Scottsboro case, as it had been in those of Mooney, Sacco and Vanzetti, and a dozen more. Its publicity machinery was excellent, it moved very quickly when it seemed that injustice was being done, and in some cases, it saved men's lives, or got sentences reduced, when almost nobody else was doing anything. On the bad side, Communist support for anybody alienated a large part of the general public. The C.P. often seemed to be looking for martyrs; it was more concerned to make propaganda than to get the victim freed. In the Scottsboro case, and some others, the party raised huge amounts of money for defense activities, amounts far in excess of what was actually spent. The surplus presumably went into the party coffers to be used for other purposes.

In the field of world affairs, some of our lost causes were shared by almost all Americans. Mussolini's wanton invasion of Ethiopia in 1935, with no real purpose except to divert the attention of the Italians from their grave domestic problems, shocked almost everybody, including the conservative businessmen who had favored him on the (false) theory that he "made the trains run on time." *The New Republic* could only watch from the sidelines as the Great Powers showed themselves willing and eager to abandon all the principles of self-determination and international fair dealing for the sake of immediate advantage. Pierre Laval, the French foreign minister, who was to be executed ten years later for treason, made a journey to Rome and agreed that Mussolini should have a free hand in Ethiopia if he would keep out of Tunisia, then a French protectorate, which the Italian was known to covet. Laval and Sir Samuel Hoare, the British foreign minister, made an even more sweeping deal with *Il Duce*, which they were forced to cancel when the terms became known and public indignation rose to a high pitch in their countries. Emperor Haile Selassie of Ethiopia journeyed to Geneva to appeal to the League of Nations against the destruction of his country; he was howled down by the representatives of Italy's Fascist allies, in a pathetic scene that is still often shown in television documentaries of recent world history.

A special committee of the League tried to appease Mussolini by offering him large fragments of Ethiopia, largely uninhabited; he refused them with a touch of grim humor, remarking, "Italy's need for expansion in East Africa is not to be satisfied by a cession of a couple of deserts, one of salt, one of stone. . . . The League Council seems to think I am a collector of deserts." His son, Vittorio, a pilot in the Italian Air Force, kept up the family tradition by calling the bombing of helpless natives from the air "magnificent sport." He reported that "one group of horsemen gave me the impression of a budding rose unfolding as the bombs fell in their midst and blew them up. It was exceptionally good fun."

I learned at this time a lesson the world seems to forget from time to time: that "economic sanctions" to bring a country to terms won't work. The League ordered such sanctions applied to Italy, but they left out the all-important matter of gasoline. They also let her continue to use the Suez Canal, vitally needed for logistic purposes. England and France solemnly embargoed arms to both Ethiopia and Italy; this was a crippling blow to the former, but Italy had no trouble in buying arms in the open market, notably from Soviet Russia. It seemed to me clear that sanctions were an act of war, and would be received as such. If they were successful in limiting the imports of food, medicine, and other consumer goods, it was women and children, the old and the ill, who would suffer. In the past thirty-five years I have seen no reason to change my opinion.

One of the important lost causes of the nineteen-thirties was the Civil War in Spain, 1936 to 1939. Most Americans rejoiced when Primo de Rivera, the dictator who had ruled Spain since 1923, was ousted in 1930. We rejoiced again when King Alfonso XIII was dethroned the following year, and a republic was established. The editors of *The New Republic* were more ignorant than they should have been of the strength of the Basque and Catalan yearning for freedom—a yearning that went back for centuries, and we did not realize the significance of the rising of the miners in the Asturias in 1934, a rising bloodily suppressed by the republic, now itself moved substantially to the Right since 1931.

When the Popular Front came to power in 1936, it seemed to us to offer hope of a viable regime, even with its odd assortment of Liberal Republicans, Socialists, Communists, and Anarcho-Syndicalists. We were not prepared, as we should have been, for the uprising of the Conservatives led by Francisco Franco, and comprised of an equally motley group—Monarchists, Carlists, the Roman Catholic Church, landowners, industrialists, the army, and of course, the Fascist Falange. But with such a lineup, we felt we had no choice; the Popular Front was acting moderately and trying to solve some of Spain's desperate problems of poverty and ignorance, and we supported it. So did almost the entire American Left.

The war promptly became a testing ground for the Second World War that was to follow only three years later. Hitler and Mussolini poured in money and men to aid the Fascists; the military men traveled dressed as civilians and pretended to be "tourists" but they were soon playing an active part in the war, especially as bomber pilots. The United States followed the lead of England and France, and embargoed military supplies "to both sides." The Loyalists' plight was then like that of Ethiopia; their enemies could get quantities of arms from Italy and Germany, while their own supplies were severely limited.

Stalin did not want to aid the Spanish Republic, in spite of the fact that the Communists played an important role in it. He didn't want to frighten the Western European powers, he feared arousing the wrath of Hitler with whom he was to make an infamous pact three years later, he disliked supporting a government which was a melange of political sects. The P.O.U.M. in Catalonia was a quasi-Trotskyist group, and the Anarchists and Anarcho-Syndicalists were almost equally anathema to him. But he could not stand aloof from a war in which the opponents were chiefly Fascists, and he dribbled a little help to the Republican forces.

He exacted a terrible price for what he did; he ordered a purge of many of the leaders he considered hostile to himself, and this bloodbath went on while the war was in progress, hidden from the outside world by the strictest of censorships. Many young Americans, not all Communists by any means, were strongly sympathetic to the Republican government, and went to Spain to fight (traveling secretly, to avoid American law). They formed the Abraham Lincoln Brigade, correlated with the International Brigade, which saw young volunteers from a score of countries, most of them disciplined Communist Party members.

The New Republic editors were inexcusably ignorant of what was going on within the Republican ranks. Ernest Hemingway became our war correspondent in Spain, largely by accident; the big, high-pay periodicals did not want to print his pro-Loyalist material, but Hemingway reported only the surface of the war. Some of the young Americans who went to Spain to fight became disillusioned when they saw what was happening; others succeeded in convincing themselves that the end was good and therefore justified the dreadful means. Some died on the battlefield, some were executed by Stalin's henchmen, some came home in various states of mind, all of them bad.

Everything considered, it was a miracle that the Loyalists held out as long as they did. In January, 1939, Barcelona fell, and Madrid followed two months later. Many of the leaders of the Republican government, and thousands of the rank-and-file, fled the vengeance of Franco into France. Most of them were still there when Hitler's leaders overran that country, and suffered tragic fates. Some American citizens who did not share their government's indifference to the fate of these hapless victims organized an underground railroad to get them out of the country and into safely neutral territory, which in most cases meant the United States. I am proud that a member of the *New Republic* family, the late Varian Fry, played an important role in this activity.

The worst of all my own lost causes came when I finally saw that it was no longer possible to keep the United States out of the Second World War. I had never been a bitter-end pacifist of the type who will not even defend himself from attack, but all my life, war has seemed to me a nightmare of compounded error that usually creates larger problems than the ones it solves.

As I have reported, I was shocked when the secret treaties among the Allies came to light after the First World War. Our Allies, who in 1917 gave lip service to Woodrow Wilson's idealism, had in fact, long before this, made firm commitments among themselves carving up the German Empire as ruthlessly as a Metternich could ever have done. These secret treaties accounted for some, though not all, of the severe terms inflicted on Germany and Austria in the peace conferences of 1919. It was clear that Lloyd George, Clemenceau, and Orlando had regarded Wilson as a babbling schoolmaster, to be indulged but not taken seriously.

During the first years of the 1920's I fought as hard as I could, in

The Globe and then in *The New Republic,* for moderating the outrageous demands made on Germany for hundreds of millions of dollars of annual indemnities, which at one point were supposed to be exacted in perpetuity. I warned, an unheeded Cassandra, that the Germans would someday become strong again and would be tempted to seek a war of revenge. It did not need special clairvoyance to see that no proud nation would stay humbled forever—but it required more insight than successive groups of British and French politicians possessed.

While *The New Republic* opposed the halfhearted sanctions applied to Italy during the invasion of Ethiopia, and the embargo on arms shipments to the Loyalists in the Spanish Civil War, and to this extent we were not neutral, it still seemed to me that it was imperative the United States stay out of the general European war which we were sure was looming ahead. With the lesson of the 1914 war vividly in mind, I felt the most useful role America could play would be, first to try to prevent the new conflict, and second, if it came, to occupy the role of peacemaker and seek a fairer and more permanent settlement than last time.

To this end, I opposed Roosevelt's suggested "quarantine the aggressors" speech in Chicago in 1937, in which he said, "Let no one imagine that America will escape, that America may expect mercy, that this Western Hemisphere will not be attacked." I was not alone in feeling at that time that we should keep out if we possibly could. His speech caused such roars of protest in Congress, in the press, and in organized labor, that the President was muzzled for a time. Washington, which had passed one Neutrality Act in 1935, now passed another one, forbidding the sale of arms or the lending of money to any belligerent. War materials must not be carried in American ships into any dangerous area.

Late in 1937 an American gunboat, the *Panay,* was sunk in the Yangtze by Japanese gunfire, and ninety-six persons were killed, of whom three were Americans. A lot of my countrymen were sounding at that time as though they wanted to go to war with Japan, and I was alarmed at their tone. I wrote an article in *The New Republic,* "This Is Where I Came In," comparing the situation then with that in 1917 just before we entered the First World War, and arguing that it would have been better if we had stayed out of that earlier conflict, remaining in a position to play the role of peacemaker. My article got a good deal of comment at the time (it was reprinted in an anthology as late as 1968), but I have no evidence it altered anything.

For the next four years President Roosevelt, who was much more aware of the dangers created by the Fascist powers than I was, took a series of steps to try to move the country closer to the side of the Allies. Sometimes he was disappointed. In 1938 he asked Great Britain to join in a conference of the leading powers to keep the peace; Neville Chamberlain brushed off his suggestion. In September of that year he reminded all the great powers of their obligations under the Kellogg-Briand Pact, to which they were all signatories; he got no response that meant anything. In April, 1939, he sent a note to Hitler and Mussolini asking them for a specific promise that they would not attack twenty small countries, which he named, for the next twenty years. Hitler solemnly read the message aloud to the Reichstag, among howls of laughter from its members; the scene, like Haile Selassie's appearance at Geneva, is often repeated in nostalgic newsreel histories of the times. You do not need to understand German to recognize the list of names which Hitler slowly and dramatically enunciates, his face wreathed in a broad grin.

On the practical side, Roosevelt did a good deal better, bending the neutrality law with the doctrine of "cash and carry." The Allies (who had command of the sea) could now have arms delivered to an American dock, paid for in cash, and transported by their own ships through the war zone. A little later came the destroyers-for-leases deal. We gave Great Britain fifty overage destroyers, which came out of a mothball fleet, in exchange for ninety-nine-year leases on naval bases in the British West Indies, Newfoundland, and Bermuda. At about the same time, the first peacetime conscription law in American history was put into effect.

A few months later came "lend-lease," a name evolved with great travail in the White House for a plan to lend the British, who by now stood alone, unlimited war supplies of every sort, with the understanding that at some time in the future these would either be returned to us, or paid for. No arrangement could have been more unbusinesslike, but the pretense served to hold the American isolationists at bay. They were a formidable group. The German-American followers of Hitler were active and arrogant. The America First organization, in which Lindbergh played an active part, seemed reconciled to a German victory in the war, and wanted the United States to keep from becoming embroiled. It was answered by the group calling itself the Committee to Defend America by Aiding the Allies, in which my old friend, William Allen White, editor of *The Gazette* in Emporia, Kansas, was a leading figure. How strong was pacifist sentiment in Congress, and in certain parts of the country like the Middle West, was shown when the renewal of conscription passed the House by a single vote—only a few months before Pearl Harbor.

I had no connection with any of these groups; *The New Republic* editors took our own line, which was that America should stay out of the impending war unless the danger of a Fascist victory became overwhelmingly great. Even after the Second World War began in September, 1939, we continued to hold this view, arguing that the United States should remain aloof and try to help make peace as quickly and as fairly as possible.

The owner of *The New Republic* was the wife of a loyal British citizen, and had been living in England for fourteen years when the war began. The pacifist position of the paper must have grated on the Elmhirsts to a high degree, but never once did they make the slightest suggestion that we should alter our course.

But alter it we did. As the war went on with one German triumph after another, George Soule and I, who collaborated in creating the policy of the paper, began to see that there was real danger that Hitler would win, and, with the other Fascist powers in his wake, would become master of the world. We decided therefore that we must abandon our plea that the country stand aloof, and advocate entrance into the war. We did so long before Pearl Harbor made such participation automatic. It was a period of anguish for me, as it was for thousands of other Americans at about that time. The *New Republic* editors were not alone in changing our views as to the course America must pursue; many other periodicals dropped their isolationism, and millions of citizens did the same.

How much influence we had on the course of events, if any, is problematical, but my own life was changed irrevocably. In spite of all my Cassandra warnings over the years about the probability of another war, trailing remnants of Victorian optimism had still clung to me; I couldn't really believe that the Fascists were as bad as they obviously were, or that a world holocaust was impending. Now I faced the fact that good intentions on the part of the democracies were not enough, and never would be. A madman like Hitler really could send a big, industrialized, highly cultured nation like Germany back into the Middle Ages. Stalin's brand of Communism was, for whatever motive, just as imperialistic, just as determined to dominate its neighbors, as any nineteenth-century big power had ever been. Hard as it was for me, I would have to live with these facts the rest of my life.

Chapter 8

TROUBLE

I think of myself as a man of peace, who hates conflict and will go to great lengths to avoid it. This being true, I don't quite understand why, as an editor, for decades I lived a life of ceaseless, sometimes violent, public dispute. I was forever publishing things that made people furiously angry; on a number of occasions I was threatened with lawsuits, and as I have recorded elsewhere, once or twice these were settled out of court for a few dollars—not because we had libeled anybody, but to avoid the expense of litigation. I was attacked in print many times, by Stalinists, Trotskyites, and the witch-hunting Far Right.

I was threatened with libel suits so many times that I developed what was practically a form letter to deal with them. I regret very much to learn, this letter said, that you feel *The New Republic* has published false and derogatory information about you. This material was published in good faith, on a basis of what we considered to be reliable information, in the public interest and without any personal malice. We shall immediately investigate the matter farther, and if we find your complaints to be substantiated by the facts, we shall at once publish a full retraction and apology.

In a surprising number of cases, this letter, all by itself, brought a complete change of heart in the complainant, and he would write back and say, in effect, Forget the whole thing. What he wanted was that somebody pay some attention to him, and this I had done.

In a few cases, when there were crooks operating on a big scale, suits were brought against us with no intention of ever having them tried, so that the plaintiff could tell people who inquired about the truth of our charges, "I have sued that paper for libel." After a couple of years, we usually got the court to dismiss such suits on the ground that they had not been brought in good faith.

Some of my troubles in regard to libel threats in the early 1930's were the result of articles by John T. Flynn. I have told elsewhere how I hired him as a cub reporter from New Haven to be real-estate editor of *The Globe;* he had a flair for reporting on finance, and after *The Globe* went under in 1923, he set up a modest syndicated column of his own, in this field.

In the late 1920's, before the crash, a great many men in Wall Street made money by exploiting the avarice of the investing public. For instance, huge public structures—hotels, apartment houses, office buildings —were built all over America with very little attention to whether they were needed at that place and time. These were heavily overcapitalized, and bonds based on them were sold by high-pressure means to small individual investors. The original builders got their money back, plus exorbitant profits, and got out; when the crash came, these buildings usually went bankrupt, and the bondholders lost all, or nearly all, of what they had put in.

Investment trusts were just coming into the American picture, and some of these were also sold in highly questionable ways. The promoters awarded themselves huge fees and expense accounts; they also conducted fictitious cash sales and ran up the per-share value to ridiculous heights. When the crash came, the gullible investors, who had been lured by promises of fantastic profits, were mostly wiped out. At that time, of course, there was no Securities and Exchange Commission, and broadly speaking, anybody could promise anything, and get away with it.

John Flynn and I were having a friendly lunch together one day, in the early 1930's, and he was telling me the inside stories of some of these Wall Street manipulations. I promptly asked him to write a weekly column for *The New Republic* on this subject, and he agreed. We used as the title a phrase Mr. Justice Brandeis had made famous, "Other People's Money," and the column soon became a great success in our pages.

Everything Flynn wrote was loaded with dynamite; he was attacking the operations of powerful, wealthy, and unscrupulous men, and week after week, I agonized about the possible consequences of that week's article. Flynn was a crusader, and while his instincts were sound, he was not always careful with his facts; checking what he said before it was printed became a major headache for me.

I remember one episode which seems humorous now, but didn't at the time. Among the few honest, well-run organizations selling shares to the public was the Massachusetts Investors Trust; Flynn went out of his way to praise it highly, and to point out how much better it was than some of the others which ruined everybody who bought their shares. For some reason I have never understood, the managers of M.I.T. decided there must be *no* public reference to the organization, no matter how favorable. On one occasion, Flynn's column referred to the Trust in highly flattering terms, and somehow, word of his reference reached the headquarters in Boston shortly after that week's issue had gone to press.

At three o'clock in the morning I was awakened at my home by a telephone call from an attorney for the Trust. He said he knew there was a reference to the organization in the upcoming issue of the paper, and I had to stop it.

I pointed out that the reference was wholly complimentary, and the attorney said this was of no importance.

I then said, "That issue of the paper has already been printed, and many thousands of copies are already in the mails. How can I possibly stop it?"

"That's up to you, don't bother me with details," was the reply. The lawyer also threatened court action, but this never materialized.

Flynn himself finally became a source of trouble. In the late 1930's he developed his extraordinary monomania of hatred of President Roosevelt, for reasons I have never understood. Years later, it developed to such a degree that he wrote a book offering the nonsensical charge that the President had deliberately incited the Japanese to bomb Pearl Harbor in order to drag America into the world war.

Gradually, Flynn's column shifted from being a report on Wall Street machinations to an account of the alleged misdeeds of the New Deal. Since the paper was supporting the New Deal, criticizing it chiefly for not going far enough, rather than too far, this made a very difficult position for us. In a few cases, I replied to Flynn's column in the same issue; in a few others, I fought with him in advance of publication and persuaded him to modify some of his worst misstatements. Once or twice I left his piece out of the paper entirely, though his salary went on. Finally, after months of wrangling, George Soule and I decided the column would have to be discontinued. Flynn was not living up to the terms of his agreement; by now he was saying hardly anything about Wall Street.

He took his dismissal very hard. He complained that we were censoring him, that we had an obligation to print material in opposition to our own views. In fact, we often did this—in the form of communications to the editors. But a signed column carried the implication of editorial endorsement, which was certainly lacking in Flynn's case.

The New Republic of course had never undertaken to be a newspaper, whose contributors could say anything they pleased. It had always carried a subtitle: "A Journal of Opinion," and our readers clearly understood that the paper had a point of view, and that its contributors were expected to—and did—share that point of view.

An endless source of trouble to me was the Newspaper Guild, with which the paper had a contract. As long as the Guild was under Communist domination, it did not press us very hard on economic matters, for what reason I do not know; but once the radicals had been purged, the union began to drive very sharp bargains with us. The fact that we were losing money did not matter to them, nor the possibility that we might be forced out of business if our expenses got too high. Union philosophy has always been to force weak organizations to the wall if necessary, on the theory that they will be succeeded by strong ones. This does not always work, as witness the newpaper situation in New York, where union demands have reduced the total number of papers for the general reader to three; but in broad terms it is probably a good principle from the union point of view.

In the case of *The New Republic* the Guild followed the principle of driving a hard bargain with us, and then using our example to coerce other publishers into line—a technique which is also standard practice. The bargaining every year or every two years usually took months of meetings at frequent intervals. Dan Mebane and I were the only representatives of management at these meetings, which always took place in my office at 5 P.M. By then I was exhausted by a hard day's work, but the Guild spokesman—never one of our employees—had presumably slept all day; at any rate, he was invariably bright and fresh. My memory of these scores of meetings is one of great fatigue; but Dan and I always succeeded in negotiating terms that would enable us to keep going.

The period of cutting back the big staff engaged for the Wallace period in the 1940's was, as I note later, a difficult one. However, we had a contract that enabled us to dismiss employees for economic reasons, and in general the union accepted our action, however reluctantly. In the case of one minor editorial man, we ran into trouble. I had notified him that he was to be let go, and he had accepted this fact. Michael Straight, now an editor, who had not studied the terms of the contract as intimately as I had, ran into this man in the hall, and casually remarked that his work had not been very satisfactory.

Bang! That did it. There was now a charge of inferior workmanship, which the Guild regarded as a very serious matter. The grievance committee of our own employees went to work, and tried to coerce me by threatening to bring an action against us before the National Labor Relations Board. Since I felt this issue might as well be faced one time as another, I myself took the matter to the NLRB; the union was furious to have its bluff called.

When the day came for the NLRB hearing, Mike Straight was out of town. I decided it was better for me to appear alone than to have a lawyer present, and that is what I did. At the hearing I sat on one side of the room, and almost the whole staff sat on the other; I had known most of them for many years, some of them had come to me for advice on their personal troubles, and I had very mixed emotions as I watched them facing me as adversaries.

The meeting did not last long, nor was it acrimonious. The dismissed man was able to produce several office memos I had written him congratulating him on jobs well done (I showered people with memos of this sort, as every editor needs to do for the sake of staff morale). The NLRB hearing officer promptly decided in the dismissed man's favor, and the meeting was ended.

We were now in the curious position of having an editorial worker whom we could not fire. I don't know whether, under the terms of the decision, he could simply have put his feet up on the desk and refused to do anything at all, but he didn't; he went on performing his duties as he had before. He and I worked as amicably together as we had done in the past.

But in a few months he stubbed his toe. The Roman Catholic Church was fighting, as it had done for many years, against the dissemination of birth-control information in Connecticut, and at some critical point, the nature of which I have forgotten, we sent our protected writer up to cover the story. He turned in a good piece, and we scheduled it for an early issue.

Just when that edition was going to press, a curious thing happened. *The Nation* was at that time printed in the same shop as ourselves, and had the same press day. The *N.R.* assistant editor whom we had sent to the press to close up the magazine was by mistake handed some proof sheets from the same week's issue of our rival, and was astonished to find a story almost identical with our own, by the same author! I promptly talked to my friendly enemy, Freda Kirchwey, of *The Nation,* and both of us pulled the articles out and made a hasty substitution of something else already in type.

The author of this bit of treachery to our interests was promptly called on the carpet, and cheerfully admitted what he had done. He had thought the fight for birth control in Connecticut so important that he wanted to give it the widest publicity, so he had written his story twice, once for us, once for our rival, without saying anything to either magazine about the duplication. We now complained to the Newspaper Guild about his action, and the Guild agreed that he should be dismissed. He was so new to journalism that he did not realize the seriousness of what he had done, and I'm not sure he does yet. He went on to a successful career as a university professor of political science.

Nobody has ever solved the old question, Do neurotics become writers? Or do writers become neurotic? Probably the two things reinforce each other. We should of course note a huge number of exceptions; there are many instances of highly talented authors who have kept their emotions strictly under control, and have been as steady and reliable as anyone could ask. Even among free-lance writers for magazines, this is probably true of many; I just don't happen to have met any large number of them. Perhaps the situation is unusually bad among writers for a magazine devoted to liberal intellectuals, both among its readers and its contributors.

An editor should be like the conductor of a symphony orchestra, trying to get the best performance he can out of each player; but at least in the three decades beginning with the 1920's, this was hard to do among the writers for *The New Republic.* It was like trying to conduct an orchestra some of whose members are disinclined to play at all, while others want to perform special compositions of their own, or to make discordant noises that are the equivalent of a Bronx cheer.

People are forever complaining that liberals don't stand together in a united front, that they don't sink their individual differences for the common good. But it is not in the nature of the liberal to stand shoulder to shoulder with anybody. He insists on acting in the light of conditions as he himself sees them; liberal organizations, like those of the radicals, are endlessly splintering into groups sometimes so small that they seem to consist of a single individual. This malaise is incurable, which may be a good thing.

Like every editor, I soon discovered that the more distinguished a man is, the less he is likely to complain of slight changes in his text for the sake of readability—always provided his meaning is not altered. John Dewey, as I have said, never once complained during the years that I virtually rewrote his articles; on the other hand, a distinguished physicist of Columbia University, whose manuscript had needed a good deal of correction for grammar and clarity, went into a tantrum and demanded that his original text be restored even though we were only minutes away from the press deadline.

In two cases, old friends of mine came to me with books they wanted serialized in our pages, and when the editors collectively voted No, they took this as a personal decision on my part; it was years before they would again have anything to do with me. Perhaps my star case was that of a well-known professor of English at Columbia who in 1956 published a book with an insulting reference to me. When I protested mildly, he explained why he was sure I was no good. "In 1946 you cut the length of a book review of mine drastically."

Another man who is now a respected, elderly, literary critic, told me sternly that I *must* print his article about Shakespeare because Shakespeare was such a great man. We agreed on at least that part of his thesis.

Against the troubles with these prima donnas must be placed the long list of contributors with whom it was a pleasure to work, from first to last. This includes most of the British group, beginning with H. N. Brailsford. It also includes many Americans who were not normally members of our circle, but turned to us when they had some special thing they wanted to say. In the late 1920's Sidney Howard, the brilliant and successful playwright, took time out to write a notable series for us on "Labor Spies"—the secret agents hired by management to infiltrate unions. Vincent Sheean, whose autobiography, *Personal History*, greatly influenced a whole generation of young Americans, generously gave us a comical piece that got endlessly reprinted, about the trouble he had getting an American restaurant to serve a raw apple for dessert. F. Scott Fitzgerald called me up and humbly asked to be allowed to write an obituary about a friend who had died; he turned it in exactly on time, and exactly of the length we had agreed was desirable. Archibald MacLeish was always fully the professional writer, a model contributor. And there were many more. All these people worked for our standard rate of two cents a word, and would probably have worked for nothing if requested; what they wanted was to reach our audience.

I had some interesting experiences with "one-shot" writers—people who have one thing to say, and in all human probability will never have another. These people usually make great difficulties for an editor, whereas the professional writer rarely clings to any one piece of his writing with such tenacious affection. He knows there will be many more pieces from his pen; the one-shot writer, consciously or unconsciously, suspects there will not.

Every editor lives in constant fear of publishing something that has been plagiarized; it is a tribute to the accurate collective memory of every editorial staff that these incidents occur so rarely. For a time, a few long-term convicts in state prisons, with access to a typewriter, used to copy whole books and submit them as their own; I believe one or two of these were actually printed, or came dangerously near to it. Attempts at plagiarism on a lesser scale, of short poems or fiction, are not uncommon, and now and then some editor gets caught.

The New Republic was victimized only once, so far as I recall. As I mentioned earlier, Robert Morss Lovett commuted between the English Department at the University of Chicago and our office, spending a few months at each end of the line. Late one spring, he sent me a delightful little sketch of life in the suburbs, which he said had been written by a girl student of his as a senior paper; he thought it was so good that we should consider it for *The New Republic.* I agreed with him, we paid the author our regular two cents a word, and the piece was published.

Within a few days we knew we were in trouble. Any ten thousand readers of almost any periodical, among them, know everything; it is impossible to print any statement, however recondite or obscure, that some reader doesn't know all about it, and takes pleasure in telling you

if you have made an error. Several people kindly told us that our charming little sketch was taken from a book of fiction, *Mr. and Mrs. Cugat,*
dealing with life in a suburb of Cleveland, Ohio. I alerted Bob Lovett,
and he called in the "author" for an explanation.

Amid tears, she told him her story. She was about to be graduated,
there were a thousand last-minute duties pressing upon her, she owed
Professor Lovett a story, had not an idea in her head, so she had copied
one from a book. She never dreamed it would be seen by any eyes but
his, was aghast when he told her he had sent it to me, could only pray
I would reject it. When she got our check for $30 or $40, she was in
misery, but still had a faint hope that nobody would identify it—a hope
that proved illusory.

Her punishment was severe; she was refused her degree, and expelled, actions which, while none of my business, I have always regretted. It is wicked to lie, certainly, but there is a difference between what
you consider will be a fairly harmless lie to one professor about one piece
of English composition and deliberately trying to sell someone else's
writing to a magazine. I never knew what became of her, but I hope she
recovered from this blow and went on to a successful life. Not, however,
as a free-lance writer.

The curse of every small organization—and every large one, as far
as I know—is office politics, and this problem seems to be incurable,
human nature being what it is. We had our share of it on *The New
Republic* in my time; luckily none of it really serious in outcome. In
retrospect, I can see that I should have kept in closer touch with the
younger members of the staff than I did, probably by going across the
street to a bar with them at 5 P.M. to sit around for a while and talk things
over. With my mild allergy to alcohol, I almost never did; at 5 P.M. I was
either still working, nearly alone in a deserted office, or hurrying home
with a briefcase full of submitted manuscript, to be read overnight.

My troubles as an editor seemed big to me at the time, especially
when I had to dismiss some member of the staff, which always gave me
a sleepless night or two (and was certainly many times worse for the
person fired). But in retrospect, they appear smaller than they did at the
time. Though I always worried over whether the magazine would survive, I didn't really think that if it did, I was likely to lose my job. This
was the exact reverse of the position of most editors of big-circulation
periodicals, who are reasonably sure the magazine will survive, but less
so about their own fate. These magazines are run to earn money, and the
owners expect ever larger circulation and advertising revenues. If either
of these items falters, the advertising and circulation managers always
blame the editor, and in many instances he is promptly decapitated,
professionally speaking. In the commercial world, every editor must
always be prepared for the axe to fall—a fact that explains a great deal
about what these magazines do and do not print.

Chapter 9

THE TERRIBLE THIRTIES

Herbert Croly never paid any attention to the size of *The New Republic*'s annual deficit, which in some of his years got as high as $100,000. I, on the contrary, worried about it all the time, and tried to keep it as low as possible; it fluctuated around $10,000, and in one or two banner years there was none. This was not a mere anxiety neurosis on my part; though it was widely believed that the paper had an irrevocable endowment, this was not true. We lived from year to year on Dorothy Elmhirst's willingness to go on. In fairness to her I should add that in twenty-five years I never heard her express any concern about money; she was only interested in the paper's influence.

One way I kept expenses down was by having a small staff that worked hard. Five editors, or sometimes only four, got out a paper with about 30,000 words a week of editorial matter, while *Time* was producing about the same quantity with, at that time, something like eighty people, including editors, writers, and researchers.

One difference was that we bought a large part of the contents of the magazine from contributors, including some men on salary who, however, took no part in the work of getting out the magazine. Among these, Stark Young wrote regularly for many years on the theater; Otis Ferguson was our movie reviewer, and by general consent one of the two most highly regarded in the country (the other being James Agee). Paul Rosenfeld wrote on music, but rarely, and this was to some extent my fault: every music critic on our magazine and on every other wanted to review New York performances as though for a New York newspaper; I argued that people in Boise, Idaho, did not care whether the Philharmonic had done well or badly last week, they wanted to hear about exciting new composers and trends. I never succeeded in converting anybody.

I inherited as poetry editor Ridgeley Torrence, himself an authentic minor voice in this field. I'm ashamed to say that we did with poetry what nearly all magazines do—used it to fill a hole at the end of a column, and since almost all our articles had to be cut to get them in, gaping holes were infrequent. Once in a long while I tried to compensate by printing an entire page, or two pages, by a single poet, but this was a poor substitute.

For about fifteen years, beginning in 1930, the editorial policy of the paper was made primarily by George Soule and myself. We saw eye to eye on almost every political and economic matter, and when we didn't, it was always possible to come to a viable compromise. George was more completely a believer in planning than I; I was more pragmatic in my approach, but these differences were unimportant compared to the list of subjects on which we agreed. He died in 1970, stilling one of the steadiest, calm voices in analytical journalism.

During most of these years Malcolm Cowley was the literary editor. He has recently stated in an autobiographical fragment published in a magazine that he was farther to the left than either George or I, and the paper was sometimes criticized for what was called "the far Left slant of our book department," but when such criticisms were shown to Malcolm, he was always able to defend the reviewers and what they had said, in terms that then seemed adequate in the light of all the circumstances. He himself often wrote the leading review, and frequently it went to the printer without being edited by anyone else; I can't recall any occasion when I felt I had reason to regret this procedure. With Edmund Wilson and Malcolm both writing for us, as was the case during most of the decade of the 1930's, I felt that we had the two best literary critics in America on our staff, a judgment I see no reason to change today.

Among Malcolm's achievements was the rehabilitation of William Faulkner, when all his books were out of print. Malcolm put together a volume of selections from his works, and wrote a long and thoughtful introduction. Perhaps the tide was ready to turn in Faulkner's favor, but if so, Malcolm helped it materially. Most of the novels went back into print, and three years after the volume of selections appeared, Faulkner won the Nobel Prize.

By the time this happened, Malcolm was no longer on *The New Republic* staff. He had always been a country boy at heart, and some years earlier a lucky windfall in the form of a grant of money enabled him to free himself from the treadmill of a weekly editor and move to Sherman,

Connecticut, where he supported himself by writing, working as a book editor, and lecturing. My opinion of his merits as a critic was reinforced by his two terms as president of the National Institute of Arts and Letters, and his membership in the American Academies of Arts and Letters and of Arts and Sciences. Today his picture of the mood of young American writers in the 1920's, *Exile's Return*, is required reading in the English Departments of scores of colleges, as are some of his other books on both the spiritual and the practical problems of the writer in America.

The fourth important figure in the *New Republic* office in the 1930's and 1940's was Daniel Mebane, the business manager. Passionately interested in public affairs, he would probably have been happier in the editorial department, but he accepted the role in which he had been cast with reasonably good grace. He and I had many conferences in which I struggled to extract from him figures on circulation and advertising revenue, and he tried to probe my mind as to what the paper was planning to say about some current national problem. It is possible that a more hard-driving person might have made us more prosperous, but I doubt it. Our problems were really insoluble. Moreover, such a person might also have tried to influence the character of our editoral policy, which Dan never did. (His own views were almost identical with those the paper expressed.)

The job of copyeditor and proofreader, in which in the early days there had been a good deal of turnover, was held for many years by Betty Huling. She knew little about the job when she was first hired, a fact she concealed until her tenure was secure, but once she had learned the ropes, she was more competent than any of her predecessors. A passionate baseball fan, she was loyal to the Dodgers, then in Brooklyn; when the World Series was on, she brought into the office a little portable radio, and she edited copy and read proof while the games were in progress; I still don't see how she managed to listen and work simultaneously without making mistakes, but she did.

I was not as well organized as Betty, and in the stress of trying to do ten things at once, I was likely to be late in giving her the copy for the upcoming issue; she extracted it from me article by article with unruffled good humor.

The weekly routine of the magazine was much the same as in Croly's day. On Tuesday we had an editorial conference, largely devoted to deciding what contributed articles should be in next week's issue, and during the next four days these were sent to the printer, with the copy from the staff reviewers such as Stark Young and Otis Ferguson. On Friday all of the paper except the section of unsigned editorials was made up into pages, and proofs of these were mailed to the three chief editors at their homes, to be read over the weekend and mailed back to reach the press Monday morning. I also wrote some of the unsigned editorial matter at home and brought it in with me on Monday morning. I thus managed to lay out a seven-day work week for myself, appropriate for a man with a work compulsion. This was especially true since for twenty years, beginning in 1927, I wrote a cable to *The Manchester Guardian* six days a week including Sunday.

The paper had by now advanced its deadline from Tuesday noon to Monday. At nine o'clock that morning George Soule and I had at most four hours in which to write whatever extra material was needed to fill five or six pages of unsigned matter. We conferred for half an hour or less and then both went to work. George wrote in longhand on foolscap; I usually dictated directly to the typewriter, since there would have been little time to transcribe shorthand or material from a dictating machine. George could sit down and instantly begin writing a cogent, thoughtful article that would exactly fill the space allotted for it; he hardly altered a word, and his handwriting was so clear that usually his piece did not even need to be typed. I could also write to an exact space, but I agonized more over my writing than he did. Either of us, if uninterrupted, could produce acceptable copy at the rate of a thousand words an hour.

Quite a number of these unsigned editorials have been reprinted in manuals of college English, with supplementary comments by the editors, and I have read some of these with astonishment. They take an editorial that George or I dashed off in half an hour and show how we had topic sentences, statement of problem, resolution of problem, conclusion, and other things. I can only say that as far as I am concerned all this elaborate planning was totally unconscious. But it is still possible that it existed.

When we felt we could afford the luxury, from time to time, we had another editorial employee. He acted as first reader of manuscript that came in without previous correspondence, "over the transom." He also helped edit material for publication, and saw visitors who came in without an appointment, a large proportion of whom were cranks with elaborate plans for saving the world with monetary or other schemes. This job was held at various times by James Benét, son of William Rose Benét, now a well-known San Francisco journalist; Tom Sancton, who plays a similar role in New Orleans; Hilary Lyons, who finally deserted us to write novels; and Bruce Bliven, Jr., who after a few months was lured away by *The New York Post* with a salary offer we could not meet.

For thirty years I read all the editorial correspondence, which was enormous in proportion to our circulation. As a writer of signed articles I have had an experience that many other men have said they shared, of getting ten times more mail from a piece in *The New Republic* than from a magazine with ten times—or a hundred times—our circulation. We had a selected audience, with a high proportion of intellectuals, a large percentage of them college graduates, who tend to express themselves readily and with ease. We usually received far more letters intended for publication than we could possibly use, and my rule of thumb was to publish as many as possible that disagreed with our position. When any important individual wrote taking us to task, he could *always* count on our publishing his letter.

When we had too many letters, or some that had a useful idea told at impossible length, I summarized them in a department called "From the *New Republic* Mailbag." One would naturally assume that the authors would be furious at such treatment, or would accuse us of inaccuracy, but I can remember no complaints of this sort.

One letter that I summarized was a formal complaint from a group of Industrial Workers of the World, who by now had lost all their prestige and influence, and were an aging group living in the past. Wallace Stegner, the novelist and teacher of creative writing at Stanford, did an article debunking the great hero of the I.W.W., Joe Hill, who had been executed for murder in 1915. The outraged Wobblies set up a picket line on the sidewalk in front of the skyscraper where *The New Republic* had its offices, with signs denouncing the paper and me.

I went down to talk to them, and discovered they hadn't bothered to communicate with us because they were sure we wouldn't give them a hearing in our columns. I said on the contrary that we'd be willing to print twelve hundred words (one page) by them complaining of Steg-ner's article. A week later, they turned in about four thousand words of turgid prose. I summarized it at the length I had previously offered, printed it, and we heard no more about it.

We of course received our proportion of letters from eccentrics or people really mentally disturbed; I should guess that we got more such letters than the big-circulation commercial magazines which did not undertake to deal in ideas. Trying to keep our readers happy, I wrote a vast number of replies to people some of whom probably did not deserve an answer. I learned to identify any letter from a real psychotic, which usually began with great clarity and logic, but got more and more unin-telligible toward the closing pages. I remember one such letter which started by making some telling points against us and ended up by saying, "I could write more if the attendants here would only take these ropes off me." I doubt he was really restrained with ropes, but he thought he was.

One man, who made no bones of the fact that he was in an asylum, complained that the authorities there refused to let him subscribe to *The New Republic* (out of his personal funds), suggesting that this was because of our editorial policy. This hit me where I lived, and I wrote a letter of protest to the director of the institution. He wrote back: "Before you complained to us, Mr. Bliven, you should have consulted your own subscription records. You would have found that this man is a paid-up subscriber for the next forty years. Since this is far more than his life expectancy, we were just trying to keep him from throwing away any more of his money."

While most of the eccentrics who called on us were harmless, a few showed signs of being really dangerous. The switchboard operators were skillful in unobtrusively asking help from a couple of stalwart office handymen, who got the visitor safely out of the building.

One caller who got past everybody into my private office was a middle-aged lady with a thick manuscript clutched firmly against her bosom. Wasting no words, she demanded, "Will you print my article?"

I made the routine reply. "If you'll leave it with us, we'll be glad to read it."

But this would not do. "If I leave it, what's to prevent you from stealing my ideas?" she wanted to know.

"How can I tell whether we want to publish it until I read it?"

"If I let you see it, how do I know you won't steal it?"

I could see that this might go on for hours, and I gently eased her out of the office. To this day, I am haunted by the idea that perhaps she had written a masterpiece.

I remember a letter we received from Henry Miller, offered for publication. Henry had already written *Tropic of Cancer*, and it had been published in Paris, but in those puritanical days it could not be published in the United States or even imported. He was living in southern California, and was broke. In his letter he said that if anybody would send him anything of value, such as nonperishable food, or clothing, he would send them an original painting of his. He made no restrictions as to the value of the merchandise he was to receive, and this worried me enough so that I wrote to ask whether he really meant what he said. He replied that he did, and I published a summary of his letter, in the *New Republic* "Mailbag." I afterward learned that quite a lot of people had accepted his offer, and he received a variety of things—food, corduroy garments, umbrellas, canes, and in one case a dinner jacket. This last he made into a scarecrow, and it survived out of doors in this form for a long time. Those who had sent him some trifle in exchange for a painting got a tremendous bargain; today any work of his brush has a substantial value.

As noted, we received in the mail many unsolicited manuscripts a week—though a tiny fraction of the number coming into the office of any of the big-circulation magazines. The two chief classes were cranks like the ones I have been discussing and ambitious young college instructors, mostly in political science, economics, history, and sociology, trying to attract attention to themselves. The cranks were hopeless, and so were most of the college professors. Either they had a native gift for bad writing, or they had sedulously imitated the bad writing of their superiors; they also tried hard to be scholarly, with footnotes, a review of the literature in the field, and all the other paraphernalia of unreadability. But even when their material was promising, it was hard to make room for it.

Our rate of payment to everybody except staff members was two cents a word, and I can't remember that we ever lost a manuscript because of the small honorarium. The professional free-lance writers, of course, almost never bothered to submit anything to us, unless they knew that for political reasons it had no hope with the magazines that paid high prices, or it had been rejected by everybody else. (Book reviewers got the same rate, and were also allowed to keep the books, which they promptly sold at half the retail price to one of the secondhand-book dealers on lower Fourth Avenue.)

Sinclair Lewis in one of his novels drew a thinly veiled portrait of our office at this time. One of his characters urges another to write an article protesting some public misbehavior, and to submit it to us. You'll find, he said in effect, that they'll accept it, pay you two cents a word, print it almost unchanged—and the evil you are protesting will continue. This last point was not quite true—but close enough to hurt.

The flood of mediocre material that came in over the transom made the occasional gem all the more precious. When William Saroyan began writing short stories, he briefly chose us, inexplicably, to receive his famous treatment of a short story a day—inexplicably because, as he surely should have known, we almost never printed any fiction at all. An upper-form student at Choate School in Wallingford, Connecticut, sent us in a few sketches so good that we broke our rule against stories and printed them, starting John Cheever on his career. Otis Ferguson began writing to us from Puerto Rico when he was about to be mustered out as an enlisted man in the Navy; when he arrived in New York we suggested he try some movie reviews, with historic results.

For a few years we had an annual writing contest each spring for college students, the prize being a summer of employment on the paper at $50 a week. A lot of young people responded eagerly to this invitation, and the winners performed acceptably doing routine editorial jobs until it was time to go back to school—or to start looking in earnest for a permanent position. One candidate sent in material with an irresistible gimmick: He wrote three short articles, parodying with deadly accuracy the writing styles of Malcolm, George, and myself. He spent a summer with us, doing well, and then departed.

Not long afterward, I got a call from him. He was about to get married, and the parents of his fiancée, old New England WASPs, objected to the fact of his being Jewish, and would have nothing to do with the ceremony. Would I be willing to serve as best man? Of course I would, and did; the wedding was performed by, as I remember, a Unitarian minister, in the New York City apartment of a woman friend, who acted as maid of honor. Stanley Edgar Hyman went on to become an outstanding writer and college teacher in the field of literary criticism; his wife, Shirley Jackson, was until her death in 1965 a distinguished novelist and short-story writer. She published hilarious reports of domestic life, like *Life Among the Savages,* and chilling baroque tales, like *We Have Always Lived in the Castle.* Inevitably, her name will always be linked with her horror-laden short story "The Lottery."

The Great Depression was a few months old when I became editor of *The New Republic* in May, 1930. It is, I know, impossible to give anyone who does not remember it any feeling of what the Depression was like. It was in some ways as bad as the world wars; in those we knew we should either win or lose, but in the Depression, nobody knew what would happen. It was like being on a falling elevator when you don't know how far it is to the bottom—or what you will find there.

For several years banks failed in increasing numbers, until by 1932 it was about fifteen every working day; people who thought themselves rich suddenly found they were penniless. There was of course no government guarantee of deposits up to $15,000 as there is today. Salaries and wages were cut, and cut again. Marriages were postponed; for this and other reasons the birth rate declined sharply, leading demographers to understate wildly what the size of the population would be twenty years later.

The school and college enrollment, oddly enough, increased; since there were no jobs, young men and women continued to study longer than they had planned. I heard of a student who was graduated from Dartmouth with honors, but was able to find only one job: the newly erected Empire State Building was almost empty of tenants, and he was hired to go from floor to floor and flush the toilets daily, so that chemicals in the water would not mar the finish.

There were supposed to be about thirteen million out of work, in a population a quarter smaller than it is today. But statistics were far less accurate than now; some economists believe the number may have been as high as twenty million. There was no unemployment compensation, no old-age social security; if you lost your job and ran out of money, you went on county relief—or were helped by the neighbors, as was more likely to be the case. When the Depression was at its worst, many hundreds of cooperatives sprang up all over the country, in which people bartered their goods and services with one another; sometimes they developed their own "script," homemade money.

The great American myth persisted that things were probably better in some other town not far away, and thousands of people in desperation took to the road, piling their children and a minimum of possessions into an old car—a "flivver." They soon discovered that things were just as bad in one place as another, but by now they were committed to the nomad's way of life, so they kept going. The adults would find a few odd jobs here and there, or would beg, in order to get money for gasoline. The gas-station attendants hated these automobile tramps, who often bought nothing at all, but asked to have their radiators filled, their tires checked, and to have news of the road ahead; they nicknamed these itinerants "I.W.W.'s," with no reference to the Industrial Workers of the World, but because all they wanted was free service—"information, wind, and water."

For every victim of the Depression who could afford a car, no matter how old and dilapidated, there were scores who had nothing but the clothes they stood in, yet for various reasons wanted to keep moving. (Sometimes lingering more than a few hours in a town meant getting arrested.) Hobos had always stolen rides on railroads, sometimes getting into unlocked freight cars, sometimes "riding the rods" under passenger cars, a dangerous business. For generations there had been a little of this, the hobos at war with the "railroad bulls" (private police) and the local authorities. Sometimes they got beaten up, or arrested, sometimes a good-natured brakeman would let them ride, or a venal one would ask a bribe of a dollar or two. Now in the Depression, there were suddenly hundreds instead of dozens, an army of itinerants big enough to frighten off the railroad employees and the local police. Most lines, especially in the Southwest, finally gave up, and ordered that the vagrants (many, perhaps most, of whom were honest working men looking for jobs), be allowed to ride.

The farm population was hard hit; in the food shortage of the First World War, land had sold at high prices, much of it on long-term mortgages, and the owners now being no longer able to keep up the payments, it went back to the banks, just as it had done forty years earlier when the mortgage and loan association for which my father worked was wiped out—and the Bliven family prosperity with it. Sometimes there were sheriff's auctions when all the property of a defaulting debtor was put up for sale. Occasionally the neighbors gathered in an ugly mood, and forced the auctioneer to sell everything back to the owner for a trifling sum. But these instances were rare; it was more common for the dispossessed farmer, who might already be an old man, to move to town and try to live on odd jobs, plus official and unofficial charity.

As I have said, the causes of the Depression were not mysterious, and it need not have come as a bolt from the blue, as in fact it did. *The New Republic* had been warning of the danger for years, thanks chiefly to the foresight and economic knowledge of George Soule. One cause was the aftermath of the inflation of the First World War, when not only did agricultural land rise to unreasonable prices, but there was a great increase in factory capacity for consumer and other goods. In the mid-twenties, industrial production increased greatly, but most of the earnings were skimmed off as profits, rents, and interest, not as wages. In a period when factory production was rising 55 percent, hourly wages rose only 2 percent. The share of the national income going to the wealthiest 1 percent increased by one-half. The overspending on industrial capacity is proved by the fact that long-term debt increased three times as fast as the national income.

In the Harding and Coolidge administrations, tariffs were raised, thus making it harder or in some cases impossible for our foreign debtors, whether governments or individuals, to pay us, since in the long run, money can only be transported across international frontiers in the form of goods. In order to keep exports high, we lent our foreign customers the money to buy them, and when the crash came, these debts were uncollectable. Washington and the banks had brought great pressure to bear on weak governments abroad—in Latin America, for example—to force loans on them that they did not need or want, in order to buy American goods that they also did not really need. From 1926 to early 1929 the Federal Reserve Board kept interest rates low and money abundant—over the mild protest, from time to time, of the then Secretary of Commerce, Herbert Hoover, who could see that our seeming prosperity was a very shaky structure.

There were other signs of trouble ahead, if anyone had bothered to look for them, aside from a few Cassandras like *The New Republic*. All through the boom, cotton and the textile trade in general were in trouble. As early as 1925 wholesale prices—always a sensitive barometer—began to drop in other parts of the world. House building in the United States slacked off in the same year, and two years later iron, steel, and automobile production turned downward. Railroads and the coal industry were in trouble.

But the Wall Street speculation went on at a feverish pace reminiscent of the South Sea Bubble, or the great tulip speculation in the Netherlands, centuries earlier. You could buy on a margin of as little as 10 percent; with $10 you could get control of a $100 share, and if it went up ten points, as often happened, you had doubled your money. The proportion of Americans who gambled was never as large as is commonly supposed, but it was substantial. A lot of people with only a few dollars in the bank drew them out, bought shares on margin, and when the crash came in the autumn of 1929 and the brokers called for collateral that they did not have, they were wiped out.

The Depression began when Hoover had been president only about eight months, and was at its deepest when he left office in March, 1933. Thirteen years earlier he had been the Great Humanitarian, the savior of the starving children of Belgium and other countries; he stepped down perhaps the worst-hated man in the country. A lifelong fervent advocate of "rugged individualism," he couldn't bring himself to believe that massive action by the federal government was necessary to keep people from starving. When Congress passed an emergency appropriation of $25 million to the Red Cross, Hoover persuaded that organization not to accept it. To aid farmers he got the railroads to cut the rates on cattle feed, but he would not take parallel action on food for human beings who were also starving.

When Congress voted a bonus of $1.3 billion to veterans of the First World War, to be paid in installments over a period of years, several thousand men, demanding that they get it at once, marched on Washington and began camping in tents and rough huts on the Anacostia Flats, just across the Potomac. After a clash between the Bonus Army and Washington police, in which two of the former were killed, Hoover ordered the U.S. Army to clear out the squatters. General Douglas MacArthur, aided by bright young Colonel Dwight D. Eisenhower, burned the whole place down. It was hardly surprising that homeless men living in old packing cases in makeshift settlements on the edges of cities began to describe their dwelling places as "Hoovervilles."

We reported the miseries of the Depression in *The New Republic*, as much as our limited finances and manpower would permit, at a time when the mass magazines were soft-pedaling the subject on the ground that the sickness was all in our minds and an optimistic attitude would end the troubles shortly. This was a common attitude in the early days; printed signs were displayed on office desks saying, "Whew! That *was* a depression, wasn't it?"—suggesting that whatever it may have been, it was now all over. John D. Rockefeller, Sr., announced that "my son and I are now buying sound common stocks." A consortium of bankers put a man on the floor of the Stock Exchange to buy a large amount of U.S. Steel at a good price. (He was Richard Whitney, who afterward went to Sing Sing prison for misappropriating money entrusted to him.) So many people made fatuous statements about prosperity's being just around the corner that a small book was made of them and sold well at a time when very few other books were selling at all.

The *New Republic* circulation prospered during the hard times. The country was in no mood for gay, amusing trifles; they wanted the hard economic analysis that we gave them, divested of any phony optimism. Some people may also have remembered our warnings, year in and year out, that all was not well with American business. We showed a steady modest increase in circulation up to the beginning of the Second World War, when the increase became noticeably larger. By then, there were few consumer goods for people to spend their money on. There were also thousands of people sitting around for hours in railroad stations and airports, in a mood to buy almost any reading matter they could get their hands on.

In addition to many unsigned editorials about the hard times, and reporting by other men, I got out into the field when I could and told what I saw. I went down to the Bowery, where the unemployed tended to concentrate, and described conditions. Every day there were long lines of badly dressed men standing in line for handouts of one kind or another. One of the longest, in 1930, was waiting to get two or three five-cent tickets good in the Y.M.C.A. cafeteria, where prices were correspondingly low; this was the enterprise of a young woman known only as "Lady Bountiful." I estimated that for a short time her charity was costing her (and, presumably, her friends) thousands of dollars a week. There were other lines in which to stand, including those under religious auspices, where the down-and-outers were a captive audience for long sermons and prayers, before being allowed a meal.

Some of the thousands who thronged the Bowery were of course alcoholics, psychotics, or other types of society's rejects. But thousands more were sober working men who simply could not find jobs. Colonel Robert McCormick, the ineffable owner and editor of *The Chicago Tribune,* kept on insisting that any man who really wanted work could find it, which if true would have meant that many millions of Americans had almost overnight degenerated into failures for no visible reason.

New York had a Municipal Lodging House, which few American cities did. I went there one rainy evening to see, again, many hundreds of homeless men standing patiently in line, who otherwise would have been without shelter. The Lodging House took care of seven thousand men a month, out of thirty thousand applicants; those who were too late to get into line in mid-afternoon begged a nickel from somebody and rode the subway lines all night; some of the guards were complaisant, others threw the men off after a couple of rides, and they had to wait in the station for the next train and hope its crew was more tenderhearted.

At the Lodging House you got a compulsory shower, and a clean nightshirt; your clothes were fumigated while you slept and returned in the morning. You got a good hot meal of stew and bread, a cot in a room with several hundred other men, and breakfast. Nobody was allowed this Elysium more than five nights a month, and if you proved to have as much as $3 on you, this wealth barred the gate. The manager, who was my guide, told me that among his nightly guests were teachers, druggists, lawyers, accountants, and musicians—many of the latter, since the sick society of America was in no mood for music. Old habits of pride dying hard, many men would not ask for help until they were desperate; it was not uncommon for someone to faint from hunger while standing in one of the interminable lines.

The manager proudly showed me an annex he had managed to arrange for several hundred men beyond the Lodging House's capacity. This was a boat tied up at a pier on the East River, not far away. It was used daytimes only, and those lucky enough to be accepted were allowed to sleep between decks on tarpaulins spread on the hard boards. The men were reasonably well protected from the rain. I paraphrase from my report:

> *All of them, my guide explained with a pride which his ingenuity well justified, were "second-night men." They had slept last night in the Lodging House, and therefore had had a bath and a medical inspection not more than twenty-four hours ago.*
>
> *A hundred yards away, in the greasy black waters of the East River, lay one of the biggest and handsomest yachts I had ever laid eyes on. She might well have been J. P. Morgan's* Corsair, *though it was too dark to read her name. It was not too dark, however, to look through the glowing portholes at the busy, happy, and presumably prosperous visitors on board.*
>
> *"That's an ironic contrast," I suggested to the manager. "What do your guests think, looking at that yacht so near, while they sleep on the deck?"*
>
> *"I never heard one mention it," said the manager, and we buttoned up our coats to face the rain.*

Anyone who traveled around the country soon realized that all was not well, if he hadn't already. On a fast train to Chicago, only a handful of travelers occupied the sleeping cars, or used the diner. As we entered every town, we came first to the Hooverville, where idle men puttered around their packing-box homes. In Chicago, in cold October, I saw scores of men huddled on the ground, sleeping under the flimsy protection of the elevated section of Wacker Drive.

I went to Europe on the new German liner, the *Bremen,* first class (my passage was exchanged for advertising, or I could never have afforded such luxury). There were only ten or twelve of us in the first-class dining saloon, meant for several hundred. With Prussian discipline, all the corps of German waiters and busboys were required to be on hand every meal, and they stood in military formation watching us, and making me nervous about my table manners.

As the Depression continued, the economic indices went farther and farther down. The national income was cut in half, from $80 billion to $40 billion, and the index of industrial production went down about the same amount, from 125 to less than 60. The drop in blue-chip stocks during the years from 1929 to 1932 was sensational. American Telephone and Telegraph went down from 304 to 70, General Motors from 72 to 8, New York Central from 256 to less than 9, Radio Corporation of America from 101 to less than 3, United States Steel from 261 to less than 22.

When prices were about at their lowest, in August, 1932, I wrote a wicked article in *The New Republic*. With the aid of a certified public accountant, Bernard J. Reis, I pointed out that for only $5.4 billion, you could buy 100 percent of the common stock of the forty-four leading corporations of America, dominating every field of activity; my article was entitled "Let's Buy America." I named the companies, told how many shares they had outstanding, the price per share, and the total price. For majority control, the government would need to spend only about $2.7 billion. Since the physical assets of these forty-four corporate giants were worth at least $12.5 billion, and their working capital was about $4 billion, the government would be getting an unparalleled bargain. I excluded the railroads from my list, because the Reconstruction Finance Corporation had lent them so much money that the government virtually owned them already.

Nothing came of my suggestion, as I of course knew would be the case. I pointed out that the Supreme Court, then still dominated by a majority of highly conservative old men, would be sure to call the plan unconstitutional. My piece caused a minor journalistic sensation, and that was all. But I have pondered many times since then as to what might have happened if my advice had been followed.

When it became evident that Governor Roosevelt was intending to run for president, we were not enthusiastic about the prospect. We felt the country needed a strong hand at the helm, and doubted whether he possessed this quality. But we did not go as far as Walter Lippmann, who called him, in the most quoted passage Walter ever wrote, "a pleasant man, without any important qualifications for the office, who would like very much to be President."

We should have known better. Roosevelt was already being aided, in Albany, by most of the men who came to be called the Brain (or Brains) Trust. They were from Columbia University, and we regarded them as being members, in varying degrees, of the *New Republic* circle; Among them were Rexford G. Tugwell, Adolph Berle, and Raymond Moley. Rex has never forgiven me for my attitude, remarking more than thirty-five years later, in his book *The Brain Trust* (Viking, 1968), that I was painfully obtuse. If so, I had plenty of company. As Tugwell himself reminds us, among those who were far from enthusiastic about Roosevelt before the Democratic Convention were John Dewey, Paul Douglas, Robert Morss Lovett, and Heywood Broun. Those who felt that a new third party was imperative included Felix Frankfurter, Harold Ickes, Amos Pinchot, and Fred Howe—famous names in the progressive movement in America.

As Tugwell admits, in those days *The New Republic* was more loyal to what afterward became known as the New Deal ideas than was Roosevelt himself. Over the years, in signed contributions and editorials, as I have said, we had discussed almost all of these problems, and possible solutions. Everyone who is old enough remembers that in 1932 Roosevelt campaigned on a promise to try even harder than Hoover to balance the budget and cut federal expenses. He had gone on record as saying that the solution to the farm problem was to dump our surpluses abroad, and that relief for the unemployed is not a federal responsibility—ideas that were of course happily forgotten once he was in the White House.

Just as it is impossible to convey to those who did not live through it any idea of what the Depression was like, it is equally hard to express the feeling of relief that swept through the country when Roosevelt was inaugurated. His buoyant self-confidence, expressed in the famous phrase from his Inaugural, that "the only thing we have to fear is fear itself," was a magic tranquilizer to the country that seemed on the brink of a real catastrophe.

The New Republic of course supported all the measures of the famous Hundred Days, and those that followed—the Works Progress Administration, the Public Works Administration, agricultural relief, the reformation of Wall Street, Social Security, the right of workers to organize and bargain collectively, and a dozen others. But we were never Roosevelt idolators, and I am still being damned to this day for my refusal to join the ranks of the hero-worshipers. I recognized all Roosevelt's enormous contributions; but I declined to close my eyes to his faults. The paper refused to become a propaganda sheet for the New Deal, much to the disgust of Thomas G. Corcoran, "Tommy the Cork," who, with Ben S. Cohen, constituted Roosevelt's invaluable team of handymen for all sorts of odd jobs in Washington.

Within a few months the conservative business community had got over its panic state of mind and had begun the long years of excoriating Roosevelt because he had used the machinery of the federal government to save them from extinction; we answered these right-wing opponents for the next seven years as vigorously as we knew how. But we also criticized the New Deal steadily from beginning to end because it did not go far enough. Roosevelt had become something of a Keynesian, under pressure from people like Tugwell who really understood the British economist (which F.D.R. never did, according to Keynes himself, after a talk with the President). He failed to accept the full implications of the doctrine, and he weakened in its practice from time to time. In 1937, when he thought the country was reasonably prosperous, he cut government spending heavily; the result was a rate of decline in business for a few months sharper even than that of the first days of the Depression. When the right wing began calling Roosevelt a Communist, they began calling *The New Republic* the same thing, on the mistaken assumption that we were heart-and-soul New Dealers. At the same moment the real New Dealers were damning us for our lukewarm attitude.

No historian, to my knowledge, has ever done full justice to the achievements of the relief projects that were started to keep people from starving but resulted in substantial accomplishments. The Federal Emergency Relief Administration, the Civilian Conservation Corps, the National Youth Administration, the WPA and PWA, brought hope into lives that had been only blank despair; they kept alive skills that are our greatest single national asset, and were rapidly deteriorating.

I still get hot under the collar at the thought of the Roosevelt-haters who had not done a day's manual labor in many years, and perhaps never, who complained of the slow pace of the men raking leaves in the parks —on the theory that they ought to work at the speed of football players. The men on relief built thousands of dams and bridges—including Bonneville Dam and New York's Triborough Bridge—as well as post offices, schoolhouses, courthouses. They built 45,000 miles of new roads and repaired 140,000 more. They planted nine million trees, renovated thirty million library books. Their flood-control work in the Tennessee Valley reduced for all time the danger of disastrous floods on the Ohio, Tennessee, and Mississippi rivers.

Painters who had been starving did murals in many hundreds of public buildings; some of them were terrible, some of them were magnificent, the work of men who are rich and famous today. The Writers' Project, on whose national advisory committee I was proud to serve, wrote a set of national guide books some of which are still the best, or perhaps the only, guides to certain regions. The Theater Project gave work to writers, directors, actors, scenic designers, stagehands, and others, and turned up some men of authentic talent. A few of their plays had long runs on Broadway, and they brought touring companies to the camps of the Civilian Conservation Corps, where hundreds of thousands of young men had been taken from despair on the city streets and set to doing useful work in the federal forests and parks. The National Youth Administration gave part-time work to huge numbers of high-school and college students, enabling them to keep on with their education. Any sane society would rejoice at this great outpouring of creative energy and its valuable results; but the rich sneered at it because it smacked of "Socialism," and the middle class, largely from ignorance, was apathetic.

While *The New Republic* always wanted the New Deal to go farther than it did, we tried to tell the story of what was happening, as very few other periodicals were doing. The President once sent me word, by a trusted caller, that he welcomed our critical comments. He was able, he said, to quote it to show his right-wing detractors that he was not a mere tool of the Left as they charged.

During the thirties I continued to visit Washington at frequent intervals, as I had done ever since 1917, to see at first hand what was happening, and to report on what I found, in signed or unsigned editorial material. The Depression, of course, never did really end until it was submerged in the rising tide of orders for war material, first from Great Britain, and then from our own defense agencies.

It has always seemed to me, as I know it has to many others, that the decade of the thirties really was finished when the Second World War began in September, 1939. It had been a terrible decade—the worst depression in history, Mussolini's assault on Ethiopia, the Spanish Civil War, Hitler's seizure of Austria and much of Czechoslovakia, Japan's stepped-up war against a China already plagued by the civil conflict between Chiang Kai-shek and the Communists. What we did not know was that the decade just ahead would be still worse, with the biggest war in history, accompanied by unparalleled human misery and thirty million deaths.

Chapter 10

LIBERALS AND COMMUNISTS

Most Americans are incapable of distinguishing among liberals, Socialists, and Communists. It is not surprising, therefore, that from the very beginning *The New Republic* was damned by the Far Right as being an organ of extreme radicalism. After the Russian Revolution of 1917, the pace and quantity of vituperation were stepped up. The paper was sometimes thrown out of high-school and college libraries, and news dealers were denounced for carrying it (as most of them did not, since we could not afford to print huge quantities of copies, spread them broadcast, and then see most of them come back to us as waste paper). Some people were afraid to be known as subscribers to the paper, and had it sent in the name of some relative or friend. If they were schoolteachers, as they often were, this was certainly a wise precaution; when witch-hunters invaded the schools one of the standard accusations was that a suspected teacher read the paper (or our friendly rival, *The Nation*).

We fought these false charges vigorously and with some success, when they were out in the open; the problem was the people who never gave us a chance to reply, but quietly boycotted us. When I became editor I had what was practically a form letter that I sent out many times, which said: I am not and never have been a Communist or fellow traveler; I have never knowingly joined a Communist-controlled organization; when Communists have infiltrated an organization of which I was a member, and I have learned of this fact, I have resigned, and have done my best to make this public. (In one case, that of the Descendants of the

American Revolution, I wrote a letter published in *The New York Times*, announcing my resignation and giving the reason.) I pointed out in this form letter that when the paper and the Communists followed the same line on anything, it was because the Communists were temporarily trying to act like liberals, as they repeatedly did. I also mentioned, when it seemed desirable, that the laws of most of the states held that a public false charge of Communist affiliation was libelous *per se*.

For many years there were various organizations in Washington that were engaged in making, and in some cases publicizing, lists of Americans they considered to be "subversive," a loose term that might cover anything from pacifism to stealing government secrets. Chief among half a dozen of these groups were the Federal Bureau of Investigation, and the House Committee on Un-American Activities (which in 1969 changed its name to the House Committee on Internal Security). These groups would accept "information" from anybody and dump it into their files, one of which was supposed to contain a million names. The overwhelming mass of this material was called "unevaluated," which meant that no effort had been made to check it, or to see whether the person sending it in was neurotic, or seeking revenge against a personal enemy. These files were elaborately cross-indexed; the various committees and agencies had salaried staffs who spent countless hours looking at letterheads, press releases, and radical and liberal periodicals. Whenever a name appeared, the fact that it did so was added to the card for the individual in question, so that in the case of some chronic "joiners," the witch-hunters were able to say that there were hundreds of items of information about him in the files, an ominous statistic that had little relation to reality.

The staffs of some of these Washington groups included former Communists who had repented their ways and gone over to the other side. As many people have commented, personalities on the Far Right and Far Left are alike in striking ways, including gullibility, the impulse to believe the worst of anybody on slight grounds, and the ability to discard facts that run counter to a preconceived idea. It must also be noted that these individuals held their good jobs because of their ability to turn up unsavory information about other people; when they ran out of legitimate subjects to expose, there was a powerful temptation to include illegitimate ones.

In my own case, for example, the HUAC files said that I had contributed to *The New Masses*, a Communist magazine, and gave the date. Since I knew this was not true, I went to the Public Library and looked up *The New Masses* for the date given. My "contribution" turned out to be a letter to the editor complaining sharply about an attack on me that had appeared in the magazine a couple of weeks earlier. What can be said of the human decency of the HUAC staff member who read my letter and solemnly recorded in the files, where it still is, the fact that I "contributed" to this magazine?

The records of the Committee soon grew to several fat volumes, and its staff members developed the habit of saying of any individual mentioned in the index that references to him appeared on pages 4613, 4985, 9862, and so on. When I discovered items of this sort about myself I went back to the Public Library to see what on earth they were talking about. I discovered that some of them were things like the "contribution" to *The New Masses,* and some of the rest were my letters of hot complaint, sent to the Committee itself. It never answered these letters—the manners of the staff were as deplorable as you might expect from people of their type—but it did put each of my protests into the record, and then printed the page number in the index as another item in the accumulating pile of evidence that I was a subversive of some sort!

No individual can win against such a policy.

I was also, of course, pilloried by the Far Right individuals who did witch-hunting on their own. The best-known of these was Mrs. Elizabeth Dilling of Chicago, an eccentric elderly lady who used the filing-card system to pile up information about a large number of people. Her book *The Red Network* was at that time the most widely circulated document of its kind. I was in it, with the list of references from the files in Washington—along with Mrs. Roosevelt and many other people who were far from being "subversives."

The witch-hunters did *The New Republic* some harm, though it is impossible to say how much. Some schoolteachers and others in sensitive positions may have been afraid to read the paper, in addition to those mentioned above who used blind addresses. But we appealed strictly to intellectuals, most of whom were Left-leaning anyhow, and very few of them paid much attention to this sort of thing. I myself may have lost some professional lecture engagements among timid women's clubs out across the country, but I never knew of an actual case of this kind. (What would happen would be, of course, that I didn't get invited at all.)

I can remember only one incident when the attitude of the witch-hunters really bothered me. When America entered the Second World War, my son was of military age and wanted to do his part. He was told that the Navy badly needed men who knew something about communications, and since he had worked on *The New Republic, The New York Post,* and *The Manchester Guardian,* he had some of the expertise required. He therefore volunteered, and his name went to Naval Intelligence to be cleared.

In the peaceful days between the two wars, Naval Intelligence had notoriously become a backwater, inhabited by the not-too-bright sons of important people with influence. They checked on Bruce, Jr., and the word came down: not cleared.

The Navy never explains these cases, but I was told on the grapevine (which in Washington is one of the biggest and most luxurious in the world) that my alleged radicalism, and that of *The New Republic*, were, at least to some degree, factors that were involved. I fired in a hot letter of protest to a man I knew slightly, James V. Forrestal, under secretary of the Navy (and later to be our first secretary of defense). Forrestal replied with an apologetic letter; he was a reader of *The New Republic*, and knew where we stood. By now it didn't matter; my son had gone into the Army, where he served throughout the war, rising from private to captain. He came home unscathed, to resume his career as a writer.

A few years later, he married a girl who seemed almost as wonderful to us as she did to him; and a few years later still, we had a grandson who seemed wonderful to all four of us.

I had one perhaps surprising ally in fighting the witch-hunters—J. Edgar Hoover of the F.B.I. Several times over the years when we were under attack I would appeal to him, and he would write me a letter saying that the paper and I were known to him not to be subversive. He was the idol of the Right, and his letters carried great weight.

While I suffered few real hardships from the activities of the witch-hunters, many others were not so lucky. The bumbling investigators, public and private, caught some non-Communists who had been reckless in permitting their names to be used on letterheads or organization lists, without proper investigation. If they were employed in radio (or in later years, television), or the movies, or other occupations where public approval is essential, they lost their jobs, could get no work, and had a hard time. Some of these stories are familiar and need not be repeated here.

The Congressional investigators also, of course, uncovered some real Communists, and these also suffered; some went to jail, some to Mexico, some tried to continue their careers under assumed names (one well-known screenwriter won an Oscar under these circumstances).

From the testimony of Russian and American defectors, we know that at this time there were at least four layers of Communists operating in this country. Nearest the surface were the admitted party members and the fellow travelers who were so closely allied that they might as well have carried cards. How important this group was is open to question; it engaged in public propaganda, usually so naïve and inept that it persuaded no one not already leaning far in the same direction. I shall always remember one of their documents that addressed the farmers of my native Iowa as "peasants," and urged them to cast off their chains—not very persuasive language. Those engaged in the really serious business of the Soviet Union had strict orders to have nothing to do with this group.

Next below them were the people secretly committed to Communism, but very careful never to admit it. These were the ones who formed hundreds of committees and organizations, all with seemingly the most laudable purposes, all with names incorporating acceptable words like "peace," "freedom," and "democracy." They followed the Russian line in international policy, but never admitted that was what they were doing. They sucked in thousands of innocent American liberals, some of whom still don't know what they joined.

The next lower level were the underground espionage agents, at the grade alleged against Alger Hiss and (until they recanted) Elizabeth Bentley and Whittaker Chambers. They stole government secrets, and transmitted them to Russian-born agents with all the elaborate machinery of microfilm, invisible ink, secret meetings on street corners, and so on. Just how valuable was the information they were able to transmit is questionable. When Whittaker Chambers turned over to the government the papers he said he received from Alger Hiss, State Department officials testified that they were indeed important, that some of them were in code, which the Russians could now break, and that in some cases they "blew the cover" of agents operating in Europe. But America was an open society (and still is, though to a lesser degree). There is evidence that some foreign spies were astonished at the amount of valuable information available by openly buying a government document or a technical magazine, for a few cents, material which in their own countries would have been closely guarded. In many cases, facts acquired in this way were copied out and sent home, no doubt with reports of the laborious and dangerous efforts with which they had been attained. In the case of Chambers and Hiss, even broad social trends seemed to be considered valuable fruits of espionage, which makes one wonder.

The fourth and deepest layer of all was the spying at the level of Klaus Fuchs, and Ethel and Julius Rosenberg, who really did steal important technical information about the making of the atom bomb. In the case of Fuchs, it is fair to add, British security services were at fault. He was one of a number of English physicists sent over by the British government, and supposedly cleared before they left. It is a fair assumption that this was the group Moscow considered most important; its judgment of the value of the others we shall probably never know.

How well did the agencies supposedly combating the revolutionaries do? Ironically, what were probably the two most important American defectors, Elizabeth Bentley and Whittaker Chambers, both changed sides voluntarily. Miss Bentley was badly shaken by the death of Jacob Golos, an important Russian spy, who died in her apartment. She was also, she afterward said, disillusioned by the rich scale of living of Earl Browder, not yet expelled from the leadership of the party as he was when it decided it should make a 180-degree turn in tactics. She went to the F.B.I. with her information, and they didn't believe her, in spite of the fact that a year or two earlier, F.B.I. men had been trailing her.

It took her many months to get anybody to listen.

Chambers had even more trouble turning himself in. He began to be disillusioned when friends came back from Russia at the time of the famous Moscow Trials in 1937, and told him what was going on there. He broke with the party the following year, and had many months of agonized hiding, believing they were sure to try to kill him. The Hitler-Stalin Pact of August, 1939, which precipitated the Second World War, was another blow, and when Miss Bentley began to testify, he felt he should no longer keep silent.

For about nine years he tried to get somebody to listen while he told them he had been a member of a Communist spy ring. He told it all to Adolf Berle, assistant secretary of state, who kept copious notes of the interview. A friend of Chambers, the former *Chicago Daily News* correspondent Isaac Don Levine, tried to tell it to Loy Henderson of the State Department, to Senator Warren Austin, and to Martin Dies, a Representative from Texas who was then head of HUAC. Levine and Chambers told the story to William Bullitt, American ambassador to France, and to Walter Winchell, newspaper columnist and radio broadcaster. Chambers told it to a reporter on *The Washington Daily News*, Will Allen, who took it in turn to the State Department, where they convinced him Chambers was a harmless nut.

Igor Gouzenko, the clerk in the Russian Embassy in Ottawa who defected in 1945, had the same problem. With the Russian secret police close on his trail, seeking to kill him and recover the documents he had abstracted from the files, he had a desperate time convincing the Canadian authorities that his defection and his peril were both real.

There were several reasons for the remarkable apathy of American officials during this period. From 1941 to 1945 Russia was an ally in the Second World War, and the U.S. Government did not want to take any action that would imperil relations with her. President Roosevelt was of a buoyant, optimistic nature, and refused to take spy stories seriously, and the people below him in government took their cue from him. President Truman, who made the disastrous comment that the investigation of Hiss was only "a Red herring," thought the action was a reflection on the security organization of President Roosevelt—and his own. American liberals had been conditioned to dislike and oppose all witch-hunting, which was so often, as I have indicated, merely a cloak for ultraconservatives seeking to prevent the righting of undoubted wrongs. And finally, the notion of cloak-and-dagger spies who could do any real harm was inconsistent with the American character, of which President Roosevelt was a good exemplar.

The record of the House Un-American Activities Committee over the years is a poor one, considering the very large amounts of money and man-hours it expended. The conspicuous exception is the work of Representative Richard Nixon in ferreting out the facts about Alger Hiss. When Whittaker Chambers at long last produced some of the State Department documents that Hiss had stolen and handed to him for transmission—part of them concealed in a hollowed-out pumpkin on his farm—Nixon was on a ship bound for a Central American vacation; he flew back to Washington and acted with great vigor and resourcefulness at a time when the Department of Justice seemed to be doing all it could to aid Hiss and injure Chambers.

The record of the F.B.I. in these years is far too long and complex to tell here. When it was finally alerted to the seriousness of the Chambers allegations, it did a very good job indeed in helping to run down the 1928 Woodstock typewriter on which many of the stolen documents had been copied, and in proving in many other instances that Chambers had told the truth and Hiss had not, about the story of their past relationship. A few years later, the F.B.I. also did well in infiltrating the highest levels of the American Communist Party; some secret agents had been given responsible positions in the organization, so that the party morale was shattered when they turned up in court as witnesses.

For many years, attempts were made to infiltrate *The New Republic,* and to influence our policy, by members of the second of the four groups I have described above—American Communists posing as liberals. Very few of them were ever publicly named as party members or collaborators. I remember only two who, years later, were so identified. Both of them tried to sell articles to the paper, but wrote so badly, and filled their material with such slavish obedience to the party line, that I rejected it out of hand.

We were saved, in large part, by the fact that our organization was so small. George Soule and I wrote nearly all the unsigned material in the paper for many years, until the great expansion at the end of 1946, of which I speak elsewhere. *Time,* with its large staff, had a strong Communist cell which fought hard to influence its editorial policy. This was also true of many other magazines and daily newspapers all over the country, during the 1930's and 1940's.

The *New Republic* office was organized into a union by the Book and Magazine Guild, which long afterward was shown to have been dominated by Communists. The paper of course had been strongly prolabor all its life, and couldn't very well have opposed the unionization even if we had wished to, which we didn't. As I have reported, some time later, as part of a deal among the left-wing unions, we were handed over to the American Newspaper Guild, also at that time Communist-dominated. We never learned why this was done, and were not even notified of it until it was over. The Guild never made any overt attempt to influence our editorial policy.

The Communists exerted a power in trade-union groups out of all proportion to their numbers, as they did in hundreds of other organizations. One of their tactics was to keep a meeting dragging on far into the night, until their opponents were tired out and went home. But they also advocated many actions which had nothing to do with radical policy one way or the other, but were just common sense. For reasons that go deep into individual psychology, the sort of individual likely to become a party member was also likely to be extremely vocal and persuasive. The members of the Communist cell cared intensely about getting their way; the non-Communists, especially at first, usually didn't care much one way or the other.

A few years later, the American Newspaper Guild fought its way free of the Communist domination, at the national and local level—a historic struggle that has never properly been told. The new leaders drove as hard a bargain with us on salaries as the old ones had, and were difficult to deal with, but we welcomed the change.

We had a union-shop contract; when a vacancy occurred in our small organization, which was rare, we notified the union, and they offered us a candidate, or several of them if the first did not satisfy us. If they had no properly qualified individual, as frequently happened, we could find our own prospective employee; if he proved satisfactory and was given a permanent place, he was then required to join the union within a specified length of time.

In the days when the Communists were going strong in the Guild, they usually had a good candidate for every job available. He was highly competent, he did not bargain much about salary, and he worked harder than the average staff member. Apparently the party attached some value to having its members in our office, even on the business side.

In the period of our great expansion, when Henry Wallace was brought in for a short time as the nominal editor, several people were added to the editorial staff who in retrospect give evidence of having been planted by the party; but I had no solid proof, then or now, that this was true. Only one person ever admitted that she was a Communist. Mr. Wallace's private secretary, apparently in an Elizabeth Bentley mood, announced one day that she was a Communist, and resigned. She did not admit that she had been planted by the party, she had done no harm that I am aware of, and we let her go.

If I sound at this point like something of a Red-baiter myself, I am. In all revolutionists in the past century or more, there has been a spark of idealism. At least in the early stages, theirs is a selfless activity; they are not seeking personal advancement, but an improvement in the lot of their fellow men. When I was a young man, the utopian Socialists of the period, people like Eugene Debs, G. B. Shaw, and H. G. Wells, proudly proclaimed their allegiance, preached their doctrine to all who would listen, and if they themselves were penalized socially or in their careers, bore the consequences without complaint.

Yet in the American Communist movement of the 1920's and 1930's, there were thousands of people who swam through seas of lies, pretending to be what they were not. I could respect the attitude of the open party members, even though I disagreed with them and thought them hopelessly naïve. But what could be said for these bright, articulate young middle-class people who entered a conspiracy of silence about what must have been the central fact of their lives? They were in no danger of being penalized to any degree that was compatible with the moral degradation of their course of conduct.

I got a clue of sorts to the motivation of many of these people in the mid-1930's, when *Redbook* magazine asked me to write an article on the psychology of the American radical. It happened that I knew one or two psychiatrists who had had a number of Communists for patients. (This would have been impossible in Soviet Russia, where psychiatry, and especially the teachings of Freud, were anathema.) Under the promise that I would not quote them by name, these psychiatrists talked to me at length about the radicals who had sought their help—of course, without revealing their identities. They helped to explain what had been something of a mystery to me.

On a trip to Russia, I had noticed that a number of the top leaders of the government (though not all, certainly) had personalities similar to those of the American pioneers who had opened the West. They were extroverts, doers rather than talkers, little interested in theories of government and very much interested in big projects like building canals, hydroelectric installations, railroads, and factories. But in America the men I knew or had good reason to suspect to be Communists were an entirely different type: they were introverted, Hamlet-like characters, more given to talk than to accomplishment.

The answer, of course, is that in Russia the road to success lay through the Communist Party, but in America it lay through embracing the underlying assumptions of capitalism. The careerist makes terms with the form of society in which he finds himself.

The psychiatrists I talked to drew a picture for me of a typical American Communist as a person who for one reason or another felt rejected by his peer group. They were unattractive physically, or had been unpopular in their youth, poor at athletics, unsuccessful with the opposite sex. Often they compensated by being brilliant at their studies, which only earned them the epithet of "greasy grinds." This was just the type of person who welcomes entrance into a group which supplies all the answers for him, gives him a powerful sense of belonging—especially if it is secret—and makes him feel that even if he cannot be a success individually, he is on the side of ultimate success—"the wave of the future."

We must also not forget what most people today are too young to remember, that in the early 1930's capitalist society seemed to be visibly collapsing before our eyes. People were going hungry, ill-shod and ill-clad, while warehouses were bursting with unsalable food, shoes, and clothing. If you had money, you did not dare put it into a bank, which might close its doors five minutes later. Until Roosevelt took control, it seemed clear that the government in Washington did not know what to do, or whether there was anything it could do. Many people turned to Communism in sheer desperation. What surprises me is not how many did so, but how few, not that there were food riots, but that so many people quietly accepted the misery of their lot.

Edmund Wilson, the brilliant literary critic, was at that time writing rather regularly for *The New Republic,* and sometimes working on salary in the office. Like so many other literary men of his time, he was attracted by the idealistic aspects of Socialism—"from each according to his ability, to each according to his need." He covered for the paper some Communist-inspired riots in New York City, and came back very much disillusioned by the personalities of the party members he saw there, who seemed to him neurotic individuals who incited the police to beat them up, in pursuance of an ill-advised policy. In January, 1931, he wrote a famous article in the paper, "An Appeal to Progressives," whose theme was "Let's take Communism away from the Communists." He argued that the ideas were better than the people who held them, and that more responsible and reliable individuals ought to take over. His article was endlessly quoted against us by the witch-hunters, even though it was only one of a series on the American dilemma, had been preceded by an editorial note explaining that this was the case, and was followed in the next issue by an article by George Soule which in large degree answered and repudiated Wilson's impractical suggestion.

Wilson, whose energy in pursuit of an idea has always been extraordinary, taught himself Russian, and went to the Soviet Union to see for himself how the ideas there were working. After nearly dying of typhoid in a hospital badly administered by American standards, he came away permanently disillusioned.

In the early years of the 1930's, when Stalin was busily betraying all the ideals of the Revolution that had been made primarily by Lenin and Trotsky, George Soule and I were unforgivably slow to realize what was happening. I can explain our attitude, but I cannot in retrospect condone it. One reason has been mentioned earlier in this book. From the moment the Revolution began in 1917, the American conservatives began exaggerating its faults so unreasonably that no individual with any common sense could accept what they said. As liberals, we were conditioned like Pavlov's dogs to reject attacks on the Soviet Union as being probably false and certainly exaggerated. Moreover, the propaganda machinery of

Stalin's government was surely the best in the world at that time. The horrors that were going on inside the country were effectively concealed, and the successes of the government (and there were some) were portrayed in bright colors. Thousands of tourists, of whom I was one, entered Russia at the very time Stalin was starving millions of peasants to death for resisting his plans for the nationalization of their land; not one hint of what was going on was permitted to leak out. Few of us spoke Russian, and those who did were in almost all cases kept very carefully from any contact with Russians except reliable party members.

In the mid-1930's plenty of complaints were made about what Stalin was doing, in addition to the ceaseless barrage from the Far Right; but most of them came from Trotskyites. I had nothing in particular against this group, in general, but it was obviously to their interest to paint the worst possible picture of what was happening. They did so in the same language as the Stalinists, and I found them no more convincing.

For reasons some of which I have already stated, I had a poor opinion of the American Communist Party. It truckled abjectly to Moscow, defending what was done in Russia with elaborate rationalizations, and changing its policy at a moment's notice whenever necessary to keep up with the constant shifts in Stalin's line.

Whittaker Chambers, in his book *Witness* (Random House, 1950), describes a typical incident of this sort. In 1929 Jay Lovestone was head of the party in America (he was soon deposed). At that time Nikolai Bukharin was contesting with Stalin for power in Russia, and Lovestone guessed that Bukharin would win. One night when Robert Minor, the ex-cartoonist, was in charge of *The Daily Worker*, he sent down to the composing room a long article lauding Bukharin, excoriating Stalin, and headed, in effect, "Lovestone Backs Bukharin." Just as the form was about to be locked up, Minor ran into the composing room; he had just received word that Stalin was winning, after all. He hastily changed the head to read, substantially, "Lovestone Denounces Bukharin," and then went through the story which was in type, changing it at every point to mean the exact opposite of what it had first said.

The greatest example of these sudden shifts was, of course, the Hitler-Stalin Pact of August, 1939. Up to that moment, anti-Fascism had been the cornerstone of Communist policy; the sudden, complete reversal of attitude would have been comical if it had not been part of such a tragedy. I believe a large number of fellow travelers "got off the train" at this time. Unfortunately for them, there was no mechanism by which they could publicly announce that they had recanted.

The attitude of the party toward *The New Republic* varied in accordance with the changes in the official line. In the 1930's, Stalin decided for a time to have a "United Front." Communists were to act like good progressives, and to stop their endless excoriation of liberals, whom they had been calling "Social Fascists." When the United Front was discarded, the party members went back happily to throwing mud at us.

By the end of 1941, the United States and Russia found themselves Allies against the Axis Powers: Germany, Japan, and Italy. Until the conflict was ended, and the Cold War took its place, there was pressure from the U.S. government, none the less strong because it was rarely openly expressed, on the media of communication not to quarrel with an ally. (Chambers says that the State Department actually forced an American publisher of Trotsky's life of Lenin to withdraw the book from circulation after the reviewers' copies had been sent out.)

In my own case, the Communists sniped at me for years except during the periods mentioned above, when they were under orders not to do so. I angered them most, I assume, in March, 1938, when I published a signed article in the paper in the form of an open letter to Stalin, criticizing him as severely as I could in the light of what we then knew, for the Moscow treason trials in which he slaughtered all the Old Bolsheviks who, in his paranoid imagination, might endanger his rule. Stalin had just issued a public call for a conference of all the non-Fascist powers, to consider ways of dealing with the menace of the Axis. I pointed out that the Moscow trials were having a bad effect on world public opinion, which in turn could help or hinder such a conference as he had in mind:

> The list of well known persons [found guilty and executed] is a staggering one, embracing a former premier, top-ranking commissars, presidents and other high officials of individual Soviet republics, foreign ambassadors and editors of chief newspapers. It must now be true that at least 90 percent of the best known men who made the Revolution have lost their places or both places and lives. . . .
>
> The series of trials in the Soviet Union has had unhappy repercussions in many parts of the world. They have made Germany, Japan and Italy more aggressive. It is not at all impossible that the internal difficulties of the USSR, have helped create the decision for Japan to attack China in 1937 rather than at a later time. They did great harm to the People's Front in France, which for this and other reasons was momentarily impotent at a major turning point in European history, when Hitler went into Austria. They have helped to alienate important and hitherto friendly sections of public opinion in the United States, including the President. Perhaps most serious of all, they upheld the hand of the anti-Soviet faction in the British government. In all human probability, they strongly influenced Chamberlain in his move toward rapprochement with Germany and Italy, which in turn gave Hitler his chance to seize Austria, and gave Hitler and Mussolini their chance to make a last desperate assault on the Loyalist Government of Spain. At a critical moment in the history of modern Europe, it was said throughout the

*world and believed by many that Soviet Russia had turned to a bloody-
handed dictatorship, that a great part of her population was in a state
of potential revolt, that Russia no longer counted, and that a new orien-
tation of the Powers must be found from which she should be excluded.
These statements may all have been false, but a false statement on which
people act may be as disastrous as a true one.*

I then went on to make a series of suggestions to Stalin: that he
change the method of conducting treason trials to one more acceptable
to Western opinion, that he make public all the evidence on which the
accusations were based, that he abolish the death sentence, and that he
offer an amnesty to all opponents who had not committed any crime
under the normal civil code. Finally, I suggested cheerfully that Stalin
himself should withdraw from public life completely for a stipulated
period of a year or eighteen months.

He never answered my letter.

Today, of course, we know far more than I did in 1938 about Stalin's
crimes—thanks largely to Khrushchev's monumental speech in 1956 in
which he recited in great detail what had been done. All the dictator's
old comrades—except Trotsky, who was out of his reach—had been
arrested and charged with treason. Months were spent forcing them to
memorize the wholly false details of their activities, making sure that
they would not slip up, and that one man's story would agree with those
of his fellows. But it did not always work. A victim testified that he had
met Trotsky in a Copenhagen hotel that did not exist at the time specified; another said he had met a fellow conspirator at an airfield when
records showed this was physically impossible. Trotsky, from his exile
in Mexico, kept denying all the charges against him, and offering documentary evidence that he could not have conspired on the dates and in
the places mentioned—until one of Stalin's assassins silenced him with
a pickaxe.

Much of Stalin's "testimony" was assembled for him by the head of
the secret police, G. G. Yagoda. When he had done his work, Stalin had
him arrested and shot; the testimony against him was created by N.
Yezhov, who was in turn liquidated. The total number of victims runs
into thousands; Trotsky made a profound observation when he said Stalin
was like a man who tries to slake his thirst with salt water. The number
of army officers executed alone is estimated as high as 20,000.

Why did all these innocent men testify in court that they were
indeed traitors to the Revolution to which they had devoted their lives,
and especially when they knew they were to be killed in any case?
Elaborate explanations have been offered, some of them probably too
elaborate. The method was simple: every variety of torture was used,
with the threat that if the victim did not play his part correctly in court

it would be renewed when he was back in his cell. In addition, the families of all these poor wretches were held as hostages; the victims doubtless hoped that if they were cooperative, their wives and children might be spared. (Often they were not.) One or two men did in fact have the courage to say before they were killed that their confessions had all been lies.

Today, with Stalin long in his grave, you must be very blind indeed not to see that Soviet Russia, in its foreign policy, is acting just as imperialist Russia has done for centuries. The almost-faceless men in the Kremlin are holding their satellite states by plain military power, with Czechoslovakia in 1968 the most conspicuous example. No group of nations in the world would be more abhorrent to Lenin, if he were still alive, than the Arab countries, with which Moscow has cemented an alliance based on the most materialistic possible considerations—including making the Mediterranean almost a Russian lake, satisfying a dream of the Tsars for centuries.

It was after the end of the Second World War that *The New Republic* had its complete, full-face confrontation with the American Communists on a big scale—a story that needs a chapter to itself.

Chapter 11

MEMOIRS OF A NAME-DROPPER

All newspapermen seem, to people outside the trade, to be name-droppers. In some cases the charge is true; but in others it comes from a misunderstanding. As I have said, it is the business of a reporter to know important people well enough to be on confidential terms with them. Everybody talks about his friends; it is only when these are high-placed that mentioning them brings the accusation of snobbery.

In 1922, when I was still with *The Globe*, Croly asked me to write a series of articles about Boston for *The New Republic*, stressing the cultural changes brought about by successive waves of immigration. I managed to do them without using any *Globe* time, by spending weekends in Boston, and doing my writing at home in the evenings. Several Bostonians were helpful to me. One was Samuel Eliot Morison, then only thirty-five, and just at the beginning of his long career as a historian. Another was the retired president of Harvard, Charles W. Eliot. Though he was eighty-eight, he showed none of the impairments of old age. I was startled by the frankness with which he spoke (of course, off the record), of his dissatisfaction with A. Lawrence Lowell, who had succeeded him as president of Harvard thirteen years earlier.

But by far my most useful informant was Professor Felix Frankfurter of Harvard Law School, whose home became my headquarters when in Boston, then and for many years. Warm, outgoing, and gregarious, he seemed to live always in a state of intense intellectual excitement, sending out showers of ideas in all directions. He had been a friend of

Croly and *The New Republic* from the beginning; year after year he wrote for the paper, sometimes signed articles but usually unsigned editorials. From 1923 until he went on the Supreme Court in 1939, it was a rare week in which I did not get at least one communication from him, frequently handwritten, praising or attacking things we had published, suggesting topics for articles, and, in many cases, nominating possible writers.

We had no one on the staff trained in the law, and Frankfurter sometimes objected to our layman's editorial comments on legal matters, and especially Supreme Court decisions. Since these were handed down on Monday, and the paper went to press a few hours later, there wasn't much time for consultation. Finally he suggested that we ask a bright young lawyer in New York to write a short unsigned editorial when there was an important decision and have it dictated over the telephone to a secretary in our office, and for some years this was done. Frankfurter as usual proved a good judge of ability; the young man he nominated, James M. Landis, went on to become head of the Securities and Exchange Commission and for almost a decade Dean of the Harvard Law School.

When Frankfurter himself went to the Supreme Court, where he served for twenty-three years, many left-of-center admirers were surprised and hurt that he often voted with the conservatives, but I was not among them. I knew that he had never been, or pretended to be, an orthodox liberal. Born in Vienna, he had come to this country as a boy, and as so often happens in such cases he had an abiding love for America, and a knowledge and respect for its institutions, that far exceeded those of most of the native-born stereotyped progressives, who on many occasions cheerfully proposed to ignore precedents and laws when these got in their way. Mr. Justice Frankfurter was, as he had always been, a conservative in the best meaning of the word, one who wishes to conserve the institutions that have stood the test of time. When he fought for Sacco and Vanzetti it was only partly because he was concerned for the lives of these men, but also because he felt the American system had been misused in condemning them to death.

My friendship with Frankfurter brought me into contact with other people as remarkable as he. One of them was Judge Learned Hand, who, about the time I first knew him, was being advanced from the Federal District Court in New York to the Federal Circuit Court of Appeals. Shy and quiet in conversation, he was in his writings one of the great prose stylists of his day, who expressed in magnificent phrases his dedication to the maintenance of individual freedom in an increasingly complex and power-ridden society. Both his decisions on the bench and his other papers stated with great eloquence the ideals of a devoted libertarian. Only a complication of politics kept him off the Supreme Court.

Judge Hand was blessed with a wife as remarkable in her way as he was in his. I served with her for many years on the board of directors of the Foreign Policy Association, where her native common-sense and devotion to the ideals of international understanding were of great value.

Through Frankfurter I came to know another great man, Mr. Justice Brandeis of the Supreme Court; for many years I capped my frequent visits to Washington with a quiet, late-afternoon cup of tea in his old-fashioned apartment. He let me do most of the talking, and I reported the gossip of the capital I had picked up in the previous few hours; if he already knew it, he never said so. For most of this time he was still on the Court (he retired in 1939 at eighty-three and died two years later), and was working hard, but he never seemed pressed for time, and answered my questions on many current topics with quiet thoughtfulness.

When Frankfurter himself came to the Court, taking Mr. Justice Brandeis's place, I called on him during my Washington visits; after he went to the bench, his torrent of letters on public matters dwindled, naturally, to a very thin trickle indeed. I rarely saw any more his universally loved wife, Marion, whose hospitality helped make their Cambridge home so inviting; I was usually trying to get a six o'clock train back to New York, and I called on the Justice in the late afternoon in his office in the handsome new Supreme Court building.

As always, he seemed almost jumping out of his skin with excitement as he talked to me on a dozen subjects in half an hour. Never, of course, did these include matters before the Court; he was as punctilious about this as Mr. Justice Brandeis had been. During the last few years of his life, when both of us were ill, and three thousand miles apart, our communications lessened, but not my admiration and affection.

Mrs. Eleanor Roosevelt was on the board of directors of the Foreign Policy Association for a few years while her husband was still governor of New York, and I had a chance to know, earlier than most people, the woman who finally became the almost universally admired First Lady of the World. In the late 1920's she was still rather shy and quiet, and said little at the monthly dinners at which the Association's course was plotted.

Almost all the members of the F.P.A. Board except me were rich, and they all knew wealthy men in Wall Street. The organization had a large annual deficit, and one of the jobs of the directors was to go and beg for donations. I declined to do this, on the ground that I could not ask a favor of a man whom I might want to attack the next week in *The New Republic*, and the F.P.A. staff saw my point.

None of the directors liked the job; our dinner meetings usually opened by having the chairman, James G. McDonald, read off a list of two or three wealthy men whom somebody should tackle. Usually there would be a long, embarrassed pause, and then Mrs. Roosevelt would say quietly, "I'll do it." She was usually successful, too.

She left the F.P.A. Board and I saw her much less frequently from then on. Our meetings were usually in her big, cluttered apartment at 29 Washington Square West, and I was usually a member of a delegation from some worthy cause, asking her to sponsor us in one way or another. I can't remember that she ever refused.

On one occasion, a few years after the end of the Second World War, I got roped into making a talk on current world affairs for some group whose name I have forgotten. I spoke in the auditorium of the old Hunter College, on Park Avenue in the Sixties, and as I talked to two or three hundred people I saw with mild astonishment that Mrs. Roosevelt was in my audience, sitting in an aisle seat in the back of the room. In the question period, somebody asked me about a New Deal policy and I responded, "There is someone in the audience who is more competent than I to comment. Would Mrs. Roosevelt care to reply?"

Few people had known she was there, and there was a splatter of applause as she stood up. She walked down to the front of the room and spoke from the floor, explaining skillfully and persuasively for four or five minutes what her husband's administration had been trying to do, and how it had succeeded.

One of the most brilliant talkers and writers of his generation was Harold Laski, whom I knew from 1923 until his death in 1950. He was the author of a long series of books on political science, mostly from a left-wing position, that are now almost forgotten; but no one who saw him in action could ever forget the impression he made. A small, round-headed man, with short black hair like a Japanese doll, he had a round face and round eyes; he always looked ten or fifteen years younger than he was. Any conversation in which he was engaged was a monologue, but so fascinating that few ever wanted to interrupt the flow of language. He was one of a very few men whom I have known—Chief Justice Charles Evans Hughes was another—who spoke in perfect sentences; Laski's casual conversation could have been recorded and printed with hardly a change of a syllable.

He was best known for his long membership in the British Labor Party, of which he was chairman for a year just after the Second World War, not because he had fought his way to the top but because the job was rotated among members of the party's Executive Committee and it was his turn. For thirty years he was on the faculty of the London School of Economics, where he greatly influenced hundreds of young men and women from many countries, but especially Great Britain and the United States. I remember visiting him in his home in London just after the Second World War, and seeing him spend an evening talking to a room packed with young people sitting on the floor and hanging on his every word.

Harold was cruelly mistreated by the popular press of both England and America, on the ground that he was a Communist. He was not; he was a Marxist of sorts, but he was for almost a decade one of the directors of the Fabian Society, which advocated evolutionary Socialism. While he lectured for a few months in the Moscow Institute of Soviet Law, he did so only during the temporary thaw of the United Front period in the mid-thirties; in general, the Russians hated the Socialists about as much as they did the capitalists, and shot a lot of them. Harold had the bad luck to be teaching at Harvard when the great postwar scare about Russia was in progress in the United States, in 1919-20, and there was an uproar in the popular newspapers over this fact.

He had a vivid imagination, which got him into some trouble because he remembered his influence on public affairs as being greater than in fact had been the case. He told me once that it was he who had persuaded Winston Churchill to put General Orde Wingate in charge of guerrilla warfare against the Japanese in Burma in the Second World War, suggesting that Churchill had never heard of Wingate. This is hard to believe; Wingate had already made himself famous by his operations against the Arabs before the war, and by beating the Italians in Ethiopia. Harold's friends learned to listen tolerantly to his stories, and not to repeat them.

While he had plenty of self-esteem (which the psychiatrists tell us is only the reverse image of an inferiority complex), Harold had enough sense of humor to laugh at himself on occasion. He once told me of being a guest of honor at the University of Edinburgh, in the home of the Provost (President). The Provost had an aged and loquacious parrot, who made so much noise that his cage was removed to the hall while Harold carried on one of his interminable monologues in the drawing room. Someone passing through the hall claimed that he heard the parrot muttering to himself, "It's the wireless! It's the wireless!" on the theory that only the radio could go on and on as Harold was doing.

My job of course threw me into contact with the outstanding progressives in Congress, and I knew them all, in varying degrees of intimacy. One of my favorites was the rough-and-ready old frontiersman, Senator William E. Borah of Idaho. He and I disagreed on some things, but agreed on others. He opposed American entry into the League of Nations, and later he fought most of the measures of the New Deal. He favored Prohibition, which I opposed as soon as I had had a good look at it. We agreed on the desirability of recognizing Soviet Russia and on the undesirability of sending U.S. Marines into various Caribbean countries.

Borah had been one of the first to advocate the Washington Conference on Limitation of Armament of 1921-22, a conference which, as I
have reported, produced no permanent reforms in the field of armament.
He also supported the Kellogg-Briand Pact.

This now almost-forgotten bit of international hypocrisy grew out
of an article in *The New Republic*, published five years before I came on
the paper. In 1918, S. O. Levinson, a Chicago businessman, wrote a piece
for Herbert Croly proposing that war should be outlawed as an instrument of national policy. Today we know that no matter how many
documents it signs, no nation will abandon its military strength unless
it feels it is entirely secure in other ways, and that no nation will hesitate
to go to war if it believes its national existence is threatened.

In those innocent days half a century ago Levinson's idea caught fire,
and there was so much support for it that finally in 1928 Frank B.
Kellogg, then American secretary of state, and Aristide Briand, then
French foreign minister, signed the international treaty that is commonly known by their names. The importance of Levinson's article, and
of the agitation he and others had carried on for a decade, in bringing
the treaty into being, were freely acknowledged in official circles.

Kellogg was a hard-boiled veteran official, who had been a U.S.
senator and ambassador to Great Britain, and I strongly doubt whether
he had much faith in the document he signed; but his action was important enough to get him the Nobel Peace Prize a year later, to be followed
by a seat for another five years on the Permanent Court of International
Justice at The Hague, the "World Court."

Borah told me a story of his youthful days in Idaho that seems to me
typical both of the man and of his times. He was district attorney in a
thinly populated county, and one day received word that a lynching
seemed likely in a small town a few miles away. The county had few
peace officers and I believe none was immediately available. Borah did,
however, have access to a railroad engine and a couple of day coaches.
He got an engineer to run this train over to the scene of the trouble, and
en route he pulled down all the window blinds on the cars. When he
arrived, he descended from the train, and walked over to the mob in front
of the local jail, a few hundred yards away. He announced that in the
train he had a company of militia, and that if the crowd did not instantly
disperse, the men had orders to come out and arrest everyone in sight.

The fact that he was bluffing must surely have been discovered in
a few minutes, but the threat lasted long enough to change the mood of
the crowd. There was no lynching.

On one occasion Borah asked me to lunch with him in the Senate
restaurant, and as we were starting our meal, a middle-aged man came
in alone and looked hesitantly about the room. Borah asked me if I would
mind if he joined us, and I of course said I wouldn't. Vice-President

Calvin Coolidge seemed glad not to eat by himself, and promptly took over the conversation. People called him "Silent Cal," but on this day he was more of a monologist. Borah had just been to Panama on a Congressional junket aboard an American warship, and the Vice-President quizzed him about it exactly as though it were a commercial packaged tour that he was thinking of taking. How were the sleeping quarters on the ship? Was the food good? Did the vessel roll much in rough weather?

When he had exhausted this topic he seemed to me to cast about rather desperately for some other. I got the feeling he was essentially a shy man who felt he must hold up his end of the conversation at any cost, and didn't quite know how to do it. At any rate, he turned to the bean soup Borah and I were eating, the Senate restaurant's justly famous specialty. Silent Cal started out to praise it, and went on for what seemed to me an incredibly long time, reporting its virtues. Finally he ran down, Borah turned our conversation to something else, and we proceeded normally through a pleasant meal.

A man I admired greatly was Robert M. La Follette of Wisconsin, who when I first knew him had been in the U.S. Senate for fifteen years. As governor of Wisconsin, "Fighting Bob" had been responsible for an unparalleled amount of liberal legislation—the direct primary, putting state employees under civil service, conservation of natural resources, control of railroad rates, and other reforms which, in combination, were known all over the world as "the Wisconsin idea."

La Follette opposed American entry into the First World War, and suffered for it. Wisconsin, with a heavy population of German origin, felt it was necessary to prove its patriotism; the state legislature formally censured him. He also narrowly escaped being expelled from the U.S. Senate. Like Borah, he also opposed American entry into the League of Nations.

In 1924, the fight over the League was a dead issue, and *The New Republic* supported La Follette when he ran for president as a third-party candidate.

He was short and sturdy, a handsome man, with a heavy head of white hair combed back. He loved to talk; I remember once sitting in his office in Washington during a long Sunday afternoon while we discussed every subject under the sun and I missed train after train back to New York.

I also knew his two sons, Robert, Jr., and Philip. Often dominant fathers have mediocre children, but both the younger La Follettes were men of substance. Robert, Jr., was his father's secretary from 1919 to 1925, and then succeeded him for more than twenty years in the Senate. The younger son, Philip, was governor of Wisconsin from 1931 to 1933 and again from 1935 to 1939.

In the interval between these two periods of service he came to lunch at our office in New York. He was on his way home from a visit to Germany, where like many other people (Charles Lindbergh, for one) he had been tremendously impressed by the seeming dynamism of the Nazi movement; the horrors of that regime were mostly still in the future, and those already existing were carefully concealed from public view. Though a sound American progressive, Philip thought that some of the Nazi techniques might be usefully employed in Wisconsin, and he had in his pocket a sketch of a symbol that might be the eqivalent of the Nazi hooked cross, as well as rough drafts of some possible slogans. Our editorial group did not think much of his ideas, but apparently they worked in Wisconsin—at least, for a while.

One of the most respected of the old progressives was Senator George Norris of Nebraska. Though he is best known as the father of the Tennessee Valley Authority, he had other important achievements to his credit. He was a leader in the fight, in 1910, to break the power of the autocratic Speaker of the House of Representatives; he wrote the Twentieth Amendment to the U.S. Constitution, changing the date on which newly elected presidents are inaugurated, and putting an end to the "lame duck" sessions of Congress in which men voted who had already been repudiated at the polls. He also put through the unicameral legislature in Nebraska, a plan that seems to work well in that state, though it has not been copied by any other.

I remember an occasion in 1939 when I was sitting in his office and he was complaining about the infirmities of old age. I made a silly remark, trying to cheer him up. "After all, Senator," I said, "I am fifty, and you are only seventy-eight. There isn't all that much difference in our ages."

He gave me a quizzical but also profoundly sad look. "Young man," he said, "the difference between fifty and seventy-eight is enormous, incalculable, a gulf between two worlds." When I became seventy-eight, several years ago, I knew what he meant.

Though he began life as a Republican, Norris ignored party lines in the Senate, and was angrily opposed by the conservatives in his state. (Finally he became an independent.) His enemies actually went to the length of finding a man with the same name to run against him in an election, hoping to confuse the voters, but the trick did not work. When he was finally defeated, at eighty-one, I believe it was chiefly because the voters of Nebraska felt that age and infirmities had impaired his usefulness, and wanted to be represented in the Senate by a younger man.

A favorite of mine, and of a great many other people, was Fiorello La Guardia, whom I knew from 1922 until his death in 1947, a personality so vivid that he became the hero of a musical comedy on Broadway. He was the son of an army bandmaster, and spent much of his childhood in Arizona. Fiorello mastered several languages in addition to English and the Italian spoken in his home as a child. He found his facility useful both while serving before the First World War in the U.S. Consular Service in Budapest, Fiume, and Trieste, and while with the American Armed Forces in Italy in 1917. He went to the House of Representatives from New York City in 1916, and again from 1921 to 1933; he teamed up with Senator Norris in sponsoring the famous Norris-La Guardia Act forbidding labor injunctions in the federal courts, by far the most advanced trade-union legislation seen up to that time in the United States. As mayor of New York for three terms, from 1933 to 1945, when he retired from this strenuous office because of impaired health, he did heroic work in cleaning up the raging corruption in the city government. He put through a badly needed new city charter, began a program of slum clearance, and took important steps toward the beautification of the town.

On one occasion Fiorello asked me to run for governor of New York. I would have been more flattered by the invitation were it not for the fact that I was one of fifteen or sixteen men sitting around a big table in the Mayor's office, each of whom was in turn asked to run, and each of whom in turn declined. Fiorello had been elected on a local third-party ticket, composed of reformers from both the major old parties, and in a new election he needed a name to complete a full slate of nominees for offices they had no possible hope of winning.

Somehow, the Mayor got it into his head that I was a storehouse of information about the political leanings of New York liberals, which was not true; I tried to follow international and national affairs, and I gave little attention to the city. Every few months, I would get a call from the Mayor's secretary toward the end of the afternoon; could Fiorello pick me up at my office (by now on East Forty-ninth Street) and take me to the Tavern-on-the-Green in Central Park for a drink? These were lively occasions; the Mayor rode in an official limousine, with a police chauffeur at the wheel and a plain-clothes detective beside him. A police radio talked incessantly, and on the back of the front seat there was a shotgun on a special rack. I felt ignorant about the intricacies of local politics, but I knew how to ask questions, when I had a chance to insert one into the Mayor's ongoing monologue. Perhaps he just wanted a listener outside the circle of his official family. I enjoyed these forays, and was sorry when they came to an end.

A man who was much less well known than he deserved to be was Morris Llewellyn Cooke, by profession a mechanical engineer, who was troubleshooter for many years for Presidents Roosevelt and Truman. Possessed of independent means, he was able to give his full time to national problems, usually without any formal title that would bring him into public view. He wrote, with a little professional help, one of the best government documents ever produced, *Little Waters*, in which he explained the importance of having many small dams far upstream, instead of the massive structures far downstream so dear to the heart of the Army Corps of Engineers. (Though the lakes behind the big dams silt up hopelessly in a few decades, the great monoliths are showy, and impress Congressmen who hold the purse strings.)

As administrator of the Rural Electrification Administration, Cooke brought the blessings of electric power to millions of farmers, eliminating billions of hours of hard manual labor. He did this over the strenuous opposition of most of the private electric companies, which couldn't or wouldn't themselves bring power to the farmer at a cost he could pay, but didn't want the government to step in and fill the gap.

In the early 1940's the United States and Mexico were embroiled in a struggle over oil wells. These were on Mexican soil, but were mostly owned by big American companies. Mexico had nationalized all subsoil mineral and other rights, but she did not have the technical skills or the capital needed to develop the wells. For years the two countries went on making faces at each other, while oil production in Mexico dwindled to almost nothing.

In this impasse President Roosevelt sent Cooke to Mexico, where he solved the problem in a few months. He persuaded the American companies to recognize Mexico's right to nationalize its natural resources —something they had stubbornly refused to do. He told Mexico to let the American companies operate the wells under lease, paying a royalty on each barrel of oil taken from the ground. Magically the angry international dispute faded away.

During the Second World War, Brazil was in serious economic difficulties, a matter of concern to the United States, since she had become one of the Allies in August, 1942. President Roosevelt sent Cooke there as head of an American Technical Mission, and he was mainly responsible for a report suggesting many things that could be done to help the country, especially by speeding up the pace of industrialization. A mountain with enormous quantities of iron ore had recently been discovered, and one of his urgent recommendations was that the steel industry should be greatly expanded.

For many years, Cooke lived in the winter at the Hay-Adams House in Washington, just across Lafayette Park from the White House. He always breakfasted at a big round table in a corner of the hotel dining room, and always with several guests, important people in the current administration, or visiting V.I.P.'s. I stayed at the hotel on my frequent visits to Washington, availed myself of a standing invitation to join the Cookes and their other guests at breakfast, and picked up a lot of information useful to a journalist, much of which subsequently appeared in the pages of *The New Republic.* Cooke died in 1960, and like many others I was astonished to learn he was more than ninety; I should have guessed he was twenty years younger.

In 1925 *The New Republic* needed a new proofreader and makeup man, and I put a small advertisement into our own pages, on the theory that someone who read the paper would probably fit well into the office group. I had half a dozen applicants, who came to see me one by one, I asked the customary questions, and then told each that since there were several of them, the decision would have to be held up for a few days. One of them was a stockily built young man whose impassive face conveyed little emotion; I surmised, correctly as it turned out, that the immobility of his countenance concealed excessive shyness, as it so often does. Tom Matthews seemed to accept the delayed decision cheerfully, as the others had done, but next morning when I arrived at the office, there was a letter from him. (Those were the days when you could mail a letter in the evening and actually get it delivered early next day.) In his autobiography, *Name and Address*, Tom says it was eight pages long, but all I remember is that he told me he was employed by a firm in Wall Street that raised money for colleges, and that he hated his job. In effect, if not in so many words, he pleaded, "Mr. Bliven, for God's sake, get me out of here." I hired him.

Tom worked for us, hard and well, for four years. He says in his book that he let many bad typographical errors get by him, but I don't recall this; ours was always a rather slapdash operation, and he was not the first or the last proofreader to let errors get into the paper. Before very long, under the friendly tutelage of Edmund Wilson, then acting briefly as book-review editor, Tom began contributing reviews to the paper, certainly no worse, and sometimes better, than the average. I remember one of them, reviewing the autobiography of a literate hobo, which began, as I recall, "Jim Tully is so god-damn tough his spit bounces."

What I did not learn (and then not from him), until Tom had been with us for many months, doing hard and grubby routine work uncomplainingly, was that he came from a distinguished and wealthy family. His grandfather had been a United States senator and a member of the Supreme Court. His father was the Episcopal bishop of New Jersey. His mother was a Procter, with large wealth from the Procter & Gamble soap firm. Tom was a graduate of Princeton, had been a Rhodes Scholar, and took honors at New College, Oxford.

A famous murder trial of that time was that of Judd Gray and Ruth Snyder, who had murdered Mrs. Snyder's husband with a window-sash weight, and then tried to set up a foolish alibi for Gray by juggling railroad tickets to prove he was far away. They were found guilty and executed. Tom, like many other people, was fascinated by the case, and wrote a novel about it.

He says in his autobiography that he came up through the ranks until, in 1929, he had become an associate editor, details I had forgotten, though I have no reason to dispute him. In 1929 he left us to go to *Time*, where he again came up through the ranks, being book editor for eight years, assistant managing editor for five years, managing editor for six years, and editor-in-chief for four years; in 1953 he resigned after a disagreement on policy with Henry Luce, and he has lived most of the time since then in England, having fallen in love with the country during his life as a Rhodes Scholar.

About the time he left *The New Republic* his first, pedestrian job there was filled by a pretty nineteen-year-old blonde girl who had de-camped from Bryn Mawr at the end of her junior year, with high aca-demic standing but an acute and growing distaste for undergraduate life. Martha Gellhorn, as she once told me, left college "having proved to them and me that I could manage the place, and not wanting a degree; not wanting any marks or signs and only wanting to work and become a writer." I wasn't smart enough to detect the potential talented author, and after some months she left us amicably to go and be a reporter on *The Albany Times Union*, a lot more fun and adventure than the staid and sober *New Republic*. A few years later she flashed across the literary sky with a book, *The Trouble I've Seen*, a poignant description of hard times in the rural South during the Depression. She went on to several mar-riages, one of them to Ernest Hemingway (and one to Tom Matthews), and a brilliant career as a war correspondent for various magazines, including *Collier's*, and, during the Vietnam War, for *The Manchester Guardian*.

In the twenties the most famous New York literary coterie was the group of editors and writers that met regularly at the Algonquin Hotel for lunch, and now and then for all-night poker sessions. Of the group the one I knew best, after Russel Crouse, was Heywood Broun, the big, untidy, shambling newspaperman who was for a quarter of a century probably the best-known columnist in the country. Heywood was a devoted liberal and follower of lost causes; he was for seven years one of the bright stars of the "opposite editorial" page of *The New York World*, where he competed with Franklin P. Adams, Laurence Stallings, Samuel Chotzinoff, the music critic, and for a time, William Bolitho, the brilliant South African author of *Twelve Against the Gods*.

I remember once running into Heywood at a baseball game, and going home with him for a drink. There were four or five in the party, who gossiped amiably for a while, until Heywood looked at his watch and remarked, "It's time I wrote tomorrow's column." He summoned a Western Union messenger, and then went into the next room, where we could hear the typewriter going with a continuous roar, as if it were actuated by high-speed tape. In what seemed like only a few minutes, Heywood appeared, handed an envelope with his copy to the boy, who was by now waiting, and went on with the conversation. Next morning I read his piece in the paper which sounded as though he had brooded over it for hours. (As perhaps he had.)

Heywood was married to Ruth Hale, a fanatical member of the Lucy Stone League, an organization devoted to the right of married women to use their maiden names. She once actually canceled a trip to Europe because the ship refused to list Ruth Hale and Heywood Broun as occupying a specified cabin together. The Brouns had a faithful domestic servant, whom Ruth had trained always to call her Miss Hale, with one exception. When she brought up their breakfast to their bedroom the maid always said, "Here's your breakfast, *Mrs. Broun*." She did not intend to address by her maiden name a woman occupying a double bed with a man.

For some years Heywood graced the lecture circuit now and then; he had only one speech, which began with a long and complicated story of how an American soldier in France had been forced to use profanity because he "he had to turn a team of mules around." Heywood was nervous about speaking, and he arranged that instead of the proverbial pitcher of water always brought on for the lecturer, there should be a pitcher of pure gin. Wetting his palate from time to time, he grew conspicuously freer and more loquacious as his lecture wore on.

He was as exercised over the Sacco-Vanzetti case as the rest of us, and his daily column in *The World* grew more vituperative about the Massachusetts authorities as the case wound to its tragic end, in spite of warnings from the paper that he was verging on libel. Finally an unusually bitter column caused him to be dismissed. I immediately asked him to write a weekly column for *The New Republic*, at our customary rate of $50 a week, and Heywood gravely accepted, though his previous salary had been $15,000 or $20,000 a year. Shortly thereafter he went back to the big money by writing for the Scripps-Howard newspapers, whose flagship was *The New York World-Telegram*, but for a year or two, he went on with a weekly article for us, always produced just before the last possible deadline, always fitting the space stipulated, within a line or two.

When Heywood had agreed to write a piece for a magazine, he had a habit of walking into the office, borrowing a typewriter, and sitting down to write the first, and also final, draft then and there. We enjoyed these occasions, even though I sometimes had to roust my secretary from her desk for him; he overflowed the secretarial chair like an elephant on a bar stool.

Heywood continued with Scripps-Howard for ten years, until he again had a falling out over editorial policy. He shifted to *The New York Post*, which seemed to have a limitless capacity for absorbing additional columnists. He died shortly afterward.

He founded the American Newspaper Guild in 1933, and was its head until his death in 1939. He intended it to be a cross between a trade union and a professional society, with a membership limited to members of the writing trade, and this is what it was for the first few years. Then the decision was made to bring in all employees of a newspaper, and the writers were soon outvoted by accountants, elevator men, and janitors, making it just another standard A.F.L.-C.I.O. union. It has been very helpful to its members in regard to wages, pensions, and working conditions, but the special quality that Heywood brought to it in the beginning has disappeared. For one thing, the Guild insists—or always did in its negotiations with *The New Republic*—that one writer is just like another, and can take his place if necessary. This might be true of strictly routine jobs, but it is ridiculously false as concerns columnists and other authors of signed material. They are just as individual as painters, sculptors, or musicians.

When the Guild was being organized, *The New Republic* of course supported its efforts; we had always favored trade unions, back to the days when they were fighting for the right to exist, harassed by labor spies and goon squads. I wrote several editorials favoring the Guild, and became a member in the easygoing days when this was permitted. I wrote a signed article entitled "Union-Card Journalist," which began:

> To my own mild surprise, I find myself a trade-union man, in good standing, dues paid, affiliated with the A.F. of L., and entitled to address William Green as Papa.

I then answered, to my own satisfaction, all the arguments that were being advanced against unions of newspaper writers, addressing myself chiefly to Roy Howard, head of the Scripps-Howard chain, who was then fighting the attempts of the union to organize his reporters, and ended:

> I am proud of my trade-union card as a member of the Newspaper Guild because I believe the people most concerned for accurate, honest, and intelligent journalism are the newspapermen who are capable of producing accurate, honest, and intelligent journalism, and that the greater the proportion of power that falls into their hands, the better. I am well aware that in the range of American industry, there are good unions and bad ones, and some of the bad ones are pretty terrible. The Newspaper Guild seems to me a good one. But even if it were bad, that

*would be no reason to abandon unionism; it would be a reason to improve
it. Newspapers will not get better by seeking to return newspapermen to
the status and responsibilities of office boys.*

The Guild responded by sending me a handsome certificate making
me an honorary life member. But when a few years later *The New
Republic*, which as noted had been organized by another union, The
Book and Magazine Guild, was handed over to the Newspaper Guild
(without our being consulted), the negotiators ignored this scrap of past
history. I was now Management, not permitted even an honorary connection with the Union, and treated just as roughly as though I had been
Roy Howard.

I knew casually or well nearly all the top figures on *The New York
Times*, over the years. Charles Merz, long editor of the editorial page, had
preceded me as managing editor of *The New Republic*. Robert Duffus,
assistant editor, had worked with me on *The Globe*. I was forever meeting
at public lunches, in the early days, Louis Wiley, the little round butter-
ball of a financial magician who brought in the money which Adolph
Ochs plowed back into the paper. I knew Carr Van Anda, the fabulously
erudite managing editor during the First World War, Charles R. Miller,
editor at the same period, Rollo Ogden, who preceded Merz, and John
H. Finley, who was better known for his prodigious feats in walking than
as a writer.

My best friend in the early days was Simeon Strunsky, who wrote
a brilliant daily column on the editorial page which in the fashion of those
days was unsigned, so that his name was known to only a few hundred
people, mostly in the trade. He used to tell me a little ruefully of a
predecessor of his who wrote charmingly for many years, but whose
name only became known when he died. In those days newspapers did
not pay the salaries they did later, and Simeon observed that this man's
column was so popular that many people were glad to contribute to the
fund to pay his funeral expenses. Toward the end of his life, Simeon
wrote a couple of novels that had a modest success, and finally broke out
of the shell of anonymity.

I met Adolph Ochs, the real genius of *The Times*, only rarely, but
I was impressed by him. On one occasion when the new home of *The
Times* on West Forty-third Street was not quite finished, I was talking
to him in his office for some reason I have now forgotten, and complimented him casually on the new plant. Learning that I had not seen it,
he promptly took me on a one-man guided tour of the whole place. He
was thirty-one years older than I, but it was I who was ready to cry
"Uncle" before the tour was completed.

One of the saddest episodes in the history of *The Times* occurred

Sunday, September 15, 1918, when the First World War was almost over. Austria, in desperate straits, sent a peace feeler to the United States by way of Switzerland. What *The Times* did about it is told by Gay Talese in his lively book about the paper, *The Kingdom and the Power* (New American Library-World, 1969). The managing editor was then Carr Van Anda, who, as I have said, was one of the most brilliant of American newspapermen, one who read Egyptian hieroglyphs as a hobby, and once found a mistaken equation in Einstein. Van Anda was at home that night, and so was Charles R. Miller, the graying editor of the editorial page. Mr. Ochs was at his summer place at Lake George.

Talese (and other historians of the paper) say that Van Anda was exultant at the news, since it indicated the enemy was cracking. He phoned Miller and Ochs, telling each of them, "This is the beginning of the end." Miller, remembering all the blood and anguish the war was causing, wrote an editorial and telephoned it in to the office for next day's paper, saying that any move toward ending the conflict should be welcomed, and that the Austrian proposal should at least be made the basis for discussion.

But America was in no mood for a negotiated peace. The country had been slow to have its emotions involved in the war, but perhaps for that very reason, virulent patriotism was now endemic, especially on the East Coast. Next morning when the paper reached its readers, the storm broke. Hundreds of telegrams and telephone calls were received denouncing the editorial; thousands of people canceled their subscriptions. Among those who were enraged was President Wilson, who wanted to keep the making of peace in his own hands. Only the end of the war, less than two months later, cooled the hot blood of the patriots.

There is an alternative version of this story which I heard immediately after it happened, and as far as I know has never been printed anywhere. As it was told to me, the editorial was written on his own initiative by a lone writer who had been assigned to keep the late watch in the office that night. Realizing the importance of the occasion, he called up Mr. Ochs at Lake George, got the aging publisher out of bed, and tried to read the editorial to him over the phone. But the connection was bad, Mr. Ochs couldn't hear, and finally he said, "Well, I can't quite hear you, but I guess it's all right." Whichever version is correct the outcome was the same.

I knew Dorothy Parker only slightly, the way a newspaperman knows so many; but like everyone else, I was impressed by her talent, and saddened by the unending series of messes she made of her personal life. Herbert Croly tried several times to get her to write something for *The New Republic*, but if she did, I have forgotten it, which is unlikely.

When she talked to any male, she had a disarming habit of holding to your coat lapel, as though she feared her attractions were insufficient to keep you from departing. Alexander Woollcott had the same habit; everybody disliked it in him, but I never heard anyone complain of it in Dorothy. On one occasion, Dorothy and I had both joined some big public committee whose purpose I have forgotten. She arrived late, and since mine was the only even half-familiar face in the room, she came and sat by me. Several people had questions to ask the chairman, and he invariably put them off by saying, "That will be answered when Mr. Weldon arrives." After this had happened three or four times, Dorothy turned and whispered to me, "God damn my filthy soul to hell, I don't even know who Mr. Weldon is."

Two sets of brothers came to see me at various times, and while I never knew them very well, I remember them. In about 1927, two young men who looked to me like good, simple, Middle-Western farm boys, dropped in unannounced. After a few minutes, one of them held up for my inspection a small metal rod about the size of a lead pencil. "This little thing," he told me, "is going to have a profound effect on the economy of the South."

I naturally thought he was crazy, but he wasn't. He was John Rust, who, with his younger brother, Mack, who was accompanying him, had invented the first practical cotton-picking machine. Its heart was the little silvery rod which, when wet, and rotated against the ripe cotton boll, caused the fibers to cling to it. The brothers estimated that the machine would eliminate about nine out of ten field hands on a cotton plantation; I don't know what the final figures were, but I am sure that enormous numbers of people, black and white, were in fact displaced. The blacks came north into Harlem and its equivalents in other cities— notably Chicago and Detroit—and forty years later their sons and grandsons participated in the riots that so troubled the last years of the 1960's.

The other two brothers came eight years later, in 1935; they, too, looked like solid, American types. They told me that, having a curiosity to see what Europe was like, they had spent three years bicycling through various countries; they were both skilled mechanics, and had managed somehow to earn their way, though some countries then, as now, had laws against letting foreigners engage in gainful employment.

They had spent quite a lot of time in Soviet Russia, where they had no trouble in getting jobs in an automobile factory. They were disgusted by the inefficiency of the operations, and the rigid bureaucracy which in many cases forced a plant to produce unusable, unwanted goods in huge quantities to fill a quota set by some ignoramus in Moscow.

The brothers told me they planned to try to get jobs in Detroit. They got them, too; Walter Reuther became president of the United Automobile Workers of America, one of the most statesmanlike of all union heads until his death in 1970, and Victor was his good right arm.

I had a few good friends in the field of radio, when it had not yet been superseded by television. One of these was Raymond Swing, who was once said by *The New Yorker* to have the best-known voice in the world. This could easily have been true, since his nightly talks were rebroadcast in many countries. I first met him some years earlier, when I was on a visit to London, and he was unhappy; he had just been fired by the American newspaper that had sent him abroad, in one of those economy waves that are forever being experienced by big organizations of every sort. He asked me for a job on *The New Republic*, and I had to tell him I didn't have one. Like E. B. White when I turned him down for *The Globe*, Ray took it hard, but it was one of the luckiest things that ever happened to him. A few months later a place opened up on the radio in New York, and somebody remembered a few broadcasts he had done for the B.B.C. in London. He was tried out, and the rest is history.

Another American I knew who had worked in London was Edward R. Murrow, whose nightly wartime broadcasts from that city to America began with the dramatic "This . . . is London." I never knew him well, but I liked him, as everybody did. I remember calling on him once at his office at C.B.S. in New York, during the short interregnum when that company had decided to make an executive of him, for heaven knows what reason. He was so obviously unhappy pushing papers around that it was easy for me to predict that he would soon be back on the air. People of my generation remember that he did more than any other single individual to end the career of Senator Joseph R. McCarthy, by the simple expedient of putting him on television and letting the country see what he was like.

My closest friend in broadcasting was Elmer Davis, whose family for a while spent its summers at a colony in the Poconos where my wife and I also had a cottage for some years. Elmer had come up through printed journalism, being a long-time star reporter on *The New York Times*. He also wrote modestly successful novels; one of them, *I'll Show You the Town*, was laid in the office of a liberal weekly, and he came down and visited the *New Republic* office to pick up local color.

Like several others, Elmer got into broadcasting by accident, filling in for a friend in an emergency. While he had broadcast under various conditions he became most famous for his five-minute talk at nine o'clock in the evening during the Second World War. He had a genius for picking out the most important things going on and summarizing them in a few words; his calm, dry, Indiana twang brought reassurance to millions made jittery by the somber, often tragic news he had to report.

Ray Swing worked ten hours a day with several researchers on his fifteen-minute broadcast; Elmer worked alone. As a guest in his home in Washington, I saw how he watched the news tickers intermittently all day long. He began writing his five-minute broadcast about four in the afternoon, kept rewriting if the news necessitated it, and drove to the studio only a few minutes before he was to go on the air.

It was an eerie experience to lunch with Elmer in a crowded restaurant. His Indiana twang was penetrating and unforgettable, and when he gave his order to the waiter, a hundred heads instantly turned in his direction. He could also be identified by his clothing; I never saw him wear anything but a gray flannel suit and a black bow tie. (Herbert Hoover had the same habit of always dressing the same; he used to order his double-breasted blue suits half a dozen at a time.)

Elmer was a cat lover; for many years his long-haired male cat, General Gray, was the master of the household. Once I entered his living room and saw that the overstuffed chairs had been shredded by sharp claws (as was the case in my own home). He saw my look, and remarked gently, "General Gray lives here, too."

When the General died, Elmer went to the office of *The Washington Post* and solemnly handed in a paid death notice. My memory is that the girl on the desk didn't recognize him, didn't realize this was a death notice for a cat, and it got printed just as written.

By a meaningless series of coincidences, I met face to face every President from McKinley to Truman. The one I knew best was Hoover, beginning with our Stanford connection. It has always seemed to me that he suffered some sort of personality change in the eight years between my magazine article suggesting him for President, and the time he actually took office. He had always had somewhat the look of a sulky baby about to burst into tears, and his pronunciation of the English language, except on rare occasions when he was strongly moved, was a difficult mumble; I felt that these things were accentuated when he got into the White House.

In his younger days he acted with great decision and effectiveness, as all the world knows from his work in getting the Americans out of Europe in August, 1914, feeding the Belgians during the war, and many other things. He could also act with equal decision in small personal matters. Once, some years before he became President, he was living in his house on the Stanford campus in the winter, and as it sometimes does in California, it rained incessantly day after day. Hoover paced up and down his living room impatiently, handling the twenty-dollar gold piece he always carried in his pocket. After a week or so of this, he got on the telephone to the U.S. Weather Bureau in Washington.

"Where in the world is there most likely to be sunshine at this time of year?" he wanted to know. The answer came back: the Aswan area on the upper reaches of the Nile in Egypt. That was enough for Herbert; he gathered up his wife and family and went there.

Though he seemed cold and humorless to the public, his close friends knew him to be a warm and generous individual, with a good sense of humor; it was unfortunate that he never managed to carry over the impression in his official appearance. His autobiography—which he produced unaided, scratching it off on big yellow sheets of foolscap—is well written, and contains many poignant reports of the worldwide suffering he saw, and helped to alleviate.

I met one more President, but long before he had achieved that position. In the fall of 1937, the debate over isolation was raging, and I was still taking the position that the United States should stay out of the European war we all saw impending, and should try to use its influence for an early and permanent peace. New York's Town Hall, on Forty-third Street, frequently staged lectures or debates, and I agreed to argue this question with a novice Representative from Texas, who had just won a special election to fill the seat of James P. Buchanan. Lyndon Johnson seemed a subdued young man, but he was a pretty good speaker, and he argued the Roosevelt position effectively. (There were no judges, or any formal decision that one side or the other had won.) Not being gifted with foresight, I brushed off the affair casually; it was just another public appearance, of which I was making a good number at that time. I believe, however, that this was Mr. Johnson's first exposure to a metropolitan audience, or to any audience outside of Texas. Our debate was reported routinely in the New York newspapers; if I had known what was to become of this young Texan I should have saved the clippings, but I threw them away.

One man I have admired increasingly over the years is David Lilienthal. The Tennessee Valley Authority is in many ways the finest achievement of the Franklin Roosevelt Administration, and once the concept had been created, Lilienthal was more responsible than anyone else for its success. While he was its head, I got together a small group of journalists from noncompeting periodicals and asked whether we could make a tour of the valley. David not only welcomed the suggestion, but he sent the T.V.A. plane to pick us up in Washington (this was in wartime, and travel was onerous when it was not impossible), and himself acted as our tour guide for the first couple of days, later turning us over to one of his associates. It was a great pleasure to see something the government was doing, and was doing right, that private enterprise could and would never have done; it was also a pleasure to see how, everywhere we went, people's faces lighted up at the sight of Lilienthal, not merely (as their conversation quickly proved) because he had done so much for the valley, but because they liked him as a man.

He went on from the T.V.A. to a trying role as head of the Atomic Energy Commission, an impossible and unhappy job, and then to a great success as the leading spirit in the Development and Resources Corporation, which combines public and private means to put through projects, some of them much like the T.V.A., in many "backward" areas of the world. For decades he has kept a journal, and selections from it have been published (by Harper & Row) in a multivolume unequaled record of our times that will grow in value as the years pass.

When the doctors exiled me from New York in my sixty-fourth year, and I came back to Stanford to live, I unexpectedly found myself presently dwelling in the same apartment house with Alexander Kerensky, who was premier of Russia when the Bolshevists took over; we became good friends. Kerensky was at Stanford writing the history of his government; the archives of the Hoover Institution on War, Revolution, and Peace were the only place in the world, as far as is known, where the necessary documents existed. (If there are duplicates inside the Soviet Union, which is highly doubtful, the government certainly would not have let Kerensky go there to work.)

When I met him, he was already eighty, but in full possession of his faculties, both mental and physical. He carried on a large correspondence with friends all over the free world; often he would tell me things he had learned from them that would turn up in newspaper headlines a month or two later. He was fluent in several languages; his English was rather heavily accented, and this accent got suddenly much worse when he had to face an audience, or appear on radio or television.

He was famous all his life for his ability as a pedestrian; he told me the secret-service men assigned to trail him in his younger days in Russia called him "the Walker," and hated the assignment because they found it so hard to keep up with him. His favorite time to start a walk was around midnight, and he rarely covered less than three or four miles. The Stanford campus had few sidewalks or footpaths, and his friends used to worry about his being struck by a car, walking on the edge of the macadam. I remember once driving him to a dinner party in the neighboring town of Los Altos; on our return journey, a little before midnight, he suddenly said, "Stop the car!" when we were still several miles from the apartment house. I pulled over onto the shoulder thinking something must be wrong, but all he said was, "I get out now. Good night!" He walked the rest of the way home.

My apartment on the ground floor had a small private porch, and in good weather my wife and I usually lunched there. Kerensky would come by, and invariably would stop and say, "What is the news?" My standard answer was, "I don't know, Mr. Kerensky, I haven't heard the radio since seven o'clock this morning," whereupon he would reply, "I will tell you." His inquiry had just been a way of starting a conversation.

Most people at this time had one of three attitudes about him. They thought he had died long ago, they assumed he had been one of the Bolshevist leaders, or they excoriated him for having lost the fight which brought Lenin and Trotsky to power. A comment I heard many times was, "Why didn't he shoot all the Communist bosses when he had the chance?" If he had been a ruthless despot like Stalin, probably he would have done so; but Kerensky was a Social Democrat, which meant in Russia in his day a mild, evolutionary Socialist; a wholesale massacre of his opponents was as unthinkable to him as it would have been to John

Kennedy. Most people have now forgotten that the government which came to power in March, 1917, of which he was a part, and of which he became the leader in July, wrote one of the most liberal constitutions in the world, and tried hard to live up to it, against hopeless odds, beset by attempted revolutions from both the Right and the Left during the few months before the Bolshevists seized power in November.

I have indicated that I am not given to hero worship, but there have been a few men during my lifetime whom I have admired very much. One of these is Fremont Older, of whom I have written earlier in these pages. Another is Roger Baldwin, for many years head of the American Civil Liberties Union. The Union fought for the civil rights of *everybody*, and Roger should have turned cynical as he saw liberals approving his activities on behalf of liberals, but unable to understand why he worked equally hard for the rights of Fascists and Communists. (The favorite argument against him was, Why seek to preserve the liberties of those who don't believe in them, who would crush you instantly if they ever came to power?) Roger is a member of the Society of Friends, which may have helped him to make a soft answer. In the fifty years and more that I have known him, I have never seen him swerve from adherence to his principles.

A third man I have greatly admired, and have known almost as long, is former Senator Paul Douglas of Illinois. He was a professor of economics at several universities, chiefly the University of Chicago; although like Roger Baldwin he was a Quaker, when the Second World War broke out he enlisted in the marines—at age fifty—and saw some of the hardest fighting in the Pacific area, including the capture of Peleliu and Okinawa. He came out a lieutenant colonel, with the Bronze Star. While he was in the Senate it was regular procedure for the Washington correspondents to vote him the most valued member of Congress. As one of the judges of the annual Sidney Hillman awards, I participated in giving him one in 1957, in recognition of his service to his country, in war and peace.

Though I never knew him very well, a man who came close to being a hero of mine was Walter White of the National Association for the Advancement of Colored People. He happened to be as fair of skin as any Iowa WASP, and could very easily have done what many other light-skinned Negroes have done, and "passed"—repudiated his black origin. On the contrary, he spent his life doing what he could to ameliorate the terrible injustices Americans have done for three hundred years to members of his race. He repeatedly went south into troubled areas when there was a good chance he would be killed, and did it so quietly few ever heard of it.

Chapter 12

THE SECOND WORLD WAR

There is not much to say, in a book like this one, about the second great war of my lifetime, even though it was the most terrible episode in history, with thirty million dead, millions more uprooted forever, irreversible changes made in the destiny of all mankind. The experience was similar for all who were of a certain age when it began; almost the only thing anyone can say of it is, I was there.

I have recorded elsewhere the slow progress in my own mind in the late 1930's from opposition to all war to a heavyhearted decision that we should make an exception of the fight against Hitler—a decision for which I was of course jeered by the true pacifists who believed in utter nonresistance to violence at all times and in all cases. The decision was taken out of our government's hands by Pearl Harbor, an episode unforgivably bungled by the State Department, the Army, and the Navy, with heavy needless loss of American lives.

Everyone who is old enough remembers where he was and what he was doing on that Sunday afternoon which came to be known as Pearl Harbor Day. I had been lying on my bed, listening on the radio to the New York Philharmonic concert, and had dropped off to sleep. I was awakened by a telephone call from a young woman friend, who wanted to know, "Is it true what they are saying, that the Japanese have attacked Hawaii?" While I was touched by this confidence in my journalistic omniscience, I said I didn't know anything about it. But a few minutes' listening told me that, while I slept, my country had got into a war.

As I have suggested, this is no place to tell over again the story of that war. America shifted with great reluctance, and slowly, from peace-time activities. President Roosevelt suspended many actions in the field of social reform on the ground that "Dr. New Deal" had to step aside for "Mr. Win-the-War." *The New Republic* argued against him on this point, urging that internal reforms made the country that much stronger and more able to carry on the conflict. We also argued that since this, like the First World War, was fought in the name of democracy, it was of great importance to correct undemocratic situations at home. I doubt that we had much influence on the course of events, but, of course, even if this had been true we should probably never have known it.

Our general policies during the war were what you might expect. We crusaded for a just and lasting peace, instead of a repetition of the unworkable provisions of the Versailles Treaty in 1919, which, as we had correctly predicted, had helped to make the Second World War more likely. We wanted conscientious objectors treated reasonably; sometimes they were, and far more often, they weren't.

We took no firm stand on the demand for "unconditional surrender" by Germany, which was formulated by Roosevelt and Churchill and announced at their Casablanca meeting. They were thinking, of course, of the muddled end of the First World War, when the Germans said the terms of the Armistice had been violated, and nursed a grievance down the years that helped Hitler come to power. Critics ever since have damned the "unconditional-surrender" formula on the ground that it gave the desperate German and Japanese people only the hardest way out, and that, in the case of the Germans at least, it tied the hands of the anti-Hitler faction who wanted to make a separate peace behind his back. (The Allies did in fact disregard their own formula in ending the war with Italy.) But a quarter of a century later, it is hard to say whether the policy was wise. Hitler was a fanatic who would not have sought a negotiated peace in any event, and the Japanese Fascists were equally intransigent. Only the enormous prestige of the Emperor, still venerated not only as the head of state, but as a divinity, made Japan's surrender possible, in spite of the terrible results of the bombing of Hiroshima and Nagasaki. When he prerecorded his radio message to the people telling them the war was over, a band of diehard militarists broke into the Imperial Palace seeking to find and destroy it. Others, in the old Japanese tradition, committed hara-kiri before the palace gates.

Our paper opposed the deal with that unsavory character, Admiral Jean Darlan, at the time of the North Africa landing in 1942, and again history gives no clear verdict as to whether we were right. As usual, immediate military necessity overruled long-range considerations. We *did* get our men ashore. Every war, if it lasts long enough, loses its ideological overtones and becomes a completely opportunistic struggle for victory.

I was staggered, like everybody else, at the concessions Roosevelt made to Stalin at Yalta, when these finally became known; but the President's conservative opponents were screaming so loudly that we did not feel much urgency about joining their uproar. The most inept thing the President did was to agree to extra seats in the United Nations for the Ukraine and Byelorussia, and then try to keep this bargain secret. Most of the other concessions at Yalta were things the Russians could, and probably would, have taken by force if necessary. The President was dreadfully wrong in thinking he could charm "good old Joe" Stalin into behaving like a Western liberal, but it is questionable whether history would have been greatly changed if he had been more astute.

The worst agreement at Yalta got little attention at the time—the arrangement that the Russians should take Berlin, which finally resulted in spreading the Communist half of Germany far to the west of that city. Only Winston Churchill seemed fully aware of the territorial ambitions of Stalin, and nobody—in America at any rate—listened to him. When the Western Allies and the Russians were racing into Germany, from both directions, Eisenhower tried hard to get a politico-military directive from the Joint Chiefs of Staff as to what he should do, and got none. It was a disastrous error, but very few of us—and certainly not *The New Republic*—had enough foresight to look ahead and see how disastrous it was.

Only one member of our staff was killed in the war. Otis Ferguson left the paper to volunteer for the merchant marine, where his Navy training would be valuable. He was put on the terrible Murmansk run, carrying military supplies to northern Russia; for some time ships on this run were not even in convoy, and they were slaughtered by German submarines. Otis was instantly killed by a direct hit by a German shell that landed amidships.

As a civilian, I suffered like everybody else from shortages, rationing, the discomforts of travel, the never-ending tension of one with a son fighting at the front. My worst physical ordeal came with the visits I had to make to Washington. Train travel often meant standing for hours in a jammed day coach, and any journey might take far longer than expected. Hotel rooms were almost impossible to get—while big corporations kept suites (whose cost was tax-deductible) standing empty night after night in case somebody from their top brass should happen to need them. These corporations were, of course, in the war effort, but this was no great consolation to a less important individual who spent the night sleeping in a chair in a hotel lobby.

The paper had no real trouble with censorship during the war. American periodicals were supposed to be under voluntary restrictions, which were made simpler because a great many important facts, some of them extremely disturbing, were suppressed at the source. I have recorded elsewhere the surprising candor of the Army with me in regard to some technological advances. I had only two brushes with the censors that I can recall, both of them over articles of my own, both after the war had ended.

In one case, *The Reader's Digest* asked me to do a science article on peacetime uses of radar. I did not go to a single governmental source; I simply consulted the files of various scientific and other periodicals, wrote my article, it was accepted, and I was paid the usual fee of several thousand dollars for it. I was under no legal or other obligation to submit it to Washington, but I felt I had better do so, and I sent it along to the Office of War Information, of which my friend Elmer Davis was no longer head. To my astonishment, word came back that this article must not be published. When I protested that everything in it had already appeared in print, I was told that while this was true, some enemy (unspecified) might not have as complete files as those I had consulted, and that my piece might fill in some important gaps for him. This was all bureaucratic nonsense, but I sadly told *The Digest* to kill the article, and gave back the money.

The other affair was rather uglier. The Office for Strategic Services, the O.S.S., was headed by the swashbuckling General "Wild Bill" Donovan, and performed many important services all over the world. Among the organizations that cooperated with it were the American trade unions, especially working with the Underground in France during the German occupation. The unions had prewar contacts with their opposite numbers there, and they sent French-speaking Americans to work with the Maquis. These performed useful services at great personal risk.

After the war, people in the C.I.O. asked me to write an article about this little-known activity. I gathered a lot of material, from documents and personal interviews, and a thrilling story it made. (In one case, two American spies, with a clandestine radio in their baggage, found themselves accidentally on board a special train carrying the German commander-in-chief!) Since some of my material had come from O.S.S. files I was obligated to show the article to that body, and I was surprised when word came back that it was not to be published. No reason was given, but from trade-union sources I got the explanation: General Donovan just didn't like organized labor, and did not want to have its contribution publicly recorded. I have no way of knowing whether he actually saw my article; it often happened that officious subordinates took it on themselves to make decisions in accordance with the real or supposed prejudices of their superiors. In any case, I had to scrap a good piece.

When the first atom bomb was dropped on Hiroshima, nobody outside a very limited circle in the government was in a proper position to realize what a terrible event had taken place. Not until long afterward did we learn the enormous loss of life in the two cities that were hit, or that Japan was already in such desperate straits that she could not have fought much longer in any case, and that she was putting out peace feelers through Stalin, which he conveniently failed to transmit in any intelligible form. We all believed that an invasion of the home islands would be necessary, and it might well have cost, as the military authorities told us, a million American lives. It was years before the nation faced the fact that the United States was the only country ever to have used in anger the most terrible of all weapons. A quarter of a century later, we can only pray that it will not happen again.

Before the fighting had ended, the Allies began the difficult task of setting up the United Nations, and I worked as a reporter on its various stages. I spent weeks in San Francisco seeing the idea of a true parliament of nations whittled down into an instrument controlled in all important aspects by the Great Powers. A few weeks after the shooting stopped, I went to London and watched some of the working committees that were trying to fill in gaps left at San Francisco, after which I continued to report the story as the organization moved to Lake Success, Long Island, Hunter College in New York, and finally, to the huge, new skyscraper on the East River.

It would not be true to say that I was disillusioned by the sordid end of a fine idea, because I had never expected anything else. Years earlier, I had reported the meetings of the League of Nations at Geneva, and on one occasion an emergency session in Paris, and I had ample evidence that the strong nations were still decades away from any important surrender of part of their sovereignty. At San Francisco I saw the cynicism of the Russian delegation, and how it blocked every effort at advance—always after a day's delay while the Russian communications ship lying in the harbor consulted Stalin in Moscow and got back orders.

The crucial issue was, of course, what it is a quarter of a century later, the veto power in the Council. Russia has exercised her veto something like a hundred times at this writing, and it is fashionable to say that the comparative ineffectiveness of the U.N. is her fault. But the correspondents at San Francisco knew that without the Great-Power veto in the Council, it was highly doubtful that the U.S. Senate would have accepted the Charter. Isolationism in the upper house was about as strong in 1945 as it had been in 1920.

In spite of all this, I was an advocate of the League from the beginning, and a supporter of the U.N. to this day. While it has never been able to prevent or end a major war, it has on several occasions halted minor conflicts that could have become dangerous. The Assembly gives a sounding board for world opinion, and in spite of all the cynicism, there is such a thing, and it does work. The U.N. operates many international

FIVE MILLION WORDS LATER

agencies of great value, among them the Educational, Scientific and
Cultural Organization, the Economic and Social Council, the World
Health Organization, the U.N. Children's Fund, the Food and Agricul-
ture Organization, the World Bank, and the International Monetary
Fund.

The meetings of the U.N. in New York, reported in the press, by
radio, and sometimes by television, throw a powerful light on the degree
to which the chief powers—the Communist ones in particular—pay only
lip service to the organization. If the U.N. did not exist it would have to
be invented; any organization is better than none, and we can only hope
it will continue to exist until at some future date, the strong powers of
the world are willing to substitute law for force. The usefulness of the
U.N. is highlighted by the character of its chief opponents in the United
States—all the worst elements of the Far Right.

Chapter 13

THE GREAT WALLACE DEBACLE

The most dramatic episode in the history of *The New Republic* was the year and a half that Henry Wallace was its nominal editor, from the end of 1946 to the summer of 1948.

When I became editor in 1930, it had been understood for some years that Mrs. Elmhirst hoped her son by her first marriage, Michael Straight, who was then fourteen, might grow up to have an important place on the paper. It seemed a little unfair for Mike to be the heir to millions for he had high intelligence, good looks, and a warm, outgoing personality. He later proved that he was also a writer of ability, not only by what he did for the paper, but by producing two novels of Western American life of seventy-five years ago, both warmly received by the critics.

When the Second World War began, Mike was already a pilot, and since he was fluent in French, he volunteered to teach flying to young Frenchmen who were sent to the United States for that purpose. The mortality rate among these instructors was high, but Mike survived, and with the end of the war he was ready to give his full time to the paper. His political views were entirely consonant with those of the editors, which is not surprising; he had been brought up on them.

By the time he had cut his journalistic eyeteeth, Mike began to have ambitions that went far beyond my own. He conceived of a *New Republic* with a circulation several times larger than the modest 45,000 or so we then had; in fact, he thought of "a liberal *Time*," which would have the wide appeal of the Henry Luce paper but would have an editorial position far to its left.

This seemed a reasonable idea at first glance, but proved in experience to be mistaken. Our readers did not want a liberal *Time*; they wanted the old, highbrow *New Republic*, printed on butcher paper, with no illustrations, but written by a group of men whom over the years they had come to like and to trust. When the change was made, our old readers deserted us in droves. The mistake, I might add, was just as much Dan Mebane's and my own as it was Mike's. Public-opinion research was only then beginning, but there was some; we should have insisted on finding out whether there was a market for such a changed paper as was planned. Instead, we encouraged him to go ahead.

The situation was enormously complicated by the matter of Henry Wallace. In fact, it is now impossible to say what might have happened to the great expansionist experiment if he had not complicated things.

Wallace was a member of the third generation of a successful Iowa family engaged primarily in agricultural journalism. His grandfather had founded *Wallace's Farmer*, and was its editor until he died in 1916. His father, Henry C. Wallace, succeeded to the editorship, and was secretary of agriculture for Presidents Harding and Coolidge until his death in 1924. Henry A. Wallace, in the family pattern, assisted his father on the paper from 1910 until 1924, when he became editor. The Wallaces had always been Republican, but Henry could not stomach the conservatism of Herbert Hoover, turned Democratic in 1928, and in 1932, helped carry Iowa for Roosevelt. He was rewarded by the same job his father had held thirteen years earlier, as secretary of agriculture, and he held that post, highly controversial in New Deal days, until 1940. He headed the Agricultural Adjustment Administration, and fought to stem the huge overproduction of farm products during the Depression—overproduction, that is, in terms of salability; there were always plenty of people who needed food and fiber, if there had been any way of getting it to them within the framework of our society as it was seen at that time.

One of the things that were in oversupply was young pigs, and in desperation, and with great reluctance, Wallace ordered large numbers of them slaughtered and used for fertilizer. Economically it was no doubt sound, by the standards of the day; but it was a fearful blow to the Protestant ethic to see so much potential food wasted, and millions of people never forgave him.

It is quite possible that long after Wallace's political career is forgotten, he will be remembered for his work as a corn geneticist. He was enormously successful in producing hybrid strains of corn that were better than anything in the past, with tremendously increased yields per acre, more sugar, less starch, and uniformity in size for machine handling. He started a business selling seed corn all over the world, which was enormously profitable; he was as important as any other individual of the time in helping to increase the food supply to keep up with the burgeoning world population.

The last fifteen years of his life were devoted to similar activity in trying to improve the breed of poultry, with substantial success. He bought a farm at South Salem, New York, and worked to develop chickens with improved size, egg-laying capacity, and resistance to disease.

In 1940, Roosevelt chose Wallace to be his vice-presidential candidate, and he served in that capacity for the next four years. But the professional politicians never liked him; they regarded him as a woolly-headed idealist, in spite of his success as a farm publisher and creator of hybrid corn. In 1944, when Roosevelt was about to be nominated for his fourth term, these politicians went on strike, and succeeded in forcing F.D.R. to choose instead Senator Harry Truman of Missouri. A few weeks after the inauguration, Roosevelt was dead, and Truman was President. He offered Wallace the post of secretary of commerce, and Henry amiably accepted.

Over the years, Wallace had become more and more a humanitarian, on a worldwide scale, and in his writings and speeches he stressed increasingly the fact that all peoples are fellow travelers on the planet Earth, and should do what they can to help one another. He developed a plan for an "ever-normal granary," which was a scheme to store up nonperishable foodstuffs in time of surplus so that they might be distributed to the hungry in times of scarcity, not only in the United States, but everywhere. He was derided for demanding "a quart of milk a day for every Hottentot," by which he meant merely that rich nations should do what they could to help the poor ones—a proposal that seems more reasonable today than it did thirty years ago.

Among the conservatives who thought Wallace was a vague, impractical idealist was James F. Byrnes, Truman's secretary of state. In September, 1946, there was a peace conference going on in Paris, and Byrnes was head of the American delegation, in head-on collision as usual with the Russians. Wallace chose this moment to make a speech in New York sharply criticizing the American foreign policy Byrnes was trying to practice. Since he knew it might cause some fireworks, he made an appointment in advance with President Truman and read it aloud to him. Wallace himself had a habit of falling asleep when anything was read to him; whether Truman shared this characteristic I don't know, but I think it more likely that like many other people he never understood anything clearly until he saw it written out. At any rate, Truman said the speech was O.K., Wallace delivered it, and hell broke loose. Byrnes, furious, gave Truman an ultimatum: either Wallace had to go, or he would. Truman promptly fired Wallace.

Henry and I had been casual acquaintances for many years, with our common Iowa heritage as a bond; I used to see him frequently on my regular trips to Washington to check on things. I once rode with him in his car as he drove a long distance from Des Moines to a small Iowa town where he was to make a speech, and back when it was over, and we talked seriously of philosophical matters. I could see that he was attracted somewhat by mysticism, to which I have always been allergic; but neither then nor ever did I see in him the fantastic beliefs attributed to him by Westbrook Pegler during the latter's smear campaign of many years.

He and I had talked from time to time of his writing a regular column in *The New Republic* when he left government service, and he seemed attracted by the idea. When Truman fired him, Mike Straight was already thinking of a great expansion of the paper, and with my enthusiastic approval, Wallace was approached about taking the job as editor, at a salary of $15,000 and a small expense account. The money was trifling compared to his profits from the hybrid-corn company, but he saw in the paper a fine forum for the statement of his liberal and humanitarian views, and agreed to come with us. He was installed in December, 1946, and my title was changed to editorial director.

His arrival coincided with the attempt to make *The New Republic* into a liberal *Time*. We added dozens of people to the staff, expanded the number of pages in an issue, went into a new typography and format, added illustrations and a second color on the cover. We spent a lot of money advertising the "new" *New Republic*, including the expensive services of Edward L. Bernays, then probably the best-known public-relations man in the country. Bernays never took a client he did not believe in; he was the father of the idea that the people he worked for should try to do something newsworthy, so that the communications media would seek them out. One of his ideas for us was to send Henry out to Des Moines to announce his new editorship, thus seeking to give the whole enterprise a Middle Western, grassroots flavor, and offsetting the ideas of radicalism and the effete East.

Henry moved to New York, and took up his new duties conscientiously, though his only actual contribution to the paper was a weekly page signed by him. Often he wrote this himself, scrawling with a pencil on a yellow pad; if he was too hard pressed or was out of town, one of the rest of us did a "first draft" which we sometimes read aloud to him; as I have suggested, he had a hard time staying awake on these occasions. These pieces he cheerfully signed, rarely altering a word. He took no other part in getting out the paper, which was done by the rest of us as in the past.

My chief personal memory of the Wallace days was the ordeal it was to go to lunch with Henry, which I had to do rather often. He was a fanatic on exercise, and got it by picking out a restaurant a mile or so away, and walking to it at such a fast pace it could be described as running. Nobody ever voluntarily "picked Henry up at the office" to take him to lunch—or at least, not more than once. After lunch, if he paid the bill, one or the other of us would surreptitiously add to the tip he left. His idea of the proper size of a gratuity had been set in his childhood in Des Moines, and was on the skimpy side.

Before long, Mike and I became aware that there were people in close contact with Henry other than ourselves. He had mysterious callers whom we did not know; speaking engagements were made for him that we had not initiated. What had happened was that the American Communist Party had closed in on him, doing a superb "snow job" to convince him that they were just a bunch of good liberals who liked and admired him, and wanted to see more of him.

In the winter of 1946-47 the Communists fully expected their party to be outlawed. Sooner than most other people, they saw the Cold War coming, and made plans to survive it. The C.P. itself would go underground, but they needed an aboveground organization to parallel it. Accordingly, they planned the Progressive Party, and found in Henry an ideal man to be its titular head. I don't mean to say, of course, that all the Progressives were Communists, just that all Communists were Progressives. In addition to them there were many thousands of innocent liberals who agreed with the carefully screened ideas that the party put forward, and were entirely unaware of the reasons for its coming into being.

Henry loved to speak in public to large audiences, and the Communists saw to it that his wishes were gratified. In Madison Square Garden in New York he addressed big crowds, and toured the other metropolitan centers across the country doing the same thing. In New York, at least, I believe the faithful were ordered to turn out to hear him. They probably did not need much coercion; the C.P. members are gluttons for punishment in the form of public oratory.

Mike Straight and I were concerned for Henry's future, and that of the magazine, and we tried to tell him that the new friends who were surrounding him were not what they seemed. He stoutly resisted this idea. "I have never met but one Communist in my life, as far as I know," he observed. This turned out to be a reporter who had interviewed him for *The Daily Worker*, who could hardly have pretended to be anything else. His new friends, Henry pointed out, got big audiences for him to speak to, everywhere. "Nobody else comes forward to arrange meetings for me," he observed. When Mike and I offered to do what we could to fill this gap, he evinced much skepticism, and he was right; we were not geared to try to arrange meetings. We had a magazine to get out.

If Henry wanted to make speeches, his new friends saw to it that his wishes were gratified; they kept him busy. Bright young men appeared in our office to help him as speech writers; they were not on our payroll, and did not seem concerned about money. They did not always succeed in getting Henry to say what they wanted said; once, for instance, in a speech in Madison Square Garden, he made a rather slighting reference to Russia, and was promptly booed by what seemed to me to be a majority of the audience. He promptly dropped from his prepared text the next couple of paragraphs, which were in the same vein. Since copies of the speech had been distributed in advance to the news media, this was not wise; the papers promptly printed the material he had left out—and very little else.

Because *The New Republic* had invested so much capital in Henry, spiritually and financially, we tried our best to accommodate ourselves to what was happening. Some of his speeches were sponsored jointly by the paper and by an organization which was to be the forerunner of the new party, and Mike Straight joined in some of the forays into the hinterland.

Meanwhile, the expansion of the paper went on at full speed. We began competing, in some salaries and in payments for contributions, with the multimillion-circulation magazines, a pace that made my head swim. We hired a high-priced art director, who bought high-priced art; we also engaged some editors and writers who have proved their worth by their subsequent careers. One was Theodore H. White, who was to go on to his famous series of books on *The Making of the President*. Penn Kimball in 1970 was on the faculty of the Pulitzer School of Journalism at Columbia, Joseph Lyford held a similar post at the University of California at Berkeley, Thomas Whiteside was on *The New Yorker*, and W. D. Patterson was publisher of *The Saturday Review*. Tristram Coffin's became a familiar Washington byline; William Walton, who soon went back to his first love, painting, was in the news during the Kennedy Administration as a close friend of the President and the First Lady. James R. Newman, before his death, became one of the bright stars of *The Scientific American* and editor of the fabulously successful four-volume anthology *The World of Mathematics*. Jack Weeks, before his retirement to Florida, was one of the top brass at *Newsweek*.

The new Progressive Party held its nominating convention in Philadelphia late in July, 1948. As everyone had known for months it would do, it named Henry as its presidential candidate. For his running mate it selected Glen Taylor, senator from Idaho, an eccentric, guitar-playing cowboy. Taylor planned to ride a horse from one coast to the other, making speeches as he went, but President Truman called Congress into session, and he had to abandon this form of electioneering.

As soon as Henry accepted the nomination, Mike Straight and I asked him to resign from *The New Republic*. We did not see how an avowed candidate for president could maintain the editorial independence that was our chief stock in trade. Also, we intended to support

Truman. Henry promptly and amicably agreed to the separation, which all of us had seen for some time was inevitable; he and I remained on good personal terms until his death nearly two decades later.

In his campaign speeches, Henry took positions that I am sure he afterward had cause to regret. He opposed not only the Truman Doctrine of armed support for democratic countries threatened by Communist uprisings, but the Marshall Plan, which offered aid to *all* countries devastated by the war and seeking to get back on their feet. When Czech Communists seized that country in a coup d'etat in 1948, with, of course, Russian backing, he condoned the action on the ground that the United States was about to engineer a right-wing takeover. All these were American Communist Party doctrines.

Some of the people and periodicals who had at first seen hope in the Progressive Party were repelled by its thick-and-thin pro-Russian policy. Frank Kingdon, a well-known liberal writer and speaker, resigned as cochairman of the antecedent organization, the Progressive Citizens of America. *The Nation* and *PM*, the New York left-wing daily, dropped off the bandwagon. So did the Amalgamated Clothing Workers, making men's clothes, and the International Ladies' Garment Workers' Union. Lacking funds for campaigning, the Wallaceites did something unusual —they charged admission to their big indoor rallies, where they had always passed the hat. Irwin Ross, in his book *The Loneliest Campaign* (New American Library, 1968), estimates that the average admission charge was $1.50—a lot of money for the kind of people who were attracted by the Progressive Party platform.

The election returns were a bitter disappointment to Wallace and his followers. Truman, whom *The New Republic* had supported, won with a little more than twenty-four million votes. Thomas E. Dewey, the Republican candidate, who had been the heavy favorite in the preelection betting, got not quite twenty-two million. Strom Thurmond, running as a splinter candidate for the States' Rights Democrats in the South, got 1,176,000 votes, and Wallace trailed him by nearly 20,000 votes, with 1,157,000—most of them in New York State where the Communists had their chief strength.

After leaving *The New Republic*, Wallace bought his farm in South Salem, New York, and began the work on chicken genetics already mentioned. How much he finally came to realize about the Communist influence in the 1948 campaign I never knew. I visited him on his farm now and then, but we did not discuss politics.

When the Communist North Korean government attacked South Korea in 1950, Wallace, like most Americans, was outraged. He issued a public statement excoriating it; the American Communists, who of course were all in favor of North Korea's action, promptly damned Henry in just as bitter terms as they would have used for J. P. Morgan.

Since Henry was of no more use to them, they felt they could afford the luxury of saying what they really thought of him.

With the 1948 election over, *The New Republic* was left in a difficult position. We had built our "great leap forward" around Wallace, and it wasn't much of a secret that we had finally been forced to ask for his resignation. Our readership had gone up, under very expensive forced draft, from about forty thousand to roughly one hundred thousand. I strongly suspect, with of course no proof, that the party members had been ordered to subscribe to "Wallace's paper," and were happy when with a clear conscience they could let these subscriptions lapse.

Within a few months it was clear that our readers didn't really want "a liberal *Time*," with or without Henry Wallace. The promotion expense was still very heavy, and there seemed no point in continuing it. Accordingly, we drew in our horns; nearly all the large number of writers, editors, researchers, and others who had been engaged were regretfully let go. Most of them took it amicably, and with the one or two exceptions we soon managed to come to an understanding.

In 1950 we decided to move the paper to Washington. Since the Second World War the government was the dominant factor in American life, as New York, the financial and intellectual capital, had been for the previous hundred years. In Washington we could get firsthand information about what was going on in every department of the government. Let me anticipate a little and say that the move was successful in every way, one of the shrewdest things we ever did.

We offered every New York employee a chance to move with the paper, but as usually happens in these cases, not a single individual was willing to do so. Their homes were in New York, their friends, their leisure activities.

Mrs. Elmhirst had not only supported *The New Republic* from its beginning, but she had given substantial support to several other magazines as well, including *Asia*, *Antiques*, and *Theatre Arts*. In 1933, she had suggested that all these magazines move into common quarters, and we did so, taking two floors of a tall office building on East Forty-ninth Street near Madison Avenue. Though each magazine maintained complete editorial independence, some of our business functions were consolidated, at a substantial monetary saving. Many of the business employees of *The New Republic* were serving all four magazines in 1950, and continued to do so. Eventually, it was decided to give up *Asia*, and for complicated reasons that have no part in this narrative, *Theatre Arts* left the group, but *Antiques* was growing, and had turned into a profitable operation.

Malcolm Cowley had left the paper some years before, as I have recorded elsewhere. George Soule did not find the atmosphere of the expanded operation under Wallace congenial, and decided to go into college teaching. He pursued this course with distinction for some years, at Bennington College and elsewhere, before he reached retirement age; he also found time to produce several books on economics for laymen which sold very well. As far as I am aware, no member of the staff suffered any real hardship because of *The New Republic*'s move to Washington.

After Malcolm's departure, and when the paper had shrunk back to its normal size and character, we had several literary editors, of whom only two stick strongly in my memory. One was Nigel Dennis, a young Englishman, who performed his duties acceptably for a while, and then went back to London. There he wrote several novels, one at least of which attracted favorable attention. I was told that a character in it was supposed to be a lampoon of me, but if so, I didn't recognize myself. (Everybody is always reluctant to identify the weaker sides of his own character.)

The other man was Alfred Kazin, who then had published only his first book, *On Native Grounds*, a study of American fiction of the past fifty years or so. The generation gap was emphasized for me when I found that Alfred had gone to the New York Public Library and there had read, one after another, all the novelists whom I had followed over the years as fast as their books were published. In 1970 he was a teacher at the Stony Brook, Long Island, branch of the University of the State of New York and widely known as critic and essayist. What seems to me his best book, up to now, is *A Walker in the City*, a beautifully written account of his childhood in a poverty-stricken Jewish home in Brooklyn.

In the fall of 1950, I went down to Washington to break in a new production crew, under the continuing editorship of Mike Straight, who had moved back to the capital, where he had lived for some years before the great Wallace episode. In a couple of months, things were running smoothly in the paper's new home, and I returned to New York, where I continued to write for the paper.

In the early 1950's, because of the way in which her estate was set up, it became impracticable for Mrs. Elmhirst to continue her financial support to the magazine. Luckily, purchasers for the paper were found in the persons of Mr. and Mrs. Gilbert Harrison. Michael Straight was beginning to get the writer's itch that finally resulted in his two fine novels of pioneer life, and a year or so later, he resigned as editor, and Gil assumed this role as well as that of publisher. He is an admirer of the type of paper Herbert Croly produced, and that I had tried to maintain.

No magazine can afford to stand still, much less to look back, but I think it is generally agreed that the new editor has succeeded in producing a paper with the intellectual quality *The New Republic* has always stood for, plus a lively journalistic impact.

The circulation in 1970 was roughly four times as large as in my day, perhaps attributable to several factors: the move to Washington, the more liberal climate since the end of McCarthyism, the urgency of our national problems today, the increase in population—especially in the colleges—plus, and foremost, Gil's own skill as an editor.

My own future was decided for me by the doctors. In 1948 I developed angina pectoris, in the form called effort angina. In 1951 and 1952 I had a couple of heart attacks (myocardial infarctions). They were not severe, but my doctor first forbade me to go to the office at all, and then decided I had better get into a milder climate than New York City. In the winter cold, my impaired circulation would leave me standing immobilized on a street corner, causing strangers to assume, no doubt, that I was drunk.

In the interval between these two medical decisions, I wrote a book of popular science, *Preview for Tomorrow*, discussing some of the world's unsolved problems on which science and technology can help, and what is being done about them. Published by Alfred Knopf, it was a very modest success, but it enabled me to get a lot of things out of my system.

In early 1953 I was getting ready to write a history of the 1930's and 1940's, told through biographical sketches of the eight most important men of that era, throughout the world. Since I had just been exiled from New York, it seemed an obviously good idea to return to Stanford, where the Hoover Institution was the world's greatest storehouse of material about world history for the past half century. Accordingly, my wife and I moved to California—back where we had started forty years earlier, and into quasi-retirement—a story that deserves a chapter of its own.

Chapter 14

"FROM OUR NEW YORK CORRESPONDENT"

In 1927, Arthur Krock was moving from *The New York World* to *The Times.* The easygoing *World* had permitted him a moonlighting job as New York correspondent of *The Manchester Guardian*, but either *The Times* was more demanding, or Krock himself decided not to scatter his energies. (He does not mention the *Guardian* job in his best-selling *Memoirs: Sixty Years on the Firing Line.*) At any rate, he offered me the post, and I accepted, beginning on March first. I filed a story of three hundred to one thousand words six days a week for the next twenty years, roughly six thousand articles.

To take on this burden was madness. I was putting in a full day as managing editor of *The New Republic*, and carrying home a fat briefcase of work every night. The deadline for filing to the London office of *The Guardian* was three o'clock in the afternoon, just when the tide of urgent business at *The New Republic* was at its flood. Krock had been on the night side at *The World;* he could write his piece at home and drop it off at a telegraph office on his way to work, but my job was in theory a nine-to-five affair, though I often imitated Herbert Croly and worked at home for an hour before coming in. The pay was not high—£ 500 a year, which then translated into roughly $2,500—worth, of course, at least twice as much as the same sum today.

The chief reason I took the job was simple egoism. *The Guardian* was then, and may still be today, the best-written newspaper in the English language, and one of the three or four most prestigious in the world. *The Times* (of London, a fact it disdained to put into its logotype), was "the Thunderer," usually closer to the government than the liberal *Guardian*, but it had little of the felicity of style that was to be encountered on every page of the *M.G.*

The editor when I started my daily messages was Charles P. Scott, the last of the great nineteenth-century journalists. He had assumed his post in 1872 when the paper was owned by his brother-in-law, and on the death of the latter in 1905, he became owner as well—an idyllic position for any editor. He was already eighty-one (which seemed to me in 1927 a huge age), but he was still in full control of the paper, and not too busy to send an occasional letter of appreciation to his New York correspondent. He retired as editor two years later, and died in 1932.

The editorship was handed over to his son, whom nobody called anything but Ted. When the latter was drowned only a few weeks later, W. P. Crozier became editor, and served until his death in 1944. He was succeeded by A. P. Wadsworth for another twelve years, continuing long after I had severed my connection with the paper. Wadsworth in turn was followed by the man still at the helm in the late 1960's, Alastair Hetherington. Newspaper editors usually live and die in anonymity, which is why I am pleased to record these names of towering if comparatively unknown figures.

The Guardian and I parted company amicably in 1947. With my steadily more onerous duties at the *N. R.*, the daily dispatch to England had become an increasing burden. My salary had never been raised—during the difficult war and postwar years the paper was just barely keeping afloat—and I had begun part-time free-lancing in large-circulation American magazines. In the spare moments of a week or two, I could turn out an article for any of half a dozen of them that would bring in more money than three hundred pieces—a year of labor—for *The Guardian*. I was succeeded by Alistair Cooke; quite apart from the fact that the paper wanted a full-time correspondent in the United States (today it has two, and sometimes three), Alistair, a brilliant writer who compensates for his British birth by knowing more about America than almost any American, was far better suited to the paper than I.

When I began, *The Guardian* was still dominated by nineteenth-century standards; all the articles were unsigned, and the foreign correspondence, in particular, was couched in stately Victorian prose. Of my six thousand articles, I don't believe more than two or three were signed; the others were all headed "From Our New York Correspondent."

I can now see that with the death of Mr. Scott, the editors wanted to liven up and modernize the paper; but for some reason they could never bring themselves to ask me to change the character of my reporting for this purpose. They tried to hint, I believe, by reading *The New Republic* and complimenting me on signed articles written in lighter, informal prose; but if this was their purpose, I was too obtuse to take the hint.

It was an exciting twenty years during which I daily reported on America for *The Guardian*—the last two years of the great speculative madness of the 1920's, the decade of the Depression, the Second World War, and the first two years of the Cold War. I did not confine my reporting to New York City; every day I picked out the most exciting thing going on anywhere in the United States and wrote an article about it that was half reporting, half editorial comment—very much, in fact, like the brief notes of which I wrote a number every week in my own paper.

Nowadays a foreign correspondent as a rule telephones in his articles; they are recorded in the home office, sometimes with an editor listening in and interrupting when necessary to ask that a sentence be repeated, or a difficult name spelled out. In my day everything went by cable or—rarely—by wireless, at the special press rate of five cents a word, collected in Manchester. To save money, we used an abbreviated type of English known as "cablese," leaving out as many words as possible, and adding Latin prefixes or suffixes to others; I was perpetually being called on the carpet by Western Union for having gone too far in putting words together.

As a random example, if I wanted to say "President Hoover does not intend to visit Latin America at this time," I wrote "Hoover unintends adlatamerica presently," cutting twelve words down to four. With the pressure on me, I learned to dictate in cablese; I doubt whether anyone eavesdropping could have made any sense out of what I was saying. On the other hand, in six thousand articles I cannot remember a single serious error made by the copyeditors in England in expanding my dispatches. Never a word was changed, omitted, or added, in all that time. American editors are accustomed to slash, rewrite, or leave out material from their foreign correspondents, but this was not *The Guardian*'s way.

When I was traveling in America, I filed every day from wherever I was, taking account of the increased time lag as I went farther west. I had nobody to fill in for me when I was unavailable; if I was on vacation, I usually wrote my daily article if I was in the United States; when I went abroad, the correspondence was simply suspended until I returned to American soil. In the summer, for many years, my family occupied a cottage in a resort area not far from New York, and I went down for weekends. On Sundays I got the New York newspapers, decided what was the leading story of the day, wrote it, and by various means got it into the hands of the nearest telegraph agent. If I was far from a town, I would sometimes drive there and dictate my story en route to my long-suffering wife, sitting beside me with a portable typewriter on her lap—and then struggle to get some frightened young woman in a Western Union office to accept a collect cable costing up to $50.

During my twenty years of service, the official attitude of Great Britain was friendly toward the United States, but some of the popular papers loved to print items from this country about the eccentric behavior of the inhabitants. *The Guardian* usually resisted this temptation, but there were a few exceptions. One of them came when Constantin Brancusi, the noted Yugoslav sculptor, tried to bring into the United States his famous brass statue *Bird in Flight* (now in the Museum of Modern Art), a needle-pointed spire which does indeed give the viewer a feeling of soaring. The U.S. customs authorities refused to concede that this was a work of art; they called it simply "a brass artifact," and proposed to impose duty on it on that basis. Brancusi took his case to court, won it, and the law was changed to permit the importation of modern art objects duty free. *The Guardian* loved this controversy, and I reported every detail in its columns.

As correspondent for an English paper, I worked closely with the British Information Service in New York, an institution so good that as an American I wished fervently we could match it with our own efforts abroad. It never indulged in propaganda as this is commonly construed; it answered thousands of inquiries a year from the general public as well as from reporters, and arranged interviews with visiting British V.I.P.'s. The effects of these things are intangible and can rarely be proved statistically, but I am confident that the B.I.S. was of enormous value in preventing discord across the ocean. The Foreign Office realized the importance of the post and saw to it that civil servants of high quality were sent to New York.

Their subsequent careers justified this impression. Sir Isaiah Berlin went on to be a well-known Oxford don, and author of a brilliant book, *The Hedgehog and the Fox.* Douglas Ritchie became a leading figure in the B.B.C., making in person the famous "Colonel Britton" broadcasts to occupied Europe during the war. Sir Alan Dudley was a distinguished member of the diplomatic service for many years. Sir Berkeley Ormerod, a major in the British Army, and known to a whole generation of New York newspapermen as "Bill," held several high posts with the B.I.S. before his retirement. D'Arcy Edmondson became British consul general in Boston. René MacColl, who had come from *The Daily Express* (London), returned to the paper after the war. I am listing only some of the men I worked with; there were a dozen others equally efficient and helpful.

The men at the B.I.S. read my work in *The New Republic,* and never quite got accustomed to the fact that I was often highly critical of what the American government was doing. They were all civil servants, trained to explain and justify British actions. When I wrote about Amer-

ica in *The Guardian* I found myself reporting and to some extent defending Washington's actions. I don't mean that what I wrote for readers on
one side of the Atlantic was inconsistent with what I wrote for the other;
it was a question of emphasis. Every American, when he goes abroad,
finds it necessary to try to correct the colossal ignorance about his country he finds everywhere, ignorance that often leads to misunderstanding
and denigration of motives. By explaining my own compatriots day after
day to the British, I believe I was helped to write with more balance and
judgment for Americans.

The *Guardian* connection was of value to me as editor of *The New
Republic* in other ways. It opened doors that would otherwise have been
closed to me, and made possible many valuable personal contacts. Articles in one paper were sometimes a dress rehearsal for those in the other.

A matter that called for tact on my part was the scandal, before the
abdication, about King Edward VIII and Mrs. Wally Simpson of Baltimore. The British press for months invoked a very tight censorship on
this subject, while the press of other countries, and especially the United
States, was full of it. Finally I cabled *The Guardian* for instructions, and
got back a stiff, British reply, saying in effect, send whatever news you
deem important. Thereupon I wrote a cable or two simply reporting the
amount of space the American papers were giving to the matter. *The
Guardian* printed this material, deadpan, and was among the first papers
in England to mention the affair.

When I visited London, I had a better inside view of Fleet Street
than would have been possible without the *Guardian* connection. I
seemed to get a sense of enormous strain, anxiety, and competitiveness
among British newspapermen. I met a number of free-lance book reviewers and writers of articles for the Sunday papers, and was astonished to
see both how hard they worked and how well they seemed to live on
earnings which, I was assured, were in some cases small.

I dined in the homes of some of these writers, and was interested
to find working journalists who, as far as I could judge, actually dressed
for dinner every night.

On one occasion I had a drink with a friend in the famous Bohemian
restaurant, the Café Royale, and was thrilled to see Augustus John, then
one of the best-known British painters, at the next table. He had come
in wearing a broad-brimmed black hat and a cape, which he piled on a
vacant chair beside him, and then sat silent for an hour, staring into space
—while I felt a long way from Emmetsburg.

I also got a sense of how loyal the chief British papers were in those
days to the Crown, part of their loyalty to the Commonwealth. During
one of my early visits, the Prince of Wales (later Edward VIII) was on
a goodwill tour to some remote part of the world, on a British battleship.
When the vessel crossed the Equator, there were the usual pranks. The

Prince dressed up as a Hawaiian dancing girl in a flimsy grass skirt, his picture was taken in this costume, and a press service sent it out for publication.

I was in the office of a leading morning paper late at night, when this picture came up for consideration. There was a hasty editorial conference and the decision was made not to run it; thereupon, one or two of the top editors quickly got on the telephone to other papers, telling them this journal did not intend to use the picture, and getting an agreement that the others would do the same. As far as I know, it never appeared anywhere.

The London editor of *The Guardian* was James Bone, who came from a distinguished family; one brother was Muirhead Bone, a noted etcher, and another was David Bone, a captain in the merchant marine, with whom Joseph Conrad always traveled when he went to sea. James wrote at least one successful book about walking in London, a city he knew well and loved. This imperturbable Scotsman, in his sixties, was on a ship that was torpedoed and sunk off the Irish coast during the Second World War; James was in the water for some time before he got into a lifeboat and was finally transferred to a ship. I could never get him to say a word about it, beyond the mild observation that it was a disagreeable experience.

I found this reticence about war experiences was true of almost all my British friends. Visiting London only a few weeks after the end of the war, I talked with people who had stayed in the city during the blitz, had slept in the subway for months on end, had had their homes destroyed, but their comment was about like that of James Bone. Britain was still very short of food, and rationing was drastic; yet when I dined out with friends, they used up many of their precious coupons to feed me, in spite of all my pleas that I was on a reducing diet. I had trouble not to gain weight.

My visits to Manchester were fascinating to an American newspaperman. The four or five writers of "leaders" (editorials), worked in cubbyholes like those I was used to at home; several of them had grown up in Lancashire, and I was interested to hear these men, some of them bearers of famous names in journalism, speaking with an accent I could hardly understand.

Once I stayed overnight in the home of the editor, and before dinner we took a walk through a broad meadow behind his house. He was accompanied by his dog, which barked at some sheep belonging to a neighbor. Instantly the owner sprang out from behind a hedge, scarlet with rage, and began abusing the editor at the top of his voice, continuing what was evidently a long-standing feud. The editor, who spoke Oxford English to me, promptly began shouting back in broad Lancashire. After a few minutes, honor being satisfied on both sides, they suddenly separated, and the editor and I continued our walk.

On one of my visits to London, my friend S. K. Ratcliffe took my wife and me to a small meeting of the Fabian Society that was to be addressed by George Bernard Shaw. We were introduced to him, and he affably invited us to sit on the platform behind him while he talked (it was a small room, with only forty or fifty chairs, all occupied). His talk was a casual affair, suited to the size of the group, about Socialist politics.

After it was over, and he had disposed of the usual contingent from the audience who wanted to shake his hand or ask a private question, my wife happened to mention that just before leaving New York a few days earlier, we had seen the Theater Guild production of *Back to Methuselah*. Instantly he was alert, and began firing questions at her about the scenic design, the costumes, how the various parts had been interpreted. My wife is blessed with total recall and a photographic memory, and she was able to answer everything he asked. This was the highly businesslike playwright speaking, the man who had remarked to Sam Goldwyn, who wanted to make a movie of one of his plays, "The trouble is, Mr. Goldwyn, that you want to talk about Art, and I want to talk about money."

On one of my visits to London and Manchester, I had one of the great experiences of my life: several hours alone with Mahatma Gandhi. He had been let out of jail in India to attend the Imperial Conference in London, knowing that he would go back into jail as soon as the conference was over, but I found no trace of bitterness in him. I saw him in the home of a friend that had been lent to him for the duration of his visit. He was sitting cross-legged on the floor, in a room with no furniture, wrapped in a huge and beautiful white blanket (it was a chilly London day), and his tiny dark head seemed smaller still against this background. He was spinning cotton on a small hand-operated wheel, which may have been a bit of theatrics for my benefit. (He had persuaded millions of Indian women to go back to home weaving of cloth as a part of his economic boycott of British goods.) He greeted me warmly; he knew that *The New Republic* had been fighting hard for Indian independence for many years, and could safely assume we should continue doing so. His lieutenant of that time, Jawaharlal Nehru, who was to become prime minister, told me years later how faithfully the paper had been read by the leaders of the independence movement.

I suggested to Mr. Gandhi that I sit down beside him on the floor, but he demurred. "You're not used to it," he pointed out. "In twenty minutes you will be stiff and uncomfortable." He ordered a small straight chair brought in for me, and the interview was conducted with my head several feet higher than his.

What he told me, which I of course published in due course, is of no importance compared to the enormous impact of his personality. He seemed to me a man of transcendent sweetness; I instantly felt at ease with him as I have with few others in my life, on such brief acquaintance. I asked him hard questions, as it is the business of a journalist to do; but when I tried to lay traps for him he saw them, and laughingly evaded them. (They chiefly had to do with whether the Indian revolutionaries would accept aid in large amounts from Soviet Russia.) If I had not already been converted to his cause, I should have become a follower that day; when I said good-bye, I felt that I was leaving the greatest man I had ever encountered—and a friend.

Another great man I met as a *Guardian* correspondent. I was one of three or four representatives of British papers invited, soon after the end of the war, to an off-the-record talk with Winston Churchill. He had just disembarked from a ship, and sat in a canvas chair on the pier while we clustered around him. As Gandhi's stage prop was a spinning wheel, Churchill's was a big expensive-looking cigar, of which he smoked only an inch or so. When one of us asked him a question, he was silent so long that we began to feel he had not heard it; but then, after preliminary rumblings like a volcano about to erupt, out came his reply, eloquently phrased, witty if wit was possible, evasive if evasion was in the interest of statesmanship, and followed sometimes by a slight gesture with his cigar, like an orchestra leader signaling the end of a movement in a symphony.

Over the years I knew a succession of editors of the British weeklies that were opposite numbers to *The New Republic,* several of which finally merged into *The New Statesman.* The editors included an alcoholic and a man who suffered for months on end from acute vertigo. This paper had been leading a hand-to-mouth existence like most liberal weeklies, until John Maynard Keynes took it in hand, recapitalized it, ran the circulation up to about 100,000, and, mirabile dictu, made it show a modest profit. Of its small staff I knew best the editor, Kingsley Martin, an able journalist but, I thought, with a blind eye to Russia's imperfections and a too sharp one for America's failings. I remember his striding into a London drawing room and demanding of me as soon as he entered, in the presence of a lot of people, "Well, what wicked thing has Uncle Sam done today?" I was glad to be able to tell him that I was aware of no misbehavior for at least twenty-four hours. *The New Statesman* had many attractive features, but as was the case with the rest of us, it was read mostly by those already converted to its views.

In Washington during the Second World War, I made friends with Israel Sieff (now Baron Sieff of Brimpton), the able head of Marks & Spencer, the British equivalent of the American Woolworth's, and in some ways remarkably enterprising and socially minded. He had been sent to this country by his government to assist in furthering economic cooperation between the two powers, and was a natural target for the isolationist, Britain-hating, bullyboys in Congress. With my *Guardian* contacts, and some knowledge of American public-relations problems, I did what I could to ease his path.

On one occasion, I remember spending a weekend with him in England at his place in the country, and somehow the subject of vintage wines came up. I casually remarked that this was a subject of which I knew nothing; this was a dreadful mistake, since apparently *all* true connoisseurs talk this way. Israel, assuming I had uttered a code phrase of the cognoscenti, began talking about burgundies. (I learned afterward that he was one of the world's great authorities on these, and had written a book about them.) Presently he was decanting several bottles for me to taste, despite my protests, in mounting hysteria, that he was wasting his riches on me. He wound up with a priceless bottle of what was, as I remember, Cheval Blanc 1921, the greatest of all recent vintage years; even I could see that this was indeed a wonderful wine. But I learned my lesson, with the discovery that to repudiate expertise is worse than to claim it.

On several occasions I combined a visit to Manchester with a swing around some of the capitals of Western Europe. I wrote for *The New Republic* a piece about each country in turn, at the rate of one a week; as every newspaperman knows, the only way to report on a nation is to stay a few days, or else several years—either superficial impressions, or a real knowledge. I relied on the foreign correspondents in each city to help me out, and they responded nobly. In Paris, Paul Scott Mowrer of *The Chicago Daily News* and Robert Dell, the great old correspondent of *The Guardian,* kept me from making a fool of myself. In Berlin, Paul's brother, Edgar Ansel Mowrer, and H. R. Knickerbocker of what was then International News Service, owned by Hearst, were helpful. I also met the Berlin correspondent of *The Guardian,* a subdued young man named Malcolm Muggeridge. Like Westbrook Pegler a decade earlier, he showed no signs of turning into the professional curmudgeon and common scold that he later became as editor of *Punch* and a bright star of British television.

In Vienna I remember three men who aided me greatly. They were John Gunther, still some years away from the first of his "inside" books (*Inside Europe*), Whit Burnett, who was already brooding over the idea of an annual anthology of the American short story, and M. W. Fodor, the skilled journalist whom we had printed in *The Globe,* who probably knew more about Eastern Europe than anybody else. In Moscow, so bewildering to the stranger, I was guided by Louis Fischer and Walter Duranty.

A few incidents of that Russian visit stick in my memory. I was interviewed by the famous old American Communist, Anna Louise Strong, for *The Moscow News,* the English-language, but of course ardently Communist, daily. She wrote a rather nasty report of our interview, putting me down as a wishy-washy apologist for capitalism. I took a somewhat malicious pleasure when years later she was abruptly expelled from Soviet Russia. After her many years of service, some Americans thought this was rather cruel, but the Russians turned out to be right; after getting her breath in California, only ten miles from where I was living, she next turned up in Peking as a propagandist for Mao.

Like every foreign visitor making a brief stay, I was in the hands of Intourist, the Russian travel agency, whose pretty girl guides were not only marvelous linguists, but also, of course, loyal defenders of the Soviet Union in all its ways. One of them took me to see some half-finished ten-story apartment houses on the outskirts of Moscow; such height seemed wonderful to her, and she asked me, "Mr. Bliven, have you anything like that in America?"

I remembered the recently erected Empire State Building, which was still having great trouble finding tenants for its offices, and I answered, "Lady, in New York we have a building a hundred stories tall, and mostly empty for lack of tenants."

Probably thinking of the terrible overcrowding in Moscow (and all other Russian cities), she looked at me with incredulity, and said, "Please, Mr. Bliven, if you want to tell me your bourgeois tall tales, try to make them reasonable." She had never heard of the Empire State Building; she shared what was to me the alarming ignorance of the outside world which then prevailed in Papa Stalin's "paradise."

Another insight I got into the Russian mind came at the Intourist hotel where I was staying. My travel ticket called for lodging and two meals a day; though the fact had been successfully concealed from me and almost all other foreigners, Russia was on very short rations at the time, and my two meals a day tended to be just alike, mostly caviar, black bread, and cabbage soup.

This went on for weeks, until one day I entered the hotel dining room as usual, and my dinner was set before me—black bread and cabbage soup. I had the same waiter every day, he spoke English, and so I asked him, "Where's my caviar?"

"No caviar," was the answer. "Your ticket doesn't call for caviar."

"But it does," I protested. "I've had caviar every day for weeks. You've served me yourself." But he was obdurate.

Next day at the accustomed hour I came into the dining room again, and the same waiter brought me my supper—black bread, cabbage soup, *and* a big helping of caviar.

"What goes on here?" I asked him. "Yesterday you said my ticket doesn't call for caviar."

Over his face spread that wonderful Russian pall of incomprehension that every visitor knows. "Must have been some mistake," was all he would say.

The answer, of course, is simple. The day before, because of some contretemps, the hotel had temporarily run out of caviar. In the Socialist paradise, you couldn't ever admit running out of anything.

The tourist lived in a dream world that had little relation to the reality of life for the Russian people. I got a couple of small glimpses of what that reality was. I had brought with me from America a big bar of bath soap, and I had an incorrigible habit of leaving it in the common bathroom down the hall. Several times the chambermaid brought it back to me; she spoke no English, but her round eyes expressed incredulity at such carelessness, with something so precious, so unattainable, as soap.

I had a letter of introduction from New York to a Russian girl, and escaped the clutches of Intourist long enough to present it to her and to be asked to tea. She shared a one-room apartment with a man, who happened to be her ex-husband, and a married couple with two small children. With perfect aplomb the three groups managed the problem of such close quarters; the ex-husband stayed in the most distant corner, with his face turned away; the married couple sent their children out to play, and themselves occupied another corner, while Elena and I had our tea in a third. I tried to talk to her on noncommittal subjects so that she would not be in trouble with the secret police if our talk was reported, which seemed likely. I never saw her again, but years later I heard that she had disappeared, presumably liquidated by Stalin; I have always hoped that my innocent dropping in for tea was not one of the counts against her.

Walter Duranty not only gave me wise advice about what was going on in Russia, but he had me to dinner—a delicious meal, and a heaven-sent release from my black bread and caviar. He had as hostess a beautiful Russian girl, his secretary, who, he and everybody else assumed, was doubtless an agent of the secret police.

Another guest at that dinner was a brash young American, a temporary visitor in Moscow, and for some incredible reason he decided to quiz Walter on his domestic life. Was he married? the young man wanted to know, and Walter said he was. But this young lady was not Mrs. Duranty? Correct. Where *was* Mrs. Duranty? Walter made what has always seemed to me the perfect answer to an impertinent busybody's query. "My wife," he said, "lives in the South of France, on top of a steep hill —and I have a wooden leg."

In the more than two decades since I left the service of *The Guardian*, the paper has moved steadily forward. Since it is a national paper, it dropped the word "Manchester" out of the logotype, and it publishes the national edition from a separate plant in the outskirts of London. Its weekly airmail version is read all over the world, and especially in the

United States, and it is holding its own in the frenetic British newspaper competition.

I look back on *The Guardian* with affection, as I do on all the five journals I served in my more than sixty years of daily or weekly journalism. Of the five, three still survive and are going strong—an unusual record in the hazardous, always stormy seas of paper and ink.

Chapter 15

THE POPULARIZER

In the late 1930's I began to write in a field that had been a lifelong interest of mine—reporting on science and technology for a lay audience. I have always winced a little at the common phrase for this— "popular science writing"—because it either sounds like boasting about one's success, or an assumption that many people are interested in the result, neither of which things is necessarily true. At any rate, I wrote for the *New Republic* audience about medicine, biology, physics, astronomy, biochemistry, and everything else in the field that seemed worth reporting. My articles got a response that surprised me. Many of them were reprinted in *The Reader's Digest,* and for years they were the *only* things in the *N.R.* that were. I wrote two books in this field, the first of which, *The Men Who Make the Future,* was largely a reprint of my articles. It was the most successful book I have produced, being published in the United States, England, and, translated into the appropriate languages, in Brazil, Argentina, France, German-speaking Switzerland, and Norway.

My second book in this field, *Preview for Tomorrow: The Unfinished Business of Science,* was, as the title suggests, a progress report on some of the problems by which mankind is confronted, and what is being done about them. Back in 1953 I was somewhat ahead of my time in writing about overpopulation, pollution of air, water, and soil, large-scale juvenile delinquency, and other things that look even more serious today than then. When science and technology overlap, as they so often do, I reported on both, in talking about such things as devices for desalinization of water, heat pumps, solar furnaces, rainmaking techniques, and civilian uses of atomic energy.

Since my own education in science had been pitifully inadequate, this meant a lot of hard work. I solved it in part by going and interviewing top experts in each of these fields, first cramming myself full of as much information as I could hold, in the New York Public Library. When I wrote on the viruses, I interviewed William M. Stanley, who probably knew more about this subject than anyone else in the world. On physics, I talked with several "fathers" of the atomic bomb, E. O. Lawrence, Enrico Fermi, and Harold Urey. On cancer research I was helped by Peyton Rous, who discovered Rous's sarcoma, and was the first to prove that some cancers, at least, are caused by viruses. I corresponded with Willard Libby, who was enormously helpful on radioactive carbon dating, and with Melvin Calvin, who was equally generous in regard to photosynthesis. All these men except one got Nobel Prizes, some before and some after I sought their aid.

As I have said elsewhere, I have had a lifetime rule never to publish an interview until the subject has seen the copy, and whenever possible, to accept all his suggestions for changes. As a result, in all the scores of articles and chapters I have written on recondite aspects of science, I can't recall ever making a real error, though of course some of the predictions that scientists have made to me and I have passed on have failed to materialize.

Among those who helped me above and beyond the call of duty I remember Harlow Shapley and Bart J. Bok, astronomers; Albert Blakeslee, geneticist of the Carnegie Institution; Robert C. Cook, biochemist, who guided my faltering steps in a report on the origins of life that got reprinted by the Smithsonian Institution; Lewis Terman, the "father of the I.Q.," whom I had known as an undergraduate at Stanford; Brock Chisholm, the psychiatrist, head of the World Health Organization of the United Nations; Warren Weaver, who in the Second World War was chairman of the committee on "difficult mathematical problems" for the U.S. Government; John J. Bittner, who found a cancer-producing factor in the mother's milk of mice bred for generations for susceptibility to this disease. Dr. Louis Katz, then president of the American Heart Association, took much trouble to set me straight on the causes of atherosclerosis. Hudson Hoagland of the Worcester Foundation for Experimental Biology was of great help to me on the always fascinating subject of the electrical processes of the brain. Flanders Dunbar's pioneering book *Psychosomatic Medicine* helped to focus attention on the relation between illness in mind and body; through her I believe I was, for a time, the only lay member of the Psychosomatic Society of America. I used to enjoy its meetings, at which psychoanalysts were deliberately rude to one another—as their own psychoanalysts had told them they ought to be!

There has been an unbelievable improvement in science writing in newspapers since I began more than thirty years ago. In those days most science in dailies was what William Randolph Hearst used to call "gee whiz" material in the Sunday supplements on "Is there life on Mars?" The only newspaper, as far as I know, with a really competent science writer on its staff at that time was, as you might expect, *The New York Times*, which had not only one man, but two. One of them, the science editor, was an old friend of mine, Waldemar Kaempffert, who had been editor of *Scientific American* before that magazine underwent its remarkable transformation at the hands of Gerard Piel. The science reporter was William Laurence, the only journalist allowed to be present at the explosion of the first atom bomb at Alamagordo, New Mexico, in July, 1945. *The New York Herald Tribune* soon followed *The Times* with, I believe, Earl Ubell. There may have been other newspapers around the country that did well at an early date; if there are any records covering the situation, I am not aware of them.

Early science writers on dailies, with a few exceptions like *The Times*, had a difficult time. They were usually general-assignment reporters who had the science beat in addition to other duties. Their mainstay was medical news, with heavy emphasis on miracle cures for various diseases, most of them greatly exaggerated as to their importance, or false. The writers were ignorant of the subjects they wrote about, and the news executives on their papers were more so. The science writer had to fight to get anything printed at all, since the news hole is always badly crowded, and they often yielded to the human temptation to exaggerate the importance of the story. A running feud began between scientific researchers and writers, which has lasted to this day, though relations are now somewhat better. (Doctors are forbidden by their professional societies to publicize themselves.)

Magazines of general circulation ignored science and technology even more than did newspapers, though the women's magazines found a perennial subject in diets for weight reduction—and sometimes did a lot of damage by suggesting menus that would do harm if followed.

An invaluable aid in bringing science to the public attention was Science Service, established and endowed by E. W. Scripps, one of the founders of what finally became the Scripps-Howard chain of newspapers in many cities. Scripps was a pioneer in believing that science was important, and in doing something about it. He established *The Science Newsletter*, reporting accurately on developments in all fields, and providing a steady, ample flow of science news to dailies, at a nominal cost. Under the leadership for many years of Watson Davis, the Scripps program had a great impact on the quality of the material in the dailies.

Another influence of great importance has been the National Association of Science Writers, of which I am now one of the longest-term members. This group has worked wonders in developing professional standards among science writers, in alerting the press to the importance of science, and in pushing scientists—and the medical profession in particular—toward a realization of the public's right to know. It has also helped on technical but important matters: the need for adequate press releases in advance of a scientific meeting, the setting of proper release dates and hours, the holding of mass interviews when necessary, and the treating of all writers alike, instead of leaking information to a favored few. The organization has stood behind its members when some scientist who has been indiscreet has tried to blame the innocent reporter. It has also collaborated in setting up annual awards for outstanding work.

It is popular to say that Sputnik, in 1957, caused a great burst of interest in science in this country, but this is only a half-truth. Space activities have lain more in the field of technology than pure science, and have encouraged physicists more than other types of scientists. The N.A.S.W. had assumed importance before Sputnik, and its influence has continued in many other fields.

Most of my own writing during the Second World War was in nonsensitive areas, and I had little trouble with censorship. When the atom bomb was under development, I interviewed the physicists mentioned above, and others, and wrote several articles about harnessing atomic energy. Today I marvel at the skill of men like John Dunning and Enrico Fermi of Columbia University, who talked to me with seeming freedom on this subject, though looking back years later I realize that they had avoided telling me anything that was a potentially dangerous secret. After Hiroshima, I had been sufficiently well briefed so that (with the aid of the invaluable Smyth Report) I was able to write a couple of articles on nuclear fission. Like everybody else, I was horrified at the terrible loss of life, especially after cracks in the censorship revealed that Japan had already been on her knees.

The Armed Services recognized my work as a science writer on several occasions. One of these came when I was one of a small group of science writers invited to visit Wright Field, near Dayton, Ohio, a center for many types of military research. There I saw the newly invented technique of using a huge spinning disk, "a human centrifuge," to simulate pressures of several times gravity, in training pilots. I saw the early work on helicopters, which involved a high level of fatalities. I also saw a captured German "buzz bomb," one of the kind that wreaked such terrible havoc on London; from it our military experts were learning the first elements of jet propulsion.

On another occasion I was given all the facts about the newly operational B-29, the last heavy bomber of the Second World War. Long obsolete today, this was at the time the most powerful plane on earth, flying higher, faster, and farther than any other. The pressurized cabin, today a commonplace of civilian life, was developed because of its needs; so was computerized aiming of guns, which takes into account all the numerous necessary factors.

So much has the atmosphere of secrecy thickened since the end of that war, that no civilian writer would today be given access to such a mass of information as I received at Wright Field and elsewhere. My articles were submitted to censorship, but my memory is that they were passed with hardly a word altered. They are museum pieces of a time before the Age of Secrecy.

A piece of technological writing that I remember vividly is my account of the raising of the French liner *Normandie* after she had sunk at her pier in the Hudson River. This ship, one of the largest in the world, had caught fire, rolled over on her side, and sunk. She was raised by creating a series of airtight compartments inside the hull, from which the water was pumped out and air pumped in. The problems involved, in wartime when there was a shortage of everything, were enormous. I was taken on a tour of the ship as she lay in the mud on her side, so that we walked far below the waterline, on what had once been the left wall of each room, with the floor and ceiling rising vertically on either hand. I was glad to get out of there.

A perennial subject for me, as for all science writers, was "cures" for the common cold. Every few months, one of these would be announced, with a great fanfare on the part of the inventor, only to fade away soon into obscurity. I speedily discovered that if *anything* is given to large numbers of people and they are told it is a cold remedy, the number of respiratory infections among this group invariably goes down by about two-thirds for the next few months. The experts have long known that there are three main causes for cold symptoms—viruses, allergies to any of many substances, and psychological factors. Apparently the last of these is more important than was once believed; people are flattered to participate in a medical experiment, and their suffering from psychic factors is reduced for a while. This may be worth remembering next time you read that some new remedy has been given to ten thousand sailors at the Great Lakes Naval Training School, and that the number of colds was reduced by two-thirds.

In the course of preparing one of my books on science, I visited a number of the great commercial laboratories, including General Electric, Westinghouse, Bell, and Du Pont, and interviewed dozens of famous inventors of various devices and products. I was amused to note that the creator of a machine never seemed able to make it work for a demonstration; invariably he would tinker with it for a while and then call for "Bill!" Bill would appear, a gnome in a dirty smock, and get things going.

The most fascinating of all scientific subjects to me is the human brain, and I have read and reread the six or seven chief books about its processes. All that you are as a human being, your memories, personality, your feelings of love and hate, are all stored somehow in the ten or twelve billion brain cells inside your skull. I am bored by articles calling a computer "an electronic brain"; there are some parallels, but the brain is a thousand times more complex and awe-inspiring than any computer is or is likely to be.

The authorities are not yet sure just how memories are stored in the brain. We know that an electric current, generated in the nerves and the brain itself, is involved, about a twentieth as strong as a flashlight battery, or less. One theory is that there are reverberating electric currents passing through loops of various numbers of brain cells, transmitted, with a short gap, from small extensions on one cell to similar extensions on the next. Such loops of cells might be only a few in number, or might be many thousands; they can be connected (if this theory is correct) in almost infinite numbers of combinations. This theory was accepted by one of the greatest authorities in this field, Sir Charles Sherrington, who shared a Nobel Prize for his work with another authority on the brain, E. D. Adrian. One of the most beautiful passages of popular writing I have ever read is Sir Charles's description, in *The Brain and Its Mechanism*,[1] of waking up:

> *A scheme of lines and nodal points, gathered together at one end into a great ravelled knot, the brain, and at the other trailing off to a sort of stalk, the spinal cord. Imagine activity in this shown by little points of light. Of these some, stationary, flash rhythmically, faster or slower. Others are traveling points, streaming in serial lines at various speeds. The rhythmic stationary lights lie at the nodes. The nodes are both goals whither converge, and junctions whence diverge, the lines of travelling lights. Suppose we choose the hour of deep sleep. Then only in some sparse and out-of-the-way places are nodes flashing and trains of light points running. The great knotted headpiece lies for the most part quite dark. Occasionally at places in it, lighted points flash or move but soon subside.*
>
> *Should we continue to watch the scheme we should observe after a time an impressive change which suddenly accrues. In the great head end which had been mostly darkness spring up myriads of lights, as though activity from one of these local places suddenly spread far and wide. The great topmost sheet of the mass, where hardly a light had twinkled or moved, becomes now a sparkling field of rhythmic flashing points, with trains of travelling sparks hurrying hither and thither. It is as if the Milky Way entered upon some cosmic dance. Swiftly the head mass becomes an enchanted loom where millions of flashing shuttles weave a dissolving pattern, always a meaningful pattern*

[1] Cambridge University Press, 1933.

though never an abiding one. The brain is waking and with it the mind is returning.

Even thirty years ago, there were many complaints that science and invention were moving too fast for humanity to catch up, that there ought to be a moratorium on new discovery for a while. Such a notion is, of course, nonsense; science cannot be stopped, no matter how disastrous its temporary consequences may be. The lag between technological innovation and social organization is probably perennial, but in the long run, mankind manages to come close enough to catching up, in order to survive—or always has.

As did many other science writers, I wrote my share of reporting on the probable origin of life on this planet—basing myself, like most others, largely on the book by the famous Russian biochemist A. I. Oparin, *The Origin of Life* (Macmillan, 1938). I also wrote on the possibility of life on other planets, as to which pessimism seems to increase, the more we learn of the facts. While it is probably true that given the right set of circumstances it is inevitable that organic life should arise, it is also true that a tremendous series of coincidences brought it into existence on the earth, if indeed it did originate here, and did not come from outer space. If a single one of the original elements that have evolved into the periodic table had been stable instead of slightly unstable, it would not have happened. Earth had to be supplied with just the right amounts of oxygen, carbon dioxide, water, and other things, and had to be just the right size to avoid losing its atmosphere, as the moon has done (if it ever had one). The atmosphere had to be thick enough to protect organisms from deadly solar radiation for the billions of years needed to develop one-celled animals and for these to grow into the vast proliferation of forms we see today.

Astronomers like Harlow Shapley like to say that the chance is high there is life elsewhere in our island universe, just on the law of probability. There are at least one hundred billion stars like our sun, and they might (or might not) have any number of planets like the ones in our solar system. This is a plausible hypothesis, though no more than that. If you start to reckon the number of conditions that must have existed in series, to bring about life here, it is also possible to say that there may be none anywhere else, in our universe or beyond it.

In any case, wherever life exists, it is doomed to extinction, as it is on earth. All stars eventually burn up their nuclear fuel and become huge "red giants," increasing their size to consume all their planets on which there is even a remote possibility that life exists. This is true of our own sun, which will one day reach out and devour the earth and all living things on it. Unless man can find some other very distant planet capable of sustaining him, and manage to migrate to it, both of which things seem unlikely, organic life in the only place where we know it to exist will end. If you take a long enough view—and it must be very long indeed— Russia's quarrel with China, or for that matter, the war, hot or cold, between two economic systems, one inhuman and the other partly humane, but both of them working well enough to keep people alive and functioning, seem trivial—children squabbling over their toys on the deck of a sinking liner.

Sir Charles Snow, who was a physicist before he was a novelist, wrote a famous paper on "The Two Cultures," arguing that scientists and humanists don't understand each other. (What he really meant was that humanists don't understand science, but he was too polite to say so.) It is worth noting that while there are some scientists who have a broadly based culture, and even a few who write well for a lay audience, the professional science writers are the only large group who can meet Sir Charles's test. We understand both the second law of thermodynamics and something of the humanities.

Chapter 16

"WE HAVE WITH US TONIGHT"

I became a professional lecturer more or less by accident. Like many other people, I discovered early that if you speak without a fee, you will be swamped with invitations from all sorts of organizations, big and little—and especially the latter. I therefore finally signed up with a lecture agent, primarily in order to be able to refer inquiries to him. (I of course went on speaking without charge to groups that I felt were "worthy causes," if they couldn't afford to pay anything.)

The agent I chose was the elderly William B. Feakins, known universally as "Pop." He was something of a liberal, and most of his stable of speakers were, like me, part-time lecturers whose views were slightly left of center. The financial arrangement was simple: Pop would either take one-quarter of the fee and let you pay your own expenses, or one-third, in which case he paid your carfare. It was safer to have the second type of contract, so that he would think twice before sending you a thousand miles to speak for $200. In those days the speaker with only a moderate appeal, like me, usually got from $150 to $300 or $400 for an appearance, unless two dates could be arranged for the same day in the same town, in which case the fee for the second might be substantially reduced.

Because of the pressure on my time, I could go out only about twice a year, in the autumn and the spring, for a week or ten days each time. When possible, the bureau arranged for me to speak every day, but sometimes there would be a day off, gratefully accepted by me, because talking daily in a new community is hard work.

The backbone of the lecture business was and is women's clubs; lecturers would starve if they depended on bookings from men's groups. The most agreeable experiences I had were in speaking for college audiences; in those days they paid small fees, or none, but their quick intelligence and easy rapport were pleasant. Over a few years I spoke in all the Ivy League colleges, and their feminine counterparts (except Bryn Mawr, which for some reason didn't want me). I appeared at many of the big state universities—Michigan, Iowa, Minnesota, Kansas, California, Washington, Utah, Louisiana, and more.

With the women's clubs, the written contract for your appearance went into careful detail. The speaker must attend a luncheon or a reception in his honor and say a few words at no extra charge. If the lecture was in the evening, sometimes it was specified that he must wear a dinner jacket; often the length of his talk was in the contract—"not less than forty-five minutes or more than an hour." These restrictions reflected painful experiences the clubs had had in the past with lecturers who talked far too long—or so briefly that the hearers felt they had not got their money's worth—or appeared in some eccentric costume. Sometimes a lecturer might arrive at the local hotel, lock himself in, and not appear until ten minutes before he was due to speak; hence the provision that he must be a guest of honor at some social function other than the one for which he was being paid.

I don't know what the situation is today, but forty years ago, the winter's social life in many a Midwestern small city was partly built around the arrival of a series of visiting lecturers. The town's chief hostesses vied for the honor of giving the party before or after the lecture; the occasion gave everybody a chance to dress up, and of course thereafter the members of the audience could name-drop, if the lecturer was well known. I remember once speaking in Peoria, Illinois, at ten o'clock in the morning, and marveling to see five hundred women dressed in their best so early in the day. The chairwoman explained it to me: "It's a great chance to pile the breakfast dishes in the sink and get out of the house." Today, of course, the dishes would be put into the automatic washer, but otherwise the situation probably remains about the same.

The compulsory acceptance of hospitality was the hardest part of a lecture trip; you had to be an important person indeed not to be forced to go through the ordeal. Many a lecturer has been so nearly killed with kindness that when he finally faced the big audience whom he was being paid to address, he was too tired to do himself justice.

The mainstay of the business (aside from illustrated travel lectures) was speakers of two types: the old professionals who went on year after year, and temporary celebrities who cashed in on a fleeting fame for a few months. One of the former was a good friend of mine, Glenn Frank, long editor of *The Century* magazine, and afterward president of the University of Wisconsin. He once told me of a chance encounter on a train with a speaker in the second classification, James W. Gerard, who had been U.S. ambassador to Germany during the First World War until America entered the conflict. Glenn asked Mr. Gerard how he liked the lecture business. He hadn't liked it at first, he said, but now things were much better.

And what had made the difference?

"I've got a clause in my contract," said the former ambassador, "that they are not to show me their God damn boulevards."

Anybody who has ever served a hitch as a lecturer will know what he meant. Every notable visitor (and a lecturer is automatically in that category) has to see the smartest new suburb of every town, where most of the wealthiest people have their homes. It never seems to dawn on the local patriots that the visitor has seen many similar areas in other places, and might prefer to be allowed to take a nap at his hotel.

In many places in those days the food in public eating places was pretty bad. My friend Fola La Follette (of the Wisconsin La Follettes, wife of the playwright George Middleton) served her turn on the merry-go-round, and once told me that only Shredded Wheat had kept her from starvation. Even the worst cook cannot do much to spoil Shredded Wheat.

A minor hazard of the lecture business is the husband of the chairwoman of the program committee of the women's club for which you are performing. It is the job of the chairwoman to greet the visitor at the railroad station or the airport, get him to his hotel, and after his lecture, get him back in time for his train or plane. Driving the car she turns over to her husband, and for some reason I have never been able to ascertain, he feels it is incumbent on him to wait until the last possible second before taking the visitor to his means of transport and then driving very fast—perhaps to show that if he is arrested he has such influence that he can fix a ticket. If you are speaking in ten towns on ten successive days, a missed connection can be a disaster, but it is worse to get killed by a show-off driver.

I finally learned how to solve both these problems. In those days air transport was too unreliable to be used by anybody on a tight schedule, and was never employed in such cases; normally, there was a Pullman car in the railroad station waiting to be connected to some train in the middle of the night. Pleading great fatigue, I would insist we start soon enough to let me go to bed before the train started. When my chauffeur began as usual to roar around corners like a get-away car in the movies, I would say to him, "Now, you don't look to me like a failure in life."

This always startled my host, who had been boasting to me that he had the best little hardware business in Zenith City, and he would turn a startled look at me. I would go on to explain: "I'm sure you know that psychiatrists say that fast drivers are compensating for a feeling of failure, a deep unconscious inferiority complex."

Rarely did my driver argue the point; instead, he would slow down at once to a pace that might make me worry again lest I miss my train.

For the editor of a magazine dealing with public affairs, lecture tours are a valuable enterprise. I learned at first hand what people were thinking, all over the country, and after each trip I reported on the mood of the area I had visited, in an article; judging by the editorial mail, these were well accepted.

If you enjoy meeting people, as I do, it was an endlessly fascinating experience to come to a new town each day, make contact with a dozen fresh personalities, and then go on next day to do it all over again. As I have noted elsewhere, I learned to have great respect for anybody brave enough to be left of center in a generally conservative community. It is easy to take an unpopular position in New York, where you are swallowed up in the anonymity of the big city; it is a very different story in a small city in Texas, for instance, where devotion to leftist causes can be followed by political and social reprisals that really hurt.

It was interesting to be engaged for an annual statewide teachers' institute, when I would speak to many thousands of educators in a short tour. In Kansas and Colorado, for example, the teachers were gathered into three cities in each state, and there were three specially engaged speakers, each of whom began in a different town and then moved forward on successive days to the second and the third. In New Jersey, the huge auditorium at Atlantic City was big enough to accommodate all the delegates at once.

After some years, Pop Feakins died, and I transferred to W. Colston Leigh, a hard-boiled, highly efficient manager who demanded much higher fees—and got them. I remember vividly what we called his "slave auction"; he would gather representatives of many women's clubs in the vicinity of New York into one lecture hall on one day, and then ask a dozen of his stable of performers to stand up and give a five-minute sample of what they had to offer. It was a memorable experience.

Over the years I barnstormed around the country, appearing before all sorts of groups on all sorts of occasions. I spoke twice to national conventions of the League of Women Voters, and was voted an honorary member—a distinction about which I was inclined to be reticent, lest it be misunderstood. Clarence Chamberlain, the aviator, came from my native state, and when he flew the Atlantic in 1927, the Iowa Society of New York honored him at a dinner. I spoke at this, and on five minutes' notice I wrote a song in his honor, duly sung by a soprano at the head table. The tune was "Iowa, My Iowa," which was at that time the unofficial state song; the tune was the old familiar "Maryland, My Maryland."

I appeared at the Conference on the Cause and Cure of War, in Washington, called by a committee headed by a wonderful old warhorse of pacifism, Carrie Chapman Catt. Many years earlier, she herself had visited Emmetsburg, had been a guest in our home, and as she said to the crowd of a thousand people, had dandled me on her knee as a baby. The audience thus reassured as to my impeccable antecedents, I got a warm welcome.

I spoke once in Emmetsburg itself, a town too small to be a part of any normal lecture circuit. They were building a hospital, the first the town had ever seen, and I came home and spoke to an overflow crowd in the high-school auditorium. They had paid to get in, I of course donated my services, and several hundred dollars were raised for a room that was dedicated to the memory of my mother.

I delivered Commencement addresses at several colleges, being a little startled to find that they sometimes found it necessary to use a lecture bureau to engage speakers for this purpose. I spoke at Chautauqua, New York, the town that gave its name to a now vanished enterprise, the traveling Chautauqua that went from town to town furnishing enlightenment and entertainment in a tent; the original, stationary Chautauqua seemed to be boycotted by the younger generation, and I spoke to an audience a startling proportion of whom were on crutches —or in wheelchairs.

In Washington I gave the Bronson Cutting Memorial Lecture in a great hall on Constitution Avenue, discovering only after I had made my address that this was considered an important highlight of the Washington social season; boxes were purchased by members of the Supreme Court, high government officials, and members of foreign legations. I spoke to a club of millionaires in Palm Beach who paid so much that lecturers could afford to make a special trip to appear there. I talked at Cooper Union in New York, thrilled to think that this was the platform on which Abraham Lincoln had first come into national prominence; unluckily, my audience, on a cold winter's night, consisted very largely of bums from the nearby Bowery who slept through my speech, having come in to get out of the cold.

One June I was engaged to speak in Des Moines to the annual meeting of the confederated women's clubs of my native state. We were having a spell of very hot weather, high in the nineties, and on the train coming in from Chicago I debated whether to wear my black dinner jacket, or a light-colored summer suit (this was one instance where the contract did not specify what should be worn). I finally decided to wear the dinner jacket, and walked out on the stage to discover that I was the only man present so attired; the many males in the audience were one and all wearing white tie and tails. The worthy clubwomen from all over

Iowa had planned for months to dress up for this night, and their men folk had to suffer correspondingly.

Teachers College, Columbia, asked me to be one of several speakers at the luncheon celebrating John Dewey's seventy-fifth birthday. Naturally, we all eulogized him, as we were expected to do, but when he rose to respond he brushed our compliments aside and sharply criticized current trends in American education. Ten years later, I had a somewhat similar experience when the American Institute of Architects asked me to speak at the dinner honoring Frank Lloyd Wright on having achieved the same age. He, too, ignored the compliments paid him, and launched into a ferocious attack on current American architecture.

The most impressive reception I ever got anywhere was in Louisville, Kentucky. The mayor was a well-known Kentucky political figure, Charles Farnsley, and when I tumbled off the sleeper at eight o'clock in the morning, here was His Honor in silk hat and morning coat, accompanied by a military guard of honor and a band! He and I entered an open carriage, and proceeded to parade through the center of town where we entered a reviewing stand and watched a substantial contingent of troops from Fort Knox march past. The military review had been planned weeks in advance, and I assume I was an afterthought. I hadn't known Mr. Farnsley, but we became good friends; he used to write to me, as he did to a lot of other people, invariably arguing the superiority of Confucius, as a human being, over Plato. I was never disposed to dispute him.

A dramatic occasion was when I spoke in Oklahoma City at a time when the Ku Klux Klan was very powerful in that state. They had been defied by Governor Jack Walton, and the situation was so tense that he had called out the National Guard; their rifles were stacked in the lobby of my hotel. Luckily, the feud did not come to bloodshed.

I remember one occasion when I had been engaged to speak in Englewood, New Jersey. The program chairman for the women's club was the wife of a professor at Columbia University, and it was arranged that he should pick me up in the late afternoon at my office on East Forty-ninth Street and drive me to Englewood for dinner at his house before my speech.

Shortly before he was due to arrive, I got an apologetic telephone call from the professor. "I'm sorry," he said, "but I'll be a few minutes late in picking you up."

I was slightly miffed at this; after all, *I* was the lecturer of the evening. But I decided to be gracious. "That's all right, of course," I said. "I hope there's nothing wrong?"

"Oh, no," said my chauffeur. "But the news has just come out that I have won the Nobel Prize for chemistry, and the press is insisting on an interview."

I began my speech that evening by repeating the news about Dr. Harold Urey, and suggesting that his Englewood neighbors stand up in tribute to him, which they did.

On a lecture tour through the Middle West in January, 1937, I spoke at the University of Michigan, at Ann Arbor. The technique of the sit-down strike had just been invented, and was being employed by a group of men from the United Automobile Workers in the Fisher Body Plant, in Flint, Michigan. After my lecture, I planned to go and visit the strikers (with the already acquired approval of the union), and I mentioned this fact to one of the students in my audience. He promptly offered to drive me to Flint, and I accepted. During the journey I wished I hadn't; his car was in the last stages of disintegration, there was a film of ice on the road, and it seemed to me we skidded about 50 percent of the way.

But these hazards were forgotten when I arrived at the scene of the sit-in. The plant was modern and handsome, set in a lawn; across the street, numbers of Flint police were keeping watch, but the strikers controlled enough of their own curbing for us to park. A committee of the strikers searched my student chauffeur and me, searched the car, and then helped us climb in through a window, the doors having been locked by the management at the beginning of the strike.

We entered a huge room, with a long row of automobile bodies on what had been beltline production, now motionless like the carcasses of so many small elephants. Fifteen hundred men had been living in this building for two weeks; it was spotlessly clean, and the routine of life was highly organized. The men slept on the floor, or in the half-finished automobile bodies; food was brought by their friends, passed in the window, and cooked (or warmed up) inside. There was a barbershop, a private post office, and an electronic paging system when any of the fifteen hundred was wanted at the front window for any reason.

A few days earlier, the scene had been much less peaceful. The police, spurred on by General Motors, had tried hard to dislodge the men sitting in. Heat was cut off, a blockade was set up for a while to keep out food supplies, and finally there was a five-hour pitched battle, in which the police used tear gas and revolvers, wounding fourteen. The strikers' battle tactics were directed by the three Reuther brothers, Walter, Victor, and Roy, from a sound truck. They were sufficiently successful so that the fight ended in a draw. Not long after, General Motors gave in, recognized the U.A.W. as a legitimate bargaining agent—and the rest is history.

There is a footnote to this story. My student guide listened while I interviewed the strike leaders inside the plant for an article for my paper, and was converted to their cause. He was the editor of the student daily at the university, and on returning to the campus, he wrote an inflamed editorial supporting the strike. The wife of a General Motors executive was a regent of the university, and promptly demanded that he be expelled. The university authorities supported his right to express his opinions, and he stayed in school. Today Marshall Shulman is head of the prestigious Institute for Russian Studies at Columbia University.

I was never in the top rank of lecturers; quite apart from any other failings of mine, I did not have the eloquence, the simplicity, or the optimism that American audiences desire. I often spoke on international affairs, and usually painted the dark picture which the period between the world wars demanded. After I had talked for fifty minutes in pessimistic terms, a number of members of the audience would come up one by one to assure me that "I have enjoyed your message *so* much." I used to wonder what I could possibly have said that they would not have enjoyed.

The most successful of the old pros of my day were men who took pains to flatter the program chairwomen in order to get asked back another year. One of the best at this was Richard Halliburton, a perpetual youth who wrote books of travel and adventure and then repeated their contents from the lecture platform. One of his little tricks was to send the program chairwoman eleven beautiful roses, with a note saying that she and these made a dozen. Halliburton, unlike most of us, always wore white tie and tails when he spoke; he would wait in the wings with his tie not yet tied, and ask whoever was to introduce him please to tie it for him; this, naturally, caused a rush of maternal emotion reflected in next season's bookings.

A successful lecturer needs what I have never possessed, instant total recall for names and faces. He meets forty or fifty people in every town, none of whom will forgive him if he forgets them. I remember speaking at the University of Colorado, in Boulder, on two occasions about ten years apart. On the second of these, a faculty wife drove me to the train, and as I got out of her car, I thanked her for doing so, and added a few conventional words about the pleasure of making her acquaintance. She turned to me a really stricken face. "Why, Mr. Bliven," she said in hurt tones, "you don't remember me! I drove you to the train the *last* time you were here."

The professional lecturer also has to develop nerves of steel or he will not long survive. You learn to endure the introducer who speaks so long (I have known one to take twenty minutes) that you have to cut your own remarks drastically. I have once or twice discovered at the last minute, while already seated on the platform, that the manager's office had made a mistake, and I was expected to speak on a completely different subject from the one listed on my schedule. Most lecturers have two or three set themes, described in the circular the manager sends out in advance, and it is usually not hard to shift from one topic to another.

I remember a rather tough moment when the United Nations was being founded in San Francisco in 1945. There was a popular radio program on a national network, The Town Hall of the Air, and its permanent moderator was a friend of mine named George Denny. He had arranged one of his weekly programs to emanate from San Francisco, and had engaged several well-known radio personalities—I remember Raymond Swing and Hans von Kaltenborn—to comment on how things were going. He had also engaged the huge Municipal Auditorium as a place from which to originate the show, and had invited San Franciscans to come and see the performance. In the days of radio there was a tremendous pent-up desire to observe one's favorite performers in the flesh, and San Francisco responded overwhelmingly, with twelve or thirteen thousand people inside the building, and four or five thousand more ready to listen on loudspeakers outside.

I had been invited to come and sit on the platform, and with some difficulty, I fought my way in through the police guard at the stage door. When I got into the wings, I met a very agitated George Denny, who seized me by the lapels. "Hans and Ray have been delayed," he told me. "They'll just barely get here when the network goes on the air, and the crowd is getting very restless. Go out there and talk to them." And so, with no preparation whatever, I ad-libbed eight or ten minutes about the Conference to sixteen or seventeen thousand people. We all survived.

Lecturing is a dangerous occupation, if followed industriously. For a full-time writer it can mean a serious encroachment on his working time. Speaking day after day to large audiences, the temptation is very strong to tell them what you know by past experience they want to hear, and to talk in blacks and whites instead of the grays where truth usually lies. You can also repeat yourself to a boring extent—a danger I partly avoided by *never* having a prepared text, and speaking always extemporaneously. George Bernard Shaw, who was so avaricious in regard to his writing, had an inflexible rule never to speak for money. Rarely did he get an audience larger than a little group of faithful Fabians who agreed with him in advance, so that he could avoid the pioneering work of the proselyter and go on to more subtle matters.

If you want to lecture—and I had some good practical reasons for doing so—you have to choose between these two types of audience. The small "in" group is appealing, your reception will be warm, but you will be preaching only to the saved. If you take money, you'll have a much larger group, you will meet more resistance to new ideas, but with luck you may be able to change their attitude somewhat, and pray that they are not changing yours. Like so many other problems in life, this one is incapable of solution, and we must muddle along as best we can.

Chapter 17

THE JOINER

From the moment I went on the staff of *The Globe,* people began asking me to join the executive committee or the board of directors or trustees of various organizations. I doubt that this was because they thought I was especially valuable for such a purpose; I suspect they hoped to get publicity for their organization in my paper. I avoided nearly all these invitations with a simple formula that almost always worked. "If I go on your board," I would say, "this would mean that I could not conscientiously continue to print more than a minimum of material about your activities." The people who had been pressing me to join them of course replied that this would not matter, but I noticed that usually their importunities diminished to a trickle.

My first exception came not long after the close of the First World War, when I heard of an organization called The League of Free Nations Association, which was holding a monthly luncheon in a midtown hotel dining room at which qualified authorities would discuss the problems of the postwar world, and especially America's role in them. This was just what I was looking for, and I promptly enrolled. The chairman was a tall, thin, blond young man with a knack for leading a discussion, James G. McDonald. When he found I was interested, he soon asked me to join the Board of Trustees of this group which presently changed its name to the Foreign Policy Association. I served there for more than twenty years, and finally resigned only because I felt that any good ideas I had for the organization must surely be exhausted by now. I thought some of the other members of the Board who had been there equally long might follow my example, but nobody did.

The F.P.A. was an active group. It gave monthly luncheons in the Astor Hotel, attended by a thousand or fifteen hundred people, at which two or three experts discussed some international problem from varying points of view; their talks were broadcast nationwide for years by what was then called the Blue Network of the National Broadcasting Company. We had many members scattered across the nation, and often those in one community would gather somewhere to hear the proceedings through a loudspeaker. We also issued quantities of documents on world problems; our research department was capably headed for a time by Raymond Leslie Buell, and then by an anti-Communist Russian refugee, Mrs. Vera Micheles Dean.

McDonald was a skillful master of ceremonies for our public meetings, managing to keep debaters who disagreed from attempting mayhem on each other. After many years he left the organization to become high commissioner for refugees from Germany, and later, the first American ambassador to the new state of Israel.

When he was not available for any reason, I sometimes took his place at the luncheons, and satisfied a long-time secret ambition to be a radio announcer by saying, on a split-second cue from a technician, "This is station WJZ of the Blue Network."

Through the F.P.A. I came to know many European visitors to the United States. Among them were three brilliant Italians: Gaetano Salvemini, Giuseppe Borgese, and Count Carlo Sforza, men of high talent, all refugees from the Mussolini regime. Salvador de Madariaga, a Spanish historian, also a refugee, disconcerted me by knowing so much about America. Count Michael Karolyi, a handsome Hungarian with a pretty wife, looked far too young to have been premier of his country as he was for a brief, stormy period after the end of the First World War; he had come to America to plead the cause of a United States of Europe, which then seemed a quixotic dream, but is now becoming something of a reality with the Common Market in the democratic West, and—under Russia's fist—the Warsaw Pact among the Communists. Jennie Lee looked like a slip of a pretty Scottish lass, but she was also a shrewd and skillful propagandist for the left wing of the British Labor Party; her husband, Aneurin Bevan, was to become minister of health in the first Labor government after World War II, and to play a major role in setting up the system of socialized medicine. All these people had axes to grind, of one sort or another, and the F.P.A. gave them a sounding board for this purpose, a legitimate enterprise, it seems to me, when we believed that their purposes were sound.

How much good is accomplished by organizations like the F.P.A.? So far as I am aware, there are no reliable statistics on this subject. When it began its operations the country was just reluctantly waking up to the fact that it was now a world power and could not avoid the obligation of that role. Radio was beginning its thirty years of influence (until succeeded in large degree by television). The news media were expanding their scope and efficiency. I can only say that during the next two decades, before the beginning of the Second World War, understanding of world affairs increased greatly in the United States, and I am confident that the F.P.A. played some part in this.

Another group for which I broke my rule against serving on boards was the Twentieth Century Fund, a foundation devoted to making economic and other studies and disseminating the results. The Fund was inaugurated by E. A. Filene, the famous Boston merchant, best known for his invention of the nationally known "bargain basement," in which prices went steadily down the longer the goods stayed on the shelves. Customers had all the excitement of a gambling game; the more they waited, the cheaper the goods became, but there was always the risk that someone else would buy the desired item.

Filene had many ideas ranging far beyond retail merchandising. He treated his employees well in many ways that were unusual at that time; he was, for instance, one of the first to permit saleswomen to sit down behind the counter, and to provide them with lounges where they could rest and relax when off duty. He believed in the doctrine of efficiency in operations and tried to spread its principles in many places, including Western Europe.

He was a pioneer in establishing credit unions, in which a group of employees of one firm, or some other cohesive group, combine to lend money to one another at low rates of interest; he spent hundreds of thousands of dollars propagating this idea, and the rash of credit unions all over the country is partly his doing. One of his ideas that always interested me was for huge, one-class ocean liners traveling the Atlantic, which would have very simple staterooms, and food served only in cafeterias and not included in the cost of the ticket. His studies seemed to show that such ships could make money at a fare, thirty years ago, of $50, and he envisioned thousands of Americans with modest incomes enjoying the experience of European travel on this basis.

Filene was a difficult man personally. He feuded with his brother, A. Lincoln Filene, for many years. Highly egotistical, he hired a succession of brilliant young men either to write his biography or to publicize his ideas in other ways, and all of them quit him in disgust after a year or two. They included Glenn Frank, afterward editor of *The Century* and president of the University of Wisconsin; Ernest M. Hopkins, later to be president of Dartmouth; Wheeler Sammons, who ended up as owner and publisher of *Who's Who in America;* and Curtice Hitchcock, later a member of the New York book publishing firm of Reynal and Hitchcock. The biography was finally written independently, years after the subject's death, by Gerald W. Johnson (*Liberal's Progress,* Coward-McCann, 1948).

I had known Filene casually for several years when in 1922 he came to see me at my office at *The Globe.* He explained that he was a bachelor, his life expectancy was not great, and he wanted to leave his fortune to serve some useful purpose. He did not want to give it to charity; he wished it to be used in socially valuable ways. Did I have any ideas?

I didn't; but I had a column to write in the paper two or three times a week, and I promptly suggested that I ask my readers for help on the problem—of course, without revealing his identity. He agreed, and I wrote a piece, which began and ended by saying that my millionaire friend would not respond to any appeals for personal aid. As you might expect, I got several hundred letters in the next few days, almost every one of which begged for money. They were the usual type of thing, gifted young musicians needing money to study; people requiring operations who couldn't afford them; old people alone in the world and not knowing where to turn. It would have taken Filene's fortune several times over to satisfy their demands—many of which, of course, should have been referred to public authorities.

All that came out of this enterprise was that Filene asked me to join the board of an organization of his. As early as 1919 he had called this the Twentieth Century Fund, but it had done very little during the intervening three years. He now proposed to turn over a substantial sum of money to it, to be augmented on his death by the rest of his fortune. Always a sucker for an unpaid job with an aura of do-goodism about it, I said I would. I began an association with the Fund that lasted thirty years, until I was exiled to California by the doctors in 1953. We soon had an office in New York, a paid executive director, and the beginnings of a staff. The trustees met once a year, at first in Filene's home in Boston, and afterward usually at the Princeton Inn, for two or three days, and set guidelines for the staff for the coming year.

The first few years, the Fund did not amount to much. Filene used its existence mainly to get out of answering appeals for charity, with which he was overwhelmed, as the response to my column had suggested. Our annual meetings at his home were something of an ordeal. For one thing, Filene had a passion for shellfish, and our meals consisted of one course after another of various types of seafood; heaven help the trustee who happened to be allergic to these. Filene himself participated in our meetings, and was a very bad expositor of his ideas, hesitating, stumbling, and repeating himself. He had lured all the trustees with the promise he had made to me, that after his death we could set our own course; I sometimes imagined he looked a little guilty at living so long.

After his death in 1937, the Fund developed a new and on the whole a successful formula for its activities. It financed studies, at the beginning primarily in the field of economics, each of which had a director, a staff when necessary, and an advisory committee of distinguished authorities in the field involved. After a year or two of research, a scholarly volume of findings would be written and published. Preparing these reports was fairly expensive, by the standards of the day, costing perhaps $100,000 to $200,000 each. The Fund had started with about $5 million but this was enhanced by skillful investment policies over the years, for which the chief credit goes to one of the trustees, H. Christian Sonne, who ran up our capital from the original sum to roughly $28 million in 1969.

Once a report was ready, the problem of distribution arose. Hundreds of documents of this sort are published every year, only to die unread—save by a handful of specialists—on library shelves. But the TCF, in accordance with Filene's original concepts, wanted to reach the general public as much as possible. There were for many years only a few people on the Board who had any contact with mass communication— W. W. Waymack, former editor of *The Des Moines Register and Tribune*, James G. McDonald, William Allen White, of *The Emporia Gazette* (for a short time), and myself. Over the persistent opposition of many "scholarly" trustees, who thought publicity was undignified, we succeeded in pushing through plans for spreading abroad the facts that would otherwise have been entombed in our fat volumes. Under the able leadership of Thomas R. Carskadon, associate director of the Fund, we sent out well-written press releases, we had our authors interviewed by the press, radio, and later television, we employed skillful popularizers, including Stuart Chase and George Soule, to write simplified books based on our research, and we even produced our own short films for use in motion-picture theaters and on television. For some of our more popular studies we got an enormous exposure in this way.

The Fund has been fortunate in having several successive full-time directors of unusual ability. The first of these was Evans Clark, who had been on *The New York Times*, and was married to Freda Kirchwey, for many years my opposite number on *The Nation*. The second was J. Frederic Dewhurst, who had been our staff economist, respected in the profession. He was succeeded by August Heckscher, who had worked on newspapers in New York and elsewhere, and was to become (part-time) White House consultant on the arts in the Kennedy administration and (full-time) parks commissioner for New York City. Long after my retirement to California, came M. J. Rossant, who, like Evans Clark, had worked on *The New York Times*.

Two towers of strength for the Fund during the years of my own activity were Dewhurst and Adolf Berle, long chairman of the Board of Trustees. Berle, who in his youth had been something of a prodigy, being graduated from Harvard at eighteen, was for many years a member of the faculty at the Columbia Law School; of his many books, perhaps the best known is *The Modern Corporation and Private Property,* written with G. C. Means. During the Second World War he took time out to serve as assistant secretary of state and ambassador to Brazil, and in 1969 he produced a brilliant, thoughtful history of the Fund's first fifty years, *Leaning Against the Dawn,* which is also a portrait of American civilization in these troubled times.

Over the years the Fund has produced a remarkably varied list of studies on such matters as relations between capital and labor, the cost of distribution, foreign trade, monopolies, population problems, agrarian and urban questions, the role of the military in modern life, old-age security, and many more. It has also produced studies of special areas— Turkey, Greece, Israel, Brazil, Haiti, Costa Rica. Notable in this field are monumental studies of Africa, by George H. T. Kimble, and of Southeast Asia, by Gunnar Myrdal. The word "megalopolis" was, as far as I know, coined by Jean Gottmann for his pioneering Fund study of the Atlantic seaboard, Boston to Washington. Under Rossant, the Fund has branched out in new directions, including the launching of a Black Academy of Arts and Letters, and a study by Lester Markel, former Sunday editor of *The New York Times,* of the relation between public opinion and public policy.

The Board of Trustees has over the years included a long list of well-known figures from many walks of life. Excluding those already mentioned, those appointed since my retirement, and those who were elected but rarely or never attended the annual meetings, I remember Robert Lynd, coauthor with his wife of the Middletown studies; Wallace Harrison, the architect; David Lilienthal of the T.V.A. and the Atomic Energy Commission; Ben Cohen of F.D.R.'s famous team of Corcoran and Cohen; Owen D. Young of the General Electric Company; Roscoe Pound, head of the Harvard Law School; Francis Biddle, once Attorney General; J. Robert Oppenheimer, and so many others that I omit their names in the interest of not boring the reader to death.

One of our most impressive studies was *America's Needs and Resources,* almost wholly the work of Fred Dewhurst, the first attempt ever made to draw up a balance sheet for the nation. First published in 1947, a revised edition appeared in 1955, and Tom Carskadon edited a summary for a popular audience, consisting largely of pictographs. All three of these volumes sold very well, and so did a companion volume done by Dewhurst in 1961, *Europe's Needs and Resources.*

I became a trustee of the Fund in a mood of skepticism as to whether foundations in general do enough useful work to justify their existence, but over the years I have become convinced that they do. My vague youthful feeling was that these things ought to be done by the state, but after nearly fifty years of observing private and public activity in this general field I am now convinced that a "mixed economy" in this regard is best. As in the case of the Foreign Policy Association, the work of the Twentieth Century Fund was aided enormously by the times, which demanded that Americans think about the economic foundations of their society as never in the past. I believe it has been of tremendous value, at a singularly small cost, as these things go nowadays.

Another organization with which I worked for almost the whole length of its life was the Union for Democratic Action, which was closer to my own field of interest than either the Foreign Policy Association or the Twentieth Century Fund. In early 1941, the American Communists had infiltrated almost every liberal organization you can think of, and some non-Communists felt it was time we had a group of our own. The U.D.A. was formed in April of that year, and I became a member of the Board of Directors a few months later.

The C.P. was following the line that had been adopted at the time of the Hitler-Stalin Pact of August, 1939, which precipitated the war, namely, that the United States should stay out of the conflict, and should at once stop the flow of arms and other supplies to Great Britain. Just two months later, Hitler invaded Russia, and as usual, the comrades changed their tune overnight. They were now more for intervention than the interventionists; before long, they were screaming for an invasion of Western Europe, to take the pressure off Russia, years before there was any possibility of such a thing.

Pearl Harbor, of course, changed everything for Americans. I was one of a U.D.A.-sponsored group which called a hasty conference shortly after it, and this was held in the Commodore Hotel later that month. It was a difficult time, because the liberals were split three ways. Some were still complete pacifists, and wanted to boycott the war. Another group still believed in cooperating with the Communists whenever these espoused liberal policies—as they always did when they thought it would suit their purpose. The third faction, to which the U.D.A. and its Board belonged, favored the war but opposed cooperation with the C.P.

Two of the important liberal organizations that had been infiltrated by the party were the National Citizens' Political Action Committee and the Independent Citizens for the Arts, Sciences and Professions. The latter had been headed by the sculptor, Jo Davidson, whose gifts as an artist were equaled by his naïveté in political affairs. Later it was chaired by the "Old Curmudgeon," Harold Ickes, Roosevelt's secretary of the interior, famous for his truculence. Never himself a leftist, he was, like Davidson, somewhat naïve about his associations. (For some time he wrote a column for *The New Republic,* and I agonized weekly over the potential libel suits he was brewing up.) The Communist smell about these two organizations finally became so strong that they merged into the Progressive Citizens of America, precursor for the Communist-dominated Progressive Party that was to run Wallace for president in 1948.

The Union for Democratic Action raised a banner to which non-pacifist, anti-Communist liberals could repair. One of its important projects was to assemble the voting record on crucial issues of all members of Congress, to be published every two years before the elections. James Loeb, the executive secretary of the U.D.A., and the *N.R.* editors worked out a successful formula. We took ten or twelve important matters that had recently been the subject of Congressional votes, explained their significance, and then told whether each member of the House and Senate had voted well or badly from the liberal point of view. (Sometimes this meant a "yes" vote, sometimes "no.") The voting record proved so valuable that it is still being carried on by the paper nearly thirty years later.

The membership of the national Board of the U.D.A. varied from time to time during its existence; the figures I remember best are Reinhold Niebuhr, of Union Theological Seminary; George Counts, of Teachers College, Columbia; Frank Kingdon, a former minister and a political activist, from New Jersey; Tom Amlie, former Representative from Wisconsin; and Robert Bendiner, a well-known free-lance writer. The man who did most for the U.D.A. was its executive secretary, Jim Loeb, who went on to be an American ambassador in Latin America and a newspaper publisher in upper New York State.

Our policies were what you would expect. We opposed segregation, then still rampant everywhere, including the armed forces; fought the poll tax, which disenfranchised so many poor Southerners, white and black; attacked the sale of oil and steel to Japan in the days before Pearl Harbor; opposed recognition of the Nazi-dominated Vichy government in France; fought the excesses of wartime censorship, which, as always, was used to cover up blunders by our own leaders as well as to conceal information from the enemy; and we had a dozen more causes, of the same sort that *The New Republic* was pushing, week after week.

The directors of the U.D.A. met in the evening in its offices in a midtown skyscraper, and my chief memory of these occasions is being terribly tired from a hard day's work, and little revived by a hastily eaten dinner in some nearby inexpensive restaurant. I was always acutely aware of the briefcase I carried, full of manuscript to be read after I got home. Next to Loeb, Niebuhr and I were the most faithful in attendance, and I recall at meeting after meeting seeing Reinhold looking as tired as I felt, but struggling on, like a man walking in thick sand.

The U.D.A. directors were almost coterminous with the founders of the Liberal Party, which had hardly any existence outside New York City. The Communists by now had got control of the American Labor

Party, and we wanted something to offset them. Our numbers were pitiful, but in New York State the Republican and Democratic strength was so nearly equal that in a tight election we could turn the balance— or at least, we pretended that we could.

Early in 1945, we tried a little power politics at the national level. Henry Wallace had been nominated for secretary of commerce, as a sop for his having been passed over for a second term as vice-president, but was having great difficulty being confirmed; the professional politicians had always hated him as a vague and wobbly do-gooder. The liberals liked Wallace (this was, of course, several years before he began his extraordinary flirtation with the Communists) and we wanted to see him in the Cabinet. We therefore gave a big testimonial dinner for him at the Commodore Hotel, attended by about a thousand people. Among those who duly sang his praises were Mrs. Franklin Roosevelt, Walter Reuther of the United Auto Workers, James Patton, head of the leftist Farmers' Union, and Henry Kaiser, the California tycoon who had accomplished such miracles in the rapid building of Liberty ships during the war. I read a letter from President Roosevelt praising the hero of the evening, and finally Henry himself responded, with his accustomed modesty and his usual plea that America use its resources to help end poverty everywhere. I don't know whether our dinner, which got a big play in the newspapers, had any effect, but a few weeks later he was confirmed.

The death of Roosevelt in April of that year brought into the White House a man much less progressive than F.D.R. had been. The liberals were disturbed by the way things were going, and in January, 1947, a large group of those known to be anti-Communist held a dinner at the Shoreham Hotel in Washington, the speakers including the omnipresent Mrs. Roosevelt, Senator Hubert Humphrey, who had made a fine record in Minnesota, and Chester Bowles. Next day the leading figures in the U.D.A. met with about a hundred and fifty people, most of whom had been at the dinner the night before, and proceeded to dissolve our organization in favor of a broader-based national group with better access to the fairly large sums needed for effective operation. The coalition was called Americans for Democratic Action, and it is still going strong a quarter of a century later. It has done many things the U.D.A. could never have accomplished; on the other hand, we had performed a useful service in preparing the ground for it.

As I have indicated in the case of the Twentieth Century Fund, I was long somewhat skeptical of the value of these organizations. Did they justify all the hard work that was put into them, both by the unpaid trustees and by the salaried staffs? It took me years to answer this question satisfactorily in my own mind. I am sure there are far too many committees of all sorts in America, and that they tend to go on long after the reason they were created has disappeared—especially if they have a salaried staff which has a vested interest in keeping its jobs. But in the case of the three I have mentioned here—and, of course, many others— I believe that they do or did indeed justify their existence. The Twentieth Century Fund has contributed notably to the education of this country in regard to many economic and other problems. The other two organizations provided a focal point where like-minded people could gather, and a means of disseminating their collective thinking to one another and to the country as a whole. This is a part, and an important part, of the democratic process. The fact that no Communist society would allow them to exist for a minute is sufficient proof that in our part of the world they have value.

Chapter 18

REFLECTIONS AT EIGHTY

Fifty years ago, there were many things in our society that troubled me and others like me. Some of them have been ameliorated in various degrees, some have grown worse, some have disappeared. A brief checklist of a few of these may be useful.

We wanted universal knowledge of and access to birth control, mainly on the ground that every woman must have the right to bear children or not as she pleases. Though we all knew of Malthus's warning, we did not foresee the terrible specter of overpopulation that would confront the world of the 1970's and 1980's.

We were all opposed to war, both on humanitarian grounds and because we could see from history how rarely it ever settled anything. But nobody foresaw the horror weapons of today, the "balance of terror," or the emergence of only three superpowers, the United States, Russia, and China.

We were conservationists, but our limited vision seems grimly ironical today. We were miles away from foreseeing man's threatened terrible damage to his total environment, air, earth, and water.

When I became managing editor of *The Globe,* I was astonished at the corruption of the New York City government, which under Tammany Hall was dishonest from top to bottom. I could not foresee that the Great Depression, more than a decade later, was to break the power of Tammany by transferring the center of authority, in distributing both jobs and charity, to federal agencies in Washington.

I was surprised, fifty years ago, at the close cooperation of the Roman Catholic Church with Tammany; the Church saw the corruption at first hand, could have fought it, and did not do so.

I disagreed with the Church on other matters, especially its opposition to birth control. In states where it had the power, it prohibited contraception not only for its own communicants, but for everybody. I was disturbed by its refusal to accept modern scientific teaching on such matters as evolution. I could not foresee that fifty years later the monolithic authority of the Vatican would be disintegrating; that in advanced countries Catholics would use contraception in the same degree as other segments of the population; and that its dogmas would be resisted on such a wide scale, and so successfully, from within its own ranks.

In the 1920's and 1930's I saw the federal government at close range and in great detail. Even then I was disturbed by many aspects of it. I saw the inferior quality of numerous members of the House and Senate, especially those from the South. I witnessed how many of these men, because of the one-party system in that part of the world, rose to the all-powerful chairmanships of important committees, at great damage to the best interests of the country as a whole. I saw the beginnings of the process of enormous growth of the Executive branch, the continuance of bureaus the need for which had disappeared, the padding of payrolls, the competition for bigger jobs and salaries by careerists who had little or no interest in the public service they were supposed to aid.

Fifty years ago, Washington was already filled with lobbyists for every kind of private interest, who exerted all possible pressure on the members of Congress to get legislation advanced or stopped, according to the wishes of the power groups whom they served. These lobbyists were in some cases even more brazen than they are today, though the situation has in fact deteriorated during the years; today's pressure groups are subtler, and more careful to avoid the limelight, but they are far more numerous and powerful, and more damaging to the public welfare.

The "military-industrial complex" was just beginning in those years; it was only a hundredth as dangerous as it now is, because the cost of weapons to keep America "secure" was insignificant compared to today.

Most of the media of mass communication did not exist fifty years ago. The news magazines were still some years in the future, television was almost thirty years away, radio had just begun, and was no more than a novel toy. Newspapers were modest enterprises compared with those of the present. Nobody, as far as I am aware, dreamed of a future when we should be overwhelmed by a Niagara of words and pictures, day and night, from almost every part of the globe, much of the material coming by satellites circling in the sky.

Withholding of information by Washington existed even half a century ago, but it was on a modest scale compared with today, when new laws requiring the releasing of important facts are regularly evaded. Today's newspapers are in general far superior in almost every way to those of the 1920's, and they and the other communication media—plus some maverick members of Congress—are fighting hard and with some success to offset the increasing tendency of the Executive departments, beginning with the Pentagon, to withhold vital information, on the dubious or false ground that to release it would endanger the national security.

In the 1920's we worried about the morals of youth, as countless generations before us had done. The advent of the automobile had suddenly removed young people from parental watchfulness, Prohibition had made illegal liquor readily available, and there was a general moral relaxation after the First World War. There was some rise in illicit sex, though probably much less than was suggested by the papers. Nobody dreamed of the problems of today, the dropouts, drug users, and the revolt in the colleges.

The liberals were of course fighting for the abolition of unequal treatment for Negroes and other minorities. In the North, where they were few, Negroes seemed to the whites (though not to themselves) to have fairly good conditions; in the South, they were either treated with cruelty, or with patronizing condescension that rankled almost as much. In the past half century, great progress has been made, but expectations have risen faster than the reality, and in 1970 it seemed likely that the worst confrontations were still to come. Most old people were still racist at heart; the hopeful note was that increasingly, young whites were not.

For several decades of my adult life, through plain ignorance, I did my best to kill myself by improper living. My weight crept up until it was more than two hundred pounds—seventy-five more than I weigh at the beginning of my ninth decade. I smoked two packs of cigarettes a day for twenty-five or thirty years; at that time nobody knew their connection with lung cancer, heart disease, and emphysema. While I ate a well-balanced diet, there was too much of it. I got sucked in by the advertising campaign of the Dairy Association, and I drank a lot of milk, with the fatuous idea that it was good for me.

I also met deadlines, daily or weekly, under great pressure, for more than forty years. Doctors are doubtful at present whether strain and tension actually contribute to the likelihood of heart attacks, but if they do, the wonder is that I held out as long as I did.

After my tight schedule of work made me suspend the long Sunday walks with the Green Mountain Club, I got little systematic exercise at all. In winter I walked perhaps a mile a day between my apartment and the nearest rapid-transit system which would carry me to and from my office. In summer, in my free hours on weekends, I played a little bad tennis and golf. For a few years my wife and I were members of the English Country Dance Society of New York, and once a month we would gather in some public gymnasium with twenty or thirty fellow enthusiasts and perform the brief, rigidly choreographed old folk dances, "Rufty Tufty," "Black Nag," "If All the World Were Paper," "Gathering Peascods," and some Morris Dances that are believed to go back to Druidical days and to symbolize human sacrifice.

An hour or two of occasional strenuous exercise is probably worse than none at all, and I should not have been surprised that, at fifty-nine, I developed angina pectoris, and a few years later had a couple of heart attacks severe enough that my doctor exiled me from New York's rugged climate, as I have told elsewhere. My wife and I returned to Stanford, where we had met and fallen in love more than forty years earlier.

For one of my temperament, a college campus is an ideal place for semiretirement. Among them, the members of the faculty of a good university—and Stanford now ranks among the top four or five in the country—know everything, and are remarkably helpful to a writer doing research. A college community, especially if it is not located in the middle of a big city, is a self-contained entity like a small town, and my wife and I both knew from early experience how to get along in a community of this type. Like any village, a college town has its clashes of temperament, and its fiercely competitive success-seekers, but their conflicts are usually within easily manageable limits, especially when the struggle takes the form of trying to be better, in research or teaching, than one's rivals. This is a small town with excellent library facilities, with a plethora of music and art, and contact with a stream of exciting personalities, both among your neighbors and imported. We came back to California in time to renew our contacts with a few teachers of our youth, and we made friends with many of the faculty of today. I was invited to teach a Senior Seminar in Communication, and did so for a few years, until another heart attack made this impossible; but it helped me to get to know some members of the rising generation.

After a third of a century in New York, holding what seems to me one of the world's most interesting jobs, I of course miss some things in my compulsory exile; but they are fewer than I expected. In the vast sea of inanity that is television, there are a dozen programs a week that are valuable. Television has banished parochialism; it gives the elderly, in particular, a sense of being present, in the best possible seat, at scores of important happenings a year. In most cities there is now at least one radio station that tells the news all day long, giving more of it than anyone can possibly want to know. Unless you are isolated in the mountains or the desert, newspapers and magazines are available as soon and as easily in one place as in another. A private library in New York sends me at trifling cost a book a week of my own selection, and I find there are rarely more than about fifty books a year in the fields of my own interest that I want to read.

The perspective of my ninth decade throws a backward light on some things about my own past self. I realize now that for many years I suffered from two maladies that are rarely identified. The first of these I call "Buyer's Disease." When you are in a position to buy something other people want to sell—in my case, manuscripts or chances at a job —you are treated with a deference beyond your deserts. When you leave your editorial chair—or your job as a buyer of anything, anywhere—and people no longer have any material reason to cater to you, it can be a traumatic experience.

The other malady is more subtle; I call it "Editorial Writer's Disease." The victim comes to feel that once he has stated a problem clearly, and told how it should be solved—which is usually easy when you don't have the responsibility for actually carrying out the amelioration—things are somehow better.

Editorial writers are, of course, not the only victims of this malady. Every wife who points out to her husband that he should earn more money, every husband who asks why his wife doesn't combine the virtues of five or six other women, every organization that passes resolutions in favor of world peace, is guilty in some degree of the belief that there is virtue in magic incantations.

Young people are not interested in the old, and the old are not much interested in one another, encapsulated as they are in the narcissism of age. But every elderly person is fascinated by his own problems, and I am therefore writing the next few paragraphs for my eyes alone.

At sixty-nine, as I have said, I had a third and almost fatal heart attack; it is probable that I survived only because of new drugs and techniques that did not exist ten or fifteen years earlier. Even before this attack, I had taken off forty-five pounds' weight, and after it, I took off another thirty pounds and went on the full heart-patient regimen—the low-sodium, low-fat diet, a rest every day after lunch, a walk of at least two miles daily, keeping my weight within a pound or two of one hundred thirty. Never overeat, never get overtired, carry nitroglycerine at all times, day and night, and put a pill under your tongue if you feel an attack of angina pectoris coming on. More methodical in old age than when I was younger, I began to weigh myself daily and write down the result in my diary. I also bought a pedometer, got it calibrated to the length of my stride, and recorded each evening the mileage covered, adding it up at the end of each month and year; nowadays I walk about 850 miles annually. Luckily the Stanford campus of nine thousand acres has a dozen beautiful short walks available, with little or no automobile traffic to interfere, and I take them in a casual rotation.

I also guard my time and energy as well as I can, thus creating the impression among my friends that I am something of a hypochondriac. This is probably true; on the other hand, I have known quite a number of people who had a condition similar to mine, and bravely went on leading a "normal" life; nearly all of them are dead.

In the decade since this bad heart attack, I have kept reasonably busy, writing two and a half books thus far, and twenty-five or thirty magazine articles. For most of this period, I dictated all my material to my angelically patient wife, using a noiseless typewriter while I lay in bed for a couple of hours after breakfast, usually listening simultaneously on earphones to an FM radio station specializing in the baroque composers. When the doctor decided that so much speaking was an undesirable effort, I learned again—after fifty years—to compose on the typewriter, and bought one light enough to hold comfortably in my lap.

When I was nearing eighty, I wrote a report on myself to be privately circulated to a few friends.

> *To paraphrase an old saying [I wrote], inside every elderly man is a young man crying to get out—and thinking he might make it, too. At seventy-nine plus, I walk with a cane so that I won't stagger into the path of a car. I go down a short flight of steps like an elephant crossing a bamboo bridge in a typhoon. I lower myself into an armchair the way they set down a Michael Angelo statue with a derrick. But in my heart I'm sure I'm only pretending these expedients are necessary, that I'm just imitating someone old, and could start gamboling any minute.*
>
> *The superannuated milk-wagon horse, left to his own devices, would faithfully follow the familiar route, stopping at every house. I run a clipping file on a hundred subjects I am unlikely ever to need again; I read a ridiculous number of newspapers, magazines, and books. I carefully correct typographical errors in printed matter before I put it into the wastepaper basket. I go to speeches, make full notes, and then throw them away. I am like the exercise fanatic who said he felt he must keep fit, to which the answer was, "Fit for what?"*

As a student of the human brain, in a modest way, I know something of the physiological symptoms of old age. Your ten or twelve billion brain cells wear out, and are not replaced by new ones. When you are old, this goes on at the rate of, probably, a few thousand a day. Everyone has been struck by the fact that old people remember things that happened in their youth better than those of a few weeks, or a year or two, ago; one reason may be that when you are young, your cells are well nourished with an ample blood supply, carrying the all-important oxygen, serotonin, and other needed materials. When you are old, the blood supply does not function so well, and neither does the creation of electricity in the nervous system. There is also the mechanism, thus far hardly understood at all, by which the brain suppresses disagreeable memories (and then dredges them up again under the influence of certain drugs, or of hypnosis).

I have found that knowing something about the process of forgetting does not prevent my being a victim of it. For years I have carried in my pocket a memorandum book, with a page for each letter of the alphabet; when I find I have a persistent block on the name of somebody, I put it into the book indexed under his occupation, or some other special characteristic, and when necessary I look it up.

I have always maintained that the poverty of my boyhood did me no special psychic harm, but there may be a few signs that point in the other direction. One might be the fact that I am a compulsive worker, forever getting into obligations to do more in a given length of time than is reasonable. Even at eighty, with almost no deadlines to meet, and no pressures on me except inward ones, I can't bring myself to sit down and read a book in the forenoon, unless I am making notes for something I am myself just about to write.

So far as I know, I have never in my life been in any real danger of losing a job, except insofar as periodicals I worked for might be suspended; however, I could never endure a vacation lasting more than two or three weeks, when I would anxiously hurry back to the office to make sure that everything was "all right." Most of my dreams are happy ones, but when occasionally I have one that is not, it is always that I have lost my place on *The Globe, The New Republic,* or *The Guardian,* and am trying rather pitifully (and ineffectually) to ingratiate myself again with the bosses.

Looking back over the years, I can see that one of my weaknesses as an editor was my inability to delegate work and authority, which could easily be a manifestation of an internal insecurity; I rationalized, as so many others have done, that it was "less effort" to do it myself than to explain to someone else what was needed. I can also see that I should have been more aggressive in asserting my own ideas, less inclined to make decisions by a majority vote of my colleagues and myself; evasion of responsibility is also a sign of unconscious insecurity. My other chief weakness, I suppose, was my insistence on writing as well as editing, though in the case of *The New Republic* this was a pattern that had been set up for all the editors years before I joined the staff.

On the other side of the scale I may set my endless curiosity about every aspect of our current civilization. Long before I became a professional science writer, I was reading every popular magazine in that field, and many professional journals. Though I am not very skillful with my hands, I have hastened to buy all sorts of household gadgets as fast as they came on the market. I am fascinated by the practical details of new developments in architecture, engineering, city and regional planning, automobiles, automated parking machines, and scores more of ways to do new things, or to do old things better. This breadth of interest was probably valuable to me as managing editor of *The Globe,* less so as editor of *The New Republic,* whose readers, as far as we could judge by the editorial mail and other indicia, were chiefly concerned only about political and social matters.

Like all old newspapermen, I get a fair number of young people who come to ask me whether they should take up journalism as a career, and I make the usual stock answer: Don't do it unless you feel a compulsion so strong you are sure you won't be happy doing anything else.

There has been a tremendous improvement in the quality of printed journalism since I started working in this field more than sixty years ago. Newspapers are big business now, and while this has obvious disadvantages, it has advantages also. The papers publish far more news, it is better written, and it is based on a keener realization of the qualities and limitations of the average reader. As I have said, news magazines, radio, and television have all been invented during my working lifetime, and all of them have on the whole, and despite some notorious weaknesses, improved greatly since they began. These media compete strongly with one another, which on the whole tends to improve all of them.

When I began in the business, there was a prejudice against college graduates so strong that the applicant would be well advised not to mention his degree. Today I believe the reverse is true, and many men planning to go into mass communication take an A.M. or Ph.D. The work of the Newspaper Guild, and the general change in the climate of opinion, have resulted in much better remuneration, adequate pensions, and a better place in the community esteem. While exceptional men have always made exceptional places for themselves, sixty years ago there was some truth in the cynical saying that "a reporter is only as good as his legs." When these began to give out, he went on the copydesk; when increasing age made him unfit for this, he was put in charge of the morgue, and when he died, in far too many cases, they had to take up a collection to bury him.

In those days we were just emerging from the era when the tramp reporter was often like the tramp printer—probably unmarried, probably an alcoholic, almost certainly a man with itchy feet, who stayed in any one city at most only a year or two. This adventurous breed was picturesque, it created some fabulous stories of intrigue and excitement, but it was far from today's successful newspaperman who probably lives in the suburbs, has two cars in his garage, and is sending his children to college.

It is still true that only a comparatively small group of men of outstanding talent achieve the heights of respect that go to a leading lawyer or doctor. People like Walter Lippmann, James B. Reston, Eric Sevareid, Howard K. Smith, and perhaps thirty or forty more, stand high on any list of the nation's valued leaders; but I should guess that a journalist has to be *more* talented than members of some other occupations, to get comparable status. This is regrettable, since communication is the lubricating oil of democracy.

The most arresting cultural development of the past few decades of my life has been the worldwide movement that I call the Cult of Unintelligibility. Gradually at first, and then with increasing rapidity, artists in every field began to produce works departing in various degrees from normal standards of rationality. The movement spread so far and so fast that it must have answered some profound need in the collective unconscious. The result, apparent to all, is novels that have several layers of meaning, or none; poetry which avowedly is intended only to stir some dim emotion in the unconscious; paintings, sculpture, and music that are intentionally void of significance, beauty, any shred of meaning, but are raw sound like a volcanic eruption, raw shape like a splatter of mud, raw visual impression like a dark midnight. Increasingly, creators have announced that they don't *want* to communicate, that they wish to stir only their own emotions, and if you don't like it, you can lump it.

The first and too-easy answer to all this is that the producers are not competent to work in the older, more familiar forms. But this is not true; some of the painters, for instance, were skilled craftsmen before they took up the new forms. It is a fact, however, that the untalented always try to follow the fashion set by the talented, and some of the results, in every type of artistic creation, are terrible, though a man of real gifts is always interesting at least now and then, no matter how hard he tries not to be.

One early result of this development in all the arts is a loss of audience. The new art forms are always accompanied by a great body of production of the old-fashioned type, and people who are alienated and angered by the experimentalists are likely to turn away to the familiar and the comfortable. Of those who profess to enjoy, or at least, to "get something out of," the new works, it is hard to say how many are honest, and how many are trying to keep in fashion. Moreover, history shows us innumerable instances of mass delusion, like the dance madness of the Middle Ages, the Children's Crusade, the tulip speculation in the Netherlands, the South Sea Bubble. The fact that the overwhelming mass of the "experts" are in favor of something doesn't necessarily mean that it will make sense a hundred years from now.

Man has existed for at least a million years, and quite possibly much longer; it is reasonable to suppose that he has been producing art objects of one sort or another for the greater part of that time. The oldest that we have, the cave paintings of Cro-Magnon man, go back about thirty thousand years. In all that time, except in the past few decades, artists have tried to produce something that will communicate to other people. It is hard to believe that these decades are right and all the rest of history is wrong.

As I look back over my eighty years of life, and what history tells us of the preceding three millennia or so, it seems to me that the worst evil by which mankind is afflicted is faith, which so easily becomes fanaticism. It is faith, in the form of religious zealotry, that has been responsible for most of the wars that have ravaged mankind for three thousand years. The awful tortures of the Inquisition, Stalin's and Hilter's unending list of cruelties, and the dreadful record of similar things down through the ages, have all been the result of the totally unverified belief that the torturer was right and the victim was wrong. Almost every religion in history has injured or killed people wholesale in the confident assumption that God, or the Gods, wanted this action to be taken. The heart of democracy, and its greatest value, is the idea that pluralism is not only possible but desirable, that people should let other people alone. Yet today many who profess faith in democracy continue to use it as a cloak for undemocratic attitudes and actions.

One of the really hopeful things about humanity is the rising tide of skepticism that rejects *all* absolutes, except possibly the one that says there are none. The pragmatic approach, which repudiates all fanatical following of any rigid ideology, is spreading as more and more people become students of science, or at least, know of the existence of the scientific method, which rejects all hypotheses unless they can be substantiated by repeated and independent verification. The need to be supported by the rod of faith is strongest among the poor and ignorant, which at present, unhappily, applies to most of the human race. But time is on the side of the nonbelievers, even in the Communist countries which have supplanted, or have tried to supplant, orthodox religion with faith in the outmoded, unscientific Marxist-Leninist zealotry. No one now living will see the end of the bondage to superstition; but our children's children may—if we are lucky.

A fact about humanity that I have never really got used to is the desperate yearning to believe what is wildly impossible, or patently false. People *want* to become the victims of voodoo of one kind or another, and I now think I know why. The conditions of life are so hard, so often almost unendurable, that most human beings see they cannot solve their problems unaided. But if there is some sort of magic at work, there is always the possibility (they feel) that a *deus ex machina* may appear out of a cloud and wave a wand. This accounts for belief in all sorts of things, ranging from unidentified flying objects and astrology to spiritualism, and the miraculous appearance of Christ or the Virgin Mary, so often witnessed by devout Catholics—miracles of which even the Vatican repudiates the great majority.

All my life, people have been coming to me, as a working newspaperman, with fantastic "inside stories" to explain public happenings. These stories almost always turn out to be nearly or entirely false, and I should have ruined myself professionally if I had published them. Only in dreams does the forty-to-one shot win often enough to matter; in real life, you should bet on the favorite.

Pragmatism gets a bad name because it is identified with opportunism, with a total lack of principles; but this is a false analogy. The pragmatist follows the scientific method; he takes nothing on faith, he accepts only what can be proved by repeated tests to have validity. When this attitude has become the standard one—and we are moving toward it with startling speed considering the long history of man as an irrational being—many of our present troubles should fade away.

Chapter 19

THE FUTURE, IF ANY

As we entered the 1970's my beloved country, with whose culture I am saturated through and through, was in the worst trouble in its whole history. We were confused and uncertain, feeling that somehow as a nation we had lost our way.

We were trying to disengage ourselves from a war in Vietnam which, however admirable our motives may have been at the beginning, we now saw we should never have entered.

At home, a disturbing proportion of our youth, though still a minority, repudiated our whole civilization, and a minority of this minority was going down the dead-end road of drugs.

Our Negro citizens, who had been unbelievably patient under three hundred years of second-class citizenship, and worse, were patient no longer.

Through technological change of which the automobile is the key, our core cities were decaying into appalling slums, where poor Americans of all races endured lives of degradation and misery from which most of them saw no way out.

Pollution of air, water, and soil were coming close to real catastrophe, and private enterprise is still so sacred in this country that it is very difficult for us to put curbs on the despoilers if they are making money out of their activities.

By a series of accidents that are nobody's fault in particular, we are living through several revolutions at once. There is the coming of auto-

325

mation, which enables machines to take over work formerly done not only by unskilled but many types of skilled labor. There is the development of the computer, making instantly available huge quantities of information, and changing the pattern of life in many ways. There is the social revolution brought about by television, whose boundaries we have not yet even begun to define; it is possible that alienation of so many of the young may spring in part from their repudiating the America of the TV commercials, which show a people seemingly with no thought or interest in the world beyond bad breath, dandruff, and perspiration.

Over all, of course, hangs the threat of nuclear war which might destroy us all, some immediately in the first blasts, the rest in the attempt to survive in the shattered remnants of a society that has grown enormously interdependent and complex. And even beyond this, there is the specter of biological and chemical warfare, going so far down the road toward utter madness that we instinctively close our minds to any serious consideration of it.

Our predicament is not isolated; it is worldwide. The demographers tell us that if the population continues to increase at the present rate it will double before the end of the century. But of course this will not happen; long before another thirty years have elapsed, there will be wholesale famine in several parts of the earth. Even if by a miracle the increase could be halted tomorrow, it is now too late to prevent a desperate and dangerous time in the late 1970's and the 1980's.

No such miracle is in sight. In poor countries like India, the bulk of the population for a variety of reasons insists on having two or three times as many children as can, in the near future, be fed. In some parts of the world, like Latin America, many religious leaders encourage this suicidal tendency. The most advanced nations, like the United States, are reducing the birthrate rapidly, because of the initiative of individuals, not that of government. Fifty years late, Washington is only beginning to approve of family planning—chiefly for poor people abroad, not at home. In 1970 we still encouraged big families, with tax exemptions for all children; countries like Canada actually give a small additional allowance for every extra child. It is clear now that people ought to be penalized, financially and perhaps in other ways, for throwing such heavy extra burdens on the resources of the state; schooling, and the provision of other social services, cost the taxpapers many thousands of dollars before each child grows up. Yet if past experience is a guide, it will be many years before we can turn our national policy around.

The ecologists have begun to study the maximum size of the population that can be sustained. North America, with only about six percent of the world's population, is using up a third or more of the global basic resources; sociologist Philip Hauser of the University of Chicago tells us that not more than a total of five hundred million people throughout the world could be supported at even the present American standard— which for many of our citizens is low enough, heaven knows. It seems probable that the optimum population for the United States would be not more than one hundred million, and even that only if we can reverse the trend toward squandering our national resources.

There are two national obsessions that do enormous harm to our country. One is the insistence that when private and public interests conflict, the former must always take precedence. The second is the universal idea that everything must always *grow*, that to stand still or retreat means death. Both of these arose naturally out of our past; both must be abandoned in the interest of our national survival.

For many years I have carried in my pocket for ready reference one of the most important statistical tables I have ever seen. It shows the proportion of people with I.Q.'s at various levels, in the American population, and it was given to me by my Stanford teacher, Dr. Lewis Terman, father of the science of intelligence testing.

In recent years, some people have decried the I.Q. test by pointing out that disadvantaged children show scores consistently below the ones they demonstrate when their disadvantages have been ameliorated, and also that the tests must be consonant with the cultural milieu of the child being examined. But this has nothing to do with the fundamental validity of these tests; all it means is that in some cases the wrong ones were given to the wrong people at the wrong time. The Terman-Binet test is still the faithful workhorse of the testing business; more than half of the millions of examinations given in the United States annually are based directly on it.

These figures show beyond dispute that in this country there are only about three million people of all ages, from infancy on, at the highest level of intelligence, an I.Q. of 140 or higher. There are about ten million who are potentially capable of a solid success in the more difficult disciplines like engineering, medicine, and law. About twenty-six million are smart enough to be graduated successfully from a good university. About sixty-three million (of whom, of course, roughly half are at present adults) will voluntarily read nonfiction books, and magazines at the intellectual level of *Time* and *Newsweek*.

Looking at the rather grimmer side of the picture, there are about ninety-four million people who cannot do any serious intellectual task. Something like seventeen million of these are unlikely to read anything beyond the comic-book and movie-magazine level. Another thirty million will read daily papers, but little else, and are unlikely to understand without help complicated questions like the causes of currency inflation, the importance of foreign trade to our economy, or the balance of power among the three branches of the federal government. While all of us live more in the world of emotion than of intellect, this group is especially likely to be swayed by a plausible demagogue.

Though the I.Q. cannot be changed beyond a few points, there are many aspects of the personality that can be altered profoundly for the better, with skillful training. For a random example, the common people of Italy, whose scatter of intelligence is the same as our own, display a remarkable degree of expertise about performances of opera. The person of mediocre intelligence who has been trained to be industrious may, and often does, exceed in performance the high-I.Q. individual with neurotic disabilities. Solid, reliable character, though it usually goes with intelligence, does not necessarily always do so. Pressing national problems can be presented in such a way that the overwhelming majority of the people can make a discriminating judgment about them. The public-opinion polls, which as a rule are not directed at any special level in the community, show a high degree of what might be called collective common sense. The scatter of intelligence is a challenge; it is not a calamity.

What is the outlook, for this country and for the world? Amid all the darkness, there are some signs of light that should be noted.

The leaders of many countries are at long last beginning to realize the dangers of unchecked population growth. India, where the problem is one of the worst, is trying hardest.

In the West, the Roman Catholic Church, long the institution with the greatest record of diehard conservatism, is changing faster than most of us would have thought possible. In 1970, while Pope Paul VI still could not face the facts, and was willing to see his policies help to bring on worldwide famine, the rank and file of his parishioners, whatever they might say, were in practice beginning to ignore his views. In Italy, the most Catholic of countries, the use of birth control was increasing with remarkable speed. Some countries where the Catholics are of less or no importance were doing well. Japan, where the annual increment of population a few decades ago was enormous, has almost brought its birth and death rates into balance, largely through government-approved abortion. In the United States, thanks chiefly to "the pill," the birthrate has dropped one-third in only about a decade, and this is paralleled by the situation in other Western industrialized nations.

The calamity of overpopulation, as noted, is partly self-liquidating. When millions have died of starvation, as seems likely in the next decades, their deaths will relieve the physical pressure somewhat. But we now know that when density of population passes a certain point, at least in the Occident, public and private discipline both begin to decay; symptoms of this may already be evident in the United States.

It is a grimly comforting fact that history shows us violent revolutions are not made by the dying, but by the vigorous populations, or fractions of populations, who have a strong grievance which they believe is remediable. The sight of wholesale famine is appalling—it has been seen in China on several occasions in my lifetime—but it does not mean great movements of population from one area to another, demanding food.

In 1970 the conflict in Vietnam still continued, though with the hope that at long last it might be ending. Israel and some of the Arab states were stepping up their guerrilla war, with great danger of another explosion in the Middle East. There was also serious tension between the two Communist giants, Russia and China. The United Nations has thus far been able to do almost nothing about any of these conflicts. The great powers encourage or discourage brushfire wars according to their political motivations of the moment.

As for the United States, it will certainly be a long time before this country sinks into another quicksand like Vietnam. Russia and China also seemed to be trying to avoid open war; China, especially, was in such domestic disarray that its effectiveness in any massive engagement was in great doubt.

When the United States and Soviet Russia were the only two powers to have a large stock of nuclear weapons, the "balance of terror" seemed effective. Communist China has now entered this situation, and the older generation of her leaders, headed by Mao Tse-tung, has suffered from a fantastic xenophobia that might have unpredictable consequences. But revolutions that are allowed to run their course have a lifespan of their own, roughly like that of a human being. The fine early fervor for foreign adventure is succeeded by a wish to safeguard the gains at home. In the case of nuclear armament, the longer you have had it, the less you are inclined to use it. Mao might talk casually of sacrificing two or three hundred million Chinese in a nuclear war and then going on to win it, but his successors will probably sing a different tune. In this matter as in others, time is on the side of the angels.

When we turn to the domestic problems of the United States, our sickness runs deep, but all the evidence available to me suggests that it is not fatal. The young radicals, of whom the press and television make so much, constitute at most, authorities tell us, 10 percent of their generation; and of this number, only another 10 percent—one student in a hundred—is with the activists. People of my generation find their manners deplorable, and this tends to conceal the fact that most of their demands are well founded, that they are, according to their own philosophy, more moral than we are, that they are true patriots, in that they are willing to undergo great hardships to bring about changes in the national objectives and methods.

If we were not so alienated by their clothing and hair styles, their sexual permissiveness, their playing with new drugs that have the attraction novelty always has for youth, we would be readier to admit that the war in Vietnam has been just about what they say it was, that the draft has been operated with great cruelty and injustice, that most of the trustees of most universities are autocratic big-business men who want to hand down orders to the students as they do to their employees, that many of the values of prosperous suburban life are questionable in the extreme.

The WASP members of my generation are still overwhelmingly racist, whatever they may say to the public-opinion pollsters; the new generation is far better, including its members in the Deep South. A large proportion of the young have no interest in making fortunes for themselves; they want to go into public service, and the generally acclaimed mores of the nation have always said this is admirable.

Among the students who are in revolt there are some who call themselves Communists, most of whom look for their inspiration to China rather than Russia. I have seen some of these young revolutionaries at close range, and they amaze me. Fifty years ago, I knew many of the youthful zealots intent on remaking the world, and they had at least a rough idea of what they were doing. They had studied the revolutions of the past, they were steeped in the ideology of the earlier radicals, they had elaborate plans for the future state.

But today's young people in this category are amazingly naïve. Their only idea is somehow to tear down the existing state, in the belief that it will magically reconstitute itself nearer to their heart's desire. I have seen revolutions, Fascist or Communist, at first hand in four countries—Cuba, Germany, Russia, and Italy—and I know that even when the new rulers are trying with all their might, society does not put itself back together again, except with heartbreaking slowness, over long years of universal suffering. Revolution in the old-fashioned sense seems to me overwhelmingly unlikely in this country, but if it ever did come, it would be taken out of the hands of these parlor radicals, and controlled by a much grimmer and more competent crew.

The pollution of our air, water, and soil has gone alarmingly far, but I do not think it is yet irreversible. The United States, which nowadays lags far behind several other countries in this as in other matters, has not yet, as I write, acted decisively against lethal insecticides as some Scandinavian countries have done, but it has made a beginning. We are at last conscious of the enormous harm being done by air pollution, and are trying to reduce the damage done by automobile exhausts, the chief though not the only factor. Public-health experts say that many people are being killed annually by bad air, but their deaths appear in the statistics as resulting from something else—emphysema, asthma, lung cancer, or cardiovascular disease. New types of automobile engines now exist, free of the disadvantages of internal combustion; when the known deaths get into the range of thousands annually, the government may summon up courage to defy Detroit and force the use of new propellants, and we may have clean air again. Our lakes and rivers are masses of sewage, and it will take decades to clean them; but we are finally aware of the existence of the problem, and are beginning to do something about it.

As we enter the 1970's, frankness in speech, in books, and on the stage, has gone to heights (or depths) no one would have dreamed possible even a decade ago. There are no more Four-Letter Words; there are only four-letter words. The speech of men in isolated groups has now become the commonplace of all society, and appears in print almost everywhere without much comment. Books describe every possible detail of sexual intercourse, and of all possible perversions, and there is no Anthony Comstock to hale the authors and publishers into court. Nudity on the stage has won acceptance in only a few years. So has the depiction of sexual intercourse of every variety, simulated or—for all the audience knows—real.

Naturally, many members of my generation draw back in Puritan horror from these goings-on. They pass back and forth among themselves stories of sexual promiscuity among the younger generation, now that contraceptives are readily available, and the great inhibiting factor of the past, fear of "getting caught," no longer operates. What these horrified elders forget is that there have been other civilizations, at other times and places, that have also practiced the greatest possible sexual freedom, and have survived and flourished in spite of it.

There is one solid benefit from the frankness of books and plays that few ever mention. Throughout my whole lifetime, practitioners of these arts have been edging ever closer to today's frankness, amid constant persecution, in this country at least, by all sorts of censors, customs officials, local police, the courts. When they have gone as far as they can go, and nobody blows the whistle, perhaps we can drop the subject and get on to more valuable activities. When writers are allowed to say anything they wish, perhaps they will stop trying to invent suggestive and salacious situations, and get back to telling real stories about the agonies of the human heart.

The John Birch Society and its allies are steeped in nostalgia, trying to force the nation back to the past of many years ago. I am older than almost all the members of this group on the Far Right, I know more than they do about the conditions of former times, and I have no sympathy with their efforts. It is impossible to turn the clock back; Thomas Wolfe was right when he said "you can't go home again." We should be better advised to try to get from the present, so abysmal in many ways, into a brighter future.

Almost all of mankind's troubles that loom so large today are of our own creation, yet the bulk of humanity is essentially good. Our problem is the inability to change fast enough to keep up with the pace of technological and scientific revolution, or to recognize new dangers before they have grown to horrendous size. Mankind has a philoprogenitive instinct, and profound impulses toward aggression, and for demanding living space, the "territorial imperative"; but all these attitudes are capable of being modified by intelligent social pressure, which we are just beginning to learn how to apply. Our culture, in the most advanced nations, is beginning to catch up with our dilemmas. I believe that mankind has enough sense—just barely—not to commit mass suicide. If we can get through the next few decades without the calamity of nuclear war—and I think there is at least a 51 percent chance of doing so—the future is bright.

INDEX

INDEX

1920 session, 131-32, 143
1924 session, 143, 179-80
Democrat (Emmetsburg), *The*, 29
Dempsey-Firpo fight, 148
Dempsey, Jack, 149
Dennis, Charles H., 129
Dennis, Nigel, 273
Denny, George, 303
Denver, Colo., 152, 169
Depression, the, 213-22, 248, 266, 277, 314
Des Moines, Iowa, 13, 268, 269, 299
Des Moines Register and Tribune, The, 308
Des Moines River, 8, 12
Descendants of the American Revolution, 223-24
Detroit, 18, 253
Development and Resources Corporation, 256
Dewey, Admiral George, 126
Dewey, John, 162, 173, 203, 219, 300
Dewey, Gov. Thomas E., 271
Dewhurst, J. Frederic, 308, 309
Dies, Rep. Martin, 228
Dietz, Howard, 105
Dilling, Mrs. Elizabeth, 225
Doheny, Edward L., 174-75
Donovan, Gen. William (Wild Bill), 262
Douglas, Senator Paul, 219, 258
Drift and Mastery, 160
Druten, John Van, 107
Dubinsky, David, 98
Dudley, Sir Alan, 278
Duffus, Robert L., 48, 115, 116, 119, 152, 155, 251
Dunbar, Flanders, 288
Dunning, John, 290
Durant, Mrs. Ariel, 147
Durant, Will, 147
Duranty, Walter, 172, 283, 285
Durstine, Roy, 105
Dutch. *See* Netherlands.

East (ideological), 130, 140, 283
East Coast (U.S.), 97, 100, 252
East Side (New York), 98, 104, 118, 142, 147
Edholm, Charlton, 97, 98
Edholm, Mrs. Lizette, 98
Edmondson, D'Arcy, 278
Edward VIII, King of England, 279
Edwards, Bobby, 109
Egypt, 255
Einstein, Albert, 252
Eisenhower, President Dwight D., 126, 152, 216, 261
El Camino Real, 43, 60
Eliot, Charles W., 237
Elk Hills oil reserve, 174-75
Elmhirst, Leonard, 167, 168, 177, 197

Elmhirst, Mrs. Leonard, 167, 168, 177, 197, 206, 265, 272, 273. *See also* Straight, Mrs. Willard D., and Whitney, Dorothy.
Emery, Rose Frances. *See* Bliven, Rose Frances Emery.
Emmetsburg, Iowa, 5, 6, 10, 11, 12-13, 15, 16, 19-38, 39, 50, 61, 64, 67, 145, 146, 279, 299
Emmet, Robert, 11
Emperor Jones, The, 109
Empire State Building, 213, 284
Emporia Gazette, The, 15, 154, 196, 308
Engels, Friedrich, 22
England. *See* Britain.
Englewood, N.J., 300-01
Erskine, Anna, 124
Erskine, John, 124
Estherville, Iowa, 15
Ethiopia, 192, 193, 195, 222, 241
Europe, 76, 118, 125, 130, 131, 142, 152, 159, 175, 187, 195, 227, 234, 248, 253, 255, 256, 278, 306
Europe's Needs and Resources, 309
Exile's Return, 208

Fabian Socialists, 22, 60, 93, 241, 281, 303
Fall, Albert B., 174-75
Far East (Occident), 157, 328
Far Left, 207, 224
Far Right, 198, 223, 224, 225, 233, 331
Farm-Labor Party, 177
Farmers' Union, 312
Farnsley, Charles, 300
Fascist powers, 195, 196, 197, 234
Faulkner, William, 207
Feakins, William B., 295, 298
Federal Bureau of Investigation, 224, 226, 227, 229
Federal Reserve Board, 215
Feisal I (Arab king), 130
Ferguson, Otis, 206, 208, 212, 261
Fermi, Enrico, 288, 290
Filene, A. Lincoln, 306
Filene, E.A., 306-07, 308
Finland, 139, 140
Finley, John H., 251
Fischer, Louis, 283
"Fiske, Mrs.," 87-90
Fitzgerald, F. Scott, 204
Five Island Lake, 6
Flaherty, Robert, 137
Fleet Street (London), 279
Flint, Mich., 301
Florence, Italy, 44
Flynn, John T., 131, 153, 199-200
Fodor, M.W., 129, 283
Fontanne, Lynn, 107
Forbes, Charles R., 175

Rome, 192
Romer, John Irving, 100, 103, 104, 110
Roosevelt, Eleanor, 225, 239, 240, 312
Roosevelt, President Franklin D., 132,
 168, 182, 195, 196, 219-21, 228, 232,
 234, 246, 256, 260, 261, 266, 267, 309,
 310, 312
Roosevelt, President Theodore, 56, 85,
 150, 158, 159, 161, 200
Rosenberg, Ethel, 227
Rosenberg, Julius, 227
Rosenfeld, Paul, 162, 206
Rosewater, Nadine, 123
Ross, Prof. Edward A., 46
Ross, Irwin, 271
Rossant, M.J., 308, 309
Rous, Peyton, 288
Ruef, Abe, 53-54, 56-58, 59
Rumania, 167
Rural Electrification Administration
 (REA), 246
Russia (Russians), 22, 129, 130, 139, 140,
 142, 144, 150, 170, 172, 183, 192, 226,
 227, 228, 231, 232, 233, 234, 235, 236,
 241, 253, 257, 261, 263, 267, 270, 271,
 281, 282, 284, 285, 293, 294, 305, 310,
 314, 329, 330
 Bolshevists, 130, 139, 170, 234, 257, 258
 Embassy in Canada, 228
 Revolution, 130, 170, 172, 223, 232, 234,
 235
 Tsarist regime, 129, 130, 236
Rust, John D., 253
Rust, Mack D., 253

Sacco, Nicola, 183, 184-86, 238, 249
Sacco-Vanzetti case, 121, 183-87, 191
Sacramento, Calif., 43, 57, 68
St. Louis, Mo., 88
St. Nicholas magazine, 29
St. Paul, Minn., 10
Salt Lake City, Utah, 178
Salvemini, Gaetano, 305
Sammons, Wheeler, 306
San Bernardino County, California, 76
San Fernando Valley, 70, 86
San Francisco, Calif., 38, 39-41, 48, 51, 53-
 54, 55, 56, 57, 58, 59, 60, 62, 63, 65, 70,
 75, 79, 102, 131, 169, 176, 182-83, 209,
 263, 303
San Francisco Bulletin, The, 49-59, 63, 65,
 95, 115
San Francisco Call, The, 56, 59, 120
San Francisco Chronicle, The, 131
San Francisco Examiner, The, 39
San Francisco News, The, 52
San Jose, Calif., 61, 64, 65, 149
San Pedro, Calif., 75

San Quentin Prison, 57, 58, 186
Sanborn, Pitts, 136
Sancton, Tom, 209
Santa Barbara, Calif., 55, 56, 177
Santa Clara Valley, 43
Santa Cruz, Calif., 64
Santa Monica, Calif., 113
Saratoga, Battle of, 17, 18
Saroyan, William, 212
Saturday Evening Post, The, 33, 92, 93,
 104, 128, 140
Saturday Review (of Literature, The), 146,
 270
Scandinavia, 16, 330
Schlesinger, Arthur M., Jr., 158, 159
Schlink, F.J., 169
Schmitz, Eugene, 53-54, 58
Schneider, Belle, 90-91. See also Bel-
 Geddes, Norman.
Schroeder, Gretchen, 36
Science Newsletter, The, 289
Scientific American, The, 270, 289
Scopes, John T., trial of, 180
Scott, Charles P., 276
Scott, Howard, 109
Scottsboro, Ala., 190
Scottsboro case, 190-91
Scripps, E.W., 289
Scripps-Howard newspapers, 140, 155,
 249, 250, 289
Sea Girt, N.J., 84
Searles, Edward, 114, 139, 153
Securities and Exchange Commission,
 168, 199, 238
Seigle, Octavio, 189, 190
Sevareid, Eric, 322
Sforza, Count Carlo, 305
Shapley, Harlow, 288, 293
Sharp, Abbie Gardner, 8-11
Sharp, Cassville, 11
Shaw, George Bernard, 162, 230, 281, 303
Sheean, Vincent, 204
Sherman, Conn., 207-08
Sherrington, Sir Charles, 292
Sherwood, Mary Frances (Mrs. Mark
 Hopkins), 114
Sherwood, Robert, 107
Shillaber, William, 139
Shipley, Rutan and Coolidge, 44
Shulman, Marshall, 302
Sieff, Israel, 282-83
Sierra Club, 91
Simonson, Lee, 107
Simpson, Jerry, 15
Simpson, Mrs. Wally, 279
Sinclair, Harry F., 174-75, 176
Sinclair, Upton, 29, 61, 109, 126
Sing Sing Prison, 216